The Trekker's Guide to The Next Generation®

COMPLETE, UNAUTHORIZED, AND UNCENSORED

Hal Schuster

PRIMA PUBLISHING

Library of Congress Cataloging-in-Publication Data

Schuster, Hal.
The trekker's guide to the Next Generation: complete, unauthorized, and uncensored / Hal. Schuster.
    p.   cm.
Includes index.
ISBN 0-7615-0573-3
    1. Star trek, the next generation (Television program)   I. Title.
PN1992.77.S732S38   1996
791.45'72-dc20   96-41950
                                            CIP

97 98 99 00 01 GG 10 9 8 7 6 5 4 3 2
Printed in the United States of America

How to Order:
Single copies may be ordered from Prima Publishing, P.O. Box 1260BK, Rocklin, CA 95677; telephone (916) 632-4400. Quantity discounts are also available. On your letterhead, include information concerning the intended use of the books and the number of books you wish to purchase.

Visit us online at http://www.primapublishing.com

Contents

Preface

A scene that never made it onto the screen: Patrick Stewart watched James Kirk, portrayed by William Shatner as always, standing on a bridge, and shouted the usual line, "Captain on the bridge." When an explosion tossed things about and the captain was buried under piles of debris, Stewart then exclaimed, "Bridge on the captain!"

And an event offstage, in real world Hollywood: Wil Wheaton returned to the studio after spending years away attending college. No one recognized the man who had once played the young Wesley Crusher.

. . . we learn the essence of *Star Trek: The Next Generation*. It is about transformation, surprise, change, and growth, both in the lives of the characters and in the world of *Star Trek*. Klingons reappeared in the *Star Trek* universe, no longer dreaded enemies but now allies of the Federation. One served as no less than the security officer of the *Enterprise*, responsible for the safety of the ship and all aboard. Spock, the Vulcan who always respected authority and acted with pure logic, reappeared as a rebel in the Romulan underground, suspected by the Federation of being a traitor because he neglected to inform anyone of his plans. And so on . . .

Wesley Crusher, the juvenile ensign who plagued the crew, leaves the story exploring the distant fringes of the universe, going places no one else in Starfleet could ever hope to go. Seemingly invincible, Tasha Yar dies . . . then returns . . . then dies again. And so on . . .

The actors, reflecting their characters, grew as well. Patrick Stewart, who dropped out of school at fifteen, delivers a college commencement address. The hotheaded, temperamental actor also develops a spirit of community with his co-stars. Michael Dorn, the last minute addition to the cast, becomes the only actor to continue as part of *Star Trek* television. And so on . . .

This book chronicles the changes and growth both on and off screen. It offers the story of a unique chapter of the *Star Trek* universe and of television history, exploring both the fictional and real worlds of *Star Trek: The Next Generation*, and of the many talented people who breathed life into an idea.

◆ ◆ ◆

I wish to thank the following people for their generous contributions to this book, which added greatly to the telling of the story. Mike Brown: The Vidiot and the Incredible People Behind Operation SNAFU contributed to Appendix A. Steven Grimm allowed me to reprint his Particles guide while Joshua Bell and D. Joseph Creighton allowed me to reprint their guides to Locations and to Ships. Mark Holtz (that maintainer of the supreme service to Trekkers everywhere) allowed me to reprint from his List of Lists.

Additional thanks to . . . Roger Stewart, Jennifer Fox, and all the Trekkers at the US Embassy in Bangkok.

—Hal Schuster

CHAPTER ONE

What Came Before

Before *The Next Generation* began, the giants of Classic Trek trod the *Star Trek* universe. Both groups of heroes look to Gene Roddenberry as their creator. He led a life as colorful and exciting as those of the characters he created.

Born in El Paso, Texas, on August 19, 1921, Gene Roddenberry spent his boyhood in Los Angeles, studied pre-law for three years in college, then transferred to aeronautical engineering and qualified for a pilot's license. He volunteered for the U.S. Army Air Corps in the fall of 1941, and entered training as a flying cadet.

Second Lieutenant Roddenberry then headed for combat in the South at Guadalcanal, flying B-17 bombers out of Henderson Field. He flew 89 missions and sorties, including missions at Bougainville and during the Munda invasion. He received the Distinguished Flying Cross and the Air Medal. Between missions, Roddenberry began to write. He sold flying stories and later poetry to numerous publications, including *The New York Times.* Eventually he was reassigned to Washington, DC, as a trouble-shooter for the Air Force, investigating the causes of air crashes.

When the war ended, Roddenberry became a pilot for Pan American World Airways and began studying literature at Columbia University. During a flight from Calcutta, his plane lost two engines and caught fire, crashing at night in the Syrian desert. As the senior surviving officer, Roddenberry sent two men to swim across the Euphrates River in search of the source of a light he had observed before the crash, while he dealt with nomads who came to loot the plane. The swimmers reached a Syrian military outpost which sent a small plane to investigate. Roddenberry returned to the outpost and relayed a message to Pan Am. He later received a Civil Aeronautics commendation.

Roddenberry continued flying in the U.S. until he saw television and immediately recognized a need for writers. He quickly relocated to Hollywood, found television in its infancy, and took a job with the Los Angeles Police Department. By the time he became a sergeant, Roddenberry had sold scripts to *Goodyear Theatre, The Kaiser Aluminum Hour, Four Star Theater, Dragnet, The Jane Wyman Theater,* and *Naked City.* Roddenberry turned in his badge, became a freelancer, then took a job as head writer for the Western *Have Gun, Will Travel.* He won the Writer's Guild Award for his episode "Helen of Abiginian," which was distributed to other writers as a model script for the series. He then created and produced *The Lieutenant,* starring Gary Lockwood and Robert Vaughn.

> **Star Trek II Episode ("The Lost Years")**
> *"In Thy Image"*
> Kirk reunites his old crew to save Earth from Vejur.

Pitching Star Trek

In 1964, Roddenberry showed his first *Star Trek* series pilot, "The Cage," to the executives of NBC. Twenty-three years later, at a screening of the same pilot, he described their reaction:

"In those days, TV was at the peak of its love affair with the Western. I had promised the network that Star Trek *would be little more than a 'Space Western'—a 'Wagon Train to the Stars'*

with zap guns instead of six-shooters and space ships instead of horses. But as I began writing that pilot, I realized that here was a chance to do the kind of drama I'd always dreamed of doing. I had seen science fiction movies before, but I'd always thought to myself, 'Not enough characterization, not enough motivation.'

"Perhaps I could use this as an excuse to go to those far-off planets—with little polka-dotted people, if necessary—and be able to talk about love, war, nature, God, sex, and all those things that make up the excitement of the human condition. Maybe the TV censors would let it pass because it all seemed so make-believe. So, instead of a Space Western, I delivered a very different kind of story.

"When the network executives saw the pilot, some of them were outraged, and I can't say I blame them. For the considerable money they'd put up, they certainly

> ### *Star Trek II* Episode ("The Lost Years")
> #### *Star Trek II*"
> While the *Enterprise* is investigating a black hole, a surge of energy engulfs the ship and the flow of time changes so that Earth was never a part of the United Federation of Planets. After picking up Spock at Vulcan, they proceed to Earth, where they find that humans are controlled by a computer. Further investigation shows that Mr. Scott somehow was thrown to the year 1937, where in an effort to help mankind he unwittingly altered history for the worse.

> ### *Star Trek II* Episode ("The Lost Years")
> #### "The Child"
> As the *Enterprise* passes through a mysterious cloud, a strange form of energy penetrates the ship's hull and enters Lt. Ilia's quarters. Dr. McCoy informs her that she is pregnant. Within three days, she gives birth to a girl who continues to age rapidly. The molecular structure of the ship's hull is breaking down. Xon learns that the girl is an entity who wants to experience being human.

did not get a Western space opera. But the network's top program executive was impressed by the fact that he'd felt as if he'd actually been flying in a space ship. In a rare move, the network ordered a second pilot—and this one had better be a familiar action adventure, or else!"

Roddenberry showed his second pilot, "Where No Man Has Gone Before," in 1965. This time the network bought the pilot.

The Creative Challenge

In 1987, Roddenberry described to the Associated Press the challenge of writing science fiction:

"You almost have too much latitude. It's hard to know how far to let your imagination go. You want the audience to feel that they're really on the Enterprise with the crew. But if you let your imagination go too far, they won't feel that way at all. The audience wants to have fun and be entertained. A writer of science fiction has to have vast knowledge. He has to know history, economics, anthropology, and many *other subjects. I'm not looking for messages, but good writers usually find something important to write about."*

But Roddenberry indeed has clear messages underlying his science fiction universe. He told the *Charlotte Observer*, "It seemed to me most certainly a way we ought to be . . . the positive force of love for the almost limitless variety within our universe." In the book *Star Trek Lives!*, Roddenberry explained another vision of the show: "*Star Trek* was trying to say . . . that to be different is not to be ugly. To be different is not necessarily to be wrong."

Roddenberry clearly projects other genres into his science fiction. Not only had he sold *Star Trek* as a Western, but his conception of the series was influenced by C.S. Forester's Horatio Hornblower books. These tales chronicled the rise of Hornblower from midshipman in the British Navy to lord and admiral of the Red Squadron. Roddenberry told the Associated Press, "One of the first things I did when we started the first series was to ask William Shatner to read the Hornblower series. I followed that same feeling of loneliness, of being wedded to a vessel.

> ### Star Trek II Episode ("The Lost Years")
> **"The Savage Syndrome"**
> Decker, McCoy, and Ilia investigate a derelict vessel in orbit around a lifeless planet and find that the crew has brutally killed each other. Meanwhile, a space mine detonates near the *Enterprise*, unleashing an energy field that attacks the crew, transforming them into savages. The other three crew members must reverse the mine's effect.

> ### Star Trek II Episode ("The Lost Years")
> **"Practice in Waking"**
> Scotty, Decker, and Sulu beam over to a sleeper ship. They find a woman in suspended animation, but activate the mechanism and collapse into a coma. They appear to awaken in medieval Scotland and protect the woman from being killed as a witch. Meanwhile McCoy struggles to awaken them.

There is no better classic series about the sea than Forester's."

The Birth of Star Trek

The first aired episode of *Star Trek,* "The Man Trap," appeared at 8:30 P.M., Thursday, September 8, 1966. This story of a salt-starved alien menacing the *Enterprise* crew changed not only television, but the world. But its initial ratings were not high. The show peaked at number 52 during the first season, ranking after *Iron Horse* and *Mr. Terrific.* It did, however, step outside of television to receive two Hugo Awards from the World Science Fiction Convention.

The series made popular heroes of William Shatner (who portrayed dashing Captain James Tiberius Kirk), Leonard Nimoy (the logical Vulcan, Spock), and DeForest Kelley (Dr. Leonard "Bones" McCoy). Nimoy recalled, "*Star Trek*'s creator had a specific look in mind for his extraterrestrial. He was very firm about it. He wanted the character to have pointy ears. I could see his point. I discussed it with my friend, Vic Morrow, and he said, 'It could be very successful, or you could be Dumbo of the Year if it doesn't work.' I've heard ear jokes for years and years, like 'what happened to your pointy ears? I sent them out to be sharpened.'"

Kelley told the *Charlotte Observer,* "Gene Roddenberry and I were old friends. He told me, 'I'm working on two pilots. One is a science fiction show, and the character I have in mind for you is half-alien. I want him to be another color, slightly green, with pointed ears.' I asked, 'What's the second pilot?' He said '*High Noon.*' And I said, 'Call me when you're ready to do that one.' And that's why I'm not playing Mr. Spock today.

"I was given somewhat of a free hand in developing my character. Gene had written the basic story bible [the outline of the show] and made him a Southerner. Bones was unmilitaristic—not a rebel, but a sort of H.L. Mencken. He wore a sweater rather than a military jacket, though we never got around to that on the show. Initially, the network backed off me for McCoy because I'd played nothing but

> ### *Star Trek II* Episode ("The Lost Years")
> #### *"A War to End War"*
> The *Enterprise* arrives at a lifeless planet in ruins, where the crew is attacked by warring android armies. A female android leads them to safety underground, where the planet's inhabitants live in peace. Eventually, the landing party leaves the androids to their war. In a rewritten version, Kirk and company find the planet's humanoid inhabitants connected to electrodes that allow them to experience the joys and pains of the war raging above.

> ### *Star Trek II* Episode ("The Lost Years")
> #### *"To Attain the All"*
> A blue-skinned alien, the Prince, boards an *Enterprise* trapped in another dimension. He tells Kirk they will receive the ultimate gift—the "All"—if they prove worthy. Decker and Xon participate in a test, including traveling through a maze-like structure. Midway through, they realize that they are assuming one another's personality. When they reach the end of the maze, an energy sphere engulfs the *Enterprise* and the crew begins to merge into a cosmic mind. Kirk and Decker resist.

heavies for years. Then they saw me in another of Gene's pilots, *Police Story,* as a criminologist and decided I'd do. The funny thing is, I figured *Star Trek* would be seven weeks' employment, and I'd be lucky if the thing went over a year!"

While making *Star Trek,* Roddenberry's reputation as a futurist began to grow. His papers and lectures earned him high professional regard, and he spoke at NASA meetings, the Smithsonian Institution, the Library of Congress, and top universities. Although ratings were low, *Star Trek* enthusiasts included physicists, aerospace engineers, senators, teachers, and intellectuals.

The first book, *Star Trek,* appeared in January of 1967. James Blish based his collection of seven short stories on TV episodes. In September of 1967, NBC moved *Star Trek* to Friday for the second season, a time when most young viewers were not at home watching television.

In January of 1968, the network canceled *Star Trek.* That began an interlude almost unique in television history—the first indication of the hidden power of *Star Trek* fandom—at a time when few people had heard of "Trekkies," or "Trekkers."

Bjo and John Trimble's association with *Star Trek* began in 1966 at Tricon, a science-fiction convention in Cleveland. There they met Gene Roddenberry, who was introducing his two pilots to fans. The Trimbles ended up becoming close friends with Roddenberry and his wife, Majel Barrett. Later the Trimbles were on hand for the filming of the second-season episode, "The Deadly Years." It was a somber set, as unofficial word was out: NBC was canceling the series. The Trimbles sprang into action, spreading the word via convention mailing lists, fan clubs, and the like. One million letters arrived at the studio offices.

Later, in their book *Inside Star Trek,* Bob Justman and Herb Solow claimed that Roddenberry said he paid the Trimbles a salary to run the "Save *Star Trek*" campaign. Bjo Trimble insisted that this wasn't true: "Possibly [Roddenberry] thought my being on the lot so often could best be accounted for by saying I was in his pay. I can't know 30 years later. We got only $100 from him during that campaign for postage when we went broke. That was his only contribution to it." Later, Roddenberry hired the Trimbles to answer the fan mail and help set up his mail order business, Lincoln Enterprises. Bjo added, "That had nothing to do with the 'Save *Star Trek*' campaign,

> ## *Star Trek II* Episode ("The Lost Years")
> ### "The Prisoner"
> Albert Einstein appears on the viewscreen, requesting help to escape from a prison planet. Kirk investigates. Logos wants to assimilate all human life because of human barbarism. Kirk tries to convince Logos that humanity has changed, starting a battle of wills.

> ## *Star Trek II* Episode ("The Lost Years")
> ### "Tomorrow and the Stars"
> A transporter malfunction transports Kirk to Pearl Harbor, days before the Japanese attack. He falls in love. Xon and Scotty attempt to recover a divided Kirk, warning the woman and returning him to his own time to let history run its course.

studios in Burbank. After the protest, Gene Roddenberry, James Doohan, David Gerrold, and other *Star Trek* production staff addressed the protesters. Two "thank you" commercials made by Shatner and Nimoy aired over KRLA a day or two after the march.

NBC renewed the show, but they also cut the budget and moved *Star Trek* to the graveyard slot: 10 P.M. Friday. It almost seemed like revenge. Many talents, including Roddenberry, were gone when the third season began, and quality visibly slipped. In February, NBC canceled *Star Trek* for the final time, and the last show aired on June 3, 1969. Oddly, the first *Star Trek* novel, *Spock Must Die!,* by James Blish, appeared in February of 1970. By then, it must have seemed that the hearty Vulcan had perished.

which was long over by that time."

Meanwhile, radio station KRLA, then the biggest rock station in Southern California, launched its own effort to save the series. In January of 1968, a series of radio ads led protesters to march on the NBC

New Life

Roddenberry moved on to other projects. In 1971, he produced the motion picture *Pretty*

Maids All in a Row, starring Rock Hudson, Angie Dickinson, and Telly Savalas. Meanwhile, the first *Star Trek* convention was held in New York City in February of 1972. Optimistic organizers hoped that hundreds would attend. Thousands showed up. After Neil Armstrong walked on the moon, America believed in science as never before. "It seemed like there was a hell of a lot of trouble in the world," D.C. Fontana, a writer on the original show, told *Time* magazine, "and it was a time when there might not have been a whole lot of hope in America. And here comes this series that says mankind is better than we might think."

Over a decade later, Nimoy told the *Charlotte Observer,* "The whole thing has been a love affair. The whole *Trek* experience. In 1965 when we first made the pilot, in 1966 when we went on the air, we had a grand ride. Then during the 1970s, when we became very popular in syndication, I had a hard time. There was no *Star Trek* product to be done, and the fans wanted a lot more of it." Fandom grew, holding conventions, publishing fan magazines (fanzines), and organizing clubs. They even met weekly in groups to discuss the hidden

> ## *Star Trek II* Episode ("The Lost Years")
> ### "Ghost Story"
> Kirk and a landing party beam down to a high-tech planet with no sign of intelligent life. Kirk is propelled into the planet's past and encounters two scientists who hook him to a mind scan. The mind scanner draws out Kirk's evil Id, which destroys all life on the planet, leaving it as the landing party first found it.

> ## *Star Trek II* Episode ("The Lost Years")
> ### "Devil's Due"
> The *Enterprise* finds a paradise planet. Its inhabitants are in a deep depression because their planet has only 20 days left. The leaders tell Kirk that 1,000 years earlier, when the planet was on the verge of environmental and social extinction, a powerful being promised them 1,000 years of prosperity in return for the planet at the end of that time. Kirk sets out to save the planet.

meanings of their favorite episodes. This kept *Star Trek* alive.

Star Trek flourished in reruns, but fans wanted more. First came the cartoons in 1973. Paramount rehired the original cast as voice actors, as well as many of the original writers. The series lasted until 1975. Meanwhile, Roddenberry continued to unsuccessfully attempt to launch new shows. He shot three new TV pilots: *Genesis II* for CBS in 1973, *The Questor Tapes* for NBC in 1974, and *Spectre* for NBC in 1977.

He actually made three different pilots for *Genesis II.* The first, *Genesis II,* starred Alex Cord and Mariette Hartley. In it, Dylan Hunt, a NASA scientist studying suspended animation in an underground lab, is buried for 500 years and emerges into a post-nuclear-holocaust world where two societies, one good and one fascist, compete. The second pilot, *Planet Earth,* included a mutant warrior race. It was set in the same future and starred John Saxon as Dylan Hunt, with Diana Muldaur and Janet Margolin in major roles. The third pilot, *Strange New World,* completely gutted the earlier attempts. It starred John Saxon in an unwatchable film. Roddenberry had his name taken off.

Spectre included standard horror elements, including H.P.

Lovecraft's "elder gods." Robert Culp and Gig Young starred in this excellent *X-Files* predecessor, as an occult investigator and his M.D. sidekick. *The Questor Tapes* starred Robert Foxworth and Mike Farrell as a noble alien and sidekick on the run from government authorities while trying to learn human emotions and fulfill a mission to help the human race. D.C. Fontana wrote the novelization of *The Questor Tapes.*

Star Trek II

While Roddenberry struggled to revive his fortunes, his brainchild, *Star Trek,* continued to show new life. Tens of thousands of fans attended conventions throughout the world, merchandise sales flourished, and the first U.S. space shuttle was named *Enterprise* after a massive letter-writing campaign. Momentum was building for new *Star Trek* stories, and in 1977, Gene Roddenberry and Paramount Pictures wanted to bring *Star Trek* back to television as the anchor of a new Paramount network. They rehired the original cast with the exception of Leonard Nimoy, who held out for past licensing royalties he believed due from Paramount, as

---

Star Trek II Episode ("The Lost Years")

"Deadlock"

The *Enterprise* is ordered to participate in war games, which nearly cause the destruction of Starbase 7. Kirk, Decker, McCoy, and Xon transport over to the Starbase to find that aliens replaced the Starfleet personnel. Kirk must convince them that humans pose no threat.

Star Trek II Episode ("The Lost Years")

"The Darker Side"

The *Enterprise* reaches a deserted planet and finds pentagrams and other occult symbols. The world's inhabitants, animal-like creatures, still live in the hills. The crew brings a disease aboard the ship, which brings out the dark side of the crew's personalities. Kirk fights the disease, returns to the planet, and confronts an evil entity.

---

did many of the writers from the original series.

Without Nimoy, there could be no Mr. Spock, but they still wanted a Vulcan on the bridge. They replaced science officer Spock with a pure-blooded Vulcan named "Xon." Other additions included Commander Will Decker, the new first officer, and Lt. Ilia, the exotic Deltan helmsman.

This near-miss marked the rebirth of *Star Trek.* The proposed series, *Star Trek II,* never aired because plans for the network were delayed for almost two decades, but without it there might never have been new filmed adventures of the starship *Enterprise.*

Star Trek II ultimately became a series of feature films. Even Decker and Ilia moved to the films, although Nimoy's, and therefore Spock's, return eliminated the need for Xon. The episodes written for *Star Trek II* represent the adventures of the Enterprise during "the lost years" between the end of the original series and the first feature film.

Highlight scripts from the series include "The Child" and "Star Trek II," the latter of which included Mr. Spock (apparently before Leonard Nimoy decided not to reprise his role as the popular Vulcan). "The Child" was used, with the same title and very few plot changes, for *Star*

Trek: The Next Generation, as was "Devil's Due," although with more plot changes. "The Prisoner" may have been used as the basis for *Star Trek: The Next Generation*'s premiere episode, "Encounter at Farpoint," in which Q puts humanity on trial. "Kitumba" showed features of Klingon society that were eventually revealed on *Star Trek: The Next Generation* when the *Enterprise* went on a suicide mission to the Klingon homeworld. "In Thy Image," originally intended as the first episode of the *Star Trek II* series, became *Star Trek: The Motion Picture.* In the story, Kirk reunites his old crew to save Earth from Vejur.

The Movies

Star Trek: The Motion Picture appeared in December of 1979. The outgrowth of *Star Trek II,* and the first new live *Star Trek* adventure in over a decade, it grossed a phenomenal $112 million and led to a series of films. The *Los Angeles Daily News* reported that "the films . . . helped *Star Trek* break out of its cult status and into mass acceptance." *Star Trek: The Motion Picture* was directed by Robert Wise, whose *West Side Story* (1961) and *The Sound of Music* (1965) had earned him Oscars as best director. Wise remembers coming to the production at the last minute, after Paramount

---

> ### *Star Trek II* Episode ("The Lost Years")
> #### *"Lords of Limbo"*
> The *Enterprise* delivers supplies to Limbo, a prison planet. Inmates capture Kirk and want the Federation to investigate conditions on the planet.

> ### *Star Trek II* Episode ("The Lost Years")
> #### *"Skal"*
> Klingon scientist Skal wants to defect to work for peace. He unknowingly carries a virus deadly to humans, planted by the Klingons. When the virus infects the *Enterprise* crew, Skal volunteers to be beamed into space; but Kirk will not sacrifice the Klingon.

---

decided to switch from a weekly series to a feature film. He told the *Charlotte Observer,* "I wasn't a 'Trekkie,' though I'd seen a few episodes. The reason I did it was I'd done [the sci-fi classics] *The Day the Earth Stood Still* (1951) and *The Andromeda Strain* (1971), which were Earthbound, and I thought it was time I got into the heavens."

Wise screened episodes, conferred with producer Roddenberry, and considered ways to create a film without Nimoy, who wasn't in the original script. When Wise's family argued that a Spockless Trek wouldn't fly, Wise and Roddenberry convinced Nimoy to beam aboard. Wise said, "The day-to-day on the set, directing the actors and working with Gene, was fine. But we were rewriting the script every day, to the very last day of shooting. We only had a third of it in good shape when we started. David Livingston did the major part of the work. Gene had some licks at it, but his writing was long and overdone. Frankly, he was almost pushed to the side during the latter part of filming."

Stephen Collins; who played the new character, Decker, told the *Charlotte Observer,* "When I see the film on television, it makes me want to put my foot through the set. It was a frustrating experience, mostly because I didn't have the chops as a film actor back then to make good use of my screen time. There were plenty of problems with the film, but the main problem, for me, was my performance. I was just so earnest and without humor that it's painful. They'd spent so much time and money on the FX [special effects], I guess they felt they had to show it all."

Pocket books began releasing their *Star Trek* novels in the same year. Most have hit the *New York Times* bestseller list, making it the best selling series in publishing history. The novels offered new adventures to satisfy impatient fans during the two-year waits between films.

Nicholas Meyer directed a far more exciting second film in 1982, when Spock died in *Star Trek II: The Wrath of Khan*. Then Nimoy directed his own resurrection in *Star Trek III: The Search for Spock* in 1984. Both were box office successes. In many ways, 1986's *Star Trek IV: The Voyage Home* marked the high point of Classic Trek. Many consider the Nimoy-directed effort to be the best film in the series. In it, the crew of the *Enterprise* walked the world of their

> ### *Star Trek II* Episode ("The Lost Years")
> #### "Only a Mother"
> Technicians on a matriarchal planet install a replicator on the *Enterprise*. It creates dozens of copies of itself. A Klingon gets one of these copies, and Kirk must get it back.

> ### *Star Trek II* Episode ("The Lost Years")
> #### "Small War"
> Kirk finds himself alone on the *Enterprise* confronting a Klingon vessel within the Neutral Zone, with a giant alien peering at him through the main viewscreen. Then Kirk is on a desert planet with Kos, the Klingon captain. Kirk and Kos join forces to survive. The alien then reveals that they were being tested.

> ### *Star Trek II* Episode ("The Lost Years")
> #### "Marla"
> Marla, the daughter of an Earth colony leader, falls for Kirk. She uses magic to win him, but fails. Kirk finds her power source, an alien crystalline computer. The colonists then use the computer to develop the colony.

audience for the first time. *The Voyage Home* was also the last film to appear before the launch of the new television series, *Star Trek: The Next Generation*, would begin a changing of the guard. The success of the films made possible what followed.

Roddenberry told the *Los Angeles Daily News*, "I doubt it's ever been completely figured out why the show has lasted so long. Most of Hollywood has been wrong in trying to find a formula that did it. I think it's because it's a very optimistic view of the future, and it's hard for young people to turn away from that. It says that mankind's adventure is just beginning."

DeForest Kelley added, "When the show started, it was during the hippie period; young people were confused. When they saw this show, it struck a chord with them, of what might be in the future. The Federation people were seeking out peaceful aspects of the universe, they approached every alien and every object as something not to destroy. It presented a positive force. In the second year of the show we were low in

the ratings, but we had broken every fan-mail record in the history of NBC."

Kelley told the *Dallas Morning News,* "In the old series, we used to do a lot of tongue-in-cheek and humorous things, and in this film, it seems like the relationships fell in place again, real nice and comfortable. It was a joy to have a light piece of material to do because the first three had been more or less on the heavy side. Hopefully, everyone will take a beat and say it's time to laugh a little bit."

Kelley noted that the lighter tone wasn't the only change: "*Star Trek IV* introduced the first female starship captain. Even in the beginning, Rodden-berry was always trying to bring women forth into the Federation. At the time, of course, that was unheard of, but I was glad to see Roddenberry kept trying.

"We've tried to deal with the age factor in a lot of subtle ways, like McCoy's gift to Kirk of the glasses for his birthday. I tried to give the impression that McCoy had mellowed somewhat with Spock." Another major change, first introduced in *Star Trek: The Motion Picture,* changed the *Star Trek* universe. The Klingons and the Federation formed an alliance, although some people on both sides, including Captain Kirk, retained their hostility.

> ### *Star Trek II* Episode ("The Lost Years")
> #### *"Pandora's Planet"*
> The *Enterprise* finds the survivors of a missing Federation ship. Then advanced reptilians attack. The survivors had taught the reptilians about Federation technology.

> ### *Star Trek II* Episode ("The Lost Years")
> #### *"Lord Bobby's Obsession"*
> Starfleet sensors detect possible penetration of the Neutral Zone by Romulans. The *Enterprise* investigates. They encounter Lord Bobby—Lord Robert Standish of 20th-century England—who claims that an alien made him immortal. Meanwhile, five Romulan ships appear and attack the *Enterprise.*

Why Star Trek?

William Shatner also speculated on the enduring popularity of *Star Trek.* He asked the Associated Press, "Is it possible that we're creating a mythology, that we touch a mythological vein somewhere? The more I read and the more I think about it, I wonder if the key to *Star Trek* is not all the wonderful stuff we talk about: the character interplay, the sci-fi, action and adventure, and all those good things that seem to be on the surface. Somewhere underneath, the chemistry and the concept touch upon a mythological need in modern culture."

David Gerrold, whose screenplay, "The Trouble with Tribbles," is widely regarded as one of the original series' finest hours, added, "The truth is that every human being has inside him some kind of vision, unformed, of what things should be like if everything worked. *Star Trek* gives people a focus for their own vision."

The multicultural *Star Trek* crew—a Russian, a Japanese, a black woman—was of symbolic importance to many viewers. "As a teen, I was a fan," Whoopi Goldberg told *Time* magazine. "I recognized the multicultural, multiracial aspects, and different people getting together for a better world. Racial issues have been solved. Male-female problems have been solved. The show is about genuine equality."

The Next Generation

The films brought *Star Trek* back to life, but Roddenberry felt left out. Though listed as executive consultant on all the films, he was largely supplanted by other producers. Writer Tracy Tormé told *Time*, "He [Roddenberry] was pretty bitter about the films. He really felt like they took the films away from him."

Roddenberry got his second chance when *Star Trek: The Next Generation* began on October 5, 1987. It needed no pilot, since they didn't have to pitch any network. Roddenberry was pleased that Paramount planned to syndicate the new series; there would be no network whose whims he must

> ### *Star Trek II* Episode ("The Lost Years")
>
> **"Kitumba"**
>
> The *Enterprise* begins a suicide mission to the Klingon homeworld to prevent interstellar war. They meet the Klingon child leader, Kitumba. Kirk tries to convince Kitumba to pursue peace between the Klingon Empire and the Federation, even as a power struggle between Kitumba and some of his aides involves the *Enterprise* crew.

please. "Encounter at Farpoint," the first episode shown, restored Roddenberry as executive producer. Kelley made a brief appearance as a superannuated Admiral Leonard "Bones" McCoy, age 137.

Roddenberry told the Associated Press that when he was asked to bring *Star Trek* back to television, he faced several choices: "The obvious way was to do a retread and use Spock and Kirk. Many people voted for that, but I said, how can you get good writers and directors and tell them to do a retread? To get the kind of energy and enthusiasm we needed you have to have new characters and a new series. You don't get the best people. You don't get the best actors. I decided the best way to do it, and it's a considerable risk, was to push it 78 years into the future. Spock and Kirk are heroes of the past."

Now a new generation ran the *Enterprise,* hoping to win the hearts of fans.

CHAPTER TWO

Launching the New Enterprise

wanted to send a message to the television industry that excitement is not made of car chases," Roddenberry told the *Los Angeles Times*. "We stress humanity, and this is done at considerable cost. We can't have a lot of dramatics that other shows get away with—promiscuity, greed, jealousy. None of those have a place in *Star Trek*." He later added, "Everyone always wants me to do space battles. Well, screw them. That's not what *Star Trek* is about."

Roddenberry had begun the daunting task of recapturing the magic of the original series while creating something new and imaginative. Millions of dedicated fans would be watching for deviation from the vision, even if by "The Great Bird of the Galaxy," Roddenberry himself. Roddenberry told *USA Today*, "We grew beyond the original show. We love the original and those actors, but we see the world differently now and our show reflects that," but his words failed to reassure the fans. Roddenberry and Paramount believed that *Star Trek* belonged to them, but the fans had other ideas. After all, they had kept the dream alive during the dark years when the studio and Roddenberry had seemingly abandoned it.

Leonard Nimoy said you couldn't capture lightning in a bottle twice. Roddenberry feared that the logical Vulcan was right and began to hand-pick his team to increase his chances of success. He brought in Robert Justman as coproducer. Justman had worked with Roddenberry as associate producer during the first two years of the original series, and he understood the task ahead. He told the *Los Angeles Daily News,* "The first thing we rejected was retreading the look of the old show. We designed some ideas from scratch. For example, this is a community flying out there in space. There are children; there are teachers."

Assembling His Team

Then Roddenberry invited a Paramount television executive to join the team. Rick Berman recalled, "I was in a meeting with other studio executives, Gene Roddenberry, and a couple of designers during the project's early stages. The next day I got a call from Gene, who asked me to have lunch with him.

"We found that we had, in odd ways, a tremendous amount in common," Berman told the *Los Angeles Times*. "He had traveled all over the world. He was fascinated that I knew what the capital of Upper Volta was, and that I had been to parts of Africa and the Middle East that he had been to. So we had a lot of fun talking about faraway places with strange-sounding names." According to Berman, Roddenberry's attorney invited him to lunch the following day and asked him to help produce the show. Berman said he already had a job as a studio vice president, but the attorney replied, "Do you want to be a vice president at a studio, or do you want to produce a television show?"

Berman understood what made Roddenberry's brainchild special: "*Star Trek* attracts people to its vision for the future. At the same time, this is a character-driven series about a family of people traveling together. There were very primal qualities in the original series that the audience was ready for a new dose of. We had to make them embrace a new group of people. Roddenberry was very, very clear about not wanting to bring back the old characters, but keeping all the rules, regulations, and nomenclature.

"Gene viewed humanity as an evolving species getting better and better. He believed the future was something to look forward to and that exploration and the development of quality of life were things that man was going to get real good at in the future. He gave a sense of hope to a lot of people, while entertaining them. We have been very, very careful to uphold that attitude.

"To do *Star Trek* without Gene Roddenberry is like doing something without a license. Gene is the license to do *Star Trek*. It has to be Gene's vision for it to make sense. Literally, we didn't need Roddenberry. Spiritually and logically, it was essential."

Describing the origins of the new series, Berman told the *Hartford Courant,* "Gene's involvement in the show was total during the conception of the series. He created the shows, he created the bible. It was his story. It was his idea. We were very close professionally and very close personally."

Berman didn't like comparisons between the new series and the original, adding, "I don't like the sense of competitiveness. There are people who run contests—'Which show do you like better? Which captain do you like better?'— what's important to me is they're two entities that are connected. [The original *Star Trek*] was created by 1960s people for a 1960s audience."

Berman saw *The Next Generation* as having a more serious edge than its progenitor, which was "a lot

more fun and more swashbuckling and sexy than our show is, but I think the television in the 1960s called for that." But Roddenberry's universe remained consistent.

Years after Roddenberry's death, Berman told *Time* magazine, "*Star Trek* was never, and hopefully never will be, my vision of the future. It's Gene Roddenberry's vision that I agreed to uphold. I went through a rather strenuous apprenticeship. I learned what was *Star Trek* and what wasn't. I learned all the nomenclature, all the rules, and regulations. I learned the difference between shields and deflectors—that was a day right there. Slowly, Gene began to trust my judgment and also to trust that I would adhere to the rules, that I would not be someone who would want to change *Star Trek*.

"There were some things that existed with Roddenberry that were very frustrating to us. Not to have conflict among your characters makes it very difficult, because all the conflict has to come from outside. On *The Next Generation,* with the exception of an android and a Klingon, pretty much everyone was human, and they weren't allowed to be involved in conflict, so that was very frustrating for the writers. The laws of *Star Trek* are totally fictional but are held by the fans with such reverence that they have to be followed as if they were Newton's. You

Chain of Command

The tech/writers guide from *TNG* season five lists the CoC as follows:

1. Captain Jean-Luc Picard
2. Commander William Riker
3. Lieutenant Commander Data
4. Lieutenant Commander Geordi LaForge
5. Lieutenant Worf (Security Division)
6. (Ships Services)
7. (Ships Defense)
8. (Sciences)
9. Commander Dr. Beverly Crusher (Chief Medical Officer)
10. Lieutenant Commander Deanna Troi (Medical)

In the case of the episode "Disaster," Troi assumed command as the ranking officer on the bridge when the lieutenant in nominal command was killed. Troi would not have assumed command had the lieutenant lived.

have to treat them very carefully, because there are people who for 25 years have considered them sacred."

Inventing the Series

After Roddenberry assembled his management team of Justman and Berman, the trio began to plan their new series. They had help from many others, including D.C. (Dorothy) Fontana. Fontana had written "Charlie X," "Tomorrow Is Yesterday," "This Side of Paradise," "Journey to Babel," "Friday's Child," "By Any Other Name," "The Ultimate Computer," and "The *Enterprise* Incident" for the original series, as well as the animated "Yesteryear." She had also written the novelization of Roddenberry's *The Questor Tapes* pilot, and the Classic Trek novel, *Vulcan's Glory*. Fontana would cowrite the first *Star Trek: The Next Generation* episode, "Encounter at Farpoint," with Roddenberry.

They invented their new series, starting with the familiar basics of the Federation, Starfleet, Vulcans, Klingons, Romulans, starships, and phasers, but they added many new elements, as promised. The new *Enterprise* would cruise the galaxies about 100 years after Kirk, Spock, McCoy, Uhura, Scotty, Sulu, and Chekov. There would be no Vulcans aboard, but there would be an android. A treaty had been signed between the United Federation of Planets and the Klingon Empire, but no episodes involving Klingons were planned. Kirk's old role would be divided between a more cautious captain and a dashing first officer.

The new *Enterprise* would be five times larger, the crew swollen from 400 to about 1,500, including entire families. Portions of the ship would be detachable, making it possible for one section of the *Enterprise* to engage in combat while nonmilitary personnel remained safe. On the new show, command and military units would wear burgundy uniforms, security and engineering mustard yellow, and science and medical teal blue. Hand-held communicators would be passé, replaced by units built into the uniforms and activated by touching the starship insignia.

Management team in place, story bible in hand, the studio sent out a call to talent representatives to fill the roles:

# # #

To: All talent representatives
Date: 3/17/87
RE: Paramount
"Star Trek: The Next Generation"
1-Hr series for syndication
2-Hr TV movie to start June 1
24 1-Hr episodes to start end of July

Please resubmit for the following roles. New York and Chicago submissions are encouraged. Please be advised that there are no scripts available. Actors may look at sides in the casting office only.

Seeking the following regulars:

- Captain Julian Picard: A Caucasian man in his fifties who is very youthful and in prime physical condition. Born in Paris, his Gallic accent appears only when deep emotions are triggered. He is definitely a 'romantic' and believes strongly in concepts like honor and duty. Captain Picard commands the *Enterprise.* He should have a mid-Atlantic accent, and a wonderfully rich speaking voice . . .

- Number One (AKA William Riker): A 30-to-35-year-old Caucasian born in Alaska. He is a pleasant looking man with sex appeal, of medium height, very agile and strong, a natural psychologist. Number One, as he usually is called, is second in command of the *Enterprise* and has a very strong, solid relationship with the Captain . . .

- Lt. Commander Data: He is an android who has the appearance of a man in his mid-thirties. Data should have exotic features and can be any one of the following racial groups: Asian, American Indian, East Indian, South American Indian, or similar racial groups. He is in perfect physical condition and should appear very intelligent . . .

- Lt. Tanya Hernandez: 26-year-old woman of Ukrainian descent who serves as the starship's security chief. She is described as having a new quality of conditioned-body beauty, a fire in her eyes and muscularly well developed and very female body, but keeping in mind that much of her strength comes from attitude. Tanya has an almost obsessive devotion to protecting the ship and its crew and treats Capt. Picard and Number One as if they were saints . . .

- Lt. Deanna Troi: An alien woman who is tall (5'8" to 6') and slender, about 30 years old and quite beautiful. She serves as the starship's Chief Psychologist. Deanna is probably foreign (anywhere from Italian, Greek, Hungarian, Russian, Icelandic, etc.) with looks and accent to match. She and Number One are romantically involved. Her alien 'look' is still to be determined . . .

- Wesley Crusher: A small 18- (or almost 18) year-old boy to play 15, his remarkable mind and photographic memory make it seem not unlikely for him to become, at 15, a Starfleet Acting Ensign. Wesley is more of an intense (not cute) teenager whose energy comes from an inquisitive nature . . .

- Beverly Crusher: Wesley's 35-year-old mother. She serves as the chief medical officer on the starship. If it were not for her intelligence, personality, beauty, and the fact that she has the natural walk of a striptease queen, Capt. Picard might not have agreed to her request that Wesley observe bridge activities; therefore letting her son's intelligence carry events further . . .

- Lt. Geordi LaForge: A 20-to-25-year-old black man, blind from birth. With the help of a special prosthetic device he wears, his vision far surpasses anything the human eye can see. Although he is young, he is quite mature and is best friends with Data. Please do not submit any 'street' types, as Geordi has perfect diction and might even have a Jamaican accent. Should also do comedy well . . .

# # #

Answering the Call

Responses came in to the casting call, but not every cast member eventually chosen responded to the original call. Patrick Stewart was a member of Britain's Royal Shakespeare Theater for 20 years, acted in such BBC programs as *I, Claudius* for television, and appeared in David Lynch's film *Dune* before donning Captain Picard's uniform for *Star Trek: The Next Generation*. He lacked "a mid-Atlantic accent," but he certainly had "a wonderfully rich speaking voice." Stewart told *Parade Magazine* that he got the part against the odds. He was doing a literary reading produced by an English professor at UCLA when Robert Justman, who was then the show's supervising producer, just happened to be in the audience. Justman turned to his wife and said, "We've found our Captain."

Stewart told the *San Francisco Chronicle* that he had become irritated by questions "implying that I was somehow slumming, going down market from having been a member of the Royal Shakespeare Company. Not only was it not slumming, but all of my years of speaking blank verse and sitting on thrones and wearing tights and striding the stage of the RSC was nothing but a preparation for sitting in the captain's chair of the starship *Enterprise*. I do find there is really a direct parallel between playing such a role [King Henry IV] and shifting to the captain's chair. In fact, there are those who would say sitting in the captain's chair on the *Enterprise* is far more important than sitting on the throne of England."

Stewart is not intimidated by following in the footsteps of William Shatner's renowned Captain Kirk. He told the *Charlotte Observer,* "In the sort of work I've done, you're inevitably following on the heels of countless great names and distinguished performers. I've sometimes looked back over my shoulder at those who have gone before. This isn't an unfamiliar situation. Last summer, for instance, in the West End [in London], I took over for Alan Bates. Therefore, that sense of stepping into someone else's shoes, very much a live man's shoes, is not unusual."

Besides, he sees Kirk and Picard as men of very different styles. Stewart told *Cinescape,* "The differences between Picard and Kirk are pretty obvious. Picard is essentially a negotiator, a talker, a diplomat. Kirk is very much a man of action. He would throw a punch first and ask questions afterward."

Stewart said, "Roddenberry told me early on that his vision of the 24th century is that there's no hunger, no greed, and the point of life is to improve the quality of life. And that's an uplifting way to spend your day. I've spent a large part of my life playing princes, leaders, everything from Shakespearean kings to Lenin. Power is interesting; how that power is used will be continually absorbing."

The aggressive side of Kirk went to Picard's first officer Riker, the leader of most *Enterprise*

Away Teams. Jonathan Frakes plays Riker. The actor told the *New Orleans Times-Picayune,* "I've never had a job that's lasted four years. I consider myself lucky to be part of this group. The writers had painted me into a very militaristic, staunch, by-the-books character, but I didn't like the stiff quality. I'm always looking for places to inject a little humor into the character."

Executive producer Rick Berman told *TV Guide,* "From the start, Data has been one of the most popular characters—if not the most popular. I think a lot of it has to do with Data being the barometer of the human condition. He illuminates human emotions by aspiring to them." Brent Spiner didn't believe that at the time he assumed the role of Data: "When I took the role, it was just another job. I figured we'd do a pilot and then go home. I really thought the odds were against us because people were initially reluctant to accept a new *Star Trek*. When I was cast as Data, my biggest fear was that he has a very small canvas to paint on."

> *"Picard is essentially a negotiator, a talker, a diplomat. Kirk is very much a man of action."*

German-born actor LeVar Burton, who cites Sidney Poitier as a major influence, told the Boston Creation Con that he wanted his character, Geordi LaForge, to start out noticeably shy around women, then evolve into more self-assurance.

Security Officer Lt. Tanya Hernandez disappeared from the crew before the first episode was filmed, and was replaced by Tasha Yar, played by Bing Crosby's granddaughter Denise Crosby. After her death during the first season, Yar would be replaced as security officer by a Klingon named Worf. Despite the

Klingon-Federation Peace Treaty, Worf is both the first Klingon to graduate from Starfleet Academy and the first Klingon officer to serve aboard a Federation starship. Worf was not considered a regular until after Yar's death, although he became one of the most popular characters and remained on television long after the others left the air. Only Worf transferred to *Deep Space Nine*, the *Star Trek* series that followed *The Next Generation*.

Michael Dorn, who played Worf, told the fans that he was the last member of the cast to be chosen. Roddenberry had belatedly decided to add a Klingon, but "the bigwigs weren't sure about it." Later everyone thought it was a great idea. Dorn told a Creation Con audience in Chicago that he tried out for *The Next Generation,* wasn't cast, then was called back two or three weeks later and asked to audition for the role of a Klingon.

Dorn went on to tell a Creation Con in Boston that he was a fan himself long before putting on the makeup to assume the role of Worf. When *Star Trek* first came out in the 1960s, he and his brother watched it and loved it. Their favorite character was Scotty. Dorn revealed that, one day on the set, he was awed by the presence of the original Trek cast members, but he was cool about it.

Gates McFadden plays Doctor Beverly Crusher. She told the fans at the Trekon in Kansas City, "I had been given the choice of all three women parts in terms of auditioning, and the scene that they gave me for Crusher

---

"Conundrum" Crew Information

During "Conundrum," the personnel files for the crew were displayed on the screen:

Picard, Captain Jean-Luc
Birthdate: 13 July 2305
Parents: Maurice and Yvette Picard
Place of Birth: LaBarre, France
Entered Academy: 2323
Graduated Academy: 2327

MacDuff, Commander Keiran
Birthdate: 27 September 2334
Parents: Joseph and Les MacDuff
Place of Birth: Gamma Cabanis II
Entered Academy: 2352
Graduated Academy: 2356

Data, Lieutenant Commander
Birthdate: 2 February 2338
Parents: Noonian Soong
Place of Birth: Omicron Theta
Entered Academy: 2341
Graduated Academy: 2345
Offspring: Lal

Crusher, Beverly C., M.D.
Birthdate: 13 October 2324
Parents: Paul and Isabel Howard
Place of Birth: Copernicus City, Luna
Entered Academy: 2342
Graduated Academy: 2350
Offspring: Wesley A. Crusher

Troi, Lt. Commander Deanna
Birthdate: 29 March 2336
Parents: Alex and Lwaxana Troi
Place of Birth: Betazed
Entered Academy: 2355
Graduated Academy: 2359

Ro, Ensign Laren
Birthdate: 17 January 2340
Parents: Ro ? and Ro Gale
Place of Birth: Bajora
Entered Academy: 2358
Graduated Academy: 2364 (2362?)

---

was the scene from 'Naked Now' where I am sort of coming on to the Captain. I said 'Ah, God I want to do this one. I like this sort of character,' because I thought it was always going to be like that."

The casting call said, "Deanna is probably foreign (anywhere from Italian, Greek, Hungarian, Russian, Icelandic, etc.) with looks and accent to match," but her origin became far more interesting before the series began. Troi became an empathic half-Beta-zoid, the daughter of an aristocratic Betazoid mother and a human Starfleet officer father. Marina Sirtis had appeared in such films as *The Wicked Lady* (1983) and *Death Wish 3* (1985) before joining *The Next Generation* as Deanna Troi. She told the *Charlotte Observer*, "Troi is a very strong person. She doesn't yell a lot or get angry often, but that doesn't mean she's not strong. Deanna Troi is a very strong person, inside and out."

Very Special Effects

A large part of the magic of *Star Trek* comes from the special effects. Major advances in computer technology had taken place between the time *Star Trek* left the air and when *The Next Generation* began. Audiences had seen *Star Wars, Close Encounters,* and the *Star Trek* films during the intervening years. Budgets were now larger, but audiences expected more, and the series creators knew they had to deliver.

The *Enterprise* has always been one of the most popular "characters" in itself. Andrew Probert designed the new Galaxy Class *Enterprise 1701*-D in 1986 based on a 30-year-old concept by artist Matt Jeffries. Probert had designed an earlier *Enterprise* for *Star Trek: The Motion Picture*. Since 1987, Rick Sternbach and Michael Okuda have made numerous modifications to the *Enterprise* and

designed dozens of smaller vehicles, alien battleships, shuttle craft, and cruisers. Sternbach first worked on *Star Trek: The Motion Picture* in 1977, designing spaceships and props, then returned for the new television series in early 1987.

Sternbach told *Wired,* "Designing a real spacecraft is for people with real mathematical and engineering backgrounds. We're safe doing what we're doing because there are no peer reviews; there are no wind tunnels. You can't test the *Enterprise* to destruction. We could, of course, come up with things the audience couldn't really identify with—driving the ship by brain waves, for example—but we don't do that. Instead we jump way ahead, then step back a few paces."

Two teams began producing most of the effects for *Star Trek: The Next Generation* before the series premiered in 1987. One team consisted of Dan Curry and Ron Moore, and the other of Gary Hutzel and effects director Rob Legato. Legato's first job on a television series was as visual effects director for *The Twilight Zone* during that program's second season. He had watched the original *Star Trek* occasionally, but he wasn't a fan of science fiction.

Legato told the *Asbury Park Press,* "We're pretty proud of the effects. It's amazing the support there is for the series. There was a plumber who came to the house to do some work. When he found out what I do, he just started to ask questions about the show. We spent the whole day talking. When I was very young, I loved movies. I was intrigued by how movies worked and how the different stunts and special effects were accomplished. I knew I wanted to be involved in movie making. I had the experience they were looking for."

Dan Curry, head of the other team, said, "We do a mixture of very high-tech and very low-tech. When one of my guys was getting out of his car one day, he stepped in something that might have been Alpo on a previous day. A close-up macro-shot of this squashed substance looked like a very interesting planet surface—once we threw it out of focus so you couldn't see the undigested corn. When I walk into a hardware store and look through the plumbing section, I don't just see plumbing supplies; I see spaceship parts in a different scale." He also kept on top of the latest technological advances. The two-time Emmy-winner noted, "A lot of what we do is transitionary technology. It sometimes makes me feel like a blacksmith at the age of the advent of the automobile."

Makeup supervisor Michael Westmore described working for a science fiction series as hard work. "You're in at 1:00 in the morning, you do three-hour makeup jobs, you're on the set all day long touching up. Even enhancing the natural beauty of, say, Counselor Troi, can take several hours." Westmore says that *Star Trek* creator Gene Roddenberry defined one primary guideline: "Gene's concept was to have a little bit of human in everybody, so you can relate to them," he said. "We never buried anybody so deep that he was just a blob."

First Voyage

Paramount committed to producing the two-hour premier and 24 one-hour episodes. "Encounter at Farpoint" first aired on October 5, 1987. The two-hour show received mixed reactions from fans and critics. The reviewer for the *Charlotte Observer* liked it:

> "Star Trek: The Next Generation *is a blast, a worthy successor to the original, brimming with strong characters, an intelligent story, flashes of humor, and special effects equal to a theatrical film. The two-hour premiere is one of the best television shows of the new season—on or off the networks. There's a strong sense of* Star Trek *continuity, starting with the credits, which appear in the wake of the U.S.S. Enterprise as she zooms across the screen. The captain and crew still describe events into the ship's log. Sideburns are still shaved to a point. But this is no cheap imitation or sappy attempt to revive familiar characters. The crew members of the new* Enterprise *share the same goals as their predecessors, but they don't ape their behavior or personality traits. If the quality of* Star Trek: The Next Generation *is maintained, it will be a pleasure riding along for many, many years to those areas where 'no one has gone before.' As in the original series, the overall tone of* Star Trek: The Next Generation *is hopeful. Sexism and racism seem to have been abolished. Even Klingons are welcome aboard in the wake of a peace treaty. Indeed, Lt. Worf (Michael Dorn) is a Klingon, but he's one of Picard's most trusted subordinates."*

Not everyone was as pleased. John deLancie, who played Q, later told fans online in Mr. Showbiz Celebrity Lounge, "The *Star Trek* format really asks for an hour rather than two hours. I had heard that the production company had originally wanted only one hour, but had been either talked into, or 'requested' to make, two hours, so they put two stories together as opposed to one. They were right in wanting to have the story for only one hour, and, of course, from then on the series has been one-hour episodes."

At the time the new series began, reruns of the original *Star Trek* series were airing on 145 stations. Then production of the new episodes almost forced them off local airwaves. The syndicator began asking for much higher prices, and stations were not allowed to buy the reruns without committing to the new episodes. WBTV program director Marion Meginnis said, "They wanted about five times what we were currently paying. They were trying to package everything as one big strip. We couldn't spend that kind of money on something we didn't know about. There's a great loyalty factor to the old show, but we weren't sure that loyalty would carry over to the new series. We couldn't gamble that kind of money on the unknown."

For these and other reasons, the original cast—then still making very popular, very profitable movies based on the classic series—rejected *The Next Generation*. On December 2, 1986, before he saw an episode, Kelley told the *Dallas Morning News,* "There is only one *Star Trek,* and I'm proud to be a part of it. My feeling is that there can be only one *Star Trek,* and that is ours. They can use the name, but I don't think they can ever duplicate the magic." The same paper later reported that Nimoy had seen only a few minutes of the new series and dismissed it with a wave of his hand.

Over time, their opinions would change, and both Kelley and Nimoy would walk the decks of the new *Enterprise*. The world slowly learned to love *Star Trek: The Next Generation,* but not before the new series faced and solved many crises.

CHAPTER THREE

Continuing the TV Voyages

*T*he *Next Generation* was launched amid both hope and scepticism. While some doubted that the new show could pick up the baton, many fans were ready for more of the atmosphere that *Star Trek* had created.

Science fiction writer Ursula K. LeGuin, the author of *The Left Hand of Darkness,* told *TV Guide,* "Naturally fearless and innovative, Gene never stopped learning. He knew television's power to persuade by showing, and wanted to use that power well. On the *Enterprise,* we see the difference of racial and alien types, gender difference, handicaps, apparent deformities, all accepted simply as different ways of being human. In this, *The Next Generation* has been light-years ahead of its predecessors, its imitators, and practically everything else on television. The continuing mission of the starship *Enterprise* has been to take us out of the smog of fear and hate into an open space where difference is opportunity, and justice matters, and you can still see the stars. Violence, on *The Next Generation,* is shown as a problem, or the failure to solve a problem, never as the true solution. This is surely one reason why the show has such a following among grown women and men."

But it took others a while to accept *The Next Generation.* "A lot of people thought that a sequel to *Star Trek* as a series wouldn't fly," *USA Today* reported in 1986. *Star Trek* movie producer Harv Bennett added, "Prior to *TNG,* people who loved Trek could watch reruns, and once every two years they could go to the theater and get a bigger dose of Trek, and you'd have a feeding frenzy." Too much *Star Trek,* executives feared, could prove as bad as no *Star Trek.*

When *Star Trek* was revived as a TV series in 1987, James Doohan, who played Chief Engineer Montgomery Scott in the original 1966-69 *Star Trek,* took his complaint about *Star Trek: The Next Generation* to series creator Gene Roddenberry. Doohan told Associated Press, "They were doing shows we had done. I said, 'What's the matter, Gene? Are you running out of writers?'" Later Doohan changed his mind, and believed that Roddenberry was trying to use *The Next Generation* to perfect things he didn't get quite right in the original series. He said, "I don't think Gene was too happy with some of the characters on the original. In a way, he was a perfectionist."

Hiring the Best

John Pike, Paramount's president of network TV, was prepared to let Roddenberry work out the kinks in the new series during its first season or two: "There was great eagerness to do *Star Trek* on television, but it was an anxious time, too. You don't want to be the one to screw up the franchise."

Music for The Next Generation

Step one was to hire the best talent available. After assembling his production team of Justman, Berman, and Fontana, Roddenberry chose Jerry Goldsmith to write the main theme music for *Star Trek: The Next Generation.* Goldsmith first met Gene Roddenberry while working on the *Have Gun, Will Travel* TV series. He had been a staff composer for CBS and had scored *The Twilight Zone, Thriller,* and *Lonely Are The Brave* (1963), his first major feature film.

In addition to his more mainstream work, Goldsmith worked on a number of genre movies, including: *Our Man Flint* (1965) and *In Like Flint* (1967); Ray Bradbury's *The Illustrated Man* (1969); *The Omen* (1976), *Damien: Omen II* (1978), and *Omen III: The Final Conflict* (1981); *Logan's Run* (1976); *Alien* (1979);

Outland (1981); *Poltergeist* (1982) and *Poltergeist II: The Other Side* (1986); *Twilight Zone: The Movie* (1983); *Gremlins* (1984) and *Gremlins 2: The New Batch* (1990); *Explorers* (1985); *Total Recall* (1990); and *Planet of the Apes* (1968) and *Escape from the Planet of the Apes* (1971). He wore an ape mask when conducting the score for *Planet of The Apes*. Goldsmith's genre television work included music for *Voyage to the Bottom of the Sea*, *The Man from U.N.C.L.E.* and *The Girl from U.N.C.L.E.*, and *The Amazing Stories*.

Goldsmith's association with *Star Trek* began in 1979 with *Star Trek: The Motion Picture*. He also worked on *Star Trek V: The Final Frontier* (1989) and *Star Trek: First Contact* (1996), as well as writing the main themes for the television series *The Next Generation* and *Voyager*.

Composer Dennis McCarthy joined the team in 1987 after a career that included nine years as arranger and composer for Glen Campbell and several more as an orchestrator for Alex North, whose scoring credits included the *V* series. He also composed music for *The New Twilight Zone* and *MacGyver*. He told the *Charlotte Observer*, "Music can augment a scene, especially an emotional scene. There's also nothing quite as fun as having an orchestra roar through a battle scene. When *The Next Generation* came up, I was already friends with people at Paramount, which produced *MacGyver*. [Producers] Rick Berman and Bob Justman were familiar with my *V* and *Twilight Zone* work."

Costumes and Sets

Veteran stage costume designer Bob Blackman moved easily from the theater to *The Next Generation* for its second season. He has put his classical background to use on the series. Blackman said, "I'll pick up a sleeve from one era, a neckline from another, cram them together, and then clean it up and make it sleeker." He changed the men's Starfleet uniforms from front-zipping spandex jumpsuits to two-piece wool gabardine numbers.

Production designer Richard James worked as a designer for NASA before he came to *Star Trek: The Next Generation* at the start of its second season. Over the seasons, James said, "We've had to slash and burn a lot. Budgets play a big part in last-minute changes. I start off with the Taj Mahal and wind up with Motel 6!" For example, he designed Data's ornate English manor home in the final episode. He pointed out, "We designed a library for it, two stories high, with a mezzanine level full of books. Then I had to cut $30,000, so out came the erasers!"

Special Effects

Rob Legato and Gary Hutzel took primary charge of special effects for the third season. Ronald B. Moore became the visual effects coordinator. He told the Byte Information eXchange that illusion is more important than reality, explaining, "In visual effects, we are interested in photographic and electronic tricks: if someone has to fly or transform; if something has to be added later like a phaser beam or a transporter effect; or an image created like a wide exterior on an alien world. The *Enterprise* or another ship all are visual effects done by Dan and me or Rob and Gary. The art department creates all the graphics, like the science station or the navigation panel or all the graphics in engineering. If a graphic is to be seen on a small panel or the viewscreen, the art department would make up the graphic, and we would put it in the screen. It was the art department that designed the *Enterprise*, though Dan has designed a few, and there are some other model builders we have used. The art department also has a lot to do with the design of the tricorders and other such equipment.

"I wish we could do more, but just before we started 'Farpoint,' we did many tests. Most effects facilities in the area were given the chance to do some tests for us. By far, Digital Production had the most convincing graphics of the *Enterprise*. They did some things we would have a hell of a time doing on film. The producers and the effects department went over and over the results, and in the end we felt that models were really the best choice. The images were more realistic. Because of that, we are locked into using models, as we must continue using the shots we already have. We are creating quite a library of ship shots. When we have tried to use graphics in other areas, we have almost always run into time and money problems. I know it could be smoothed out, but we have so little time that we don't use it as much as we could.

"The *Enterprise* models are custom-made at a great cost. Now we have three models: one six feet, one four feet, and one two feet long. They are quite different from each other. They all photograph differently, and we have a lot of control with cameras and lenses. If you look at the models, they look different, but we use them for different purposes and make them look alike. Sometimes we do better than other times. The four-foot model was seen for the first time in 'The Defector.' I think you will see it in almost every show.

"We plan to reshoot some of the stock shots from ILM [George Lucas's special effects company]. We have a better model now and can improve them a lot. We have been shooting a lot of ships the last few years. Hundreds of shots. We hate to use the older shots that you guys are starting to pick out."

Moore described how the special effects team worked with a Malibu location shoot for "Survivors." "It was shot at a house that looks like what you see. We made some changes there but not to the house itself. However, the only time you see the house in a long shot, it is a painting, and the only real part is the area where our guys beam in. It was a tough shot in that we were moving in to the guys while they were beaming in. It was a grand attempt, but it could have been better. We try to add touches like that when we can to add some interest. Most transporters are locked down during the transporting action. It was an unusual shot."

He added, "The idea for the cigar gag at the end [of 'Deja Q'] was from the Captain himself! The Q flashes are very difficult to do in that you have to try to remember exactly how someone is standing. John is really good at it. I think he studied *Tai Chi* or something like it. If you watch frame by frame, I am sure you can see imperfections, but I think in context they work. It is a very quick effect. I feel that it is best to put the money where it will show the most."

The effects teams have some input on the scripts. Moore said, "The scripts can be detailed: *Enterprise* fires photon torpedoes at Ferengi ship. Or the crew marvels at the screen while mind boggling image fill them with feelings of impotence! We sometimes have many long talks with the producers and director before the shoot, then it's pretty much up to us. It's good for us if they like what we do 'cause they will let us keep doing them. We do surprise, inspire, and sometimes disappoint them."

Giving Life to the Characters

Then, of course, there's the on-screen acting talent who give life to the characters. How well they grow into their parts and interact with one another determines the success of a TV series. Roddenberry's team went looking for the best to sign to five-year contracts.

Patrick Stewart told *Cinescape,* "Before my Americanization, I blush to recall that I'd say, 'All right, Number One can have the bridge, but he stays in his own chair.' Can you believe anyone would behave like that? Happily, those days are behind me. I was fortunate enough to work with a group of people who liked me enough to not want me to go on being a pompous ass.

"I do remember a company meeting I called during the first season—Denise Crosby was still on the show—and I said that I felt that the set was much too undisciplined and that we should all exhibit much more self-control. I remember Denise saying, 'Come on, Patrick, it's just fun.' I said, very adamantly, 'We're not here to have fun!' Well, they wore me down. They wouldn't do the things I wanted them to do. They just laughed at me. As it turned out, I had the best time of my life in the last five or six years of the show."

Stewart told *TV Guide* that the close personal relationships he formed during *TNG*'s run have much to do with his affection for the show. He said, "I'm entertaining half [the *Star Trek* cast] at my house this weekend. We do all kinds of things together. I've just finished directing four of them in a play. It never occurred to me to cast anybody else. I wanted to work with my pals and I wanted to have a new experience with them. I'm told that it is unusual. And we have fun. I've laughed more in the last six years than I have in my entire life." He told a Creation Convention in Palo Alto, "They're the silliest bunch of people imaginable. LeVar isn't silly, but they're working on him."

At the end of the first season, Paramount announced that Gates McFadden had left the series "to pursue other career options." McFadden maintained that the news she wouldn't be returning was a surprise to her. She told the *San Jose Mercury News,* "I got a call from my agent saying that they had decided to go in another direction with the character. And that was literally all I heard." Stewart said that he was opposed to dumping Gates but didn't want to propagate dissension. He felt that the chemistry with Gates was good, and that she had been forced to leave for political reasons.

Diana Muldaur was briefly brought aboard as the starship's new doctor for one season. Stewart said that Muldaur's Dr. Pulaski was never really pinned down as a character: "They started off with chains and never let the character become firmly rooted."

> "As it turned out, I had the best time of my life in the last five or six years of the show."

McFadden was surprised to be asked back for the third season, saying, "I certainly missed working with my fellow cast members." After she returned, she still wasn't happy with the way the series presented her character. She told the Trekon in Kansas City, "I would like to see Beverly used more. She is someone who has a very high rank, and you sort of lose that. I would like to see more humor, and I would like to be involved in more command decisions. Anyone on the bridge would have to be able to serve in combat. I have often felt straightjacketed. I wish that the character could occasionally loosen up outside of the operating room. There are wonderful things about the character that I have tried to develop, and I hope that part comes across."

Expressing a more positive side, she said, "Brent's trailer is right across from mine, so we play practical jokes across to each other, but nothing that is, well, repeatable."

Denise Crosby also left at the end of the first season, but unlike Gates' Crusher, Crosby's Tasha Yar never returned. When she died in "Skin Of Evil," she stayed dead. Crosby had been so disgruntled with her back-burner status that she begged to leave. Crosby told *TV Guide,* "If Gene Roddenberry hadn't been alive and in complete control of the show, there's no way I would have gotten out. Paramount certainly wouldn't have let me go. [Roddenberry] told me if he was hungry and in his twenties, he probably would have done the same thing."

Crosby later told the *Charlotte Observer,* "Tasha meant a lot to a lot of people and I'm grateful for that. There was a sort of diamond-in-the-rough street kid element that people just related to." An alternate-time-line Yar returned two seasons later, in the episode, "Yesterday's Enterprise." "That gave Tasha the chance to die with a sense of meaning," explained Crosby. "It was a beautiful episode, moving, exciting and with a real emotional payoff." Crosby appeared one last time as Yar, in the series finale, "All Good Things. . . ."

Wil Wheaton played Wesley Crusher for 83 episodes, then left during season four's "Final Mission." He returned during the seventh season. Roddenberry liked Wesley best of all his characters, but the viewing audience never accepted the Will Robinson clone and hoped he would become "lost in space." The character left to attend Starfleet Academy, while actor Wheaton told *TV Guide* he wanted to "go out and experience my life."

Denise Crosby told a convention in Adelaide, South Australia, "It was very difficult for Wil [Wheaton]. He wanted to be a part of 'the group' and do things with us. Of course, he was 14 when the show started, and he simply couldn't. Also, when all the adults went to lunch, Wil would go to school for a couple of hours. And we had to watch what we said, since there was always this kid around.

"I have acquired the nickname 'Pookie' amongst the cast and crew. I don't know where it came from but I got it and it stuck. Anyway, I was on the set doing the episode before the last one and I heard a voice behind me saying, 'Pookie.' I turned around and here was this person I had never seen before. So I put on that stupid expression which meant, 'do I know you?' Wil said, 'Denise. It's me. Remember, it's me, Wil.' I couldn't believe it. All of the sudden he'd turned into a man!"

In 1990, Jonathan Frakes, who played Commander William Riker, told Associated Press, "The show's come a long way. It would be great to go back and redo the pilot knowing what we know now. The actors have all settled into their roles. The writing's gotten so good. We've relaxed into our characters and their clothes. The new ease is captured on screen." In 1991, he thought they had come to the end of the road, telling the *New Orleans Times-Picayune,* "It probably will be our final year. At the end of the season, they'll have more than 200 episodes altogether including the old show, and that's plenty. I've never had a job that's lasted four years. I consider myself lucky to be part of this group."

Michael Dorn (Worf) told a Creation Con in Boston that working on the show was incredible because the cast hung out at one

> *"The show's come a long way. It would be great to go back and redo the pilot knowing what we know now."*

another's houses and went out together. He said, "Marina and I are very close. Jonathan Frakes and I hang out a lot when he's not in New York or directing. It's really turned out to be a wonderful cast to be around. It kind of shows on screen, but when we're rehearsing and being together, we just have a good time. This really has become a family."

Marina Sirtis told the *New Haven Register,* "The success of our show was that we brought a whole new audience to *Star Trek* who were regular people." After the later debut of *Deep Space Nine,* Marina Sirtis told the *Charlotte Observer,* "I was a little bit sick of reporters coming up and saying, 'How does it feel to finally see strong women on *Star Trek?*' I wanted to punch their lights out. What do these reporters regard as being strong? To me, strength is a character thing and Troi is a very strong person. She doesn't yell a lot or get angry often, but that doesn't mean she's not strong. Gene Roddenberry and the show's writers inadvertently thrust Troi and Dr. Crusher into a dramatic black hole by assigning them 'nurturing' professions. When they created the females on *Deep Space Nine,* Rick [Berman] and Michael [Piller] couldn't let themselves fall into the same trap. The professions for the women had to be ones men or women could handle. I'm happy for Nana and Terry."

Whoopi Goldberg's fame almost worked against her. When her friend, LeVar Burton, forwarded her request to join the crew to *The Next Generation* production team, they thought it was a joke. They didn't think that anyone as big as Goldberg would sign on for a TV show. She told *Starlog,* "One of the cast members left the show and I heard about it, so I approached the show's producers again and said, 'Listen, I don't know if you know it, but I've been trying for a long time now to get on

this show.' They said LeVar had told them about it and they thought he was kidding. I told them I can't do all the episodes but I would like to do some of them."

Goldberg sees her character, Guinan the alien bartender, as "a cross between Yoda and William F. Buckley," but freely admits she's put a lot of herself into the role. "Well, she's a wise old owl," she told *Star Trek: The Official Fan Club* newsletter. "She's several thousand years old. She can change a lot of things for the folks on the *Enterprise,* but chooses not to."

Brent Spiner gets the most mail. He told *TV Guide,* "I get a lot of romantic mail. They're just curious about my availability or they're telling me about themselves, their problems, and how difficult life is for them. But the letters are really written to Data; he's a really accessible personality. He's vulnerable and innocent and there's a feeling that he's somebody who would be kind. That's why he would make a good partner or somebody to tell your troubles to.

"I think Data is the most clearly evolved character. When this series started—when I thought, 'Oh, sure, we'll do a pilot and that'll be it'—what appealed to me most about Data was that if this show could get a foothold, Data had the most growth potential. In the very first episode ['Encounter at Farpoint'], Riker calls Data 'Pinocchio,' in reference, of course, to this thing that wants to be human. And the challenge to me and the writers at that moment was to begin this journey toward Data striving for humanity, little by little."

He told *Cinescape,* "It couldn't have been a better job. I remember in the very beginning that Gene Roddenberry and I discussed where we wanted the character to go and his notion was, and I quite agree with him, that the journey my character would be on was that with each passing year he would get closer and closer to humanity and, finally, would be extremely close but still not a human. I think that's the way it went and it's still going that way."

Ursula K. LeGuin agreed, telling *TV Guide,* "It's been fascinating to watch Brent Spiner develop the physical and psychological subtleties of a role that might have been just another jerky android.

"The casting of the show was superb from the start. Gates McFadden, Marina Sirtis, and Majel Barrett brought depth and complexity to the conventionally feminine roles of Dr. Crusher, Counselor Troi, and Lwaxana Troi. Many of us wish that Tasha Yar [Denise Crosby] and Ensign Ro [Michelle Forbes] had stayed on board to shake things up, but at least we got Whoopi Goldberg wearing those great hats.

"The lead male actors, all impressive separately, were also great team players, their characters changing and deepening in relation to one another. Worf [Michael Dorn] was my first love. The glimpses of Klingon dynastic struggles were like Shakespeare's plays about the kings of England, full of quarrels and treachery and kinfolk at each other's throats, just like a family Christmas. I love that stuff. Worf, caught between two worlds, was a powerful figure, tragic."

Controlled Conflict

Villains added power to *The Next Generation.* Klingons had come to terms with the Federation, but that other warlike race from Classic Trek, the Romulans, clearly had not. They frequently returned to plague the *Enterprise. The Next Generation* introduced its own evil race of Borgs in "Q Who?" They, too, returned often. Data met his evil twin in "Datalore." The writ-

ers introduced the Ferengi in "The Last Outpost" as a threat, but the floppy-eared creatures soon became the Keystone Cops of the Alpha Quadrant. They would prove controversial. Perhaps Q, a member of the Continuum, proved to be the most interesting character in the series. Each provided *The Next Generation* with needed conflict and menace.

In 1991, the *L.A. Times Magazine* reported that, "*Star Trek* has certainly evolved light-years beyond the frequent punch-ups and photon torpedo blasts that characterized the original TV series. Death and strife have not been entirely banished from the universe some 400 years hence. But the new show, which is set some 85 years after the old series transpired, generally eschews violence and bluster for diplomacy and intellectual guile. Phasers are rarely set to kill. The new *Enterprise*—a plush, high-rent hotel in space—seeks out its new worlds gingerly, fearing, with a politically correct 1990s sensibility, that outright human interference may irrevocably muck up physical and cultural ecologies."

This change was carefully engineered by Roddenberry against great resistance. Roddenberry's original bible limited the boundaries of what *Star Trek* characters could and could not do, giving his writers a unique challenge: how to generate genuine human drama on TV without drawing on the baser motives—greed, lust, and power—that appear to drive other TV characters.

The writers' bible contained an entire list of "thou shalt not's," which included the admonition: "We are not in the business of toppling cultures that we do not approve of. We are not 'space meddlers.'" Item 10 on the list urged writers to "Beware of spaceship battles: They cost enormous amounts of money and are not really as interesting as people conflicts." His bible mandated that writers "Show a somewhat better kind of human than today's average. Regular characters all share a feeling of being part of a band of brothers and sisters. As in the original *Star Trek,* we invite the audience to share the same feeling of affection for our characters." The *Writers'/Directors' Guide for the 1989 Season* stated: "Our continuing characters are the kind of people that the *Star Trek* audience would like to be themselves. They are not perfect, but their flaws do not include falsehood, petty jealousies, and the banal hypocrisies common in the 20th century."

Few writers successfully dealt with this format, so Roddenberry rewrote the first 15 episodes. Berman said, "The show needed a helmsman who would set a strong course. By rewriting the first 15 scripts, Gene set the course for the rest of us."

Years later, Berman told *Time,* "There were some things that existed with Roddenberry that were very frustrating to us. Not to have conflict among your characters makes it very difficult, because all the conflict has to come from outside. On *The Next Generation,* with the exception of an android and a Klingon, pretty much everyone was human, and they weren't allowed to be involved in conflict, so that was very frustrating for the writers."

Tracy Tormé served as the creative consultant for the first season. He also wrote "Haven," "The Big Good-bye," "Conspiracy," and "The Schizoid Man." Years later, he told *Cinefantastique* of his struggles with these constraints during his brief tenure on *The Next Generation.* There was an atmosphere, Tormé said, of, "We can't do this, and we can't do that. I think the show was unbelievably static. All of these characters like each other all the time, and for me that was a real big disadvantage." Writers came and went. Fontana, the story editor, complained about the additions grafted onto her script for "Encounter at Far-

point." Both Fontana and David Gerrold claimed they had contributed to the development of the series concept. Roddenberry denied them credit. They left the series.

Berman began to act as a buffer between Roddenberry and the disgruntled writers. He told the *Hartford Courant,* "In the second season, [Roddenberry] began to step away. And by the third season his involvement was quite a bit less." Patrick Stewart said, "Rick was a little more broadminded about what I was permitted to explore as a character."

The Changing of the Guard

On Thursday, October 24, 1991, five years after *The Next Generation* began, a 70-year-old Roddenberry suffered a heart attack in his doctor's office. He was taken across the street to Santa Monica Hospital Medical Center, where he was pronounced dead at 2:46 P.M. Roddenberry had been ailing for six weeks. He was survived by his wife Majel Barrett, and their 19-year-old son, Gene Roddenberry, Jr., as well as two grown daughters from a previous marriage, Darlene and Dawn, two grandchildren, and his best-known offspring, the *Star Trek* universe.

Paramount Pictures Chairman Brandon Tartikoff said, "Few ideas in the annals of motion picture and television history have inspired more passion and allegiance on the part of the audience than has *Star Trek.* Twenty-five years ago, Gene Roddenberry imagined an optimistic future for us all, and his vision will live on well into that future."

Nimoy told the Associated Press that Roddenberry "had an extraordinary vision about mankind and the potential of mankind's future." George Takei added, "Gene was a dear friend as well as someone who shepherded my career. We call him the 'Great Bird,' and he really was for me."

Roddenberry's ashes were taken into orbit aboard a space shuttle sometime after his death. Majel Barrett Roddenberry divulged at a local Space Congress banquet that the ashes were returned to Earth. She said her husband "would have given anything to have been able, just once, to go into that great galaxy he dreamed about, where so few men have gone before. While he lived, it was not possible. Some time between the last day of Gene's life and today, nearly three years later, a beautiful space shuttle broke the bounds of Earth and disappeared into the final frontier. It carried the ashes of Gene Roddenberry." NASA spokesman Brian Welch confirmed the words, saying, "It is true. It was approved as a personal effect." It was appropriate.

Barrett is quick to defend her husband's memory. When Joel Engel wrote an unauthorized biography, *Gene Roddenberry: The Myth and The Man Behind Star Trek,* that portrayed Roddenberry as a sexually insatiable, widely disliked glory hog who overhyped his "vision" while burying the contributions of those who made it a reality, she told *TV Guide,* "Apparently the best way for inadequate talent to achieve recognition is by being negative." She called Engel "one of those people who'd accuse Santa Claus of abusing children," insisting that, "Even if some things in the book are true—even if everything in the book is true— it should never have [been written]. Gene instilled a hope and a brightness in people. He gave us reason to look forward to the future and he did it with a great deal of love and energy—so leave it alone! People like [Engel] absolutely disgust me. What he's done reflects more on his own attitude and self-image than that of his subject."

At the time of Roddenberry's death, Barrett told *TV Guide,* "Gene reached the point where he felt he'd done enough. He was retired and was resigned to the fact [that Berman] would go on without him. When Rick talked about [the possibility of] doing a third series, Gene just said, 'Go with God, I wish you well.'" She told the *Charlotte Observer,* "They were upholding Gene's vision before he passed away. Gene picked talented people, trained them, then stood back and let them work."

"Gene brought Rick down from the white-collar world, in his blue suit and tie, and he taught him *Star Trek,*" Barrett told the *Los Angeles Times,* "There were all the people who were saying, 'Hey, nobody can do it like Roddenberry,' and that's not true. Rick understands the basic idea, the Prime Directive, and his main objective is toward a better, kinder, more gentle world."

Barrett warned Berman of the job demands, after herself being locked in a legal battle with Paramount for years over merchandising rights. "Rick has been the guy behind the badge, really, for a long time. Now he's got the weight of the empire hanging all over him that Gene had for so long. I hope he's strong enough to take it, because we put up with it for 25 years. And believe me, they will come at you with knives drawn. I have to say, it can be horrific."

Berman became executive producer of *Star Trek: The Next Generation.* On December 3, 1991, he told the *Hartford Courant,* "If you're producing a medical show, you've got to learn all the rules of medicine. If you're producing *L.A. Law,* you've got to learn all the rules of jurisprudence of the state of California. When you're producing *Star Trek,* you have two sets of rules you've got to follow. You've got to get involved with [the] astronomy and physics and science that are very important elements of every episode, and at the same time, you've got to familiarize yourself and adhere to the rules of *Star Trek*, which are made-up rules, but have existed for 25 years. And there are millions of fans who take these rules as seriously as they take Newton's."

"Gene Roddenberry laid a mantle on me, of sorts," Berman told the *Los Angeles Times*, "and I feel very lucky. Gene wanted me to carry the ball for him, and to try to maintain his vision. He saw that I had respect for his vision—not because it's my vision. I don't believe the 24th century is going to be like Gene Roddenberry believed it to be, that people will be free from poverty and greed. But if you're going to write and produce for *Star Trek*, you've got to buy into that. I'm like a quality-control guy. My job is to keep this show good, and to keep it believable, and to keep it entertaining, and to keep whatever messages are in it true to what Gene wanted.

"He wanted to paint a picture of hope in the world, and I would much rather paint a picture of hope than a picture of despair. Whenever there is an instance in a story or a in piece of casting, or in the general fabric of society, I always feel Gene sitting on my shoulder. We have 25 million viewers who watch *The Next Generation*, 20 million who watch *Deep Space Nine*, and hopefully just as many who will watch *Voyager*. I like to think that we're doing this show for the vast majority of fans who bring this *Star Trek* family of characters into their home every week, and who embrace the ideas we try to portray on the show."

Berman saw his role as continuing the dream of the man who had been his mentor and friend, not to attempt to replace him. He told *TV Guide*, "Right after Gene Roddenberry died, I was asked to take his place

as the final speaker at a big *Star Trek* convention in Los Angeles. A year later, I again spoke at the same convention, and those are the only public appearances I've made. I have tried my best to stay away from them because it's not my job. My job is to turn out pieces of television that are thought-provoking, intelligent, entertaining, and on budget.

"Gene was elevated from television writer to a highly esteemed place in the hearts of millions, and that esteem has not changed. Yes, in certain ways he passed the baton to me, but I'm not comfortable with the honors that come with that baton. I don't think it's appropriate for me to step into his shoes and be beatified."

If Berman is not the visionary Roddenberry was, he did become a better executive producer. Roddenberry, a writer first and foremost, drove other writers to despair as a producer. Berman, on the other hand, had been a fresh young vice president at Paramount. Michael Piller, series writer and eventual executive producer of *TNG*, told the *Times*, "Rick has a remarkable ability to have an awareness of everything that's going on. I give him personal credit for saving the pilot of *Deep Space Nine* in the editing room. [The raw film] was long, slow, confusing. He went in there with the editors and

> *"He wanted to paint a picture of hope in the world, and I would much rather paint a picture of hope than a picture of despair...I always feel Gene sitting on my shoulder."*

33

came out with what was reviewed universally as a terrific piece of television film."

Berman later said, "I was involved in the birth of all these characters. I was involved with the selection of every actor. They're all very close to me. Worf has grown a great deal. Worf was originally not even a member of the regular cast. He was going to be a recurring character. With Michael Dorn, the character took on a life of its own and slowly became a member of the family. Data has grown. When we met him, he was an android meeting all these people for the first time. His search for humanity has gone on, and he has become a very complex personality. All the characters have grown."

New Writing Talent

As Berman took the reins, he showed his sense of humor, placing a bust of Roddenberry blindfolded by a red bandanna on his desk. He also brought in additional production talent, beginning with Michael Piller. In looking back on his initial relationship with *The Next Generation,* Piller said, "I'd been working on *Hard Time on Planet Earth* at Disney," Piller said, "I called Maurice Hurley, who was then co-executive producer, and asked him about a science fiction writer we wanted to hire. In the course of that conversation, I told him how much my family and I liked the show. He then approached me about meeting Gene Roddenberry. They asked me to write a free-lance script, 'Evolution,' which my agent advised against, but I decided to do. The third season was quite turbulent. Michael Wagner was leaving and Gene asked if I wanted to come on board and run the staff.

"By the end of my first season [the series' third], my nerve endings were raw. I wrote the season cliffhanger, 'The Best of Both Worlds'

with no idea of how it would end at the start of next season or if I would even come back. Obviously, I did come back and now I look back, and that third season—both difficult and exhilarating for me—is the one most fans regard as the turning point of the series. Suddenly it became more than just the sequel to the old *Star Trek*; it became *The Next Generation,* a show you must watch.

"It became its own phenomenon—transcending the original—with quality stories, about the characters and the human condition. The people who watch feel they have discovered something on their own. They've brought other people in, and they all feel part of this cult experience. The show's become part of their lives in a very special way; it gives them optimism and hope and shows that there is a future."

Piller had begun his Emmy-Award-winning broadcasting career with CBS News in New York. He then served as Managing Editor of the WBTV-TV News in Charlotte, North Carolina, and Senior News Producer at WBBM-TV, the CBS affiliate in Chicago. His first job in entertainment television was as a censor in the CBS docudrama unit. Piller later spent two years as a Programming Executive before leaving CBS to write full time. Piller's credits as a writer-producer include the series *Simon & Simon, Cagney & Lacey, Miami Vice, Probe,* and *Hard Time on Planet Earth.*

Jeri Taylor joined the show's writing staff in 1990. Taylor had been a producer for the series *Quincy, M.E.* (for which she also directed episodes), *Blue Thunder, Magnum, P. I., In the Heat of the Night,* and *Jake and the Fat Man.* She had also co-written and produced the CBS television film, *A Place to Call Home* (starring Linda Lavin), and two ABC Afterschool Specials, *But It Wasn't My*

Fault, and *Please Don't Hit Me, Mom,* for which she earned Writer's Guild and Emmy Award nominations. Taylor had also written for the television series *Little House on the Prairie, The Incredible Hulk,* and *Cliffhangers,* but had never seen *Star Trek.* She came to executive producers Gene Roddenberry, Rick Berman, and Michael Piller through a recommendation from producer Lee Sheldon. Taylor co-wrote the script for the fourth-season episode, "Suddenly Human," became a staff writer, then was promoted to producer.

Taylor told the New York Times Syndicate, "I had to take a crash course in *Star Trek* history. It wasn't easy, but maybe, not having any preconceptions whatsoever about *Star Trek,* I was able to bring some kind of fresh perspective to it. It's immensely gratifying to be involved in helping to create another part of the *Star Trek* legend. It's a rare show in that I feel a difference is being made. When you write something for *The Next Generation,* it's going to be seen by millions of people and it can affect their lives in a profound way. The moral structure of our show, what it espouses, is good and positive. We have a wonderful staff of people I work with and like. All of these very positive things definitely make it worthwhile."

Brannon Braga had never seen an entire original *Star Trek* episode, and had watched few *The Next Generation* episodes before beginning an internship with the show's writing staff in 1990. He later wrote many of the series' most highly praised episodes, including "Realm of Fear," "Phantasms," "Cause and Effect," "Timescape," and "Parallels," and rose to the position of co-producer. He told the *Charlotte Observer,* "I was here for about eight weeks and going through a lot of the experiences a staff writer goes through, not knowing much about television production at all. I was learning about *The Next Generation,* the show

itself. I was given an assignment to rewrite [the fourth-season episode] 'Reunion.' It received a very favorable response, and after that I just never left."

Frustration and Acclaim

In 1990, *TV Guide* reported that Paramount Network Television was waging an aggressive campaign to secure Emmy nominations for their popular cult series, *Star Trek: The Next Generation.* The studio ran ads and promotional spots touting the show. In addition, reruns of its best episodes were shown. In the previous year, *Star Trek: The Next Generation* had been nominated for eight Emmys, but all in technical categories. Berman told *TV Guide,* "In some demographic groups, this is the number-three or -four show. Few people would argue that actor Patrick Stewart is one of the best actors on television. And we are hoping through promotion to garner the recognition that we deserve."

The campaign failed. In 1991, *Broadcasting* reported, "For the fourth consecutive year, *Star Trek: The Next Generation,* which garnered a slew of technical nominations, was shut out of performing, writing, directing, or outstanding drama series categories." John Pike, president of Paramount Television, told the magazine, "I don't want to sound like sour grapes, but *Star Trek* has certainly deserved more recognition in the series, acting, writing, and directing categories. We submit nominations for most technical and creative categories, but I really believe most voters think series from the broadcast networks are the cream of the crop. As far as budget, production value, and the performances, I'd put this against any network series."

In 1993, Patrick Stewart told *TV Guide,* "*Star Trek* is only dismissed by people who don't watch it. Even though it's full of fun, high adventure, dazzling technology, and all kinds of creatures, it's a very serious show, and that's the way serious things should be presented. Shakespeare wrote entertainment, but clearly his plays could be very serious, too. We're conscious that some people think of us as 'that syndicated kids' show,' and as far as a large part of the TV industry is concerned, we are. Otherwise, how can you explain the total absence of Emmy nominations for directing, writing, and acting?

"Oh, I was angry for a while. I wondered: 'Are we so bad? Are we getting it wrong? Are our numbers somehow totally misleading as to the quality of the work?' I watch the show and I think it's very good. In fact, it's as good as anything I've ever been around in my life as an actor. So how do we explain this? It's interesting that on the first American Television Awards show we got a nomination from reviewers and critics, but never from the industry, unless it's a technical nomination for special effects or makeup. It's somehow a curse to be too popular."

The real problem may have been that *The Next Generation* was not a network series, but rather proved that audiences could be attracted to syndicated drama. The Academy of Television Arts and Sciences, the organization which issues Emmys, was still dominated by ABC, CBS, and NBC.

Awards

The Next Generation did win a Peabody and a Hugo, and was the first non-network show to be endorsed by the Viewers for Quality Television. *TV Guide* chose the show as "Most Improved Series" in 1991 and "Worthiest Enterprise" in 1994. In 1993, the magazine also picked Patrick Stewart as best dramatic actor of the 1980s, saying, "We simply feel that Stewart's work on *Star Trek: The Next Generation* took a dubious notion—a *Star Trek* retread—and made it fly. He gave his role unexpected humanity, gravity, and literate grace. His formidable screen presence raises others to his level." *TV Guide* even named Stewart "the most bodacious man on TV."

In 1993, *TV Guide* also said, "*TNG* succeeds in ways that the original never did, or could. And while it retains Trek's story-telling style, it expands on it both technically and imaginatively. In this future, aliens and Earthlings mix more freely, even aboard the *Enterprise*. Its endless creations—the charming, omnipotent 'Q;' the fearsome Borg collective; the enigmatic Guinan [Whoopi Goldberg]—keep it fresh week after week. We're glad this starship is on a 'continuing' mission."

Criticisms

Not everyone was pleased with the show, though. Donald Frew, a scholar of religions and a member of the San Francisco Bay Area Interfaith Council, studied all 250 characters in the *Star Trek* series (films included), and decided that the show has a Jewish problem. In its seven movies and four television series, Frew noted to the *San Francisco Chronicle*, not once had there been a Jewish character. Frew said that "no one has even mentioned a bar mitzvah." His biggest problem is with the Ferengi: "short, swarthy and shifty-eyed," they have big ears, "wear a distinctive piece of headgear," and "are wanderers without a home" depicted as greedy merchants and "social pariahs." Frew added, "It could just as easily be a description of the Jewish people from a Nazi propaganda tract."

This claim appears dubious. Both stars of Roddenberry's Classic Trek, Shatner and Nimoy, are Jews, as is Whoopi Goldberg. The famous Vulcan hand signal came from a Jewish ritual recalled by Nimoy. Roddenberry's philosophy left no room for anti-Semitism, but could possibly abide militant atheism and hostility to all religion. If we never saw a bar mitzvah, it is also difficult to recall a Christmas tree. Although it is unlikely that Berman would allow anti-Semitism, the Ferengi first appeared while Roddenberry firmly held the helm, during the first-season episode "The Last Outpost."

An unhappy Timothy Perkins, the director of the Voyager Visibility Project, has been trying to get the producers of *Star Trek* to add a gay cast member to one of the crews. He said, "It's sad that a TV program known for such a progressive vision now lags behind situation comedies and soap operas in regard to the inclusion of gay and lesbian characters."

Popularity

The Next Generation also won the hearts of the viewers. The series first ranked number one among hour-long syndicated shows in 1989, and held that rank until it left the air. Only *Wheel of Fortune* and *Jeopardy!* ranked higher. In 1991, *The Next Generation* even beat *Wheel of Fortune* to take top spot for Nielsen Syndication Service program rankings as the number-one show for the week of November 11-17, 1991. The episode that beat *Wheel* was part two of a story featuring Leonard Nimoy reprising his famous Vulcan role from the original series for the 25th anniversary of *Star Trek*'s debut on NBC. It was one month after series creator Gene Roddenberry had died, and the sixth theatrical movie was set to open in theaters.

There were many other signs of popularity:

- When Patrick Stewart graced the *TV Guide* cover (January 2, 1993), it ranked as the best-selling regular issue of the year.

- Patrick Stewart's stint as guest host of *Saturday Night Live,* on February 5, 1994, won ratings ranked among the top five *Saturday Night Live* programs.

- A 1993 Purdue University study found that children learn more about science from *Star Trek* than anything else outside the home.

- A 1991 Los Angeles *Star Trek* convention drew 12,000 fans.

- The Charlotte Chamber of Commerce chose a "Charlotte: The Next Generation" theme for its annual meeting, complete with a Klingon and Starfleet uniforms.

- *Star Trek* novels, published monthly by Simon & Schuster's Pocket Books, reach the top of the New York Times bestseller list and generate close to a million dollars a year.

- Franklin Mint conducts a brisk trade with high-end *Star Trek* items, including 25th-anniversary commemorative coins, pewter models of the various *Enterprise*s, and even ornate chess sets costing nearly $1,000.

- Timex offers a complete line of Trek watches.

- Associates National Bank, headquartered in Dallas, offers Trek credit cards.

- *Star Trek* and *The Next Generation* are seen in 40 countries.

- There are at least 250 product licensees worldwide; merchandise sales have passed the $1-billion mark.

- Nimoy said, "People have not gotten a real sense of what *Star Trek* fandom is really all about. I talk to people in various professions all the time who say, 'I went to college to study this or that because of *Star Trek*.'"

- Fans include General Colin Powell, Robin Williams, Mel Brooks, physicist Stephen Hawking, Los Angeles Laker James Worthy, Mae Jemison (first African-American woman in space), Emmy and Tony award winner Bebe Neuwirth, *Entertainment Tonight*'s John Tesh, Mick Fleetwood of Fleetwood Mac, all-around entertainer Ben Vereen, film legend Jean Simmons, the Dalai Lama, comic Joe Piscopo, and Rachelle Chong, a member of the Federal Communications Commission. Chong decorated her office with Trek paraphernalia and dressed up as Captain Picard for Halloween, saying, "I like the show because it shows me tomorrow." Many scientists admire the show for its faithfulness to the scientific method. "They have a respect for the way science and engineering work," said Louis Friedman, a former programs director at Pasadena's Jet Propulsion Laboratory.

- Associated Press reported one of the oddest enterprises of all. Some *Star Trek* fans were calling for help in a bold new mission to establish a North Carolina community where the virtues played out on the science fiction television show would become a reality. Advertisements in *The News and Observer* of Raleigh and *Starlog* magazine called on mature Trekkers interested in a structured community where they could live out the high moral code set by the Starfleet gang.

Tibetan monks from the Dalai Lama's monastery in India once visited the set of *The Next Generation*. Their spiritual mentor, the Dalai Lama, is a *Star Trek* fan. Roddenberry told the *L.A. Times Magazine,* "It has become a crusade of mine to demonstrate that TV need not be violent to be exciting. I'd often felt that no one was catching on. But if the Dalai Lama likes us, I suppose the message is getting out. I finally feel I have become a philosopher, junior grade. There's hardly a subject you could mention I haven't spent time thinking out while writing *Star Trek* scripts. You spend years dreaming up strange new worlds, and they build up into something quite real."

Stewart once explained why he believes *Star Trek* plays a special role in the history of television, telling the *L.A. Times Magazine,* "[What Trek offers] is the kind of narrative power that our earliest ancestors knew around their fire in the cave. It's what kept people together. It's what gave meaning to their lives. It's what validated them, or placed them in time and space. It still does. One of the ways any culture will be judged by history will be by the quality of its entertainment. In this business, one can never attempt to see into the future. I don't know what people will say of this show 100 years hence, but *Star Trek* has maintained its grasp for 25 years. 'Where are we going?'—if there are still any of us left to inquire—will continue to be asked then."

Stewart related a dramatic personal anecdote to the *Seattle Post-Intelligencer,* which made clear how important his role has become to the world. He said, "About 18 months ago, I foolishly went to a bank machine after midnight in Los Angeles. As I did, a car ominously pulled up, this huge man jumped out, and seemed about to do me in. But then he suddenly pointed at me, cried out, 'You're Patrick Stewart . . . You're Jean-Luc Picard!' Then he threw his arms in the air and cried out, 'God, I love this town!' and drove off. Who knows, [being Picard] may have saved my life!"

Summing Up

Summing up his career with *Star Trek: The Next Generation* at the end of its television run, Berman said, "I have held the rudder firmly. I've been in charge in many respects for seven years and it has gone smoothly. We have a cast, crew, writers, producers, production people, and post-production people pretty much still intact who still get along. That's an accomplishment. The show has maintained its dignity, clarity, and purpose. I have kept the show true to Gene Roddenberry's image, and I think I've been very, very clever in selecting wonderful people to make this television show. There are a lot of people on the show who make me look very smart.

"The series began with the 'Encounter at Farpoint' episode seven years ago. It was the beginning of a journey of exploration. The last episode brings our characters back to that episode in many respects. It reintroduces Q, who we've seen numerous times in between, and it is going to again explore man's standing at a threshold of exploration. This episode will make people think about humanity. That's what the show represents: an opportunity to think about things in a different way."

Perhaps Sirtis summed it up best, telling the *Charlotte Observer,* "We all fit together like an old glove now. It's strange to think this will all come to an end pretty soon. I'm getting withdrawal pangs just thinking about it. We're going to go off to make our movies and I'm excited about that. But, I could go on. We really haven't done it all yet. There's more to do, to explore, to learn about our characters. But it's off to the movies we go."

But first the final episode would air, and the world would pay tribute to an old friend even as it prepared to wait two years for the first movie.

CHAPTER FOUR

The End of the TV Years

On October 2, 1993, *TV Guide* reported: "Rumors are buzzing on the set of *Star Trek: The Next Generation*. Will there be an eighth season in 1994–1995, or is the current one the last? 'Anything is possible with *Star Trek*,' says star Patrick Stewart. But executive producer Rick Berman claims the series will 'pretty definitively' close down." It did. "All Good Things . . ." aired as the final TV voyage during the week of May 23, 1994.

Puzzling Decision

Everyone puzzled over Paramount's decision to cancel the series. *The Next Generation* was still the highest-rated syndicated drama in the history of television, with 15 to 20 million viewers a week, and the number-one-rated hour-long series among men age 18 to 49. Joel Berman (no relation to Rick), Paramount's executive vice president of domestic television, told *Entertainment Weekly*, "It's always tough to cancel a series that's doing as well as *The Next Generation*, but the bottom line is that a successful feature film franchise can be more profitable than a TV series. We thought it was time to launch *The Next Generation* as a movie franchise, and we didn't think we could do the television series at the same time. Why would people go to movie theaters to see *The Next Generation* if new episodes were available on TV every week? The movie wouldn't be as special."

Rick Berman admitted to *Entertainment Weekly*, "A slight little pang of despair runs through me every time I realize we're going to be on the bridge or in Picard's quarters for the last time, but there's no real sense of closure. The movie certainly softens the blow of separation. There are a lot of reasons why this decision has been made, and I'm not aware of all of them." Retreating a little from the strength of that statement, he told *TV Guide*, "All I can tell you is that the decision to end *The Next Generation* after a seven-season run was made at least two years and two Paramount regimes ago. This plan has been around a long time, since before the studio asked us to do Voyager. You'd have to ask Paramount why they did it."

Gene Roddenberry's widow, Majel Barrett, was the only performer to have spanned all *Star Trek* incarnations, appearing as the first officer in the original pilot for *Star Trek*, then recast as Nurse Christine Chapel for the series, continuing as Chapel in *Star Trek: The Motion Picture* and *Star Trek IV: The Voyage Home*, and later becoming Lwaxana Troi on both *Star Trek: The Next Generation* and *Star Trek: Deep Space Nine*. She's also the voice of the Enterprise computer. Barrett told *TV Guide*, "Paramount has come up with a whole bunch of excuses and reasons, but so far none of them holds water. One [executive] will point in one direction, one will point in the other. I have a feeling it has to do with what goes on behind that little door marked 'Accounting.' Maybe I'm wrong, but I don't think we've heard the truth yet. Maybe it's Rick Berman. Maybe he just wants to go on to something that has no more of Gene Roddenberry in it. [Berman has been left] with the [burden] of the whole thing. If nothing is out there with Gene's name on it, it might make Rick's role a little easier. I could [understand] it."

Rumors persisted that series' star Patrick Stewart had forced the end and had been uncooperative in filming the last episode, supposedly refusing to loop segments on weekends—even that other cast members were fed up with Stewart's supposed prima donna behavior on the set. Berman told *TV Guide*, "Totally, totally untrue. This last episode is very complex and demanding. That's why

Stewart's been less patient with outside stuff. He's been working 14-hour days in three different wardrobes and three different makeups. He's in every damn shot. He's totally fried."

Mixed Feelings

Stewart wasn't sorry to see the series end. He told *Entertainment Weekly,* "For me, the timing is perfect. I had been increasingly feeling that I'd given the best of my work on the series. The last two years especially have found me feeling intense restlessness. I needed to go on to something else. This is the toughest job I've ever done, except maybe when I worked on a building site unloading cement blocks; that was marginally more difficult. And the last three months have been especially tough, culminating with this epic two-hour special. There were moments when I thought I wouldn't be able to finish the episode, I was so tired. And yes, it did lead to some outbursts like the one [with *Entertainment Tonight*], for which I apologized personally to everyone concerned. It was turning into a three-ring circus with press on the set every day."

He told *TV Guide,* "My feelings when I knew this was to be the last season were a mixture of intense relief, sadness, and an inevitable sense of loss and regret. When it first started, I didn't think that I would survive beyond the pilot. I did not unpack. I didn't see the point. I thought the producers would come to their senses and realize they'd made a grave error in casting me. I was certain that I'd be on my way back to London. Eventually, it became clear to me that not only wasn't I going to go away, the series wasn't going to go away. I stayed, and have relished every moment. There comes a time when you've given all you can to a project, and I've liked to roam from job to job. I'm ready now to tackle a different kind of work."

Stewart told *Cinescape,* "I started to fear that I, as an actor, might begin to repeat myself. The days were not as fresh and exciting or as interesting as they had been, and I was looking for new pastures."

LeVar Burton pointed out that the cast is an ensemble with very different needs. As he told *Entertainment Weekly,* "We're a family in crisis. This is the end of seven years of shared experience. You can't end something like this without pushing people's buttons. It's going to bring up strong emotions, and everybody is going to handle it differently." He told *TV Guide,* "I actually feel great about it. This has been a very fulfilling seven-year cycle in my life, but I feel in my very being that it's time to move on. Time to do what I've been preparing to do: tell stories that are near and dear to my heart." Burton had established his own production company, Eagle Nation Films, in 1991.

Some other cast members were, like Stewart and Burton, ready to move on. Michael Dorn told *TV Guide,* "I reached the apex of Worf about three years ago, and around that time, I, and Patrick, too, I think, started counting down. Emotionally, I really haven't come to grips with the end of the series yet. However, I do know one thing: I'm gonna be glad to get out of this makeup! Gene Roddenberry gave me great creative leeway and, as a result, I feel I've been the architect for all Klingons."

> *"This is the toughest job I've ever done, except maybe when I worked on a building site unloading cement blocks…"*

43

Despite being ready to move on, Dorn was happy with his life since joining Trek, telling the *L.A. Times Magazine,* "If what happened to the first cast is called being typecast, then I want to be typecast. Of course, they didn't get jobs after Trek. But they are making their sixth movie. Name me someone else in television who has made six movies!"

Brent Spiner echoed his castmates, telling *Cinescape,* "We'd done 178 hours of the series, and 178 hours of anything is enough. It was a brutal seven years of work and I am glad that I don't have to get up at 5:00 in the morning any more. Maybe a couple of people would have been interested in doing an eighth season, but not many of us. I think we felt we'd done enough for seven years, and with luck we'll get to come back and do it every couple of years as a film." But he went on to tell *Entertainment Weekly,* "Right now I'm in plain old denial. I have absolutely no feelings about it whatsoever. I'm serious. To me, it's just another season-ender, like all the others."

> "Of course, they didn't get jobs after Trek. But they are making their sixth movie. Name me someone else in television who has made six movies!"

Others felt differently. Gates McFadden believed there was more she could do with her character, telling the *Charlotte Observer,* "There's just so much we never learned about [Dr. Crusher]— about her as a person, as a doctor, as a mother. But I must say we made some real headway the last two seasons. Since Jeri Taylor took over [as day-to-day executive producer] my character really did blossom. And I'm pleased to say I have some nice stuff in this last double episode."

Jonathan Frakes agreed with Gates; he didn't want to leave his role, and didn't understand why a popular TV series was being canceled. Frakes told *Entertainment Weekly,* "I haven't been given any reason that holds water. Maybe [Paramount] thought they couldn't do the movie and the TV show at the same time, although I don't know why the movie had to be made this year. Some of us kept hoping there would be an eleventh-hour reprieve, that Paramount would realize how much money the show has made for them and change their minds."

He told *TV Guide,* "If there's any truth to the rumor that our show makes Paramount $80 million a year, why in God's name do they take off the cash cow? But they don't ask us, do they? One wonders if they aren't going to the well one too many times. I hope not. But it's certainly got to be a fear the creators have. [The *TNG* producer] was more interested in talking about going on to *Voyager.* She's on her way and I felt like an old shoe. It's sorta like [they are saying], 'Hey, we've got a new group showing up, it's been wonderful, see ya later, have a good finale.' There was a different feeling when we first came on board. If there was an answer you needed, you could always go right to Gene, and the answer made sense. It was well thought out because it was his vision. And we're kind of a conglomerate now. We're lost in the machinery. We have all the affection in the world for each other. I don't know if we're ever going to have this much fun on any future job."

Marina Sirtis also believed that she could do more with her role. She told the *Charlotte Observer,* "I'm really very sad. In my head I thought we had another season left in us. So I feel a little cut short. I'd love to have done a little more with Deanna and then wrap it up. Although I'm really very excited about the film, which I'm sure will be great, I'd be lying if I didn't say I wish everything were one more year away."

"Psychologically, I think everyone is trying to detach themselves from the show and each other," she told *Entertainment Weekly.* "People are subconsciously being pissy on the set so that it won't hurt so much when the show is finally over."

Final Voyage

Berman told *TV Guide,* "We wanted to end with a sweeping story that embodies the themes that have made *Star Trek* important to us. The episode will bookend the series by once again exploring the concept of mankind being put on trial—the theme of our premiere show, 'Encounter at Farpoint.' We don't tie up every loose thread because, hopefully, there will be a series of movies. But there is a very strong sense of finality. We owe that to the audience. Riker will not wake up in the shower and say it's all been a dream."

The story, "All Good Things . . ." adds to the legend, portraying the futures of the command crew of the *Enterprise.* The future, revealed courtesy of Q, shows La Forge doffing his VISOR (Visual Input Sensory Optical Reflector) to become a novelist; Riker pining for Deanna Troi and angry at Worf, a rival for Troi; Dr. Crusher commanding a medical ship, divorced from Picard; and Data teaching at Cambridge while living in Isaac Newton's old house. Colm Meaney returns from *Deep Space Nine* as Transporter Chief Miles O'Brien, and Denise Crosby comes back as

Security Chief Tasha Yar, while Picard leap frogs between past, present, and future.

John deLancie, who portrays Q, said, "It's a bookend to the whole series. It's really a wonderfully poignant conclusion." He also told fans in Prodigy's Celebrity Lounge, "For the final episode of *The Next Generation,* I think that people were in a heightened sense. They were leaving a job, but they were also beginning the movie, so it wasn't like they were really, really leaving a job. They were going on to another one. What happens on sets, especially toward the end, is that people are extremely tired. As they get closer to the end, they think of what's going to happen for the rest of their lives. A lot of the thought at that point had to do with what was going to happen in the future instead of what was happening on the set."

The work load helped everyone keep their minds on the job, though. McFadden told *Entertainment Weekly,* "It's been crazy here these past few weeks. Last Friday I was on the set for literally 23 hours. These have been inhuman hours. People are just exhausted."

TV Guide reported that when the scene was finally finished, and the camera clicked off for the final time, Stewart stood on a scaffold above the bleary-eyed production crew and delivered a farewell address, saying, "I've been cleaning out my trailer and I found a piece of paper. It's a quote that I read at [Gene Roddenberry's] memorial, and it suddenly seemed really appropriate.

"'To, walk, we have to lean forward,'" he read from the writings of British psychotherapist Robin Skynner, "'lose our balance, and begin to fall. We let go constantly of the previous stability, falling all the time, trusting that we will find a succession of new stabilities with each step. . . . Our experience of the past, and of those dear to us, is not lost at all, but remains richly within us.'"

After The Next Generation

Stewart looked back, as well as toward the future, telling *TV Guide,* "I cannot yet say the world is my oyster. The English are uncomfortable with too much success. We see it to be in somewhat bad taste. The 25 million people who watch *The Next Generation* every week is not insignificant to producers. Most curious to see what possibilities will open for a film career in Hollywood. It opened up an area of work for me that I'm delighted with, because I never anticipated romantic roles would be accessible.

"There are far worse fates than being permanently identified with the legend that is *Star Trek*. I'll take a career like William Shatner's or Leonard Nimoy's any time. Cash in some chips at Paramount so they'll let me direct *Deep Space Nine* and their new series, *Voyager.* Hey, I was around and struggling long before *The Next Generation* came along. I don't have to be kicked in the head to recognize a good job."

Spiner told the magazine, "There's no getting around it: for the rest of my life, I'm Data. I would love to think the audience will instantly accept me as another character, but, in reality, the best I can hope for is that they'll see me in future parts and say, 'Oh, my God, that's Data!' and then forget about it 10 minutes later."

Spiner will miss working with his costars. He told the *Charlotte Observer,* "It's the friendships. Work is work. I've done a lot of jobs I enjoyed and a lot of jobs I didn't particularly enjoy. The one constant on this show has been the relationships with the cast. We've developed some really rich friendships and I expect those will go on forever."

British actress Sirtis agreed, telling *TV Guide,* "For the love to have lasted this long is extraordinary. Everyone has said that they've never known actors to get along this well after two years, much less seven. We've all heard horror stories about other sets, but we have no horror stories here. Not one. . . These people, and my husband, are the only family I have in this country."

McFadden added, "This experience has changed all of us in a really positive way, but by now we're all excited about the prospect of new things," while Stewart only noted, "After a few days of break, I shall be back on the bridge of the *Enterprise* again." Four days after they wrapped up the TV finale, they moved down the Paramount lot to Stage 7, and began their first film adventure together.

"All Good Things . . .," the final TV episode of *Star Trek: The Next Generation,* went on to win the "Best Dramatic Presentation" Hugo Award at the World Science Fiction Convention.

CHAPTER FIVE

Reborn on the Big Screen

Rumors about the new movie began to spread almost immediately. First the word was that the entire cast of the Classic series would appear in the film. Then a story spread that Scotty (James Doohan) and McCoy (DeForest Kelley) would not appear because at their advanced age (both are 74), Paramount wouldn't insure them. Some guessed that Data would be given an emotion chip and make love to Klingon sisters; others guessed that Riker would die, or that the *Enterprise* would be destroyed.

Rumors also spread that Shatner didn't recognize Frakes on the set, that Shatner and Stewart fought, then, after a Stewart spokesperson announced that he and Shatner "get along great," that Shatner and Stewart had bonded. Berman said the pair, who hadn't yet shot their scenes together, had become "fast friends."

Fans were desperate for news. On December 9, 1994, Associated Press reported that a producer had accused two memorabilia dealers of selling a bootleg script, an early draft. "For this reason, Paramount does not authorize sale of draft scripts. They will lead to a false impression of the final product. By learning every detail of the works, it is very likely that much of the public will not find it necessary to revisit the story by seeing the feature film." Paramount Pictures Corp. asked a U.S. District Court judge in Atlanta to shut down the memorabilia dealers.

Kerry McCluggage, chairman of Paramount Television Group, told the *Los Angeles Times:* "People are always hungry for details, to the point where scripts disappear from the lot. Almost everything you do is subject to all kinds of scrutiny and wild speculation." The entire *Generations* [the eventual name of the first *TNG* movie] script found its way onto the Internet.

Brent Spiner later told Boston Con, "Everybody had a copy of the last movie before we did. Folks got in trouble for that. When we first got our copies, they went according to the number on the call sheet: Patrick was number 1, Jonathan was number 2, I was number 3, and so on. Every page of my script had a big number '3' on it in red, so they could be sure, if the script got out, they would know who did it. By the time we had it, it was on computer [bulletin boards]."

One enterprising fan had odd collecting habits. "We came in on the third day of the shooting of the film, and the captain's chair was missing," Spiner said. "Someone took the chair off the Paramount lot without anybody seeing it. You've gotta wonder how they did that. It took a couple of hours for them to construct another chair. We came back the next day, and the chair was gone again! Somebody, again, had stolen the chair."

Star Trek VII—*Not!*

"The next Trek movie won't be called 'Star Trek VII.'" Rick Berman told *TV Guide*. "That would imply it's a continuation of the first six, which, in a sense, it is not. Right now we're calling it *Star Trek: The Next Generation: The Movie,* but that's strictly for the people in payroll."

Berman had written two story outlines and hired separate teams of *Next Generation* alumni screenwriters to develop them. Only one would go before the cameras. Berman had added, "And if both scripts work out well, we've got fodder for the eighth movie."

Patrick Stewart told *Cinescape,* "I had the most passionate voice for this being a truly transitional movie. Three years ago when rumors of a feature film were whirling around,

I said, 'This film must include as many members of the original crew as possible.' When it became a reality and there would be a role for Bill [Shatner], I was so anxious about whether or not he would want to do it. It would have been a bitter disappointment if he had pulled out. I felt we had the makings of a really nice team."

Generations marked the first time the *Star Trek* movies and TV series were produced by the same person. After the first film, Paramount took the sequels away from Roddenberry. Berman produced *Generations* the same way he produced his TV series, and he shares story credit for the film.

Ever since Roddenberry's death, *Star Trek* fans had been watching Berman for signs of deviance. Roddenberry used to rally his fans with speaking engagements, but Berman admits he doesn't understand the fierce devotion of fans. "The people who talk on their computer networks all night long, or the people who go to conventions—it's all a little overwhelming to me. I can't relate that much to people who take this a little bit more seriously than this should be taken. It is, after all, a show," he told the *Los Angeles Times*.

Changing Plans

Berman first called Nimoy to direct. Nimoy had successfully directed *Star Trek III* and *Star Trek IV*, and had been executive producer and cowriter for *Star Trek VI*. Each phone call to duty had come from a powerful studio executive—Michael Eisner, Jeffrey Katzenberg, Frank Mancuso—and Nimoy had been involved in script development from day one. This time a TV producer called with a finished script in hand. Nimoy wasn't pleased with the script and wanted a major rewrite,

but there was no time, so he declined to direct. Nimoy also turned down an offer to play Spock one last time.

When DeForest Kelley also turned down an offer to come back, Berman had to change his plans. Berman told *Entertainment Weekly*, "Both felt they had made a suitable departure in the last film."

"Once we knew we weren't going to have Leonard and DeForest," Berman told the *Los Angeles Times*, "it seemed silly to have all the rest. So we decided just to pick two." Berman turned to David Carson, a frequent director of *The Next Generation*, to direct *Generations*. He persuaded Sherry Lansing, chairman of Paramount Motion Picture Group, to go with the untested feature director by showing her his work on the two-hour series premiere of *Deep Space Nine* (which had begun its TV run before *TNG*'s was over).

British-born Carson had directed more than 50 plays throughout Great Britain and had moved into television work in 1980, earning acclaim for his productions of *Sherlock Holmes, Souvenirs,* and the short film *Waiting for Godot*. He had become disillusioned with the paralyzed British film industry and moved to Los Angeles, directing the pilot and two episodes of *Deep Space Nine*, and episodes of *Star Trek: The Next Generation*, as well as *L. A. Law, Northern Exposure, Homefront,* and *Beverly Hills, 90210*.

Carson told the *Los Angeles Times*, "People in the industry have said to me, 'Why would you want to direct *Star Trek*?' Well, the amazing thing about *Star Trek* is that you have the opportunity to tell stories that actually say something about the human condition."

"David is incredibly tenacious," Patrick Stewart observed. "I know of no other director that has the kind of determination and energy for work that he has. He's utterly tireless. The erroneous assumption that those who work in television are somehow less talented than those who work in film is the most monstrous snobbery and very unfair to those who do extraordinary work in television. I had no doubt very early on in production that, with David, this was a major film career in the making."

Changing Script

Brannon Braga co-wrote the screenplay with Ronald D. Moore. He told the *Charlotte Observer* that "At its heart and core it's a *Next Generation* film. It begins with the original-series crew and picks up later with *The Next Generation* crew. And, in a strange way, the two crews connect."

Their script went through rewrites prior to filming, then more changes when the actors and director read the words, then again when the footage went to the editing room. Actors and crew were called back to the set. The original draft changed in many ways. Berman and Carson changed Data's opening scene. Originally, the *Enterprise* suffered fatalities in an engagement with the Romulans. Riker reminded his captain that he must speak with the families of the dead crew members, but Picard ordered Riker to handle it. The producers

felt this didn't fit the character, and in the revised version the captain dealt with the death of his brother without neglecting his duties. This original script included all the major characters from Classic Trek in the opening sequences. The only characters to appear were Chekov, Scotty, and Kirk.

Whoopi Goldberg was not going to do the movie at first. Paramount called her agent, who turned them down for offering too little money. Whoopi heard about this while talking with Paramount and said, "What? Screw him, I'm doing the movie!" Her motivation was that Nichelle Nichols was in the original script, which called for Uhura to comfort Guinan after she was 'rescued' from the Nexus. Uhura was Goldberg's role model when she was growing up. When she later realized Nichols wasn't asked to be in the movie, she was extremely upset. She dreamed of acting with Nichelle.

Preview screenings for the movie rated it a 65 to 75 (a mark of 50 means the movie will do 'okay,' while a mark of 75 means the movie will make good money), but reactions to the ending were negative, so it underwent some changes. Originally, Kirk and Picard arrived back from the Nexus, and Kirk knocked Soran from the ridge over the canyon to the rocks below. Kirk and Picard then ran to turn off the missile,

---

Generations' SNAFUs

Revealing mistakes: Geordi's right eye is momentarily visible through his visor just before he inserts Data's emotion chip.

Factual errors: A chemically powered rocket launched from a planet inhabitable by humans would take significantly longer than 11 seconds to reach a yellow sun. The effects of the sun being destroyed would not be seen immediately on such a planet.

Continuity: Worf's sash when he is blown over the console.

The model of the Veridian system that Data shows Picard indicates that the ribbon will miss Veridian III unless the sun is destroyed, and yet the ribbon enters Veridian III's atmosphere with the sun still in existence.

Plot holes: The ribbon should not have made any course changes due to a sun not being destroyed.

---

mission accomplished—a happy ending until a half-dead Soran shot Kirk in the back and both died. Carson and several cast members went back to Nevada to reshoot the scene. Berman told the *Los Angeles Times* they went back to inject "a little more excitement, a little more action."

When asked why those elements weren't there to begin with, Berman said, "It might have been a problem with the writing, or it might have been a problem with the directing, or it was probably due to the fact that when we first wrote this movie it was much bigger than we could afford. There were some limitations made to the last sequence that were probably a mistake. We storyboarded this movie at five or six days longer than we had, and we had to compress the time. When you have less time to do something, you have to do it less well, especially when you're dealing with action."

They also changed the opening sequence. Originally, shots of Kirk "space-diving," free-falling, and eventually entering the atmosphere were interspersed with those of the wine bottle floating through space. Paramount didn't think that Kirk falling to Earth with his butt on fire—where the heat shields were—

What the critics said about
Star Trek: Generations
Roger Ebert, *Chicago Sun-Times*

"The *Star Trek* saga has always had a weakness for getting distracted by itself, and *Star Trek: Generations,* the seventh film installment, is undone by its narcissism. Here is a movie so concerned with in-jokes and updates for Trekkers that it can barely tear itself away long enough to tell a story. From the weight and attention given to the transfer of command on the Starship *Enterprise,* you'd think a millennium was ending. Leave it to Kirk to be discontent with just one death scene. Kirk's first death is a very long silence, but he has dialogue for his second one. I, for one, will miss him. There is something endearing about the *Star Trek* world. *Star Trek* seems to cross the props of science fiction with the ideas of Westerns. Watching the fate of millions being settled by an old-fashioned fist fight on a rickety steel bridge, I was almost amused by the shabby story-telling. In *Star Trek: Generations,* the starship can go boldly where no one has gone before, but the screen-writers can only do vice versa."

---

would be popular with viewing audiences. They cut the sequence.

One cut scene left residual dialog behind. The scene involved Soran torturing Geordi; in the missing portion, he had put nanites in Geordi's heart. When Soran was asked, "Did you get any information out of him?" he replied, "His heart wasn't in it." Beverly later mentions "damage to the coronary artery." These lines lose their meaning without the cut scene.

Sirtis didn't like the cutting of one of her scenes. When the bridge blew up, the helmsman died, and Riker told Troi to take the helm. She moved into the seat, then jumped up and yelled, "Ouch!," ruining the shot. The director yelled, "Cut! Cut! Marina, what's the problem? That was perfect!" Marina replied, "My bum's on fire! Look, I've got a hole burnt right through the uniform!" During the explosions on the bridge, flaming pieces had fallen onto the chair where Troi was to sit. It was too expensive to reshoot the sequence because they already had blown up the bridge.

Walter Koenig (Chekov) originally declined to appear in the film. He told the *Charlotte Observer*, "Rick Berman then called and asked me to come in and discuss it with the writers.

A little tweaking was done and I felt more comfortable. Even though it would be a small role, it was an opportunity to do something significant with the character. Indeed, I was very pleased with the scenes we shot, particularly one that had Chekov and Scotty [James Doohan] dealing with what we think is Kirk's death. Then they started editing the film, and I've been apprised that my work is eviscerated, including that particular little moment. There's no bitterness on my part, just disappointment. It's just not the way I wanted to go out as Chekov."

Controversies

Kirk's death proved controversial. During a *Time* magazine–hosted forum on America Online (AOL) on November 22, 1994, Berman said, "Gene [Roddenberry] felt very strongly that James Kirk was dead and gone before *The Next Generation* ever began. All we've done is resurrect him for one final adventure."

Malcolm McDowell played the man who killed Kirk. He told the *Charlotte Observer*, "I killed him for real, blasted him, actually, the first time we shot the ending. Now, as it turns out, I'm involved in Kirk's death by shooting the bridge he's on and causing it to fall, so his demise is not quite at my door anymore, and I'm actually quite glad about that, but I must be honest with you. For an actor, even though I may be killing a legend like Captain Kirk, the fact is it's just a scene to me, no more, no less. I've always thought the villain is the best part. They're the most fun. I think the big danger is that you can overdo it. There has to be a core of total reality to these parts. If they get too cartoonish, you belittle your audience."

Before killing Kirk, the actor had appeared in Stanley Kubrick's *A Clockwork Orange* (1971), *Caesar in Caligula* (1979), *Bopha!* (1993), *if. . .* (1968), *O Lucky Man!* (1973), *Time After Time* (1979), and *The Player* (1992). The non-Trekker knew Stewart from his days with London's Royal Shakespeare Company. Stewart and McDowell worked together on the production of *Henry V* 30 years ago. McDowell said, "I enjoyed working with him again. It was a good experience."

Shatner told an audience, "I didn't really want to die, but the whole thing about dying. . . Paramount decided to do *Next Generation* movies. They approached me and said, 'How would you like to die in this movie and give the character an end?,' and I agreed.

"There is a funny story about the death scene as we reshot it. When I was jumping over on the bridge that was about to give way, Patrick Stewart yelled out during one of the takes, 'Captain on the bridge!' Then, after the bridge breaks off and falls with me on it, and I'm lying under it, broken and bloody, Patrick is supposed to run down the hill and look at me, and he says, 'Bridge on the Captain!'"

Shatner enjoyed working with the horses, which came from his ranch. He raises horses, and noted, "I'm working on two sets of horses: reining horses here [in Los Angeles] and the saddlebreds in Kentucky [where he has a farm]. There is a great deal: the beauty of the horse, the feeling of two entities joining. The athleticism, the competition, the excitement of a galloping horse, and the art that is needed to control and yet be free."

Data's emotions chip also proved controversial. Spiner told a Grand Slam III audience, "I had some reluctance when I first saw the [*Generations*] script. I didn't know if the emotion chip was such a good idea for the first feature. I thought maybe somewhere down the line it would have been more interesting. I was vetoed on that suggestion.

"I know people objected and wanted Data to stay the way he was. It's interesting to watch a character you've known for seven years grow. *Star Trek* is about exploration, enlightenment, and growth. Data had steady growth. There was nowhere else to take him. There is room to play if he has the emotion chip. Obviously, in the last film, it was childish emotion. Data's always been a childlike character. In the movie, he was a childish character who suddenly had emotions and didn't know how to deal with them. As he grows, a maturing will take place. Instead of the really bad jokes he was making, he'll be tossing off *bon mots* from Oscar Wilde."

Spiner enjoyed working on the film. He told *Cinescape*, "The film was a real opportunity to cut loose and be wild. When I first read the script, I was a little concerned because it was so different, even though it represented the natural evolution of the character. Thinking about it, I finally came to the conclusion that, in a worst-case scenario, at least

> **What the critics said about**
> **_Star Trek: Generations_**
> **_Route 66 Online_**
>
> "*Star Trek: Generations* production values may be high, but the writing is frequently appalling, and instead of a script has a collection of references, in-jokes, and ill-defined characters. I don't think it is an insult to fans of *Star Trek* to suggest that to a certain extent, the particulars of a plot are not really the most important elements in a Trek film. It's about a chance to visit with old friends. But even that interpretation assumes that characterization has to be consistent, and in *Generations* that just doesn't happen. Data (Brent Spiner) is particularly victimized by this sloppy writing. If the rest of *The Next Generation* cast fares any better, it's only because they're on the screen so little that they're simply window dressing.
>
> "But this story isn't really about the new crew. It's about Kirk and Picard, the cowboy and the politician. The huge surprise is that William Shatner blows Patrick Stewart away. Stewart's edginess is indicative of what may be a very bad sign for Paramount's hopes to turn the new cast into the same kind of franchise the original cast was: these are clearly the Not Ready for Big Screen Players."

they'd love me in France. The character went from being childlike and naive in the series to being a different kind of child in the movie, because of the newness of the emotions and the inability to control them. So he was a child with emotion. I think the obvious place to take the character is into a gradual emotional maturity. That can only mean romance, can't it? What I hope would occur is a deepening of understanding of emotion and how to deal with that."

He told Boston Con, "[The emotion chip] wasn't just comic relief. It wasn't all good; it wasn't all fun. Geordi's life was jeopardized as a result of it; Data went through guilt and remorse. I enjoy evolution. The character grew. If he had stayed the way he was in the pilot episode, it would be a very tedious thing. The emotion chip, in some form, is there to stay.

"If you look at Captain Picard, he's very different now than he was initially. That's valuable. Worf is a different person than he was initially, and the same for the rest of ship. *Enterprise*-D was destroyed. I'm certain there will be an *Enterprise* E that will grow and change."

Reception

Star Trek: Generations was nominated for Best Science Fiction Film in 1995's 21st Saturn Awards. In the United States, as of March 12, 1995, the film had grossed over $75 million. Walter Koenig started his talk at Monadno-Con 2 in Ridge, New Hampshire, by revealing some of the numbers. He said the final take of the seventh Trek film was between $72 and $75 million dollars. He said *Star Trek:*

Generations cost $33 million to make, and came in as the second lowest money-maker of the series, just ahead of *Star Trek V: The Final Frontier,* which made $52 million dollars. He said it seemed that *Star Trek: Generations* was not looked at by Paramount as a major hit because it did not pass the magic $100-million-dollar mark of many other *Star Trek* films.

According to *Variety,* however, *Generations* opened strong in Germany and England, pro-

Week	Position	#Screens	$/Loc	Weekend Gross	Total Gross
Gross Income for *Star Trek: Generations*					
1 (11/18)	1	2,659	$8,694	$23,116,934	$26,146,569
2 (11/25)	2	2,681	$4,920	$13,190,324	$49,016,317
3 (12/02)	2	2,681	$2,177	$5,836,333	$57,630,192
4 (12/09)	4	2,245	$1,282	$2,877,922	$62,428,934
5 (12/16)	7	1,739	$1,062	$1,846,963	$65,328,308
6 (12/23)	15	1,201	$1,380	$1,657,871	$68,186,934
7 (12/30)	15	1,029	$1,752	$1,803,245	$71,293,610
8 (1/06)	17	678	$1,149	$778,732	$72,448,184
9 (1/13)	283		$1,459	$412,980	$73,114,817
10 (1/20)	235		$1,039	$244,060	$73,434,334
11 (1/27)	215		$790	$169,773	$73,676,885
12 (2/03)	133		$665	$88,489	$73,824,232
13 (2/10)	82		$751	$61,610	$73,919,128
14 (2/17)	65		$960	$62,423	$74,009,623
15 (2/24)	47		$617	$29,021	$74,048,309
16 (3/03)	20	665	$799	$531,55	$74,588,117
17 (3/10)	502		$587	$294,61	$75,074,114
18 (3/17)	264		$609	$160,88	$75,355,531
19 (3/24)	155		$586	$90,769	$75,510,568
20 (3/31)	83		$567	$47,054	$75,595,908
21 (4/07)				$16,319	$75,628,782
22 (4/14)					$75,638,153
23 (4/21)					$75,645,682
24 (4/28)					$75,652,048
25 (5/05)					$75,657,647

viding evidence that the worldwide popularity of the *Star Trek* phenomenon continues to grow. The opening weekend in Britain was the largest for any Paramount film in history. After five weeks and four days, the film's box office total in Britain was $11,339,616. In Germany, after five weeks and five days, the gross was $11,561,706. Other countries include Brazil at $406,000 in four days, Belgium at $186,000 in seven days, and Singapore at $151,300 in five days. But Trek collapsed by 50 percent after a "socko" start Down Under—$1.8 million in 13 days—and by about the same after a fair debut in France, $1.3 million total.

Brent Spiner told *Grand Slam III,* "Patrick [Stewart] and Bill Shatner and I were in Germany for the opening of *Generations* in Berlin. It was thrilling. There were thousands of people outside when we got there. The same thing happened in England when they opened the movie in London. We were convinced that we were Beatles that day. It was unbelievable, but Germany was incredible. Bill Shatner came in and they literally broke through the barricades to get to him. It was thrilling."

But George Takei told the *Charlotte Observer,* "[*Generations*] was blandly going where the original cast had been before. When you compare Spock's death [in *Star Trek II: The Wrath Of Khan*] with Kirk's, it's night and day. Spock's was a noble sacrifice, a painful loss. *Generations* had Kirk in this strange netherworld with no one there to grieve over him."

Gates McFadden told the *Charlotte Observer,* "I'm intrigued by the films, but must say I think the first one [*Generations*] is a little fast. I was hoping there'd be more time before it happened. My life has been much enriched by the entire experience, and now I'm excited about the future."

Stewart told the *Seattle Post-Intelligencer,* "We had to go directly into this movie, and a 51-day shoot in god-awful places like the Valley of Fire in the Nevada desert. I wasn't excited about the prospect. I was tired. It just seemed a chore." Then the chore turned into a pleasure. "It was a revelation. I loved having the luxury of time. Television is a prison with no time off. But with a movie, you always have time. The ability to stay with something until you got it right. My great fear was that it would be an extended version of a TV episode. And I don't think there is a scent of TV anywhere around the film. It's a tribute to David Carson and [cinematographer] John Alonzo. It's a substantial feature. I'm very proud of it. I now look forward to doing more *Star Trek* movies, maybe one every two years or so. That's quite a novelty for me—looking forward to *Star Trek*."

Bruised egos resulted from the effort to combine the two TV casts for a passing of the torch in the new movie. Nimoy had declined a role after he saw how small his part would be. "I told them," he said, "'The lines that you've written to be spoken by somebody named Spock can be easily distributed to any of the other characters on the screen.'" Which is what happened. Several members of *The Next Generation* cast, meanwhile, were also less than

> *"It was thrilling. There were thousands of people outside when we got there…We were convinced that we were Beatles that day."*

Star Trek: Generations (1994)
Boldly Go
Two captains. One destiny.

USA 1994 Color (DeLuxe)

Produced by: Paramount Pictures
Sound Mix: DTS/Dolby Stereo Digital
Certification: Finland: K-10/K-7/UK: PG/USA: PG
Runtime: Germany: 116/UK: 117/USA: 123

Directed by:
   David Carson

Cast (in credits order):

Patrick Stewart	Capt. Jean-Luc Picard
Jonathan Frakes	William T. Riker
Brent Spiner	Data
LeVar Burton	Geordi La Forge
Michael Dorn	Worf
Gates McFadden	Dr. Beverly Crusher
Marina Sirtis	Deanna Troi
Malcolm McDowell	Dr.Tolian Soran
James Doohan	Montgomery 'Scotty' Scott
Walter Koenig	Pavel Chekov
William Shatner	James T. Kirk
Whoopi Goldberg	Guinan
Alan Ruck	Capt. Harriman
Jacqui Kim	Demora Sulu
Jenette Goldstein	Science Officer
Thomas Kopache	Com Officer
Glenn Morshower	Navigator
Tim Russ	Lieutenant
Tommy Hinkley	Journalist
John Putch	Journalist
Christine Jansen	Journalist
Michael Mack	Ensign Hayes
Dendrie Taylor	Lieutenant Farrell
Patti Yasutake	Nurse Ogawa
Granville Ames	Transporter Chief
Henry Marshall	Security Officer
Brittany Parkyn	Girl With Teddy Bear
Majel Barrett	Computer Voice
Barbara March	Lursa
Gwynyth Walsh	B'Etor
Rif Hutton	Klingon Guard
Brian Thompson	Klingon Helm
Marcy Goldman	El Aurian Survivor
Jim Krestalude	El Aurian Survivor
Judy Levitt	El Aurian Survivor
Kristopher Logan	El Aurian Survivor
Gwen Van Dam	El Aurian Survivor
Kim Braden	Picard's Wife
Christopher James Miller	Picard's Nephew
Matthew Collins	Picard's Kid
Mimi Collins	Picard's Kid
Thomas Alexander Dekker	Picard's Kid
Madison Eginton	Picard's Kid
Olivia Hack	Picard's Kid

Written by:
   Rick Berman (story)
   Brannon Braga (also story)
   Ronald D. Moore (also story)

Cinematography by:
   John A. Alonzo

Music by:
   Dennis McCarthy

Production Design by:
   Herman Zimmerman

Costume Design by:
   Robert Blackman

Film Editing by:
   Peter E. Berger

Produced by:
   Rick Berman
   Peter Lauritson (co-producer)
   Bernie Williams (executive)

Other crew:
   Yudi Bennett (assistant director)
   Ken Dufva (foley)
   Douglas Fox (property master)
   Terry Frazee (special effects)
   Jane Haymore (makeup)
   John Knoll (visual effects supervisor)
   Patricia Tallman (stunt double)

thrilled with their small amount of screen time. LeVar Burton said, "Hopefully, if we do another one of these, we will have an opportunity to spread the wealth more."

Berman understood their disappointment, telling an AOL audience, "When you make a motion picture based upon an ensemble cast of seven characters, some of those characters are going to undoubtedly get less screen time than they deserve. You can't please all of the fans all of the time. Over the last eight years, I've done my best to satisfy myself and my colleagues, the mass viewing audience, and the fans. It ain't always easy. It is our intention to produce *Next Generation* films as long as there is an audience to see them."

Rumors of the Second TNG Film

As noted, Paramount was unhappy with how quickly confidential information became public while filming *Generations*. While filming the sequel, Paramount mounted a massive disinformation campaign, feeding various *Star Trek* actors false, and sometimes conflicting, stories. The reader, having seen the film, will know far more about that sequel than this writer now does in July of 1996. Rather than reporting on the film—which has been known at various times as *Generations II, Resurrection,* and *First Contact,* and variously reported to include Tom Hanks, Christopher Walken, and Yaphet Kotto among its cast—it will prove far more interesting to follow the many twists along the rumor trail.

The rumors of a second film began in August of 1993, before *Generations* appeared, when Armin Shimerman (who plays the Ferengi, Quark) told the Phoenix convention that four movies were planned.

November 1993 to March 1994

By November of 1993, rumors were circulating that the second film would be one of two stories, either with a "heavy Data theme" or a "heavy Riker theme." In March of 1994, fans learned that Paramount would build new sets for the second film, and Michael Dorn told the South Bend, Indiana, Creation con that he had signed on for three films.

December 1994

In December Doug Murray said that Picard would be promoted to Commodore and Riker would finally permanently get the Captain's seat on board the *Enterprise*-E. That same month, Richard Arnold told the York Multimedia Society that a second movie would show Borg still a dangerous force, unaffected by Hugh's return, attacking the Federation in spectacular space battles.

January 1995

A month later, in January of 1995, Creation Con heard that all of the *Next Generation* cast except Brent Spiner and Patrick Stewart had signed for five motion pictures, to be produced over a period of ten years, contradicting Dorn's earlier statement. Spiner had expressed concern over typecasting and Stewart wanted more money. They also heard that Picard would not command the new *Enterprise,* but be promoted to commodore, if he appeared.

February to November 1995

In February, a London convention learned there would be a new ship for the next movie, the Borg would appear, and that Patrick Stewart

57

and Brent Spiner had signed on for three movies. Then, in March, an Edmonton heard that Spiner and Stewart had not signed, but that there would be an *Enterprise* 1701-E with Captain Riker at the helm. They also heard that Q would bring the crews of Classic Trek and *TNG* together a year after *Generations. Starlog* reported that Brent Spiner had come aboard for the eighth Trek movie, and that Paramount Pictures had entered into an agreement for Berman to produce and co-write. In June *Cinescape* ran a story confirming the Borg involvement.

Then, in October, a script appeared on the Internet in which the Borg decimated *Deep Space Nine;* Worf took the *Defiant* to Earth, ramming a Borg vessel kamikaze-style, and was beamed out by Picard to rendezvous with the cast, including Captain Riker and First Officer Data in the *Enterprise* E. No fan knew if it was authentic.

In November, *Hollywood Reporter* stated that Stewart had signed for $5,000,000 while Spiner was still in negotiations. The following month, *Star Trek Communi-*

cator reported that the Borg would be co-villains with other undisclosed bad guy(s), and Picard would have a love interest.

January 1996

As filming grew closer, Berman approved staff illustrator John Eaves' *Enterprise* E design in January. It featured long nacelles, like the Excelsior class, but a flat, *Voyager*-like profile. It had a recognizable saucer/engineering section and two dart-like nacelles. *Variety* reported that plans to call the film "Resurrection" were dashed when Fox used that title for the fourth *Alien* film, and that a script completed by Brannon Braga and Ronald Moore pitted the *Enterprise* crew against the Borg. The newspaper also said that there was no shortage of aspirants to direct the feature but Patrick Stewart and Brent Spiner had lobbied for their shipmate, Frakes. His longtime agent, Paradigm's Sam Gores, said a deal hadn't yet been made, but indicated that negotiations were proceeding at warp speed.

Star Trek: First Contact (1996)

Produced by: Paramount Pictures

Directed by:
  Jonathan Frakes

Cast (in credits order):

Patrick Stewart	Capt. Jean-Luc Picard
Jonathan Frakes	Cmdr. William T. Riker
LeVar Burton	Lt. Cmdr. Geordi LaForge
Michael Dorn	Lt. Cmdr. Worf
Gates McFadden	Dr. Beverly Crusher
Marina Sirtis	Counselor Deanna Troi
Brent Spiner	Lt. Cmdr. Data
Alfre Woodard	Picard's Woman/Zefram's assistant
James Cromwell (II)	Zefram Cochrane

Rest of cast listed alphabetically:

Alice Krige	Borg Queen
Lincoln Sohn	Zefram Cochrane
Patti Yasutake	Nurse Ogawa

Written by:
  Rick Berman
  Brannon Braga
  Ronald D. Moore

Music by:
  Jerry Goldsmith

Produced by:
  Rick Berman

Other crew:
  Michael Westmore (makeup)

February 1996

New rumors spread in February of time travel to the founding days of the Federation, the American Civil War, the Romulan Wars of the 22nd century, and Renaissance England—or that the Borg would travel back in time to assimilate Zefram Cochrane before he could invent warp drive, changing the future. Other rumors predicted Sisko's limited appearance, the death of a major character, negotiations with Christopher Walken and Yaphet Kotto to play villains, and the casting of Emma Thompson for the role of Picard's love interest.

That same month, Marina Sirtis told the *New Haven Register* that she hadn't read the script yet, but "apparently I get to get drunk in a bar." The "Inside Trek" newspaper column reported that Ron Moore and Brannon Braga had completed their second draft of the screenplay to Paramount's satisfaction and that, despite rumors, Wil Wheaton, John deLancie, Whoopi Goldberg, and Jonathan Del Arco would not appear, nor would any members of the Classic Trek cast appear. *Entertainment Weekly* said Paramount had picked Jonathan Frakes as director, to follow in the footsteps of former Trekkers Leonard Nimoy and William Shatner. Frakes said, "They wanted someone

> ### What the critics said about
> ### *Star Trek: Generations*
> #### *Charlotte Observer*
>
> "After watching *Star Trek: Generations,* I can't see why Trek movies couldn't continue in this vein for all eternity. That's not a compliment. The seventh in the series confirms what five and six suggested: This franchise has become a handsome, efficiently produced version of James Bond in space. In *Generations,* there's even a Bondian changing of the guard. Kirk hardly figures in the picture, leaving it after 15 minutes and returning for the limp final battle. The bulk of our time is spent with Picard and cohorts from *The Next Generation* TV show. If we ignore some extremely fuzzy scientific concepts, we're left with the same powerful-alien-who-might-kill-us-all plot as in Star Treks two, four, five, six, and even one, if you count the *Voyager* spacecraft as an alien. Yet fans, who don't want change, should be satisfied."

familiar with the language of Trek. I'm under strict orders to bring the fun back. I can't say [who the villains would be], but beware the Borg . . . they're like cockroaches. They always come back."

Michael Dorn told Creation Con in Chicago that he liked the script and "what my character has to do." He had complained about the "Worf in the water" scene from *Generations,* so when Berman asked him for notes on *Star Trek VIII,* and he had none, Berman yelled at him and said, "C'mon, I know you have some, let me have it, spit it out." Michael replied, "No, really, it's great," and Berman said, "Oh. Okay."

As to how Worf gets from *DS9* to the *Enterprise,* Dorn would only say, "The writers were quite clever." Notably, in the *DS9* episode "Accession," Worf mentions that he will be away from the station visiting his parents in seven months, which is about when the second movie will take place.

When asked if he's back at *DS9* at the end, he only replied, "In this case, again, the writers were very clever," adding, "You think that I don't know that if I whisper one thing, it'll be crawling all over the Internet in minutes?"

He confirmed that the Borg are back, and that Frakes is directing, saying, "We're not gonna get anything done on that set," regarding cast and crew goofing around.

STAR TREK Communicator reported on new costumes, different from the ones for *Star Trek: Generations*. Costume designer Robert Blackman re-evaluated them after the Generations premiere and was thrilled at the decision not to use them again, saying, "They [the costumes] were frankly slapped together, incorporating bits and pieces of past movies and the TV show. They came off looking fairly uninspired . . . way too militaristic and austere."

Also in February, Paramount took the unprecedented step of bumping the budget up to $40 million, a 25 percent increase, making it the most expensive Trek film. Although $40 million is not a massive budget, it is extraordinary for frugal Paramount Pictures. The movie will have to turn a $110 million domestic box office to make a profit.

March 1996

In March, *Globe*, the tabloid that accurately reported the general story-line of *Generations* almost 18 months before its release, reported that Data will receive human flesh from a "Borg Queen" and proceed to have sex with her. Frakes told the *New York Daily News* that an offer was out to Alfre Woodard to play the love interest of Picard, but that they were still casting for the key roles of "Zefram Cochrane,

the man who discovered warp drive, and the Borg Queen; she's half-woman, half-cyborg and our most vicious and hostile villain."

April 1996

In April, *Variety*, then *Entertainment Tonight*, reported that James Cromwell had accepted the part of Zefram Cochrane, the character played by Glenn Corbett in the original series episode "Metamorphosis." Cromwell had previously played an alien character in the *Deep Space Nine* episode "Starship Down." Cromwell was born in Los Angeles in 1942 and educated at Carnegie Institute of Technology. He occasionally draws op-ed cartoons for the Lancaster, PA, *New Era*, and has made guest appearances on *The Client*, *Three's Company*, and *Little House on the Prairie*. He appeared in *Babe* (1995) as Farmer Hoggett; he later said, in reference to his Academy Award nomination for Best Actor in a Supporting Role, "Andy Warhol said everybody gets their 15 minutes of fame. And if this is mine, I couldn't imagine a better 15 minutes." He also appeared in numerous TV movies, including *Revenge of the Nerds III: The Next Generation* (1992), *China Beach* (1988), and *The Rainmaker* (1982), and several films, including *Revenge of*

> ### What the critics said about
> ### *Star Trek: Generations*
> #### Toronto's eye WEEKLY
>
> "Kirk is summoned from cosmic-whip-limbo to prop up [*Star Trek: Generations*]. Chicken feed, but there you have it. The purist will hate it; Spock isn't in it, and the Great Scott and the cherubic Chekov are given short shrift. And whereas the six previous *Star Trek* films could mine the pop culture phenomenon created by the original series, *Generations*, as the title suggests, mixes old with new—to an unsavory result. Against the vintage series, *The Next Generation* is unfermented grape juice; rather than creating an exciting new flavor, the two cancel each other out. The Next Generationist is going to be disappointed. Much time is wasted re-establishing familiar characters. The garden variety Trekker will be satisfied. Special effects and technical gadgetry abound. Stars burst and planets are pulverized. The *Enterprise* gives as good as it gets."

the Nerds (1984) and *Murder by Death* (1976). He also appeared in a number of TV series, including the role of Stretch Cunningham in *All in the Family* (1971).

Alfre Woodard had also joined the cast, playing the part of a civilian who must accompany Picard on a journey to save the Earth from the Borg. Woodard was born in 1953, in Tulsa, Oklahoma. Her numerous film credits include *Primal Fear* (1996) and *How to Make an American Quilt* (1995). Her TV work includes the movies *The Piano Lesson* (1995), *Race to Freedom: The Underground Railroad* (1994), *Blue Bayou* (1990), *A Mother's Courage: The Mary Thomas Story* (1989), *The Child Saver* (1988), *Mandela* (1987), *L.A. Law* (1986), *Unnatural Causes* (1986), *Go Tell It on the Mountain* (1984), *The Killing Floor* (1984), *Sweet Revenge* (1984), *The Ambush Murders* (1982), *The Sophisticated Gents* (1981), *Freedom Road* (1979), and the TV series *Gulliver's Travels* (1996), *A Century of Women* (1994), *Sara* (1985), *St. Elsewhere* (1982), and *Tucker's Witch* (1982).

Warp 10 reported that *Star Trek: Borg,* now the working title, featured bad Borg, with a Borg queen controlling them, who could remove her head, arms, legs, and other parts, and that Tom Hanks had wanted to play Zefram Cochrane, but that scheduling hadn't worked out. Marina Sirtis reported that Patrick Stewart was anxious to show off his

> ### What the critics said about
> ### *Star Trek: Generations*
> #### The Syracuse Newspapers
>
> "There's a Nexus—a waving pink ribbon where life is total joy. There's a plot that wobbles back and forth in time and eventually makes no sense. If it did, Capt. James T. Kirk feasibly still could be alive. But, as we all know by now, the good commander of the Starship *Enterprise* has died. There are few pieces of him left to bury at the end of *Star Trek: Generations.* It's on with the Next Generation cast from the TV show. For those who admired *Star Trek II: The Wrath of Khan* and *Star Trek IV: The Voyage Home,* like myself, this comes up short."

new sculpted bod, and would be taking off his shirt in the movie.

May 1996

The first major news came in May, when *Entertainment Tonight* showed shots from the new movie, including the new uniforms, the new bridge, the briefing room, and Geordi's implanted cyber-eyes. In other news, Dwight (Lt. Barclay) Schultz and Robert (The Doctor) Picardo confirmed their cameo appearances.

Lolita Fatjo confirmed at a Bonn convention that the new title was *Star Trek 8: The First Contact,* that Marina (Troi) Sirtis and Gates (Dr. Crusher) McFadden would have bigger roles than in *Generations,* that no *TNG* main character would die, that the Borg homeworld would not be seen, and that there would be no Cardassians or Romulans. She also said that Alfre Woodard would play Millie, who develops a friendship, though not a love affair, with Picard.

The title *Star Trek: First Contact* cleared MPAA on May 1. Jerry Goldsmith signed on to create the soundtrack. Frakes told Goldsmith to do a "dark" theme. GNP Crescendo Records secured the rights to the original soundtrack featuring Goldsmith's original score.

A merchant at Grand Slam IV in Pasadena tried to sell a batch of scripts downloaded from the Internet, just a stone's throw from the Paramount offices. They were promptly caught, and the scripts confiscated and carted away.

The early buzz was positive. Director Frakes was reportedly acting like a "kid in a candy store," and going to great lengths to get back the *TNG* on-screen family.

Patrick Stewart said the script was great—a good story that happens to be *Trek*—which could open the movie up to more people. He is enjoying getting reacquainted with Picard, filming in Tucson in a Titan missile silo—the only one with a missile still in it!—and night shots in the mountains east of L.A.

Spiner told Star-Fest, Denver, "Jonathan Frakes is a terrific director. He is really skilled, has great energy. We all have a great time on the sets."

Alice Krige signed on to play the part of the Borg queen. "I love to work in both [film and stage]," she told MIT's *The Tech*. "There is something about the cinema that gets me wildly excited. It's incredibly real, and it takes me away. Theater does something else." Krige was born and raised in South Africa, and has an obvious British accent. She originally went to Rhodes University (in South Africa) to follow

---

What the critics said about *Star Trek: Generations*
Entertainment Weekly

"With *Generations*, responsibility for the future of the movie outpost of Star Trek's empire passes from the original cast to that of *The Next Generation*. The pleasure of any Star Trek movie lies in experiencing the familiar mixed with the inventive. There's the deep, nostalgic joy of seeing the faces of old friends. There's the thrill of the iconic. There are the luscious astrophysical possibilities: Soran chases a shimmering ribbon of time called the Nexus, a kind of El Dorado as addictive as a drug, in which a visitor can be anywhere he wants to be, forever. And there is the grandiloquent dialogue.

"Shatner (who ambles through his relatively brief on-screen time like the winningest of retired football coaches) and Stewart (who stalks the screen like he personally owns the props) spar bemusedly. But my problem is, this enjoyable journey doesn't make the chances of success grim enough. As steered by David Carson, *Generations* is fun but not particularly bright, big but not particularly magnificent, loud but not particularly resonant. I'm enjoying the trip. I'm ready to drink Dom Perignon. And the flight attendants are serving Korbel."

Grade: B

---

in the footsteps of her psychologist mother, but when the university started a drama school, and she had one free credit, her parents urged her to take an acting class. She then took her honors degree, a degree earned after the bachelor's, in drama, and left home to attend acting school in London. She debuted on British television in 1979. Her TV work since includes *Devil's Advocate* (1995), *Joseph* (1995), *Sharpe's Honour* (1994), *Scarlet & Black* (1993), *Double Deception* (1993), *Jack Reed: Badge of Honor* (1993), *Judgment Day: The John List Story* (1993), *Ladykiller* (1992), *The Strauss Dynasty* (1991), *L'Amerique en otage* (1991), *Max and Helen* (1990), *Baja Oklahoma* (1988), *Second Serve* (1986), *Wallenberg: A Hero's Story* (1985), *Ellis Island* (1984), and *A Tale of Two Cities* (1980). Her films include *Institute Benjamenta* (1995), *Barfly* (1987), and *Chariots of Fire* (1981).

Sci Fi Universe reported that the script involved the Borg beginning the transformation of the *Enterprise* into a Borg hive and tempting Data with humanity. Riker and Geordi must help Zefram Cochrane make his first warp-drive flight to keep history from being changed.

June 1996

In June, the TV series, *Today in New York,* and E! Network's *Weekend Extra* ran segments on *Star Trek: First Contact.* They included a new Conn officer, Lt. Hawk, played by Neal McDonough. He said the cast calls him "a young stud-buck" because he is really in shape and wears a tight suit, while everyone else has the usual loose-fitting suits. He added that sometimes Patrick Stewart will say during a break, in his English accent, "Mr. Hawk, are you sure you shouldn't eat another donut?" McDonough went on to talk about his position, about how anyone who sits in his seat at the end of the movie or during the series . . . dies. Another *Entertainment Tonight* segment included: scenes of a ship bearing the Starfleet registry number NCC-74654 and firing an antimatter spread at a Borg cube ship; a Borg cutting-beam slicing away at a Galaxy-class vessel; Picard standing on an alien ship firing a disruptor rifle as Data moves in to stand beside him; James Cromwell as Zefram Cochrane; a Reliant-class vessel firing on a cube ship; a worn-looking crewman reporting to Worf that "they control Decks 26 to 11. They have assimilated more than half the ship!"; a missile silo, followed by a scene of Alfre Woodard as Lily Sloane blazing away at the Borg; a cube ship firing on a Starfleet vessel with the registry number NCC-3181; and Picard in the *Enterprise*'s ready room, saying "A line must be drawn here."

Internet *Star Trek* newsgroups were flooded following *Entertainment Tonight*'s preview clips of the new film. The show, broadcast in the U.S. on May 22, provided the first clues about what they can expect from the new film. Judging by the pictures of the bridge and conference lounge, the new *Enterprise* E appears little different on the surface, but rumors persist that it will include a cloaking device as well as an arsenal of weaponry to take on the film's bad guys, the Borg. As revealed previously, the plot will also involve some form of time travel, and many people are speculating that the movie could see Starfleet on the losing side of a Borg war, with the *Enterprise* traveling back in time to effect a rescue.

Aside from various conjectures about the plot, the thing that really seems to be getting the newsgroup crowd hot under the collar is Geordi's new eye implants. The VISOR has allegedly been dropped at the request of LeVar Burton, which has annoyed fans who believe that any cosmetic change should be brought about because of the story, rather than for the convenience of an actor.

Picard will have less of a role than he did in *Star Trek: Generations* because Patrick Stewart is supposedly asking for too much money. Paramount will most likely cut back on his scenes.

Other rumors from the set suggest that Robert Picardo will make an appearance as the *Enterprise*'s emergency doctor, and that Dwight Shultz will be reprising his role of the born loser, Lt. Reginald Barclay. There are also stories that this film will see the death of Commander Data.

Trouble in Paradise

On May 4, *Entertainment Weekly* reported, "Even as the next installment in Paramount's $1-billion-grossing Trek feature franchise gears up for its November premiere, ratings for both the syndicated *Star Trek: Deep Space Nine* and UPN's [United Paramount Network's] *Star Trek: Voyager* seem to have fallen prey to the

Vulcan death grip. *DS9* has seen its audience shrink from an average of 10.9 million viewers per episode last season to 9.3 million this year. More dire is the situation at UPN, where *Voyager,* its flagship show, took a nose-dive from 11.1 million viewers to 7.5 million viewers."

Berman put his finger on the problem. "Trek is up against not just other sci-fi shows, but other Trek shows," he told *Entertainment Weekly.* "*DS9* has to play against repeats of *Next Generation,* the original Trek, *Voyager,* and even repeats of *DS9.*"

Entertainment Weekly noted, "Many fans have yet to embrace the new shows because they're still angry over Paramount's decision to kill off the phenomenally popular *Next Gener-*

ation series in order to parlay the show into a big-screen franchise. While the short-term math worked—the first flick, *Star Trek: Generations,* racked up $75.7 million at the box office—Paramount was left with two weaker shows to carry on *Star Trek*'s TV line, and a host of disgruntled fans and merchandisers."

UPN entertainment president Michael Sullivan dismisses *Voyager*'s weak showing. "A minor downtrend may be happening," he told *Entertainment Weekly,* "but our core viewers are still there. And the feature film will definitely punch things up."

"It's going to be a lot of fun," said Frakes. "There's a new *Enterprise,* the Borg have been redesigned, and the whole cast's back."

CHAPTER SIX

A Guide to the 24th Century

By the time the 24th century rolls around, as depicted in *The Next Generation,* many social customs have changed. In addition, new planets, solar systems, and life forms have been discovered, each adding its language, culture, and starships to the expanding informational *Star Trek* universe.

The Measurement of Time

In the 24th century, stardates have replaced our system. For example, in "stardate 45076.3," the 4 represents the 24th century, the 5 represents the season number of *TNG,* and the 076 represents the part of the season. The .3 represents the part of the day.

During pre-recorded sub-space messages and recorded logs of Away Teams, both the current stardate and the current time (in 24-hour military format, down to the second) are given.

Money in the Future

Money continues to be used. People still offer to buy each other drinks in the Ten-Forward Lounge, but no one is ever shown paying.

In "Encounter at Farpoint," Beverly Crusher buys a roll of cloth, and has it billed to her account on the *Enterprise.* The Ferengi in "The Last Outpost" called the comm badges a shameful use of a precious metal.

Ditalics Mining Corporation owned the planet Ditalics B, where the Starship Captains met in "Conspiracy," showing that companies continue to seek profit. Picard says that they no longer use money in "The Neutral Zone," though, but this could mean they use "smart" cards and a system of debits and credits.

A bidding war goes on for the use of a wormhole in "The Price," and Picard mentions how much toll the Ferengi might charge if they get the rights to use that wormhole. In "A Matter of Perspective," Dr. Apgar wants to develop and sell the Krieger wave generator to the highest bidder. And the pursuit of an ancient Romulan artifact is accompanied by a promise of gold-pressed latinum in "Gambit."

In "Peak Performance," Riker plays strategema against Kolrami, and Worf whispers to Riker that he has bet a "sizable amount" on Riker in the ship's pool. When Riker enters the bar in "Unification II," he is asked to toss coins into the jar for a song. Riker responds that he doesn't have any money.

Races of the Alpha Quadrant

Many races populate the familiar Alpha Quadrant in the 24th century. Some are friendly, others hostile, but all are interesting in their differences.

Bajorans

Bajorans recently submitted an application to become members of the Federation. They are a deeply spiritual people. The humanoid race flourished for 25 thousand years, beginning before humans walked upright. Bajoran history includes great architects, artists, and philosophers.

Cardassian occupation caused Bajoran culture to decline in the 24th century. Most Bajorans were driven from their homeworld after occupation in 2328 and formal annexation in 2339, until the resistance drove them away in 2369. The Bajoran government then gave the Federation control of orbital starbase Deep Space Nine, near the only known stable wormhole leading to the Gamma Quadrant.

Under Bajoran custom, a person's family name comes first, followed by the given name. Most Bajorans wear an ornamental earring on their right ear. Bajorans look to their spiritual leader, the Kai, for guidance. Bajorans believe that prophets guide ships safely through the wormhole and that the Celestial Temple dwells within the passage. Some conservative Bajoran religious leaders, notably Vedek Winn, tried to suppress scientific theories of the wormhole's creation. Religious faith helped the Bajoran people survive the brutal Cardassian occupation.

Betazoids

Betazoids resemble humans. They are charter members of the Federation. The normal gestation period of a Betazoid is ten months. Betazoids usually develop telepathic abilities in adolescence. They are incapable of telepathy with Ferengi, Breen, or Doptherian minds. Betazoids are a matriarchal society, and believe men to be a commodity.

The Borg

The Borg were created by Maurice Hurley. Bearing a societal resemblance only to the Binars of the Federation, the Borg are the greatest threat to all galactic cultures.

Borg are cybernetic organisms from Delta Quadrant that act and think as one. Perhaps millions in number, they exist only to absorb unfortunate civilizations. Individual Borg begin life as normal humanoid infants, but are equipped with different bionic components based on their assigned lifelong duties. This addition of parts continues until adulthood. Each Borg is tied into a sophisticated subspace communications network, forming the Borg collective. Borg may have developed a method for accelerating growth, perhaps taking each Borg drone unit from infancy to adulthood in mere months.

Borg design cube-shaped vessels purely by function, with no aesthetic considerations. The structures have great firepower and speed unaccounted for by Federation science. The Borg appear to be centered in an area of space beyond the Romulan Empire. The first known contact between the Borg and the Federation was in 2265, when Q transported the *Enterprise*-D into the flight path of a Borg vessel. Following this first contact, Starfleet put Commander Shelby in charge of preparations for a Borg offensive, as Federation technology is attractive to the Borg.

A Borg vessel entered Federation space, heading for Earth, in 2366. Starfleet tactical planners were unprepared. *Enterprise*-D Captain Jean-Luc Picard was captured and assimilated at the beginning of the offensive. He became known as Locutus of Borg. Starfleet massed an armada in hopes of stopping the Borg ship at Wolf 359, but the fleet was decimated. Following the rescue of Picard from the Borg ship, a destructive computer command was implanted into the Borg collective, destroying the Borg ship in Earth orbit.

Two more Borg vessels were found to have reached Federation territory when a crashed Borg scout ship was discovered on the surface of a moon in the Argolis Cluster in 2368. One surviving Borg, Third of Five, later renamed Hugh, was rescued from the crash by *Enterprise*-D, and nursed back to health. An invasive program was introduced into Hugh, designed to cause a fatal overload in the Borg collective consciousness.

Following the return of Hugh, his new sense of individuality began to infect a portion of the collective. Deprived of group identity, individual Borg ceased to function as a unit. The android, Lore, changed this, and appointed himself leader of the Borg.

In 2369, Lore led the Borg in a major new offensive against the Federation outpost at Ohniaka III. The offensive ended when Lore was dismantled by Data.

Cardassians

Humanoid Cardassians were once a peaceful, spiritual people. Starvation and disease ran rampant on their resource-poor planet. People died by the millions until the military rose to power and acquired new territories and technology by violence, leading to extended conflict with the United Federation of Planets.

An uneasy truce was reached in 2366. Starfleet captain Edward Jellico was partially credited for the negotiations. Ambassador Spock publicly disagreed with his father, Ambassador Sarek, over the treaty. Starfleet captain Benjamin Maxwell, commanding the starship *Phoenix,* violated the treaty later that year. Starfleet believed Maxwell's suspicions of illicit Cardassian military activity were correct, but his actions were illegal.

In 2369, it was believed that Cardassia was developing a metagenic weapon to use in an incursion into Federation space. *Enterprise*-D captain Jean-Luc Picard, along with Chief Medical Officer Beverly Crusher and Security Officer Worf, covertly entered Cardassian space to investigate. The reports were found to be a ruse, designed to lure Captain Picard into Cardassian captivity. Also in 2369, the Bajoran resistance movement forced the Cardassians from Bajor. They abandoned Deep Space Nine. The station became of major value when a wormhole was discovered.

Cytherians

The humanoid Cytherians reside on a planet near the center of the galaxy. They bring space travelers to them with probes that reprogram computers with instructions to come to their world.

The *Enterprise*-D encountered one such probe in 2367. It programmed Lieutenant Reginald Barclay's mind to bring the ship. The crew spent 10 days exchanging cultural and scientific information with the friendly Cytherians.

Ferengi

Technologically sophisticated, humanoid Ferengi first contacted the Federation at planet Delphi Ardu in 2364. Ferengi entrepreneurs quickly entered Federation commerce.

They maintain a strict code of honor based on distorted principles of capitalism. The sexist Ferengi do not allow their females to wear clothing. Ferengi males find female humans attractive.

Betazoids can't read Ferengi minds due to the four-lobed design of the Ferengi brain.

Humans

The influential human race co-founded the United Federation of Planets. Peaceful human society wants to explore the universe. Humans come from the planet Earth, in Sol, in sector 001.

Klingons

This aggressive humanoid warrior race, originally from the planet Qo'noS, values tradition and honor. The death of a warrior who has died honorably is not mourned, but celebrated as a freeing of the spirit. Their military power is respected and feared. Klingons recently ended a 100-year alliance with humans by an unprovoked attack on Deep Space Nine.

The tall, muscular Klingon race grows to adult height at a younger age than humans. Genetically pure Klingons exhibit a ridged forehead crown. Klingon blood is lavender. They have no tear ducts. Klingon science, although technologically advanced, lacks sophisticated medicine because of a cultural bias that favors the strong and offers no sympathy to the weak, including the aged and infirm.

The R'uustai ceremony bonds families. Family background determines public and private action. Tests of warrior combat skill are rites of passage. Most Klingon disputes are settled using ancient hand-to-hand weapons.

Klingons have pistol-like disruptor units. Large disruptors are the primary weapons of the Klingon fleet, effective against shields and hulls. Klingon vessels also have photon torpedoes acquired during the brief Klingon/Romulan alliance.

That alliance led to scientific advances for both cultures. Romulans acquired Klingon D-7 battle cruisers and the warp drive in exchange for their cloaking device and their Bird-of-Prey cruiser.

Nausicaans

Hot-tempered Nausicaans quickly resort to violence. While on leave at Starbase Earhart shortly after graduating from Starfleet Academy, Ensign Jean-Luc Picard fought three Nausicaans. One stabbed Picard through the heart.

The Q Continuum

Q lives in the extradimensional Q Continuum. He once possessed near-godlike power, but was banished from the Continuum and stripped of power in 2366 for spreading chaos.

A selfless action later persuaded the Continuum to return his powers.

The *Enterprise*-D made first contact with Q in 2364. Q later caused the first encounter with the Borg.

Romulans

This offshoot of the Vulcan race descended from a rebel colony that broke away from its homeworld before Vulcans turned away from violence. They now live on the planets Romulus and Remus. Romulans conducted a brutal attack on the Klingon Narendra III outpost in 2344. The *Enterprise*-C responded to distress calls to aid the Klingons, leading to closer Klingon-Federation ties. Romulans consider Klingons too barbaric to trust. They fear the current Federation-Klingon alliance and wish to see it dissolved. Romulan military intelligence unsuccessfully tried to undermine this alliance. Sensor scans of the Romulan Neutral Zone show a dramatic increase in patrols, indicating a fear of invasion.

The Romulan Star Empire wants to expand. It grew though conquest and rules with an iron fist. Starfleet first encountered Romulans two centuries ago. A treaty ended that first encounter. The physical nature of the Romulan race wasn't learned until decades later, after another confrontation. Current Starfleet intelligence indicates that a growing underground movement within Romulan society wants to return to their Vulcan heritage.

Romulan starships equal those of the Federation. Their powerful new Warbird has become the mainstay of their space forces. Larger than Starfleet's Galaxy class, and equipped with an improved cloaking device, the Warbird poses the single greatest threat to the Federation. The vessel is equipped with disruptors and photon-torpedo-launch units, a Romulan innovation.

Trills

A joined species comprised of a humanoid host and a small vermiform symbiont that resides in an internal abdominal pocket of the host body. Most personality and memory resides in the long-lived symbionts, although the host contributes personality traits. Upon the death of a host body, a symbiont can be transplanted to a new host. Volunteers undergo rigorous competition to determine who will be accorded this honor. Once joined, the host and symbiont become biologically interdependent, and neither can survive without the other.

Trills have cold hands. Hosts can feel sexual urges, but they try to ignore them.

Ullians

Ullians are telepathic humanoids characterized by skull skin involutions. Other telepathic species can't read Ullians.

Violence plagued Ullian society before 2068. Many fell victim to telepathic rape. Ullians evolved into a peaceful race by the 21st century. Ullians used telepathic retrieval to build a library of individual memories from 11 planets in the 24th century. Sadly, Researcher Jev was convicted of multiple telepathic rapes.

Vulcans

Humanoid race native to the planet Vulcan. Terrible wars wracked Vulcan until Surak led his people to reject their emotions in favor of pure logic 2,000 years ago. Display of emotion is now considered bad manners. Those who rejected Surak's teachings left Vulcan to found the Romulan Star Empire.

Vulcans revert to ancient mating rituals during "pon farr," a period of total emotional abandon, every seven years. It is a price they pay for totally suppressing emotion. Parents select a mate for their children at age seven. The children are joined in a telepathic linking ceremony. When the children come of age, they must join together in marriage.

Vulcans demonstrate greater physical strength and more acute hearing than humans because of Vulcan's higher gravity and thinner atmosphere. Intense sunlight caused Vulcans to evolve a secondary eyelid. Injured Vulcans enter a trance and concentrate strength, blood, and antibodies to individual organs.

Vulcans may have originated on another world, possibly Sargon's planet. The telepathic race practices the mind meld.

Locations in the Alpha Quadrant

Table 6.1 Regions, Bodies, and Phenomena

Location	Series or Film	Episode
Alpha Quadrant	*Star Trek VI*	
Alawanir Nebula	*The Next Generation*	"Rightful Heir"
Amargosa Diaspora Cluster	*The Next Generation*	"Schisms"
Amatha Sector, Cardassian Space	*Deep Space Nine*	"Defiant"
Andromeda Galaxy	Classic	"By Any Other Name"
Argolis Cluster (six systems)	*The Next Generation*	"I Borg"
Argosian Sector	*Deep Space Nine*	"Babel"
Argus Sector	*The Next Generation*	"Gambit, Part I"
Bajoran Sector	*The Next Generation*	"Chain of Command, Part I"
Belati Sector	*The Next Generation*	"Ethics"
Betreka Nebula (site of "incident" between Cardassians and Klingons, which lasted 18 years)	*Deep Space Nine*	"The Way of the Warrior"
Black Cluster, Sector 97	*The Next Generation*	"Hero Worship"
Borgolis Nebula	*The Next Generation*	"Lessons"
Brechtian Cluster	*The Next Generation*	"Silicon Avatar"
Cavis Alpha Sector	*The Next Generation*	"Evolution"
Crab Nebula	*The Next Generation*	"Manhunt"
Deltived Asteroid Belt	*The Next Generation*	"Deja Q"
Demilitarized Zone (DMZ) (between Federation and Cardassian space)	*Deep Space Nine*	"The Maquis, Part I"
Denorios Belt (charged plasma field)	*Deep Space Nine*	"Emissary"
Dorias Cluster (at least twenty star systems)	*The Next Generation*	"Bloodlines"
Epsilon 9 Sector	*The Next Generation*	"Samaritan Snare"
FGC13(cluster)	*The Next Generation*	"Schisms"
FGC47(nebula)	*The Next Generation*	"Imaginary Friend"
Fledka Asteroid Belt	*Deep Space Nine*	"Rivals"
Galaxy M-33	*The Next Generation*	"Where No One Has Gone Before"
Galdon Terr	*Deep Space Nine*	"Blood Oath"
Gamma 7 Sector	*The Next Generation*	"Unnatural Selection"
Garamin Sector	*The Next Generation*	"Rightful Heir"
Giles Belt	*The Next Generation*	"The Most Toys"
Glaceen Sector	*Deep Space Nine*	"Babel"
Hanoli Rift	*Deep Space Nine*	"If Wishes Were Horses"
Hekarus Corridor	*The Next Generation*	"Force of Nature "
Helosplant Nebula	*Deep Space Nine*	"The Adversary"

Table 6.1 Regions, Bodies, and Phenomena *(continued)*

Location	Series or Film	Episode
Heugoran Nebula (Federation space; near DMZ)	*The Next Generation*	"Preemptive Strike"
Horadin Sector	*The Next Generation*	"The Big Goodbye"
Horami Cluster	*The Next Generation*	"The Vengeance Factor"
Hyralan Sector	*The Next Generation*	"Gambit, Part II"
Igo Sector	*The Next Generation*	"Realm of Fear"
Ikalian Asteroid Belt	*The Next Generation*	"The Mind's Eye"
Kadasian Sector	*The Next Generation*	"The Wounded"
Kaleb Sector	*The Next Generation*	"Face of the Enemy "
Karaya Sector	*The Next Generation*	"Birthright, Part I"
Lantar Nebula	*Deep Space Nine*	"Q-Less"
Legana Sector	*The Next Generation*	"Second Chances"
Lonka Cluster	*The Next Generation*	"Allegiance"
Lorenze Cluster	*The Next Generation*	"Arsenal of Freedom"
McAllister C-5 Nebula (11 light-years from Minos Korva)	*The Next Generation*	"Chain of Command, Part I"
McCorda Sector	*The Next Generation*	"Emergence"
McPhereson Nebula (supernova remnant)	*The Next Generation*	"Emergence"
Mar-Oscura Nebula	*The Next Generation*	"In Theory"
Mempa Sector	*The Next Generation*	"Redemption"
Mikoria Quazar	*The Next Generation*	"The Pegasus"
Mogawna Quadrant	*The Next Generation*	"Where Silence Has Lease"
Morab Sector	*The Next Generation*	"Time's Arrow"
Murasaki 312	Classic	"The Galileo Seven"
Murasaki Quasar	*The Next Generation*	"Data's Day"
Mutara Nebula	*Star Trek II*	
Mutara Sector	*Star Trek III*	
Nagami Nebula	*The Next Generation*	"Clues"
NGC321 (star cluster)	Classic	"A Taste of Armageddon"
Onias Sector (near Romulan Neutral Zone)	*The Next Generation*	"Future Imperfect"
Outer Cometary Cloud	*The Next Generation*	"Sins of the Father"
Paulson Nebula	*The Next Generation*	"The Best of Both Worlds"
Pelloris Asteroid Field	*The Next Generation*	"Cost of Living"
Phoenix Cluster	*The Next Generation*	"The Game"
Phyecus Sector	*The Next Generation*	"Up the Long Ladder"
Pleiades Cluster	*The Next Generation*	"Home Soil"
Quad L-14	*Star Trek: The Motion Picture*	
Quadrant 9	*The Next Generation*	"Heart of Glory"
Quadrant 448	Classic	"The Deadly Years"
Romboy Droniger Sector	*The Next Generation*	"Samaritan Snare"

Table 6.1 Regions, Bodies, and Phenomena *(continued)*

Location	Series or Film	Episode
Sector 001	*The Next Generation*	"The Best of Both Worlds"
Sector 5	*Star Trek IV*	
Sector 23	*The Next Generation*	"The Measure of a Man"
Sector 30	*The Next Generation*	"The Neutral Zone"
Sector 31	*The Next Generation*	"The Neutral Zone"
Sector 63	*The Next Generation*	"Conspiracy"
Sector 97	*The Next Generation*	"Hero Worship"
Sector 396	*The Next Generation*	"The Offspring"
Sector 1156 (over two sectors away from Darcaya System)	*The Next Generation*	"Masks"
Sector 1607	*The Next Generation*	"The Pegasus"
Sector 2520	*The Next Generation*	"Aquiel"
Sector 9569	*The Next Generation*	"Transfigurations"
Sector 19658	*The Next Generation*	"Parallels"
Sector 21305	*The Next Generation*	"Ensign Ro"
Sector 21459	*The Next Generation*	"The Chase"
Sector 21503	*The Next Generation*	"The Wounded"
Sector 21505	*The Next Generation*	"The Wounded"
Sector 21527	*The Next Generation*	"Chain of Command, Part II"
Sector 21947	*The Next Generation*	"Suddenly Human"
Selcundi Drema Sector (five systems)	*The Next Generation*	"Pen Pals"
Septimus Minor	*The Next Generation*	"The Ensigns of Command"
Solarian Sector	*The Next Generation*	"Inner Light"
Staleeby Asteroid Belt, Sector 396	*The Next Generation*	"The Offspring"
Talos Star Group	Classic	"The Cage"
Teleris Cluster	*Deep Space Nine*	"Q-Less"
Typhon Expanse	*The Next Generation*	"Cause and Effect"
Vega Omicron Sector	*The Next Generation*	"The Icarus Factor"
Volon Colonies, DMZ	*Deep Space Nine*	"The Maquis, Part I"
Vodrey Nebula	*The Next Generation*	"Firstborn"
Volterra Nebula	*The Next Generation*	"The Chase"
Zed Lapis Sector	*The Next Generation*	"Skin of Evil"
Zeta Gelis Cluster	*The Next Generation*	"Transfigurations"
<Unnamed nebula>, Dorias Cluster (three lightyears from unnamed pulsar)	*The Next Generation*	"Bloodlines"
<Unnamed cloud>, Bryma System	*Deep Space Nine*	"The Maquis, Part II"
<Unnamed nebula>, DMZ	*Deep Space Nine*	"Defiant"
<Unnamed nebula>, Amleth System (emission nebula)	*Deep Space Nine*	"Return to Grace"

Table 6.2 Solar/Star Systems

System	Series or Film	Episode
Acamar	*The Next Generation*	"The Vengeance Factor"
Alpha Centauri	Classic	"Metamorphosis"
Alpha Leonis	*The Next Generation*	"The Vengeance Factor"
Alpha Omicron (seven or more planets)	*The Next Generation*	"Galaxy's Child"
Alpha Onias	*The Next Generation*	"Future Imperfect"
Altair	Classic	"Amok Time"
Amargosa (star collapsed)	*Star Trek: Generations*	
Amleth	*Deep Space Nine*	"Return to Grace"
Argaia (near Cardassian border)	*The Next Generation*	"Lower Decks"
Argo	*The Next Generation*	"Silicon Avatar"
Atalia	*The Next Generation*	"The Chase"
Barradas	*The Next Generation*	"The Emissary"
Bersallis (three or more planets)	*The Next Generation*	"Lessons"
Beta Aurigae (binary system)	Classic	"Turnabout Intruder"
Beta Casius	*The Next Generation*	"Haven"
Beta Coupsic	*The Next Generation*	"The Icarus Factor"
Beta Magellan	*The Next Generation*	"11001001"
Beta Renna	*The Next Generation*	"Lonely Among Us"
Beta Stromgren	*The Next Generation*	"Tin Man"
Bilaren	*The Next Generation*	"True Q"
Borratas	*The Next Generation*	"Gambit, Part I"
Bras Lota (two or more planets)	*The Next Generation*	"Peak Performance"
Bryma	*Deep Space Nine*	"The Maquis, Part II"
Cabral	*The Next Generation*	"Homeward"
Calder	*The Next Generation*	"Gambit, Part I"
Cambus	*The Next Generation*	"Firstborn"
Camor	*The Next Generation*	"Bloodlines"
Carraya	*The Next Generation*	"Rightful Heir"
Clarus	*Deep Space Nine*	"The Nagus"
Colla	*The Next Generation*	"Firstborn"
Cornelia	*The Next Generation*	"Where Silence Has Lease"
Dala	*The Next Generation*	"Symbiosis"
Dapo (almost three days from Korma)	*Deep Space Nine*	"Return to Grace"
Darcaya (over two sectors away from Sector 1156)	*The Next Generation*	"Masks"
Delphi Ardu (eleven planets; unexplored)	*The Next Generation*	"The Last Outpost"
Delta Rana	*The Next Generation*	"The Survivors"
Detrian (newborn star)	*The Next Generation*	"Ship in a Bottle"
Devidia, Morab Sector	*The Next Generation*	"Time's Arrow"
Devolin	*The Next Generation*	"The Pegasus"

Table 6.2 Solar/Star Systems *(continued)*

System	Series or Film	Episode
Devron, Romulan Neutral Zone	*The Next Generation*	"All Good Things . . ."
Diamidian	*The Next Generation*	"Clues"
Dichon Alpha (Class Nine Pulsar)	*The Next Generation*	"Emergence"
Dozaria	*Deep Space Nine*	"Indiscretion"
Dracana	*The Next Generation*	"Legacy"
Draken	*The Next Generation*	"Face of the Enemy"
Eladrell	*The Next Generation*	"Darmok"
Endicor	*The Next Generation*	"Time Squared"
El Orean	*Deep Space Nine*	"Rivals"
Epsilon Indi	Classic	"The Enemy Within"
Epsilon Mynos	*The Next Generation*	"When The Bough Breaks"
Epsilon 119 (dead sun; reborn)	*Deep Space Nine*	"Second Sight"
Epsilon Silar	*The Next Generation*	"Conundrum"
Falla (mirror universe system)	*Deep Space Nine*	"Crossover"
Fealin	*The Next Generation*	"The Outcast"
Ferrius Prime	*Deep Space Nine*	"The Maquis, Part I"
40 Eridani A	Classic	"Amok Time"
Galador II	*Deep Space Nine*	"The Maquis, Part I"
Galvin V	*The Next Generation*	"Data's Day"
Gamelan	*The Next Generation*	"Final Mission"
Gamma Arigulon	*The Next Generation*	"Reunion"
Gamma Eridon	*The Next Generation*	"Redemption II"
Gamma Hydra	Classic	"The Deadly Years"
Garth (neighboring system to Malkor III)	*The Next Generation*	"First Contact"
Guernica	*The Next Generation*	"Galaxy's Child"
Halee	*The Next Generation*	"Heart of Glory"
Hanoli (destroyed by subspace anomaly expansion in the mid-23rd century)	*Deep Space Nine*	"If Wishes Were Horses"
Hekarus	*The Next Generation*	"Force of Nature "
Hokton VII, DMZ	*Deep Space Nine*	"The Maquis, Part II"
Hyashi	*The Next Generation*	"Tin Man"
Hittarian	*The Next Generation*	"Firstborn"
Ilecom	*The Next Generation*	"We'll Always Have Paris"
Indri	*The Next Generation*	"The Chase"
J Two-Five	*The Next Generation*	"Q Who?"
Karaya, Karaya Sector	*The Next Generation*	"Birthright, Part II"
Karrats	*Deep Space Nine*	"The Siege"
Kataan (six planets; star went nova 1000 yrs ago)	*The Next Generation*	"Inner Light"
Kazeus Binary	*The Next Generation*	"The Neutral Zone"

Table 6.2 Solar/Star Systems *(continued)*

System	Series or Film	Episode
Kerlan	*The Next Generation*	"The Chase"
Kilarn	*The Next Generation*	"The Nth Degree"
Kleone	*The Next Generation*	"The Game"
Korridon	Classic	"Journey to Babel"
Krios	*The Next Generation*	"The Mind's Eye"
Lapolis	*Deep Space Nine*	"Emissary"
L-370 (seven planets; all destroyed)	Classic	"The Doomsday Machine"
L-374 (at least four planets; two left)	Classic	"The Doomsday Machine"
Lima Sierra (four planets)	*The Next Generation*	"Loud as a Whisper"
Loren	*The Next Generation*	"The Chase"
Lygos	*The Next Generation*	"Rascals"
Lysia	*The Next Generation*	"Conundrum"
Maricor	*The Next Generation*	"Ethics"
Maxia Zeta	*The Next Generation*	"The Battle"
Meldrar I (lunar prison)	*Deep Space Nine*	"Necessary Evil"
Mesalina	*The Next Generation*	"Ethics"
Minos Korva (11 light-years from McAlister C5 Nebula)	*The Next Generation*	"Chain of Command, Part II"
Minos Korva (site of a Cardassian incident)	*The Next Generation*	"Gambit, Part I"
Mira (six planets)	*The Next Generation*	"Conspiracy"
Moab	*The Next Generation*	"The Masterpiece Society"
Modean	*The Next Generation*	"Imaginary Friend"
MS	*The Next Generation*	"Descent"
M-24 Alpha	Classic	"The Gamesters . . ."
Myrichri VII	*The Next Generation*	"Interface "
Nel Bato	*The Next Generation*	"The Most Toys"
Nel (two or more planets)	*The Next Generation*	"Violations"
Nelvana, Romulan Neutral Zone	*The Next Generation*	"The Defector"
Nequencia	*The Next Generation*	"Birthright, Part II"
Ohniaka	*The Next Generation*	"Descent"
Omega	Classic	"Requiem for Methuselah"
Omega Sagitta	*The Next Generation*	"The Outrageous Okona"
Omicron	*The Next Generation*	"Manhunt"
Omicron Pascal	*The Next Generation*	"11001001"
Onepherus	*Deep Space Nine*	"Improbable Cause"
Operlyne	*The Next Generation*	"Symbiosis"
Orelious Minor	*Deep Space Nine*	"Paradise"
Orhyis	*Deep Space Nine*	"Defiant"
Oxmal	*The Next Generation*	"Power Play"
Paradas (at least four planets)	*Deep Space Nine*	"Whispers"

Table 6.2 Solar/Star Systems *(continued)*

System	Series or Film	Episode
Parvenium	*The Next Generation*	"Inner Light"
Pegos Minor	*The Next Generation*	"We'll Always Have Paris"
Peliar	*The Next Generation*	"The Host"
Pentath	*Deep Space Nine*	"Rules of Engagement"
Pheben	*The Next Generation*	"A Matter of Honor"
Praxillus (star destroyed in experiment)	*The Next Generation*	"Half a Life"
Quayar	*The Next Generation*	"The Wounded"
Rakella Prime (protostar)	*Deep Space Nine*	"The Maquis, Part I"
Ramatis	*The Next Generation*	"Loud as a Whisper"
Ramazad	*The Next Generation*	"The Chase"
Rechelli	*The Next Generation*	"The Child"
Regulan	*Deep Space Nine*	"The Maquis, Part I"
Rigel	Classic	"The Doomsday Machine"
Ruah	*The Next Generation*	"The Chase"
Rubicun (adjoining Strenab)	*The Next Generation*	"Justice"
Rymus Major (two suns)	*Deep Space Nine*	"Profit and Loss"
Secarus	*Deep Space Nine*	"Blood Oath"
Selcundi One, Selcundi Drema Sector	*The Next Generation*	"Pen Pals"
Selcundi Two, Selcundi Drema Sector	*The Next Generation*	"Pen Pals"
Selcundi Three, Selcundi Drema Sector	*The Next Generation*	"Pen Pals"
Shelia	*The Next Generation*	"The Ensigns of Command"
Shiralea Six	*The Next Generation*	"Cost of Living"
Sigma Draconis	Classic	"Spock's Brain"
Sigma Erandi	*The Next Generation*	"The Most Toys"
Sigma Three	*The Next Generation*	"Hide and Q"
6-11	Classic	"The Return of the Archons"
Sol	Classic	All episodes
Solarion	*The Next Generation*	"Ensign Ro"
Soltok IV	*Deep Space Nine*	"The Maquis, Part I"
Space Quadrant 904	Classic	"The Squire of Gothos"
Strenab (adjoining Rubicun)	*The Next Generation*	"Justice"
T'lli Beta	*The Next Generation*	"The Loss"
Talos (eleven planets)	Classic	"The Cage"
Tambor Beta Six (white dwarf)	*The Next Generation*	"Emergence"
Tau Cygna	*The Next Generation*	"The Ensigns of Command"
Taugus	*The Next Generation*	"Gambit, Part II"
Tellun	Classic	"Elaan of Troyius"
Terlina	*The Next Generation*	"Inheritance"
Theta 116	*The Next Generation*	"The Royale"

Table 6.2   Solar/Star Systems *(continued)*

System	Series or Film	Episode
Tiarchanon	*The Next Generation*	"Identity Crisis"
Topin (binary; unstable protostar)	*The Next Generation*	"Preemptive Strike"
Triacus	Classic	"The Enemy Within"
Tycho	Classic	"Obsession"
Tyran	*The Next Generation*	"The Quality of Life"
Ufandi (at least three planets)	*The Next Generation*	"Firstborn"
Valo	*The Next Generation*	"Ensign Ro"
Vandor	*The Next Generation*	"We'll Always Have Paris"
Veridian (star collapsed in alternate timeline)	*Star Trek: Generations*	
Veyton	*The Next Generation*	"Suspicions"
Vilmoran (seven planets)	*The Next Generation*	"The Chase"
Wolf 359	*The Next Generation*	"The Best of Both Worlds"
Xendi Kabu	*The Next Generation*	"Bloodlines"
Xendi Sabu	*The Next Generation*	"The Battle"
Zairtzi Seven	*The Next Generation*	"When The Bough Breaks"
<Unnamed> (Dyson Sphere)	*The Next Generation*	"Relics"
<Unnamed pulsar>, Dorias Cluster (Class Four; 3 light-years from unnamed nebula)	*The Next Generation*	"Bloodlines"

Table 6.3   Planetary Classifications

Classification	Series or Film	Episode
Class D: ?	*Voyager*	"Emanations"
Class J: gaseous giant	*Deep Space Nine*	"Starship Down"
Class K: adaptable for humanoid use with pressure domes	Classic	"I, Mudd"
Class L: oxygen/argon atmosphere	*Voyager*	"The 37s"
Class M: oxygen/nitrgen atmosphere		

Table 6.4   Planets

Planet	Series or Film	Episode
Adelphous IV	*The Next Generation*	"Data's Day"
Acamar III, Acamar	*The Next Generation*	"The Vengeance Factor"
Akrayde VII	*The Next Generation*	"Captain's Holiday"
Aldea, Epsilon Mynos	*The Next Generation*	"When the Bough Breaks"
Aldebaran III	*Deep Space Nine*	"Past Tense, Part I"

Table 6.4 Planets *(continued)*

Planet	Series or Film	Episode
Aldebaron	Classic	"Where No Man Has Gone Before"
Aldron IV	*The Next Generation*	"Coming of Age"
Algeron	*The Next Generation*	"The Pegasus"
Alpha 177	Classic	"The Enemy Within"
Alpha Aradoni II	Classic	"Wolf in the Fold"
Alpha Carinae V	Classic	"Wolf in the Fold"
Alpha Majoris I	Classic	"Wolf in the Fold"
Alpha Moon, Peliar Zel	*The Next Generation*	"The Host"
Alpha Onias III, Onias	*The Next Generation*	"Future Imperfect"
Altair III	*The Next Generation*	"Encounter at Farpoint"
Altair IV	*Deep Space Nine*	"Prophet Motive"
Altair VI	Classic	"Amok Time"
Altec, Omega Sagitta	*The Next Generation*	"The Outrageous Okona"
Altoor VII	*The Next Generation*	"Birthright, Part I"
Amleth Prime, Amleth (inside an emission nebula)	*Deep Space Nine*	"Return to Grace"
Andoria	*Deep Space Nine*	"Prophet Motive"
Angel One	*The Next Generation*	"Angel One"
Angosia III	*The Next Generation*	"The Hunted"
Antide III	*The Next Generation*	"Manhunt"
Antos	Classic	"Whom Gods Destroy"
Antos IV	Classic	"Whom Gods Destroy"
Arakang VII	*Deep Space Nine*	"Q-Less"
Archer IV	*The Next Generation*	"Yesterday's Enterprise"
Argelius II	Classic	"Wolf in the Fold"
Argus X	Classic	"Obsession"
Ariannus	Classic	"Let That Be Your Last Battlefield"
Arlof IX	*The Next Generation*	"The Neutral Zone"
Armus IX	*The Next Generation*	"Angel One"
Arret	Classic	"Return to Tomorrow"
Atalia VII, Atalia	*The Next Generation*	"The Chase"
Atrea IV	*The Next Generation*	"Inheritance"
Axanar	Classic	"Whom Gods Destroy"
Babel (planetary code name)	Classic	"Journey to Babel"
Bajor (at least five moons)	*Deep Space Nine*	"Emissary"
Bajor (under Cardassian occupation for over 50 years)	*Deep Space Nine*	"Accession"
Bajor VII (at least three moons)	*Deep Space Nine*	"Whispers"
Bajor VIII (six colonies)	*Deep Space Nine*	"Past Prologue"
Balisty	*Deep Space Nine*	"The Nagus"
Barisa Prime	*Deep Space Nine*	"The Adversary"

Table 6.4 Planets *(continued)*

Planet	Series or Film	Episode
Barkon IV	*The Next Generation*	"Thine Own Self"
Barradas III, Barradas	*The Next Generation*	"The Emissary"
Barson II	*The Next Generation*	"Eye of the Beholder"
Barzan II	*The Next Generation*	"The Price"
Benzar	*The Next Generation*	"Coming of Age"
Bersallis III, Bersallis	*The Next Generation*	"Lessons"
Beta Agni II	*The Next Generation*	"The Most Toys"
Beta Antares	Classic	"A Piece of the Action"
Beta III, 6-11	Classic	"The Return of the Archons"
Beta XII-A	Classic	"The Day of the Dove"
Beta Moon, Peliar Zel	*The Next Generation*	"The Host"
Beta Thoridar	*The Next Generation*	"Redemption"
Betaline Kel	*The Next Generation*	"Redemption II"
Betazed	*The Next Generation*	
Bilana III (approximately three light-years from Layma II)	*The Next Generation*	"New Ground"
Binus, Beta Magellan	*The Next Generation*	"11001001"
Blue Horizon (developed by Gideon Seyetik)	*Deep Space Nine*	"Second Sight"
Borka VI	*The Next Generation*	"Face of the Enemy "
Bopac III, Bopac (uninhabited; six weeks away from nearest Dominion outpost)	*Deep Space Nine*	"Hippocratic Oath"
Boraal II (atmosphere dissipated)	*The Next Generation*	"Homeward"
Boreth (Klingon monastery)	*Deep Space Nine*	"The Way of the Warrior"
Brax	*Deep Space Nine*	"Q-Less"
Bre'el IV	*The Next Generation*	"Deja Q"
Brekka, Dala	*The Next Generation*	"Symbiosis"
Brentalia	*The Next Generation*	"New Ground"
Browder IV	*The Next Generation*	"Allegiance"
Cairn	*The Next Generation*	"Dark Page "
Calder II, Calder	*The Next Generation*	"Gambit, Part I"
Caldos IV (terraformed)	*The Next Generation*	"Sub Rosa"
Caldonia	*The Next Generation*	"The Price"
Callinon VII, Callinon	*Deep Space Nine*	"The Search, Part I"
Camor V, Camor	*The Next Generation*	"Bloodlines"
Campa III	*Deep Space Nine*	"Defiant"
Camus II	Classic	"Turnabout Intruder"
Capella IV	Classic	"Friday's Child"
Carraya IV, Carraya	*The Next Generation*	"Rightful Heir"
Cardassia	*The Next Generation*	"The Chase"

Table 6.4 Planets *(continued)*

Planet	Series or Film	Episode
Cardassia III	*Deep Space Nine*	"Prophet Motive"
Cardassia IV	*Deep Space Nine*	"The Homecoming"
Cardassia V	*Deep Space Nine*	"Shadowplay"
Cardassia Prime	*Deep Space Nine*	"The Wire"
Castal I	*The Next Generation*	"Suddenly Human"
Celais V	*Deep Space Nine*	"The Adversary"
Celfala Prime (near Draylon II)	*Deep Space Nine*	"Sanctuary"
Celtris III	*The Next Generation*	"Chain of Command, Part I"
Cestus III	Classic	"Arena"
Cestus III (other side of Federation territory; 2 weeks for subspace messages)	*Deep Space Nine*	"Family Business"
Cestus III (8 weeks from Deep Space Nine at max. warp)	*Deep Space Nine*	"The Way of the Warrior"
Ceti Alpha V	Classic	"Space Seed"
Cetlic III	*Deep Space Nine*	"Emissary"
Chalna	*The Next Generation*	"Allegiance"
Chandra V	*The Next Generation*	"Tin Man"
Chantil III	*The Next Generation*	"Darmok"
Cheron	Classic	"Let That Be Your Last Battlefield"
Choltok IV (Romulan research colony)	Voyager	"Time and Again"
Chya VII	*The Next Generation*	"Booby Trap"
Clauvdia III	*The Next Generation*	"The Dauphin"
Colendia IV	*Deep Space Nine*	"Playing God"
Colla III, Colla	*The Next Generation*	"Firstborn"
Corcoroli V	*The Next Generation*	"Allegiance"
Cosla II	*Deep Space Nine*	"The Alternate"
Costalane	*The Next Generation*	"Cost of Living"
Daled IV	*The Next Generation*	"The Dauphin"
Davlos III (on Klingon border)	*Deep Space Nine*	"Visionary"
Dayas IV	*Deep Space Nine*	"Blood Oath"
Deanius III	*The Next Generation*	"Contagion"
Deilos IV	*The Next Generation*	"Remember Me"
Delb II	*The Next Generation*	"The Drumhead"
Delta IV	*Star Trek:TMP*	
Delta Vega	Classic	"Where No Man . . ."
Deneb II	Classic	"Wolf in the Fold"
Deneb IV	*The Next Generation*	"Encounter at Farpoint"
Deneb V	Classic	"I, Mudd"
Deneva	Classic	"Operation: Annihilate!"
Deriben V	*The Next Generation*	"Aquiel"

Table 6.4 Planets *(continued)*

Planet	Series or Film	Episode
Desica II (site of Picard's apparent murder in a bar)	*The Next Generation*	"Gambit, Part I"
Devidia II, Devidia	*The Next Generation*	"Time's Arrow"
Dilicium IV	*The Next Generation*	"Unification: Part II"
Dilula II	*The Next Generation*	"The Best of Both Worlds, Part II"
Ditalix B, Mira	*The Next Generation*	"Conspiracy"
Doraf I	*The Next Generation*	"Unification"
Dorvan V	*The Next Generation*	"Journey's End"
Dozaria, Dozaria	*Deep Space Nine*	"Indiscretion"
Dracana IV, Dracana	*The Next Generation*	"Legacy"
Drago IV (within three light-years of Cardassian space)	*The Next Generation*	"Homeward"
Draken IV	*The Next Generation*	"Gambit, Part I"
Draycon IV, Draycon	*The Next Generation*	"Face of the Enemy "
Draylon II (near Celfala Prime)	*Deep Space Nine*	"Sanctuary"
Drema IV, Selcundi II	*The Next Generation*	"Pen Pals"
Dynomicus VII	*The Next Generation*	"A Fistful of Datas"
Earth, Sol	Classic	All episodes
Eden	Classic	"The Way to Eden"
Eden	*Star Trek V*	
892 IV	Classic	"Bread and Circuses"
Ekos	Classic	"Patterns of Force"
Elas, Tellun	Classic	"Elaan of Troyius"
El-Adrel IV, El-Adrel	*The Next Generation*	"Darmok"
Elba II	Classic	"Whom Gods Destroy"
Emila II	*The Next Generation*	"A Matter of Perspective"
Eminiar VII	Classic	"A Taste of Armageddon"
Ennan VI	*The Next Generation*	"Time Squared"
Epsilon Canaris IV	Classic	"Metamorphosis"
Epsilon Hydra VII	*Deep Space Nine*	"Q-Less"
Excalbia	Classic	"The Savage Curtain"
Exo III	Classic	"What Are Little Girls..?"
Ferenginar (Ferengi homeworld)	*Deep Space Nine*	"Bar Association"
Feris VI	*Deep Space Nine*	"Life Support"
Fahleena III	*Deep Space Nine*	"Dramatis Personae"
Forkis III	*The Next Generation*	"Parallels"
Galen IV (Federation colony)	*The Next Generation*	"Suddenly Human"
Galas II	*The Next Generation*	"Darmok"
Galor IV	*The Next Generation*	"The Offspring"
Galora Prime	*Deep Space Nine*	"Rules of Engagement"
Galorndon Core	*The Next Generation*	"The Enemy"

Table 6.4 Planets *(continued)*

Planet	Series or Film	Episode
Gamelan V, Gamelan	*The Next Generation*	"Final Mission"
Gamaras V	*The Next Generation*	"Captain's Holiday"
Gamma II	Classic	"The Gamesters . . ."
Gamma Canaris N	Classic	"Metamorphosis"
Gamma Hromi II, Hromi Cluster	*The Next Generation*	"The Vengeance Factor"
Gamma Hydra II, Gamma Hydra	Classic	"The Deadly Years"
Gamma Hydra IV, Gamma Hydra	Classic	"The Deadly Years"
Gamma Tauri IV	*The Next Generation*	"The Last Outpost"
Gamma Trianguli VI	Classic	"The Apple"
Gault	*The Next Generation*	"Heart of Glory"
Gagaran IV	*The Next Generation*	"Unnatural Selection"
Garadias IV	*The Next Generation*	"The Next Phase"
Garon II	*The Next Generation*	"Ensign Ro"
Garon IV	*The Next Generation*	"The Next Phase"
Garushda	*The Next Generation*	"Tin Man"
Germulon V	*Deep Space Nine*	"Paradise"
Gideon	Classic	"The Mark of Gideon"
Gonal IV	*The Next Generation*	"Disaster"
Gravesworld	*The Next Generation*	"The Schizoid Man"
Harrakis V	*The Next Generation*	"Clues"
Harod IV	*The Next Generation*	"The Perfect Mate"
Harrok IV, Latar Nebula	*Deep Space Nine*	"Q-Less"
Hattoria (near Romulan Neutral Zone)	*The Next Generation*	"All Good Things . . ."
Haven, Beta Casius	*The Next Generation*	"Haven"
Heirata III	*The Next Generation*	"Violations"
Hekarus II, Hekarus	*The Next Generation*	"Force of Nature "
Hercoze III	*The Next Generation*	"The Price"
Hogas II	*The Next Generation*	"Brothers"
Holberg 917G	Classic	"Requiem for Methuselah"
Hottar II	*The Next Generation*	"The Offspring"
Iconia	*The Next Generation*	"Contagion"
Indri VIII, Indri (biosphere destroyed)	*The Next Generation*	"The Chase"
Iotia	Classic	"A Piece of the Action"
Iratin V	*The Next Generation*	"The Most Toys"
Isis III	*The Next Generation*	"Too Short a Season"
Ivadni IV	*The Next Generation*	"Clues"
Izar	Classic	"Whom Gods Destroy"
Jaforay II	*Deep Space Nine*	"Improbable Cause"
Janus VI	Classic	"Devil in the Dark"

Table 6.4 Planets *(continued)*

Planet	Series or Film	Episode
Jeraddo (fifth moon of Bajor)	*Deep Space Nine*	"Progress"
Juri IV	*The Next Generation*	"The Best of Both Worlds"
Kabatris	*The Next Generation*	"Angel One"
Kafka IV	*Deep Space Nine*	"Invasive Procedures"
Kaldra IV	*The Next Generation*	"Violations"
Kaelon II	*The Next Generation*	"Half a Life"
Kanda IV	*The Next Generation*	"Darmok"
Karil Prime	*Deep Space Nine*	"The Jem'Hadar"
Kataan, Kataan	*The Next Generation*	"Inner Light"
Kelva, Andromeda	Classic	"By Any Other Name"
Kenda II	*The Next Generation*	"Remember Me"
Kentanna	*Deep Space Nine*	"Sanctuary"
Kerl, Kerlan (civilization died out 12,000 years ago)	*The Next Generation*	"The Chase"
Kesprit III	*The Next Generation*	"Attached"
Khitomer	*The Next Generation*	"Yesterday's Enterprise"
Keeair	*The Next Generation*	"The Chase"
Klaestron IV	*Deep Space Nine*	"Dax"
Kling	*The Next Generation*	"Heart of Glory"
Kora II	*Deep Space Nine*	"Duet"
Koltair IV	*The Next Generation*	"We'll Always Have Paris"
Korbin II	*The Next Generation*	"New Ground"
Korma (Cardassian space)	*Deep Space Nine*	"Return to Grace"
Korridon	Classic	"Journey to Babel"
Krios	*The Next Generation*	"The Mind's Eye"
Kresalia	*The Next Generation*	"The Price"
Kronos (Klingon spelling: Qo'noS)	*Star Trek VI*	
Kronos (verified as Klingon homeworld)	*Deep Space Nine*	"The House of Quark"
Ladonia III	*Deep Space Nine*	"The Wire"
Lagobus X	*Deep Space Nine*	"Second Sight"
Lalya IV	*The Next Generation*	"Identity Crisis"
Lambdo Paz (moon of Pentarus III)	*The Next Generation*	"Final Mission"
Landris II	*The Next Generation*	"Lessons"
Lapa IV	*The Next Generation*	"Menage a Troi"
Largo V	*Deep Space Nine*	"Babel"
Larieshe IV	*The Next Generation*	"Darmok"
Lemma II (approximately 3 light-years from Bilana III)	*The Next Generation*	"New Ground"
Ligon II	*The Next Generation*	"Code of Honor"
Loren III, Loren	*The Next Generation*	"The Chase"

Table 6.4 Planets *(continued)*

Planet	Series or Film	Episode
Loval (civilian outpost; subspace relay station; secret weapons research installation)	*Deep Space Nine*	"Return to Grace"
Lyar	*The Next Generation*	"Liaisons"
Lygos VII, Lygos	*The Next Generation*	"Rascals"
Lysepia	*Deep Space Nine*	"Indiscretion"
Lysia, Lysian	*The Next Generation*	"Conundrum"
Lunar V (moon of Angosia III)	*The Next Generation*	"The Hunted"
Lunar V Base (Bajoran moon)	*Deep Space Nine*	"The Siege"
M-113	Classic	"The Man Trap"
Mab-Bu VI (single moon)	*The Next Generation*	"Power Play"
Makus III	Classic	"The Galileo Seven"
Malena II	*The Next Generation*	"Violations"
Malcor III (over 2000 light-years from Earth)	*The Next Generation*	"First Contact"
Malkus IX	*The Next Generation*	"Loud as a Whisper"
Malona IV (stripped of life by crystaline entity)	*The Next Generation*	"Silicon Avatar"
Maranga IV	*The Next Generation*	"Firstborn"
Mariposa, Phyecus Sector	*The Next Generation*	"Up the Long Ladder"
Markus II	Classic	"Requiem for Methuselah"
Markus XII	Classic	"The Enemy Within"
Marlonia	*The Next Generation*	"Rascals"
Mars, Sol	*The Next Generation*	"The Best of Both Worlds, Part II"
Mars, Sol (colonized by Earth in 2103; currently 2371)	*Voyager*	"The 37s"
Mekemus III (Tzenkethi settlement)	*Deep Space Nine*	"The Adversary"
Melas II	*The Next Generation*	"Ship in a Bottle"
Melindy VII	*The Next Generation*	"Darmok"
Melnos IV	*The Next Generation*	"Lessons"
Melvala IV	*The Next Generation*	"Inheritance"
Memory Alpha	Classic	"The Lights of Zetar"
Merak II	Classic	"The Cloudminders"
Meridian, Triala	*Deep Space Nine*	"Meridian"
Milika III	*The Next Generation*	"Tapestry"
Minara	Classic	"Turnabout Intruder"
Minas (moon of Saturn)	*The Next Generation*	"The First Duty"
Minas V	*The Next Generation*	"Tapestry"
Minos	*The Next Generation*	"Arsenal of Freedom"
Mintaka III	*The Next Generation*	"Who Watches The Watchers?"
Miradin	*Deep Space Nine*	"Q-Less"

Table 6.4 Planets *(continued)*

Planet	Series or Film	Episode
Miridian VI	*The Next Generation*	"Future Imperfect"
Mizar II	*The Next Generation*	"Allegiance"
Moab IV, Moab	*The Next Generation*	"The Masterpiece Society"
Mordan IV	*The Next Generation*	"Too Short a Season"
Moria IV	*Deep Space Nine*	"Dramatis Personae"
Morikin VII	*The Next Generation*	"Tapestry"
Mudor V	*The Next Generation*	"Disaster"
Muendella, Telleris Cluster	*Deep Space Nine*	"Q-Less"
Narenda III	*The Next Generation*	"Yesterday's Enterprise"
Nahmi IV	*The Next Generation*	"Hollow Pursuits"
Neinmen, Zairtzi Seven	*The Next Generation*	"When the Bough Breaks"
Nel III, Nel	*The Next Generation*	"Violations"
Nelvana III, Nelvana	*The Next Generation*	"The Defector"
Nervala IV	*The Next Generation*	"Second Chances"
Neural	Classic	"A Private Little War"
New Bajor	*Deep Space Nine*	"Crossover"
New Gaul	*The Next Generation*	"Bloodlines"
New Halana	*Deep Space Nine*	"Second Sight"
Neygor	*The Next Generation*	"Birthright, Part I"
Nibok, DMZ	*Voyager*	"Prime Factors"
Nimbus III	*Star Trek V*	
Norpin IV	*The Next Generation*	"Rascals"
Norpin V	*The Next Generation*	"Relics"
Oceanis IV	*The Next Generation*	"The Game"
Odet IX	*The Next Generation*	"The Child"
Ohniaka Three, Ohniaka	*The Next Generation*	"Descent"
Omecla III (Obsidian Order shipyards)	*Deep Space Nine*	"Defiant"
Omega IV	Classic	"The Omega Glory"
Omicron IV	Classic	"Assignment: Earth"
Omicron Ceti III	Classic	"This Side of Paradise"
Omicron Theta	*The Next Generation*	"Datalore"
Onara III, Dala	*The Next Generation*	"Symbiosis"
Ophiucus III	Classic	"Mudd's Women"
Orelious IX (asteroidal planetoid)	*The Next Generation*	"Booby Trap"
Organia	Classic	"Errand of Mercy"
Orhyis III, Orhyis	*Deep Space Nine*	"Defiant"
Orion	Classic	"Journey to Babel"
Pacifica	*The Next Generation*	"Conspiracy"
Parada II, Paradas	*Deep Space Nine*	"Whispers"

Table 6.4 Planets *(continued)*

Planet	Series or Film	Episode
Parada IV, Paradas (seven moons)	Deep Space Nine	"Whispers"
Pasiphony V	The Next Generation	"Too Short A Season"
Parliament, Beta Renna	The Next Generation	"Lonely Among Us"
Peliar Zel, Peliar	The Next Generation	"The Host"
Pelleus V	The Next Generation	"11001001"
Pentarus II	The Next Generation	"Final Mission"
Pentarus III	The Next Generation	"Final Mission"
Pentarus V	The Next Generation	"Final Mission"
Pentath III, Pentath	Deep Space Nine	"Rules of Engagement"
Penthara IV	The Next Generation	"A Matter of Time"
Phendouse V	The Next Generation	"Loud as a Whisper"
Pholar III	The Next Generation	"Dark Page "
Platonius	Classic	"Plato's Stepchildren"
Polloc V (Cardassian space; first off-planet raid by the Bajoran Resistance)	Deep Space Nine	"Shakaar"
Pollux IV	Classic	"Who Mourns for Adonais?"
Praxis (Klingon moon; over 3/4 destroyed)	Star Trek VI	
Proctol II	The Next Generation	"In Theory"
Prophet's Landing (Bajoran colony nearest Cardassian border)	Deep Space Nine	"Heart of Stone"
Psi 2000	Classic	"The Naked Time"
Pyris VII	Classic	"Catspaw"
Pythra V	Deep Space Nine	"Rivals"
Q	Classic	"Conscience of the King"
Quadra Sigma III, Sigma III	The Next Generation	"Hide and Q"
Qualor II	The Next Generation	"Unification"
Rakkal (at least four moons)	Deep Space Nine	"Return to Grace"
Ramatis III, Ramatis	The Next Generation	"Loud as a Whisper"
Rahm-Izad, Rahm Izad	The Next Generation	"The Chase"
Rana IV, Delta Rana	The Next Generation	"The Survivors "
Raynas VI	The Next Generation	"Q Who?"
Regula, Mutara Sector (class D)	Star Trek II	
Regulus III (Science Academy; over 300 light-years from Deep Space Nine)	Deep Space Nine	"Fascination"
Regulus V	Classic	"Amok Time"
Reina VI	The Next Generation	"Pen Pals"
Rekag-Seronia	The Next Generation	"Man of the People"
Relva VII	The Next Generation	"Coming of Age"
Renol VI	Deep Space Nine	"Heart of Stone"

Table 6.4 Planets *(continued)*

Planet	*Series or Film*	*Episode*
Rigel III	*The Next Generation*	"All Good Things . . ."
Rigel IV	Classic	"Wolf in the Fold"
Rigel V	Classic	"Journey to Babel"
Rigel VII	Classic	"The Cage"
Rigel XII	Classic	"Mudd's Women"
Rigley's Pleasure Planet	Classic	"Man Trap"
Risa	*The Next Generation*	"Captain's Holiday"
Rochani III	*Deep Space Nine*	"Dramatis Personae"
Romulus	Classic	
Ruah IV, Ruah	*The Next Generation*	"The Chase"
Rubicun III, Rubicun	*The Next Generation*	"Justice"
Ruso V (astroidal planetoid)	*The Next Generation*	"The Dauphin"
Rutia IV	*The Next Generation*	"The High Ground"
Sarona VIII	*The Next Generation*	"We'll Always Have Paris"
Saturn	*The Next Generation*	"The First Duty"
Scalos	Classic	"Wink of an Eye"
Seary IV	*The Next Generation*	"The Most Toys"
Setlik III	*The Next Generation*	"The Wounded"
Septal Minor IV	*The Next Generation*	"The Best of Both Worlds"
Sherman's Planet	Classic	"The Trouble with Tribbles"
Sicoura Prime, Alpha Quadrant	*Voyager*	"Dreadnought"
Signa XIV	Classic	"Tomorrow is Yesterday"
Solais V	*The Next Generation*	"Loud as a Whisper"
Solarion IV	*The Next Generation*	"Ensign Ro"
Sorata IV	*The Next Generation*	"Shades of Gray"
Sosha III	*The Next Generation*	"The Chase"
Straleb, Omega Sagitta	*The Next Generation*	"The Outrageous Okona"
Styris IV	*The Next Generation*	"Code of Honor"
Suvin IV	*The Next Generation*	"Rascals"
T'Lani III	*Deep Space Nine*	"Armageddon Game"
T'Lani Prime	*Deep Space Nine*	"Armageddon Game"
Tagra IV, Argolis Cluster	*The Next Generation*	"True Q"
Takara	*The Next Generation*	"Suspicions"
Talos IV	Classic	"The Cage"
Tantalus Five	Classic	"Dagger of the Mind"
Tanuga IV	*The Next Generation*	"A Matter of Perspective"
Tarella	*The Next Generation*	"Haven"
Tarsas IV	Classic	"Conscience of the King"
Tasus III	*The Next Generation*	"11001001"

Table 6.4 Planets *(continued)*

Planet	Series or Film	Episode
Tartaras V	*Deep Space Nine*	"Q-Less"
Tau Alpha-C	*The Next Generation*	"Where No One Has Gone Before"
Tau Ceti III	*The Next Generation*	"Conspiracy"
Tau Cygna V, Tau Cygna	*The Next Generation*	"The Ensigns of Command"
Taurus II	Classic	"The Galileo Seven"
Tavela Minor	*The Next Generation*	"Imaginary Friend"
Taygus III	*The Next Generation*	"Qpid"
Tazna V	*The Next Generation*	"Darmok"
Terlina III, Terlina	*The Next Generation*	"Inheritance"
Terosa Prime	*Deep Space Nine*	"Second Sight"
Tessen III	*The Next Generation*	"Cost of Living"
Tethys III	*The Next Generation*	"Clues"
Thalos VII	*The Next Generation*	"The Dauphin"
Thanatos VII	*The Next Generation*	"Phantasms"
Thasus	Classic	"Charlie X"
Thelka IV	*The Next Generation*	"Lessons"
Theta VII	Classic	"Obsession"
Theta VIII, Theta 116	*The Next Generation*	"The Royale"
Theydat IV	*The Next Generation*	"When the Bough Breaks"
Tiarchanon III, Tiarchanon	*The Next Generation*	"Identity Crisis"
Tiburon	Classic	"The Savage Curtain"
Tilonus IV	*The Next Generation*	"Frame of Mind "
Titan (moon of Saturn)	*The Next Generation*	"The First Duty"
Titus IV	*The Next Generation*	"Realm of Fear"
Tohvun III	*The Next Generation*	"Chain of Command, Part II"
Torman V	*The Next Generation*	"Chain of Command, Part I"
Torona IV	*Deep Space Nine*	"The Sword of Kahless"
Triacus	Classic	"And the Children Shall Lead"
Trill	*Deep Space Nine*	"Equilibrium"
Trill (Trill homeworld)	*Deep Space Nine*	"The Way of the Warrior"
Triskelion, M-24 Alpha	Classic	"The Gamesters . . ."
Troyius, Tellun	Classic	"Elaan of Troyius"
Turkana IV	*The Next Generation*	"Legacy"
Tycho IV, Tycho	Classic	"Obsession"
Tyrus VII-A, Tyran	*The Next Generation*	"The Quality of Life"
Udala Prime	*The Next Generation*	"Gambit, Part I"
Ultima Thule	*Deep Space Nine*	"Dramatis Personae"
Umith VIII, DMZ	*Deep Space Nine*	"The Maquis, Part II"
Vacca VI, Cabral	*The Next Generation*	"Homeward"

Table 6.4 Planets *(continued)*

Planet	Series or Film	Episode
Vadris III	*Deep Space Nine*	"Q-Less"
Vagra II, Zed Lapis	*The Next Generation*	"Skin of Evil"
Valo I (three or more moons)	*The Next Generation*	"Ensign Ro"
Valo II	*The Next Generation*	"Ensign Ro"
Valo III	*The Next Generation*	"Ensign Ro"
Valt Minor	*The Next Generation*	"The Perfect Mate"
Vandor VI, Vandor	*The Next Generation*	"We'll Always Have Paris"
Vega IX	Classic	"Mirror, Mirror"
Velara III, Pleiades Cluster	*The Next Generation*	"Home Soil"
Velos VII	*Deep Space Nine*	"Babel"
Vendikar	Classic	"A Taste of Armageddon"
Ventax II	*The Next Generation*	"Devil's Due"
Venus	*Deep Space Nine*	"Past Tense, Part I"
Veridian III, Veridian (destroyed by star collapse in alternate timeline)	*Star Trek: Generations*	
Veridian IV, Veridian (destroyed by star collapse in alternate timeline)	*Star Trek: Generations*	
Vilmor II, Vilmoran	*The Next Generation*	"The Chase"
Volchok Prime	*Deep Space Nine*	"The Nagus"
Volon II, Volon Colonies, DMZ	*Deep Space Nine*	"The Maquis, Part I"
Volon III, Volon Colonies, DMZ	*Deep Space Nine*	"The Maquis, Part II"
Vulcan, 40 Eridani A	Classic	"Amok Time"
Yadera Prime	*Deep Space Nine*	"Shadowplay"
Yonada (asteroidal body)	Classic	"For the World is Hollow and I Have Touched the Sky"
Zalkon	*The Next Generation*	"Transfigurations"
Zeon	Classic	"Patterns of Force"
Zeta Alpha II	*The Next Generation*	"The Best of Both Worlds"
<Unnamed planet>	Classic	"Requiem for Methuselah"
<Unnamed planet>	*The Next Generation*	"Descent"
<Unnamed planet>	*The Next Generation*	"Liaisons"
<Unnamed planet> (160 million km from Orelious Minor)	*Deep Space Nine*	"Paradise"
<Unnamed planet> (Karemma homeworld)	*Deep Space Nine*	"The Search, Part I"
<Unnamed planet>	*Deep Space Nine*	"The Jem'Hadar"
<Unnamed rogue planet>, Omarian Nebula (Dominion homeworld)	*Deep Space Nine*	"The Search, Part I"
<Unnamed planet> (Tzenkethi homeworld)	*Deep Space Nine*	"Adversary"
<Unnamed moon>, Rakkal (fourth moon)	*Deep Space Nine*	"Return to Grace"
<Unnamed planet> (Bolian homeworld, Alpha Quadrant)	*Voyager*	"Dreadnought"

Table 6.5 Other Locales

Place	Series or Film	Episode
Aerowath Colony	*Deep Space Nine*	"The Wire"
Amargosa Observatory, Amargosa (destroyed by star collapse)	*Star Trek: Generations*	
Argus Array (deep space telescope)	*The Next Generation*	"The Nth Degree"
Arkaria base	*The Next Generation*	"Starship Mine"
Benecia Colony, Beta Aurigae	Classic	"Turnabout Intruder"
Bersallis III Outpost, Bersallis (Federation outpost; destroyed by firestorm)	*The Next Generation*	"Lessons"
Bryma Colony, Bryma, DMZ	*Deep Space Nine*	"The Maquis, Part II"
Camp Khitomer (near Romulan border)	*Star Trek VI*	
Colony Beta Six	Classic	"The Squire of Gothos"
Communication Relay Station 47 (near Klingon border)	*The Next Generation*	"Aquiel"
Communication Relay Station 194	*The Next Generation*	"Aquiel"
Corvat Colony	*Deep Space Nine*	"Blood Oath"
Crasnar Outpost (massacred by Talarian forces)	*The Next Generation*	"Suddenly Human"
Darmok Colony, Melindy VII	*The Next Generation*	"Darmok"
Darwin Station, Gagaran	*The Next Generation*	"Unnatural Selection"
Deep Space Three Station	*The Next Generation*	"Interface "
Deep Space Four Station	*The Next Generation*	"The Chase"
Deep Space Five Station (Regula 1 type)	*The Next Generation*	"Parallels"
Deep Space Nine Station; Cardassian name: Terek Nor (Cmdr Benjamin Sisko; Capt Benjamin Sisko as of Stardate 48960.9)	*Deep Space Nine*	All episodes
Earth Colony II Research Station	*The Next Generation*	"Tapestry"
Earth Station Babruisk	*The Next Generation*	"Family"
Earth Station McKinley	*The Next Generation*	"The Best of Both Worlds, Part II"
Elumsbur Detention Center, Bajor	*Deep Space Nine*	"Second Skin"
Experimental Colony, Gamma Hydra IV	Classic	"The Deadly Years"
Farpoint Station, Deneb IV (dissolved)	*The Next Generation*	"Encounter at Farpoint"
Fastbase Starbase Earhart	*The Next Generation*	"Samaritan Snare"
Federation Penal Settlement, New Zealand	*Voyager*	"Caretaker"
Feloris Colony	*The Next Generation*	"The Perfect Mate"
Gallitep Labor Camp	*Deep Space Nine*	"Duet"
Hailium Experimental Station	Classic	"Mudd's Women"
Hanolin Colony	*Deep Space Nine*	"The Siege"
Jupiter Outpost Nine-Two	*The Next Generation*	"The Best of Both Worlds, Part II"
Khitomer Outpost (destroyed)	*The Next Generation*	"Heart of Glory"
Klingon Outpost, Narendra III	*The Next Generation*	"Yesterday's Enterprise"
Laizon II Labor Camp	*Deep Space Nine*	"Defiant"

Table 6.5 Other Locales *(continued)*

Place	Series or Film	Episode
Lithium Cracking Station, Delta Vega	Classic	"Where No Man Has Gone Before"
Lya Station Alpha (orbital)	*The Next Generation*	"Ensign Ro"
Lysian Central Command (15,311 people)	*The Next Generation*	"Conundrum"
Mars Defence Perimeter	*The Next Generation*	"The Best of Both Worlds, Part II"
Mars Station	*The Next Generation*	"Booby Trap"
Martian Colony	Classic	"Wolf in the Fold"
McKinley Rocket Base, Earth (1968)	Classic	"Assignment: Earth"
Minas Station, Minas, moon of Saturn	*The Next Generation*	"The First Duty"
Milona IV Colony (destroyed)	*The Next Generation*	"Silicon Avatar"
Mission District, San Francisco, Earth	*Voyager*	"Non Sequitur"
Morska (Klingon listening post)	*Star Trek VI*	
MS One Colony	*The Next Generation*	"Descent"
Navigation Control Post 24 (Cardassian outpost)	*Deep Space Nine*	"The Homecoming"
New Berlin Colony	*The Next Generation*	"Descent"
New Paris Colony, Makus III	Classic	"Galileo Seven"
New Providence Colony, Juri IV (destroyed)	*The Next Generation*	"The Best of Both Worlds"
Norcan Outpost	*The Next Generation*	"The Defector"
Norpin Colony, Norpin IV	*The Next Generation*	"Rascals"
Norpin Colony, Norpin V	*The Next Generation*	"Relics"
Outpost 06	*The Next Generation*	"The Defector"
Outpost 23 (location Top Secret)	*The Next Generation*	"Future Imperfect"
Outpost 47, Amatha Sector (Cardassian outpost; destroyed by Maquis)	*Deep Space Nine*	"Defiant"
Outpost 61, Amatha Sector (Cardassian outpost; destroyed by Maquis)	*Deep Space Nine*	"Defiant"
Outpost MZ 5	*The Next Generation*	"Heart of Glory"
Outpost Seran T-1	*The Next Generation*	"Booby Trap"
Outpost Terra 9 (destroyed)	*The Next Generation*	"The Neutral Zone"
Paralex Colony, Sherlaya VI	*The Next Generation*	"Cost of Living"
Pellios Station	*Deep Space Nine*	"Invasive Procedures"
Pentarus Station	*The Next Generation*	"Final Mission"
Proxima Maintenance Yards (Admiral Drasman)	*Deep Space Nine*	"Past Tense, Part I"
Relageth Refugee Camp, Bajor	*Deep Space Nine*	"Shadowplay"
Research Station 75	*The Next Generation*	"Face of the Enemy "
Remmler Array	*The Next Generation*	"Starship Mine"
Rigel Colony, Rigel	Classic	"The Doomsday Machine"
Rog Prison (Ferengi)	*The Next Generation*	"Bloodlines"
Rura Penthe (dilithium mine and penal asteroid)	*Star Trek VI*	
Sanctuary District A, San Francisco, Earth (year 2024)	*Deep Space Nine*	"Past Tense, Part I"

Table 6.5 Other Locales *(continued)*

Place	Series or Film	Episode
Science Station 402, Kilarn	*The Next Generation*	"The Nth Degree"
Science Station Delta 05 (destroyed)	*The Next Generation*	"The Neutral Zone"
Science Station Tango Sierra	*The Next Generation*	"The Child"
Singa Refugee Camp, Bajor	*Deep Space Nine*	"Shadowplay"
Solarion IV Colony (destroyed)	*The Next Generation*	"Ensign Ro"
Spacedock, Earth (orbital)	*Star Trek:The Motion Picture*	
Space Station K7	Classic	"The Trouble With Tribbles"
Space Station Regula 1, Regula (orbital)	*Star Trek II*	
Starbase	*The Next Generation*	"Home Soil"
Starbase, Hottar II	*The Next Generation*	"The Offspring"
Starbase 2	Classic	"Turnabout Intruder"
Starbase 4	Classic	"The Enemy Within"
Starbase 6	Classic	"The Menagerie"
Starbase 9	Classic	"Tomorrow is Yesterday"
Starbase 10	Classic	"The Deadly Years"
Starbase 11 (Commodore Stone)	Classic	"Court-Martial"
Starbase 23	*The Next Generation*	"Suspicions"
Starbase 24	*The Next Generation*	"Redemption"
Starbase 35 Sierra	*The Next Generation*	"The Neutral Zone"
Starbase 41	*Deep Space Nine*	"Playing God"
Starbase 47	*The Next Generation*	"Parallels"
Starbase 55	*The Next Generation*	"Relics"
Starbase 67	*The Next Generation*	"Disaster"
Starbase 73	*The Next Generation*	"Time Squared"
Starbase 74, Tasus III (orbital)	*The Next Generation*	"11001001"
Starbase 82	*The Next Generation*	"The Game"
Starbase 83	*The Next Generation*	"Q Who?"
Starbase 84	*The Next Generation*	"Heart of Glory"
Starbase 87	*The Next Generation*	"Homeward"
Starbase 105	*The Next Generation*	"Yesterday's Enterprise"
Starbase 112	*The Next Generation*	"Identity Crisis"
Starbase 123	*The Next Generation*	"Tin Man"
Starbase 129	*The Next Generation*	"Parallels"
Starbase 133 (orbital, Earth)	*The Next Generation*	"Remember Me"
Starbase 152	*The Next Generation*	"Tin Man"
Starbase 153	*The Next Generation*	"The Emissary"
Starbase 157	*The Next Generation*	"The Best of Both Worlds"
Starbase 173	*The Next Generation*	"The Measure of a Man"
Starbase 179	*The Next Generation*	"A Matter of Honor"

Table 6.5 Other Locales *(continued)*

Place	Series or Film	Episode
Starbase 185	*The Next Generation*	"Q Who?"
Starbase 200	Classic	"The Alternative Factor"
Starbase 211	*The Next Generation*	"The Wounded"
Starbase 214	*The Next Generation*	"A Matter of Time"
Starbase 218	*The Next Generation*	"Lessons"
Starbase 219	*The Next Generation*	"Phantasms"
Starbase 220	*The Next Generation*	"Night Terrors"
Starbase 231	*The Next Generation*	"Thine Own Self"
Starbase 227 (Admiral Jakotay)	*The Next Generation*	"Gambit, Part I"
Starbase 234	*The Next Generation*	"Redemption II"
Starbase 247	*The Next Generation*	"The Pegasus"
Starbase 247 (Admiral Riker; 25 yrs after Stardate 47988)	*The Next Generation*	"All Good Things . . ."
Starbase 260	*The Next Generation*	"In Theory"
Starbase 295	*The Next Generation*	"Descent, Part II"
Starbase 301	*The Next Generation*	"Conundrum"
Starbase 310	*The Next Generation*	"Journey's End"
Starbase 313	*The Next Generation*	"Galaxy's Child"
Starbase 324	*The Next Generation*	"The Best of Both Worlds"
Starbase 328	*The Next Generation*	"Eye of the Beholder"
Starbase 336	*The Next Generation*	"The Emissary"
Starbase 343	*The Next Generation*	"The Vengeance Factor"
Starbase 401	*Deep Space Nine*	"Whispers"
Starbase 410	*The Next Generation*	"Clues"
Starbase 416	*The Next Generation*	"Brothers"
Starbase 440	*The Next Generation*	"Violations"
Starbase 495	*The Next Generation*	"Interface "
Starbase 514	*The Next Generation*	"Hero Worship"
Starbase 515	*The Next Generation*	"Samaritan Snare"
Starbase 621	*The Next Generation*	"Sub Rosa"
Starbase 718	*The Next Generation*	"The Neutral Zone"
Starbase G-6, Quadra Sigma III	*The Next Generation*	"Hide and Q"
Starbase Lyra 3	*The Next Generation*	"The Hunted"
Starbase Montgommery	*The Next Generation*	"The Icarus Factor"
Starfleet Headquarters, San Francisco, Earth	*Star Trek:TMP*	
Star Station India	*The Next Generation*	"Unnatural Selection"
Station Lya 4	*The Next Generation*	"The Most Toys"
Station Negala 4	*The Next Generation*	"Deja Q"
Station Salem 1	*The Next Generation*	"The Enemy"

Table 6.5 Other Locales *(continued)*

Place	Series or Film	Episode
Surplus Depot Z-1-5, Qualar II	*The Next Generation*	"Unification"
Tanika IV Research Station (orbital; destroyed)	*The Next Generation*	"A Matter of Perspective"
Terenko Colony	*The Next Generation*	"Thine Own Self"
Tyran Partical Fountain, Tyra VII A (orbital)	*The Next Generation*	"The Quality of Life"
Utopia Planetia, Mars Station	*The Next Generation*	"Booby Trap"
Velos VII Internment Camp (closed Stardate 46302)	*Deep Space Nine*	"Babel"
Yaderan Colony, Yadera Prime	*Deep Space Nine*	"Shadowplay"
<Unnamed> Federation Outpost, Calder II	*The Next Generation*	"Gambit, Part II"
<Unnamed> Klingon Outpost, Maranga IV	*The Next Generation*	"Firstborn"
<Unnamed> Romulan Outpost	*Star Trek: Generations*	
<Unnamed> Terraforming Stations, Venus	*Deep Space Nine*	"Past Tense, Part I"
<Unnamed> Cardassian Outpost, Korma (destroyed by Klingon Bird of Prey)	*Deep Space Nine*	"Return to Grace"
<Unnamed> Cardassian Station, Amleth Prime	*Deep Space Nine*	"Return to Grace"
<Unnamed> Cardassian Base, fourth moon of Rakkal	*Deep Space Nine*	"Return to Grace"

Table 6.6 Countries, Provinces, States, Cities

Location	Series or Film	Episode
Aberdeen, Scotland, Earth	*The Next Generation*	"Sub Rosa"
Alameda, California, USA, Earth (20th cent.)	*Star Trek IV*	
Anchorage, Alaska, Earth	*The Next Generation*	"The Icarus Factor"
Antwerp, Earth	*Deep Space Nine*	"Homefront"
Arizona, Earth	Voyager	"The 37s"
Atlanta, Earth (1864)	*Voyager*	"Death Wish"
Australia, Earth (21st cent.)	*The Next Generation*	"Attached"
Bozeman, USA, Earth (19th cent.)	*The Next Generation*	"A Fistful of Datas"
Brussels, European Alliance, Earth	*The Next Generation*	"The Price"
Cambridge, Earth (25 years after stardate 47988)	*The Next Generation*	"All Good Things . . ."
Canada, Earth	Classic	"The Trouble With Tribbles"
Calgary, Alberta, Canada, Earth	*The Next Generation*	"The First Duty"
Chicago, Illinois, USA, Earth (20th cent.)	Classic	"A Piece of the Action"
Deadwood, USA, Earth (19th cent.)	*The Next Generation*	"A Fistful of Datas"
D'kor Province, Bajor (home province to Major Kira Nerys)	*Deep Space Nine*	
Edinburgh, Scotland, Earth	*The Next Generation*	"Sub Rosa"
First City, Klingon Imperial Empire	*The Next Generation*	"Sins of the Father"
France, Earth	*The Next Generation*	"We'll Always Have Paris"

Table 6.6   Countries, Provinces, States, Cities *(continued)*

Location	*Series or Film*	*Episode*
Glasgow, Scotland, Earth	*The Next Generation*	"Sub Rosa"
Heliopolis, Alpha Aradoni II	Classic	"Wolf in the Fold"
Hindrics Pool Province, Bajor	*Deep Space Nine*	"Shadowplay"
India, Earth	Classic	"Space Seed"
Indianapolis, USA, Earth	*The Next Generation*	"The Neutral Zone"
Iowa, USA, Earth	*Star Trek IV*	
Japan, Earth	Voyager	"The 37s"
Jolan City, Bajor	*Deep Space Nine*	"Return to Grace"
La Barre, France, Earth	*The Next Generation*	"Family"
Leningrad, Russia, Earth	Classic	"I, Mudd"
Marseilles, France	*Voyager*	"The Cloud"
Marta Community, Southern Continent, Malkor III	*The Next Generation*	"First Contact"
Nahalek Province, Rakkar	*Deep Space Nine*	"Vortex"
Nairobe, Earth	*Deep Space Nine*	"Prophet Motive"
New Berlin	*Deep Space Nine*	"The Maquis, Part I"
New Marteem-vaz, Atlantic Ocean, Earth	*The Next Generation*	"The Survivors"
New Orleans, Earth	*Deep Space Nine*	"Explorers"
Old Bandi City, Deneb IV	*The Next Generation*	"Encounter at Farpoint"
Onkor Village, Prit border	*The Next Generation*	"Attached"
Paradise City, Nimbus III	*Star Trek V*	
Paris, France, Earth	*The Next Generation*	"We'll Always Have Paris"
Pike City, Cestus III	*Deep Space Nine*	"Family Business"
Portland, Earth	*Deep Space Nine*	"Past Tense, Part I"
Rakantha Province, Bajor	*Deep Space Nine*	"Shakaar"
Rapid City, USA, Earth (19th cent.)	*The Next Generation*	"A Fistful of Datas"
Resic, Northern Province, Kataan	*The Next Generation*	"Inner Light"
Ropol City	*Deep Space Nine*	"The Maquis, Part I"
Roswell, New Mexico, USA (circa July 1947)	*Deep Space Nine*	"Little Green Men"
Russia, Earth	Classic	"I, Mudd"
San Francisco, California, USA, Earth	*Star Trek:TMP*	
Sausalito, California, USA, Earth (20th cent.)	*Star Trek IV*	
Scotland, Earth	Classic	
Secaucus, New Jersey, USA, Earth	*The Next Generation*	"The Neutral Zone"
Tombstone, Arizona, USA, Earth (19th cent.)	Classic	"Spectre of the Gun"
Tongve, Kronos (historical ref.)	*Deep Space Nine*	"Rules of Engagement"
United States of America (USA), Earth	Classic	"The Omega Glory"
Valdez, Alaska, Earth	*The Next Generation*	"The Icarus Factor"
Wellington, New Zealand, Earth	*Deep Space Nine*	"Explorers"
Washington, DC, USA, Earth	*Voyager*	"The 37s"

Table 6.7 Non-Starfleet Ships in the Alpha Quadrant

Name	Type	Notes	Series or Film	Episode
Bajoran				
ANTARES CLASS				
<Unnamed>	Cruiser	Destroyed by Cardassian war ship	*The Next Generation*	"Ensign Ro"
OTHER CLASS/TYPE				
<Unnamed>	Scout	Captain Tahna Los	*Deep Space Nine*	"Past Prologue"
<Unnamed>	Transport		*Deep Space Nine*	"Battle Lines"
<Unnamed>	Assault vessel		*Deep Space Nine*	"The Circle"
<Unnamed>	Assault vessel	Destroyed by Bajoran sub-impulse raider	*Deep Space Nine*	"The Siege"
<Unnamed>	Sub-impulse raider	Crash landed on Bajor	*Deep Space Nine*	"The Siege"
<Unnamed> [2]	Interceptor		*Deep Space Nine*	"Sanctuary"
<Unnamed>	Transport		*Deep Space Nine*	"Shadowplay"
<Unnamed>	Transport		*Deep Space Nine*	"The Collaborator"
<Unnamed> [6]	Transport		*Deep Space Nine*	"Defiant"
<Unnamed>	Transport		*Deep Space Nine*	"Life Support"
<Unnamed>	Solar sail	Crash landed on Cardassia Prime	*Deep Space Nine*	"Explorers"
<Unnamed>	Solar sail	Captain Benjamin Sisko	*Deep Space Nine*	"Explorers"
<Unnamed>	Transport		*Deep Space Nine*	"Crossfire"
<Unnamed>	Light sail	Captain Akorem Laan; left Bajor in 9174 (over 200 years ago); caught in ion storm	*Deep Space Nine*	"Accession"
UNKNOWN CLASS/TYPE				
<Unnamed>			*Deep Space Nine*	"In the Hands of the Prophets"
<Unnamed>	Parallel warring universe		*The Next Generation*	"Parallels"
<Unnamed>		Captain Razka	*Deep Space Nine*	"Indiscretion"
Cardassian Union				
GALOR CLASS TYPE 3				
Aldara	War ship	Gul Danar	*Deep Space Nine*	"Past Prologue"
Kraxon		Gul Renor	*Deep Space Nine*	"Defiant"
Reklar		Gul Lemec	*The Next Generation*	"Chain of Command, Part I"
Trager		Gul Macet	*The Next Generation*	"The Wounded"
Vetar		Gul Evek	*The Next Generation*	"Journey's End"
<Unnamed> [2]			*The Next Generation*	"Ensign Ro"
<Unnamed>	Patrol ship		*The Next Generation*	"Lower Decks"
<Unnamed>		Gul Dukat	*Deep Space Nine*	"Emissary"

Table 6.7 Non-Starfleet Ships in the Alpha Quadrant *(continued)*

Name	Type	Notes	Series or Film	Episode
\<Unnamed\>		Gul Jasad Cardassian Guard; 7th Order	*Deep Space Nine*	"Emissary"
\<Unnamed\> [2]		Cardassian Guard; 7th Order	*Deep Space Nine*	"Emissary"
\<Unnamed\> [2]			*Deep Space Nine*	"The Homecoming"
\<Unnamed\>		Gul Ocett	*The Next Generation*	"The Chase"
\<Unnamed\>			*The Next Generation*	"The Chase"
\<Unnamed\>			*The Next Generation*	"Parallels"
\<Unnamed\> [9]			*Deep Space Nine*	"Defiant"
HEDEKI CLASS				
\<Unnamed\>		Gul Evek Patrol ship	*Deep Space Nine*	"Tribunal"
KALEN CLASS				
\<Unnamed\>		Cloak capable	*Deep Space Nine*	"The Die is Cast"
KELDON CLASS				
\<Unnamed\> [6]			*Deep Space Nine*	"Defiant"
OTHER CLASS/TYPE				
Bok'Nor	Freighter	Merchantman class design; destroyed by impulse overload/sabotage	*Deep Space Nine*	"The Maquis, Part I"
Gromal	Freighter	Gul Dukat; destroyed by Klingon Bird of Prey under Gul Dukat in orbit over Loval	*Deep Space Nine*	"Return to Grace"
Koranak	Cruiser	Destroyed by the Jem'Hadar	*Deep Space Nine*	"The Die is Cast"
R'Bal	Transport		*Deep Space Nine*	"Indiscretion"
Ravenock	Bajoran prisoner transport	Crash landed on Dozaria over six years ago	*Deep Space Nine*	"Indiscretion"
\<Unnamed\>	War ship	Destroyed by *U.S.S. Phoenix*	*The Next Generation*	"The Wounded"
\<Unnamed\>	Supply ship	Destroyed by *U.S.S. Phoenix*	*The Next Generation*	"The Wounded"
\<Unnamed\>	Shuttle		*Deep Space Nine*	"Necessary Evil"
\<Unnamed\> [2]	Attack vessel	Destroyed by Federation support courier	*Deep Space Nine*	"The Maquis, Part I"
\<Unnamed\> [26]	War ship		*Deep Space Nine*	"Defiant"
UNKNOWN CLASS/TYPE				
\<Unnamed\>		Gul Toran; Cardassian Guard; 6th Order	*Deep Space Nine*	"Defiant"
\<Unnamed\> [2]	Cloak capable	Mirror universe	*Deep Space Nine*	"Through the Looking Glass"
\<Unnamed\>		Gul Dukat; destroyed in Klingon attack	*Deep Space Nine*	"The Way of the Warrior"

Table 6.7 Non-Starfleet Ships in the Alpha Quadrant *(continued)*

Name	Type	Notes	Series or Film	Episode
Ferengi Alliance				
B'REL CLASS (Klingon Bird of Prey)				
<Unnamed>	DaiMon Lurin	Renegade Ferengi ship; captured by *U.S.S. Enterprise*	*The Next Generation*	"Rascals"
<Unnamed>		Renegade Ferengi ship; captured by *U.S.S. Enterprise*	*The Next Generation*	"Rascals"
D'KORA CLASS				
Krayton	DaiMon Tog		*The Next Generation*	"Menage a Troi"
Kreechta	DaiMon Bractor		*The Next Generation*	"Peak Performance"
<Unnamed>	Transport ship		*The Next Generation*	"Force of Nature"
<Unnamed>	DaiMon Taar		*The Next Generation*	"The Last Outpost"
<Unnamed>	DaiMon Bok		*The Next Generation*	"The Battle"
FERENGI POD				
Quark's Treasure	Shuttle	Crash landed near Roswell, New Mexico (circa July 1947); sold for salvage	*Deep Space Nine*	"Little Green Men"
<Unnamed>	Shuttle	Lost via wormhole in Delta Quadrant	*The Next Generation*	"The Price"
<Unnamed>	Shuttle	Self-sabotaged; containment failure	*The Next Generation*	"The Perfect Mate"
<Unnamed>	Nagus' ship		*Deep Space Nine*	"Rules of Acquisition"
UNKNOWN CLASS/TYPE				
<Unnamed>	Trading ship		*The Next Generation*	"Descent"
<Unnamed>	DaiMon Goss		*The Next Generation*	"The Price"
Klingon Empire				
B'REL CLASS				
<Unnamed>	Advance Scout		*The Next Generation*	"Yesterday's *Enterprise*"
D12 CLASS				
<Unnamed>		Commanded by Lursa and B'Etor; destroyed by *U.S.S. Enterprise*, NCC-1701-D, over Veridian III	*Star Trek: Generations*	
K'T'INGA CLASS				
IKC T'Ong		Captain K'Temoc; found after extended dormancy	*The Next Generation*	"The Emissary"
<Unnamed>		Destroyed by DS9	*Deep Space Nine*	"The Way of the Warrior"
<Unnamed>			*Deep Space Nine*	"Rules of Engagement"
K'VORT CLASS				
IKC Pagh	Cruiser	Captain Kargan, Commander William Riker (temporary)	*The Next Generation*	"A Matter of Honor"

Table 6.7 Non-Starfleet Ships in the Alpha Quadrant *(continued)*

Name	Type	Notes	Series or Film	Episode
<Unnamed>		Destroyed in battle with *U.S.S. Enterprise* NCC-1701-D	*The Next Generation*	"Yesterday's *Enterprise*"
<Unnamed> [2]			*The Next Generation*	"Yesterday's *Enterprise*"
TORON CLASS SHUTTLECRAFT				
<Unnamed>		Captain Koral	*The Next Generation*	"Gambit, Part II"
VOR'CHA CLASS				
IKC Bortas		Captain Gowron	*The Next Generation*	"The Defector," "Redemption"
IKS Drovana		Massive hull breach from cloaked mine	*Deep Space Nine*	"Sons of Mogh"
IKC Maht-H'a			*The Next Generation*	"The Chase"
Qu'vat		Commander Morag	*The Next Generation*	"Aquiel"
Toh'Kaht		Captain Tel-Pah; destroyed (bomb placed near reactor core)	*Deep Space Nine*	"Dramatis Personae"
<Unnamed>		Captain K'mpec	*The Next Generation*	"Reunion"
<Unnamed>			*The Next Generation*	"The Mind's Eye"
<Unnamed>		Governer Torak	*The Next Generation*	"Aquiel"
<Unnamed> [2]		Mirror universe Association ships	*Deep Space Nine*	"Crossover"
<Unnamed>		Emperor Gowron	*Deep Space Nine*	"The Way of the Warrior"
<Unnamed>[2]		Destroyed by DS9	*Deep Space Nine*	"The Way of the Warrior"
BIRD OF PREY TYPE				
IKC Buruk		Captain Gowron	*The Next Generation*	"Reunion"
Hegh'ta		Captain Kurn	*The Next Generation*	"Redemption"
IKS Korinar			*Deep Space Nine*	"Sons of Mogh"
M'Char		Commander Kaybok (executed by General Martok)	*Deep Space Nine*	"The Way of the Warrior"
IKC Vorn		Captain Duras	*The Next Generation*	"Reunion"
<Unnamed> [2]	Warship		*The Next Generation*	"The Defector"
<Unnamed> [2]			*The Next Generation*	"The Mind's Eye"
<Unnamed>		Destroyed by IKC Bortas	*The Next Generation*	"Redemption"
<Unnamed>			*The Next Generation*	"Redemption"
<Unnamed> [2]		Destroyed in battle with the Hegh'ta	*The Next Generation*	"Redemption II"
<Unnamed>			*Deep Space Nine*	"Past Prologue"
<Unnamed>			*Deep Space Nine*	"Blood Oath"
<Unnamed>		Destroyed by *U.S.S. Defiant*	*Deep Space Nine*	"The Way of the Warrior"
<Unnamed>			*Deep Space Nine*	"The Way of the Warrior"
<Unnamed>[4]		Destroyed by DS9	*Deep Space Nine*	"The Way of the Warrior"
<Unnamed>		Captain K'Temang; boarded and taken by Gul Dukat	*Deep Space Nine*	"Return to Grace"

Table 6.7 Non-Starfleet Ships in the Alpha Quadrant *(continued)*

Name	Type	Notes	Series or Film	Episode
<Unnamed> [2]		(Escorts for IKS Drovana?)	*Deep Space Nine*	"Sons of Mogh"
<Unnamed> [3]			*Deep Space Nine*	"Sons of Mogh"
<Unnamed>			*Deep Space Nine*	"Rules of Engagement"
OTHER CLASS/TYPE				
Negh'Var	Flagship	General Martok with Chancellor Gowron; same design as seen in *The Next Generation* "All Good Things . . ."	*Deep Space Nine*	"The Way of the Warrior"
IKC Prang	Cruiser		*The Next Generation*	"The Emissary"
<Unnamed>	Cruiser		*The Next Generation*	"The Royale"
<Unnamed>	Freighter		*Deep Space Nine*	"The Maquis, Part I"
<Unnamed> [2]	Negh'Var design	One destroyed by *U.S.S. Enterprise* NCC-1701-D [Refit] 25 yrs after stardate 47988	*The Next Generation*	"All Good Things . . ."
<Unnamed>	Civilian transport	Crashed on Galora Prime	*Deep Space Nine*	"Rules of Engagement"
<Unnamed> [5]	Civilian transport		*Deep Space Nine*	"Rules of Engagement"
<Unnamed>	Civilian transport	Destroyed by *U.S.S. Defiant*	*Deep Space Nine*	"Rules of Engagement"

Romulan Star Empire

Name	Type	Notes	Series or Film	Episode
D'DERIDEX CLASS (B-Type)				
Decius		Admiral Picard	*The Next Generation*	"Future Imperfect"
Devoras		Admiral Mendak	*The Next Generation*	"Data's Day"
Haakona		Sub Commander Taris	*The Next Generation*	"Contagion"
IRW Khazara		Commander Toreth	*The Next Generation*	"Face of the Enemy"
Terix		Commander Sirol	*The Next Generation*	"The Pegasus"
Terix		Commander Tomalak (25 years after stardate 47988)	*The Next Generation*	"All Good Things . . ."
<Unnamed>		Destroyed by Gomtuu	*The Next Generation*	"Tin Man"
<Unnamed>			*The Next Generation*	"Tin Man"
<Unnamed>			*The Next Generation*	"The Neutral Zone"
<Unnamed>	Illusionary		*The Next Generation*	"Where Silence Has Lease"
<Unnamed> [2]			*The Next Generation*	"The Enemy"
<Unnamed>		Commander Tomalak	*The Next Generation*	"The Enemy"
<Unnamed> [4]			*The Next Generation*	"Data's Day"
<Unnamed>			*The Next Generation*	"The Mind's Eye"
<Unnamed>		Disappeared from this dimension	*The Next Generation*	"Timescape"
<Unnamed>			*The Next Generation*	"Unification: Part II"

Table 6.7   Non-Starfleet Ships in the Alpha Quadrant *(continued)*

Name	Type	Notes	Series or Film	Episode
SCOUT TYPE				
Pi		Crashed, unseen	*The Next Generation*	"The Enemy"
<Unnamed>		Admiral Jarok; destroyed in self-detonation	*The Next Generation*	"The Defector"
<Unnamed>	Science vessel		*The Next Generation*	"The Next Phase"
UNKNOWN CLASS/TYPE				
Belak		Presumed destroyed by the Jem'Hadar	*Deep Space Nine*	"The Die is Cast"
Gasko			*Deep Space Nine*	"Paradise"
Makar		Presumed destroyed by the Jem'Hadar	*Deep Space Nine*	"The Die is Cast"
<Unnamed>			*The Next Generation*	"Sins of the Father"
<Unnamed>	Illusionary		*The Next Generation*	"Peak Performance"
<Unnamed> [4]		Vulcan vessels; destroyed by Romulan Warbird	*The Next Generation*	"Unification: Part II"
<Unnamed>			*Deep Space Nine*	"Visionary"
<Unnamed>		Colonel Lovok; destroyed by the Jem'Hadar	*Deep Space Nine*	"Improbable Cause"

Other Ships by Name

Name	Class/Type	Notes	Series or Film	Episode
Batris	Antares Class/ Talarian Freighter	Destroyed after sustaining severe damage	*The Next Generation*	"Heart of Glory"
Cleponji	Promellian battle cruiser	Destroyed by *U.S.S. Enterprise*	*The Next Generation*	"Booby Trap"
Dorian	Transport ship	Captain Talmit	*The Next Generation*	"Man of the People"
Ekina	"Cargo ship" (rogue terrorist ship)		*Deep Space Nine*	"Invasive Procedures"
Erstwhile	Cargo Carrier Class 9	Captain Okona	*The Next Generation*	"The Outrageous Okona"
Gomtuu	Living space vessel		*The Next Generation*	"Tin Man"
Jovis	Zibalian tradeship	Captain Kivas Fajo	*The Next Generation*	"The Most Toys"
Kalondin	Kressari ship		*Deep Space Nine*	"The Circle"
Kallisco	Cargo ship	Destroyed by Crystalline Entity	*The Next Generation*	"Silicon Avatar"
Karama	Karaman ship	Abandoned in gas giant atmosphere	*Deep Space Nine*	"Starship Down"
Lakul	El-Aurian refugee transport ship	Destroyed by energy ribbon	*Star Trek: Generations*	

Other Ships by Name *(continued)*

Name	Class/Type	Notes	Series or Film	Episode
SS *Milan*	NDT-50863	Transport ship	*The Next Generation*	"New Ground"
Mondor	Antares Class	Pakled ship	*The Next Generation*	"Samaritan Snare"
Nanut	Tygarian freighter		*Deep Space Nine*	"The Homecoming"
Nenebec	Mining shuttle	Captain Dirgo; crash landed on Lambda Paz	*The Next Generation*	"Final Mission"
Norkova	Freighter	12-member crew	*Deep Space Nine*	"The Passenger"
Q'Maire	Talarian warship	Captain Endar	*The Next Generation*	"Suddenly Human"
Rak-Miunis	Kobheerian freighter		*Deep Space Nine*	"Duet"
Rayat	Kobliad transport ship		*Deep Space Nine*	"The Passenger"
Sanction	Onaran Freighter		*The Next Generation*	"Symbiosis"
Santa Maria	Erewhon Class/ Personnel transport	Crash landed on planet in Orelious Minor system	*Deep Space Nine*	"Paradise"
Sherval Das	Valerian Transport		*Deep Space Nine*	"Dramatis Personae"
Taris Murn	J'naii shuttle	Abandoned in null space pocket	*The Next Generation*	"The Outcast"
T'van	Vulcan ship		*Deep Space Nine*	"Vortex"
Xhosa	Freighter	Captain Kasidy Yates (name identified in *Deep Space Nine* "The Way of the Warrior")	*Deep Space Nine*	"Family Business"

Table 6.8   Other Ships by Race

Race	Type	Notes	Series or Film	Episode
Alean	Transport		*The Next Generation*	"The Chase"
Andorian	Transport		*Deep Space Nine*	"Rules of Acquisition"
Angosian	Transport vessel	Destroyed in escape attempts by prison inmate	*The Next Generation*	"The Hunted"
Angosian	Security Transport		*The Next Generation*	"The Hunted"
Atlec	Class 7 Interplanetary		*The Next Generation*	"The Outrageous Okona"
Bartesian	Merchant ship		*Deep Space Nine*	"The Maquis, Part I"
Bolian	Freighter		*Deep Space Nine*	"Whispers"
Bolian	Transport		*Deep Space Nine*	"The Maquis, Part I"
Bolian	Freighter		*Deep Space Nine*	"Tribunal"
Borg	Cube		*The Next Generation*	"Q Who?"
Borg	Cube	Power overload caused self-destrution in Earth orbit	*The Next Generation*	"The Best of Both Worlds"
Borg	Scout cube	Crew of five; crash landed on moon within Argolis Cluster	*The Next Generation*	"I Borg"

Table 6.8 Other Ships by Race *(continued)*

Race	Type	Notes	Series or Film	Episode
Borg	Scout cube		*The Next Generation*	"I Borg"
Borg	Warship		*The Next Generation*	"Descent"
Boslik	Freighter	*Deep Space Nine*	"The Homecoming"	
Boslik	Freigher	Talarian warship design	*Deep Space Nine*	"Sons of Mogh"
Corvallen	Antares Class Freighter	Destroyed by IRW Khazara in Kaleb Sector	*The Next Generation*	"Face of the Enemy"
Costalane	Diplomatic ship		*The Next Generation*	"Cost of Living"
Cravic	Homeship	Automated Unit 122	*Voyager*	"Prototype"
El-Aurian	Refugee transport ship	Destroyed by energy ribbon	*Star Trek: Generations*	
Fernalian [3]	Science vessel	Talarian warship design	*Deep Space Nine*	"Emissary"
Flaxian		Captain Ratiya destroyed; Romulan sabotage	*Deep Space Nine*	"Improbable Cause"
Galador	Freighter		*Deep Space Nine*	"The Maquis, Part I"
Galipiton	Freighter		*Deep Space Nine*	"The Wire"
Hekaran			*The Next Generation*	"Force of Nature"
Husnock	Illusionary Warship		*The Next Generation*	"The Survivors"
Kaelon	Starship [2]		*The Next Generation*	"Half a Life"
Katarian			*The Next Generation*	"The Game"
Klaestronian			*Deep Space Nine*	"Dax"
Kotakian			*Deep Space Nine*	"The Maquis, Part I"
Kovarian	Freighter [3]		*Deep Space Nine*	"The House of Quark"
Lyaaran		Shuttle crash landed	*The Next Generation*	"Liaisons"
Lysian	Destroyer	Destroyed by *U.S.S. Enterprise*	*The Next Generation*	"Conundrum"
Lysian	Sentry Pod [7]	Destroyed by *U.S.S. Enterprise* (47 in total, all presumed destroyed)	*The Next Generation*	"Conundrum"
Lysepian	Supply ship		*Deep Space Nine*	"Heart of Stone"
Miradorn	Theta Class	Captain Arkel; destroyed by igniting Toh-mair field in Chamra Vortex	*Deep Space Nine*	"Vortex"
Rekok	Battle cruiser [2]		*The Next Generation*	"Man of the People"
Satarran		Pilot: Kieran MacDuff; destroyed (possible self-destruction)	*The Next Generation*	"Conundrum"
Sheliak			*The Next Generation*	"The Ensigns of Command"
Skrreean	Emigrant ship	Stolen; destroyed by Bajoran Interceptors	*Deep Space Nine*	"Sanctuary"
	Emigrant ship [100s]		*Deep Space Nine*	"Sanctuary"
Straleb	Security ship	Class 7 Interplanetary	*The Next Generation*	"The Outrageous Okona"

Table 6.8 Other Ships by Race *(continued)*

Race	Type	Notes	Series or Film	Episode
Suffite	Freighter		*Deep Space Nine*	"The Homecoming"
T'Lani	Cruiser	Talarian design	*Deep Space Nine*	"Armageddon Game"
Taask	Hunted ship		*Deep Space Nine*	"Captive Pursuit"
Taask	Hunter ship		*Deep Space Nine*	"Captive Pursuit"
Talarian	Observation craft		*The Next Generation*	"Suddenly Human"
Talarian	Warship		*The Next Generation*	"Suddenly Human"
Tamarian	Captain Dathon		*The Next Generation*	"Darmok"
Tarellian			*The Next Generation*	"Haven"
Tarellian	Cargo freighter	Crash landed	*The Next Generation*	"Liaisons"
Teldarian	Cruiser		*The Next Generation*	"The Mind's Eye"
Tellerite	Freighter		*Deep Space Nine*	"Shadowplay"
Trill	Transport		*Deep Space Nine*	"Rejoined"
Valtese	Chancellor Alrik		*The Next Generation*	"The Perfect Mate"
Venoben	Transport		*Deep Space Nine*	"Vortex"
Vergillian	Freighter		*Deep Space Nine*	"Vortex"
Wadi			*Deep Space Nine*	"Move Along Home"
Xepolite	Freighter	Headman Droofu Awa	*Deep Space Nine*	"The Maquis, Part II"
Yridian	Warp-capable tradeship		*The Next Generation*	"Birthright, Part I"
Yridian	Destroyer	Destroyed by *U.S.S. Enterprise*	*The Next Generation*	"The Chase"
Yridian	Freighter		*The Next Generation*	"Firstborn"
Zalkonian		Commander Sunad	*The Next Generation*	"Transfigurations"
OTHERS/UNKNOWN				
	Farpoint "ship"	Elasamorph being	*The Next Generation*	"Encounter at Farpoint"
	Gatherer's ship	Pakled design	*The Next Generation*	"The Vengeance Factor"
<Unnamed>	Sublight freighter	Radioactive waste product ship	*The Next Generation*	"Final Mission"
<Unnamed>	Jovis escape pod		*The Next Generation*	"The Most Toys"
<Unnamed>	Alien ship		*The Next Generation*	"Night Terrors"
<Unnamed>	Time pod (26th century)	Berlingoff Rasmussen (22nd century; from New Jersey)	*The Next Generation*	"A Matter of Time"
<Unnamed>		Captain Jaheel; destroyed by containment field breach	*Deep Space Nine*	"Babel"
<Unnamed>	Mercenary ship	Peregrine Class Courier (?)	*The Next Generation*	"Gambit, Part I"
<Unnamed>	Black combat vessel; Jovis design	Destroyed by *U.S.S. Enterprise*	*The Next Generation*	"Unification: Part I"
<Unnamed>	Mulzirak transport		*Deep Space Nine*	"Q-Less"
<Unnamed>	Jem'Hadar vessel [2]		*Deep Space Nine*	"The Jem'Hadar"
<Unnamed>	Jem'Hadar vessel	Destroyed by ramming *U.S.S. Odyssey*	*Deep Space Nine*	"The Jem'Hadar"
<Unnamed>	Jem'Hadar warship [7]		*Deep Space Nine*	"The Search, Part I"

Table 6.8 Other Ships by Race *(continued)*

Race	Type	Notes	Series or Film	Episode
\<Unnamed\>	Jem'Hadar warship	Destroyed by *U.S.S. Defiant*	*Deep Space Nine*	"The Search, Part I"
\<Unnamed\>	Jem'Hadar vessel [2]	Destroyed by *U.S.S. Defiant*	*Deep Space Nine*	"Starship Down"
\<Unnamed\>	Alliance fighter	Captain Miles O'Brien; mirror universe	*Deep Space Nine*	"Through the Looking Glass"
\<Unnamed\>	Alliance fighter	Captain Benjamin Sisko; mirror universe; destroyed by Cardassians	*Deep Space Nine*	"Through the Looking Glass"
\<Unnamed\>	[150] Jem'Hadar vessel	6 destroyed by *U.S.S. Defiant*	*Deep Space Nine*	"The Die is Cast"
\<Unnamed\> [2]			*Deep Space Nine*	"The Visitor"
\<Unnamed\>	Alien vessel		*Deep Space Nine*	"Hippocratic Oath"
\<Unnamed\>	Jem'Hadar vessel	Crashed on Bopac III, Gamma Quadrant three years ago	*Deep Space Nine*	"Hippocratic Oath"
\<Unnamed\>		Jovis design	*Deep Space Nine*	"Sons of Mogh"
\<Unnamed\>		Jovis design	*Deep Space Nine*	"Sons of Mogh"

Table 6.9 Ship Statistics

	Constitution Class (pre-2270) UFP	*Constitution Class (post-2270) UFP*	*Galaxy Class, UFP*	*Oberth Class, UFP*	*Bird of Prey, Klingon Empire*
Classification	heavy cruiser	heavy cruiser	explorer	science	scout
Mission	multi-purpose vessel	multi-purpose military and exploration vessel	exploration, science, defense	science, transport	scout
Service	commissioned 2245 (est.); decommissioned 2270 (est.)	re-commissioned 2270 (est.) and decommissioned 2295 (est.)	2360 -	2270s-2370+	2270s-2370+
Design	UFP, Earth	Earth, Starfleet	Utopia Planitia Fleet Yars, Mars, UFP	UFP	Klingon Empire (Kronos?)
Ships	NCC-1017 *U.S.S. Constellation* NCC-1700 *U.S.S. Constitution* NCC-1701 *U.S.S. Enterprise*	NCC-1701 *U.S.S. Enterprise* NCC-1701A *U.S.S. Enterprise*	*U.S.S. Galaxy* NCC-76037 *U.S.S. Yamato* NCC-71807 *U.S.S. Enterprise* NCC-1701-D	*U.S.S. Grissom* *S.S. Vico* *U.S.S. Tsiolkovski* *U.S.S. Biko* *U.S.S. Pegasus*	*Barruc* *Hegh'ta* *Pagh* *Vorn*

Table 6.9 Ship Statistics *(continued)*

	Constitution Class (pre-2270) UFP	Constitution Class (post-2270) UFP	Galaxy Class, UFP	Oberth Class, UFP	Bird of Prey, Klingon Empire
	NCC-1705 *U.S.S. Excalibur* NCC-1706 *U.S.S. Exeter* NCC-1702 *U.S.S. Farragut* NCC-1707 *U.S.S. Hood* NCC-1703 *U.S.S. Lexington* NCC-1711 *U.S.S. Potemkin*				
Structure: X (width) =	127.1 m	140.4 m	467 m docked; 259 m stardrive only	103 m	85 m atmospheric; 83.5 m spaceflight
Y (height) =	72.6 m	70.6 m	137 m docked; 126 m stardrive only	59 m	16.5 m atmospheric; 35.8 m spaceflight
Z (length) =	288.6 m	301.9 m	642 m docked; 360 m stardrive only	148 m	51.2 m atmospheric; 51.2 m spaceflight
Displacement Mass = Area = Decks =	1.9e8 kg	2.2e8 kg	10e7 m^3 4e9 kg 8e5 m^2 42	4e7 kg	3
	(the following describes the *U.S.S. Enterprise* NCC-1701)				
Warp Systems: Power	M/AMR lithium-augmented; M/AMR dilithium-augmented (2267 refit)	M/AMR dilithium-augmented linear; M/AMR dilithium-augmented linear/pulse (2285 refit)	M/AMR (secondary hull)	M/AMR (core in secondary hull)	M/AMR (dilithium mediated)

Table 6.9 Ship Statistics *(continued)*

	Constitution Class (pre-2270) UFP	Constitution Class (post-2270) UFP	Galaxy Class, UFP	Oberth Class, UFP	Bird of Prey, Klingon Empire
Nacelles	2	2	2 (secondary hull)	2 (inboard)	2 (inboard)
Cruising	Warp 5 (TOS); Warp 6 (2267 refit)	Warp 8 (TOS); Warp 7.4 (TNG) (2285 refit)	Warp 6	Warp 5	Warp 5
Maximum	Warp 7(TOS); Warp 8 (TOS) (2267 refit)	Warp 12 (TOS): Warp 9.0 (TNG) (2285 refit)	Warp 9.6 (12 hours max.)	Warp 8	Warp 8
Emergency	Warp 8+ (TOS)	Warp 12+ (TOS); Warp 9.2+ (TNG) (2285 refit)	Warp 9.8		Warp 9.6 (<5 min)
Failure	Warp 14.1 (TOS) due to propulsion meltdown	Warp 15+ (TOS); Warp 9.4+ (TNG) (2285 refit) due to propulsion meltdown	Warp 9.9		Warp 9.92
Impulse Systems:					
Power	fusion	fusion	fusion reactors	fusion	fusion
Engines	1 twin-port	1 twin-port	1+2; one (main) on secondary hull, two on primary hull	2	2
Design	TOS	TFS	Ambassador Class; impulse engines equipped with subspace field sustainer coils	Oberth Class (specific)	TFS Klingon
Tactical Systems:					
Lasers	(pre-2260)				
Type	capacitor-driven medium power, mechanical ball turrets				
Location	dorsal forward (x2); ventral port-starboard (x2=4)				
Phasers	(2260 refit)	9 banks of 2			

Table 6.9 Ship Statistics *(continued)*

	Constitution Class (pre-2270) UFP	Constitution Class (post-2270) UFP	Galaxy Class, UFP	Oberth Class, UFP	Bird of Prey, Klingon Empire
Type	warp coil-augmented from capacitors (transtator technology); medium power	Warp coil-augmented from warp core (transtator technology); high power mechanical ball-turrets	Type X, strips	transtator-induction	
Location	dorsal forward (x2); ventral port/starboard (x2=4); ventral secondary hull port/starboard (x2=4)	dorsal/ventral forward (x2 = 4); dorsal/ventral port/starboard (x2 = 8); ventral secondary hull port/starboard (x2 = 4); secondary hull aft (x2)	2 strips on primary hull (300 degrees firing arc); 6 strips on secondary hull (one covered while docked)	forward (x2); aft-starboard (x2); aft-port (x2)	
Photon Torpedoes:					
Type	M/AM warp-capable low power	M/AM warp-capable medium power	M/AM, warp sustainer coils, variable yield		M/AM, variable yield
Location	ventral forward, 1 twin launcher	dorsal secondary hull forward, 1 twin-launcher	primary hull, aft, 1 (covered while docked); secondary hull, forward, 1; secondary hull, aft, 1		forward (1)
Casings	100 duranium-terminium general-purpose casings	100 duranium-terminium general-purpose casings	300		16
Disruptors:					
Type					projectors
Location					port-starboard wing (x1 = 2)

Table 6.9 Ship Statistics *(continued)*

	Constitution Class (pre-2270) UFP	Constitution Class (post-2270) UFP	Galaxy Class, UFP	Oberth Class, UFP	Bird of Prey, Klingon Empire
Shields	navigation deflectors; tactical deflectors and screens (form-fitting)	navigation deflectors; tactical deflectors and screens (form-fitting)	4 primary grids, 7.3e8 W dissipation rate	navigation deflectors; projected tactical (hull-conforming)	grid-projected (TFS); distance-projected (TNG)
Cloak					old Romulan design (hull conformal)
Crew & Auxiliary Systems:					
Crew	203 (pre-2260); 430 (2260)	500	760 + 252 non-Starfleet (standard); 5000 (maximum life support)	88 (typical)	12; 24 (maximum life support)
Medical	8 beds in sickbay	14 beds in sickbay	50 beds in sickbay + triage in holodecks		
Transporters	4 standard; 5 emergency; 2 cargo	4 standard transporters; 4 emergency; 2 cargo	6 + 22 emergency + 8 cargo		1x4 person/cargo
Tractor Beam	1 emitter, ventral forward secondary hull	1 emitter, ventral forward secondary hull			
Auxiliary Spacecraft:					
Shuttlebays	1, secondary hull aft	1, secondary hull aft	1 (main) on Primary Hull; 2 on Secondary Hull		
Shuttlecraft	6 general-purpose; 1 aqua-shuttle	4 general-purpose shuttlecraft; 6 workbees	10 Type-15 Shuttlepods; 3 Type-7 Personnel shuttles; 5 Type-6 Personnel shuttles; 3 Type-9 Cargo Shuttles; 4 Sphinx Workpods		

Table 6.9 Ship Statistics *(continued)*

	Constitution Class (pre-2270) UFP	Constitution Class (post-2270) UFP	Galaxy Class, UFP	Oberth Class, UFP	Bird of Prey, Klingon Empire
Captain's Yacht			docked to primary hull; impulse only, w/ sustainer coils; X = 18m, Y = 8m, Z = 10m		
Runabout Class Starships			1-3, mission variable		

Key to abbreviations:

    M/AMR: Matter/Antimatter Reactor

    TNG: The Next Generation

    TOS: The Original Star Trek

CHAPTER SEVEN

Trek Tech

Star Trek's science has always had a strong foundation in reality. Top scientists advise the series. This chapter serves as a guide to the science and technology of the Star Trek universe.

Is It Trek, or Is It Real?

One of the fascinating aspects of the Star Trek phenomenon is in the crossovers between the science fiction and current science and culture. For instance, the original *Enterprise* is now displayed in the Smithsonian, alongside real spacecraft, and both the sickbay diagnostic bed and the hypospray moved from fiction to reality. The VISOR appears to be following close behind.

The Future Is in Sight

Geordi LaForge wore a prosthetic device, called VISOR, to correct his blindness. Now medicine offers that same device. The Pennsylvania College of Optometry has unveiled the Low Vision Enhancement System (called LVES and pronounced "Elvis"), a video headset that electronically manipulates images. LVES was developed by the National Aeronautics and Space Administration and Johns Hopkins Medical Center. It serves as a real-time electronic magnifier and allows the user to tune the focus, magnification, and contrast. It contains three miniature video cameras, two miniature television screens, and a series of finely tuned mirrors.

LVES is currently available only at the William Feinbloom Vision Rehabilitation Center of the Pennsylvania College Of Optometry in Philadelphia, Pennsylvania. Teenager Chris Escuti of Cherry Hill was one

of the first people to use the device on a daily basis. He suffered optic nerve damage as a result of radiation treatments for a brain tumor. While the LVES doesn't yet equal the VISOR, it is a major step toward making the *Star Trek* dream a reality.

The Production of Antimatter

Reuters news service carried a story on January 5, 1996, reporting that, "European scientists have managed to create fleeting atoms of antimatter for the first time, bringing a dream of science fiction a step closer to fact. The European Laboratory for Particle Physics (CERN) said Thursday nine anti-hydrogen atoms were created in experiments last September, although each lasted only about forty billionths of a second before being annihilated by ordinary matter.

"'If you watch *Star Trek,* you'll know the *U.S.S. Enterprise* was driven by antimatter power,' said CERN spokesman Neil Calder in a reference to the U.S. cult television series. 'We're not there yet, but this is a major step.'"

The Enterprise Legacy

After the loss of the *U.S.S. Enterprise* NCC 1701-A, Starfleet Command kept the name alive by baptizing an Excelsior-class battleship, the new workhorse of Starfleet, as a new *Enterprise,* retaining the "1701" and adding the letter "B".

The *U.S.S. Enterprise* NCC 1701-B had a distinguished career. Loosely assigned to Starbase 12, the ship took part in many engagements in the Neutral Zone and the Triangle. It also served on four five-year galaxy exploration tours, recording a number of first contacts.

The ship boasted the least crew losses for six years.

The *Enterprise* often transported dignitaries, including the Klingon Emperor and his consort, the Romulan Praetor; six powerful Orion families; the whole Vulcan political hierarchy; fifty Starfleet Admirals; and the entire Federation Council.

The *Enterprise*'s career ended on stardate 2/9208.12, when it engaged an IKS (Klingon) L-24 battleship and a Romulan Nova-class battleship. The Romulan and Klingon vessels won a pyrrhic victory, and the Klingons pulled back into the Neutral Zone, ending their raids.

> One of the fascinating aspects of the Star Trek phenomenon is in the crossovers between the science fiction and current science and culture.

After the destruction of the Excelsior-class *Enterprise* NCC 1701-B, Starfleet assigned the name to an Alaska-class battle cruiser. Vulcans in the Federation Council had insisted that the name was synonymous with exploration, discovery, and the ideals of IDIC, the Vulcan philosophy of Infinite Diversity in Infinite Combinations. They argued that giving the name to a research vessel or Exploration Command cruiser was more logical. Starfleet officials listened, but awarded the name to the Alaska-class on stardate 2/9301.

This *Enterprise* was relegated to patrol duties for five years. Then Starfleet Command assigned the ship to a 10-year Galaxy Exploration mission that would take it beyond the UFP's frontier in the Northwest Quadrant.

Two and a half years later, the *Enterprise* sent a distress call to Starbase 67. The ship was declared lost and presumed destroyed on stardate 3/0006.30.

Starfleet Command then gave the designation *U.S.S. Enterprise* NCC 1701-D to the new Galaxy-class exploration vessel. This vessel had an enviable record under the command of Jean-Luc Picard before being destroyed. It was the second ship lost under his command.

Only two Galaxy-class exploration cruisers were built: the *Enterprise* and the *U.S.S. Yamato* NCC 1305-E. The *Yamato* was destroyed by a computer virus.

Warp Drives

Starfleet vessels depend on warp drive to travel faster than the speed of light. The stress-energy tensor mathematically describes each point in four-dimensional space-time. It is linked to the mass and energy distribution of normal space (non-subspace). This distribution and flow of stress-energy of matter is dependent on the surrounding stress-energy tensor which defines the curvature of four-dimensional space-time. Matter-energy within the warp (or subspace) field is dissociated from the matter-energy outside of the field due to the violent change in the frame of reference produced by the plasma stream within the warp field coils in the nacelles.

This violent change in the local stress-energy within the subspace coils would rip the fabric of space, if not for the fact that nature produces a subspace field around the event to gradually fix the tear. This, in effect, spreads the event over a general area in a subspace field that looks similar to a gravity field originating from a gravity well, protecting the

115

space-time continuum. It can be manipulated into asymmetric propulsive fields.

Matter within the field is removed from normal space and anchored to the frame of reference of subspace. The effect of this is to allow matter within the field to almost completely bypass relativity's obstacles and to allow phenomena such as FTL (faster than light) travel.

The limiting factor is the amount of energy required to dissociate the matter from normal space. This energy must be continuously applied, or the subspace field will gradually dissipate and bring the matter back into normal space.

> **The original Enterprise *is* now displayed in the Smithsonian, alongside real spacecraft, and both the sickbay diagnostic bed and the hypospray moved from fiction to reality.**

Subspace is a field that defines a particular frame of reference at all points in known space. It is composed of an infinite number of cells, like a honeycomb. A ship entering warp uses subspace so as to keep its frame of reference regardless of speed. The asymmetrical peristaltic warp field propels a ship by pushing against each anchored reference frame of subspace. The first field coil anchors the ship to the occupied position in subspace, then passes the field along to the next coil, along with its anchored position in subspace, and so on down the nacelle.

It is not necessary to add extra nacelles to increase warp speed. Once a warp field is established, it takes pure engine power to push toward Warp 10. The nacelles create the warp field and sustain it. The number of nacelles is determined by the size and mission of the starship, although three nacelles is a very unstable design (the *U.S.S. Tritium Warp 4 Cruiser,* designed with three nacelles, was canceled in 2155 due to severe instability during warp flight). Two extra nacelles made the Constellation-class starships very agile. Starships that go faster than Warp 5 pollute space with localized "rifts."

Transporters

Starfleet uses transporters to move people and goods over short distances. Transporters are matter-energy conversion devices that take an object or a being and transform it into a pattern of phased energy that can be transmitted as a complex trans-barrier signal through the first-level subspace (hyperspace) domain to a set of desired coordinates, and then re-transformed into its original form. They employ Heisenberg compensators, pattern buffers, phase transition coils, biofilters, matter streams, annular confinement beams, matter-energy converters, and phased matter. An entity remains conscious during transport, but can be held in stasis. While in transport, a person feels whole.

The annular confinement beam locks onto and disassembles a subject via the phase-transition coils, causing it to take on an energy-like state called "phased matter," somewhat akin to plasma. The matter stream is then fed into the pattern buffer, piped through waveguide conduits to one of the beam emitters on the hull of the starship, and then relayed to a point on the ground, where the annular confinement beam reconstructs the subject.

The annular confinement beam maintains a "lock" on the subject to identify what to beam out and what to leave behind. The beam also transports the intact subject.

The pattern buffer, a cyclotron-like tank, holds the whirling matrix of phased matter in the annular confinement beam while the subject is beamed out and beamed in. It keeps track of the subject's particles in the beam.

"Virtual focus molecular imaging scanners" perform a trace at the quantum level. The transporter ID trace keeps a verification record of the trace after transport. This compressed sample also includes the subject's name and logs of the transport cycle.

Ionizers and phase transition coils perform the quantum matrix manipulation to transform an object into phased matter in what is known as the "dematerialization process." This is what produces the familiar gold "sparkles" of the older-style Federation transporters, and the red and blue effects of later Federation systems, as different dematerialization and phase transition processes were developed.

The Heisenberg Principle states that you cannot know both the position of a subatomic particle and its momentum. The Heisenberg compensators help keep track of the particles in the beam by compensating for what is not known.

The biofilter identifies elements of the pattern and erases unwanted particles. It can be used to filter out unwanted viruses or bacteria and to manipulate DNA strings.

Pattern degradation occurs because annular confinement beams aren't perfect, even when amplified by Heisenberg compensators. The matter stream shifts out of alignment. A subject can be suspended in transport for up to 420 seconds before degradation becomes too severe to reform the subject. Locking the transport controller in a diagnostic loop keeps

Games Tech Manuals Play

The *Star Trek: The Next Generation Technical Manual* (Pocket Books, ISBN 0-671-70427-3) is the complete technical guide to the Treknology used in *TNG*. It is written by Rick Sternbach and Michael Okuda, who work in *TNG*'s Art Department. Their responsibilities include making sure everything is technically consistent from show to show. However, they have been known to clown around, and some of that clowning has shown up in the technical manual:

Page 7: The line drawing of the *Enterprise* is the mirror image of what it should be. Shuttlebay 3 (the wide bay) should be on the right hand side, and Shuttlebay 2 (the narrow bay) on the left side. The descriptions, however, point to the correct relative positions. This has been confirmed with the onscreen image of the *Enterprise* and the other drawings throughout the manual.

Page 11: In the saucer section, above the Captain's Yacht, is a duck. A half inch to the left, and a little bit down, is a mouse. Slightly to the right of the mouse, is a "Slippery When Wet" sign. In the shuttle bay are three big shuttles, two small shuttles, and a Porsche. About one inch to the right of the duck is a DC-3 cargo aircraft, and, in that same rectangle, is a symbol of a woman and a child (the symbol for Canada's "Family" rating for movies). Also, right under the warp pylons is a registered trademark symbol. In addition, an image of NOMAD is lying on its side in the center of the saucer section and forward. Those items show up in the ship diagram in Engineering on the show.

Page 77: One control not seen is the "Infinite Improbability Generator," a reference from the *Hitchhiker's Guide to the Galaxy*.

Page 120: The tricorder display shows: "TR580 TRICORDER VII," a reference to the old Radio Shack TRS-80s.

Page 159: One shuttle is named "Hawking."

pattern degradation to a minimum, but phased-matter "bugs" reside in the plasma environment.

Emitter array pads reside at various sites on the surface of the *Enterprise* hull. "Long-range virtual-focus molecular imaging scanners" handle remote disassembly of the subject, and facilitate reassembly.

Holodecks

Starship crews amuse themselves on shipboard "holodecks." Holodeck walls can generate holographic images that appear to extend for an unlimited distance. Holograms can also be projected into space and can be augmented with force beams to simulate solid, tangible objects or with replicator technology to create actual solid matter such as foodstuffs.

Holodeck matter can imitate real matter even at the molecular level. Molecule-sized magnetic bubbles replace molecules in full-resolution holo-objects. The computer can manipulate them individually in three dimensions. The computer may use large magnetic bubbles to simulate surfaces and textures rather than create an object at the molecular level.

Computers cannot duplicate the complexity of electron-shell activity and atomic motions that determine biochemical activity in living creatures. This prevents replicators from duplicating life or resurrecting the dead. Advances in computer technology may allow this, permitting a person to live forever in any chosen environment while interacting with real people and objects visiting the holodeck. On the other hand, a person can be injured on the holodeck.

All foods eaten on the holodeck are replications. No simulation would survive outside of the holodeck.

The holodeck includes a forcefield treadmill. Approaching a wall causes an instant shift away. The holodeck can change gravity in three dimensions, so occupants don't notice the change.

Any technology has limitations. "Reality gaps" can become apparent.

The Chemistry and Physics of Star Trek

Star Trek has presented a kaleidoscope of particles, substances, waves, fields, fissures, and anomalies. A guide to these phenomena, including their properties and their significance in the Star Trek universe, follows.

amnion Artificially generated by crew. Disrupts the phase of matter. Harmless to humans.

Appeared in *The Next Generation:* "The Next Phase." Data tried to use amnions to decontaminate the ship when he detected bursts of anyons caused by the presence of Geordi and Ro in phased form. A sufficiently large flood of amnions was enough to bring the two back into phase with the rest of the crew and the walls of the ship.

amniotic fluid Naturally occurring. In real life, protects embryos from disease while in the womb.

Appeared in *The Next Generation:* "Genesis." Cured the outbreak of Barclay's Protomorphosis Syndrome.

antigraviton Artificially generated by aliens. Can act as "antigravity."

Appeared in *The Next Generation:* "Attached." Was used by aliens to deflect a transporter beam to a new set of coordinates.

antimatter Artificially generated by crew; naturally occurring in real life. Matter with electrical charge properties that are the opposite of "normal matter." (It is not well understood why the universe is overwhelmingly made of matter, since most reactions that produce particles produce equal amounts of matter and anti-matter. The imbalance could have started as a minor percentage in the early moments of the Big Bang, with resulting annihilation keeping the excess only; the rest is the photon background.)

Appeared in classic *Star Trek*. Mentioned in all series and episodes. The word was used when describing what was wrong with the warp engines or their status.

antineutrino Naturally occurring. In real life, a byproduct of beta decay.

Appeared in *Voyager:* "Prime Factors." After B'Elanna installed the Sikarian space "folding" mechanism, the device generated antineutrino particles as a part of the process of its normal operation. These particles proved harmful to the Federation warp core and almost caused a core breach. Fortunately, B'Elanna thought quickly and phasered the device out of existence before any serious harm was done.

antineutron A real particle; the antimatter version of a neutron.

Appeared in the movie *Voyage Home.* The computer prompts Spock to "adjust the sine wave in the gravity envelope so that antineutrons may pass but antigravitons cannot."

antiproton Naturally occurring. Also generated by ships. Can penetrate Romulan cloaking devices. In real life, the antimatter version of a proton.

Appeared in *Deep Space Nine:* "The Search, Part 1" and "Defiant." Used by Jem'Hadar in "The Search" and by the Cardassians in "Defiant" to detect the cloaked Defiant.

Appeared in classic *Star Trek:* "The Doomsday Machine." Decker called the Doomsday Machine's weapon an antiproton beam.

Appeared in *The Next Generation:* "Face of the Enemy." *Enterprise*-D used it to determine who destroyed the smuggler's ship.

Appeared in *The Next Generation:* "Silicon Avatar." Crystalline Entity is tracked by gamma radiation from antiproton decay.

Appeared in *Voyager:* "The Threshold." Used to slow down the mutation of Lt. Paris' DNA.

antitime Naturally occurring. Analogous to "antimatter" but refers to time, not matter.

Appeared in *The Next Generation:* "All Good Things. . ." Produced as a result of the time rupture, which was caused by the intersection of three dechyon beams from different time frames.

anyon Artificially generated by crew. Caused by the interaction between phased and normal matter. In real life, an anyon isn't a real particle; it's a theoretical construct formed by confining a normal fermion (and possibly boson) to a two-dimensional region. The exchange arguments which lead to the parity operator eigenvalues being ±1 no longer apply, and these theoretical constructs can have arbitrary quantum phase changes under exchange.

Appeared in *The Next Generation:* "The Next Phase." Data hypothesized that the bursts of anyons were caused by phased matter. When Geordi and Ro set off a disruptor on overload, a huge burst of anyons were detected, leading Data to sweep the area with amnions, thereby saving Geordi and Ro.

badlands Naturally occurring. Stormy region of space; plays havoc with sensors and warp drives.

baryon Naturally occurring. In real life, these are "heavy" particles like protons, as opposed to "light" particles (leptons) like electrons.

Appeared in *The Next Generation:* "Starship Mine." The ship needed to undergo a "baryon sweep" to remove the accumulation of these particles.

Berthold radiation Artificially generated by aliens.

Appeared in *The Next Generation:* "Deja Q." A form of radiation used by the aliens to scan the *Enterprise*-D when looking for Q.

Berthold rays Naturally occurring. Nature unknown. Harmful or fatal to humans.

Appeared in classic *Star Trek:* "This Side of Paradise." Emotion-affecting spores granted immunity to Berthold rays, allowing a colony to survive.

calendenium Naturally occurring chemical; possibly an element

Appeared in *The Next Generation:* "Night Terrors." Combined by the alien ship with hydrogen released by the *Enterprise* in order to produce a massive chemical explosion to free both vessels from the Tychon rift.

carbon neutronium Artificially generated by aliens.

Appeared in *The Next Generation:* "Relics." The shell of the Dyson sphere was composed of carbon neutronium. A phaser blast was ruled out as an option to get out of the sphere because it would be ineffective.

carbrodine Origin unknown. When mixed with infernite, it becomes explosive.

Appeared in *Deep Space Nine:* "In the Hands of the Prophets." Used by Neela to destroy Keiko's schoolroom.

castridinium Naturally occurring. The hardest substance known to Federation science. (Might be "cast rhodinium.")

Appeared in classic *Star Trek:* "Balance of Terror." The outer protective layers of Federation outposts along the Romulan Neutral Zone are composed of this material. However, even with an outpost buried miles underground, it provided insufficient defense against the Romulan energy weapon. A piece of the destroyed shield was crushed by Spock.

chemicite Origin unknown. A highly explosive compound, dangerous to transport; can be sold for a good profit on Orion.

Appeared in *Deep Space Nine:* "Little Green Men." A cascade reaction in the chemicite caused Quark's shuttle to be flung through time.

chroniton Artificially generated by aliens. Created by a problem of some sort in the cloaking device.

Appeared in *Deep Space Nine:* "Past Tense." Used to travel back to 21st-century Earth.

Appeared in *The Next Generation:* "The Next Phase." Chroniton particles cause Geordi and Ro to be phased so they can pass through walls (not floors).

Appeared in *Deep Space Nine:* "Visionary." Sent O'Brien back and forth in time whenever a cloaked Warbird came near Deep Space Nine.

corbomite Artificially generated by Captain Kirk. A fictional substance which supposedly reflects weapon fire back at the attacker.

Appeared in classic *Star Trek:* "The Corbomite Maneuver." Kirk tells the First Federation captain that the *Enterprise* is equipped with corbomite, a bluff that prevents the alien from firing his weapons.

Appeared in classic *Star Trek:* "The Deadly Years." Kirk uses the same ploy to escape Romulans.

cordrazene Artificially generated by crew. A drug.

Appeared in classic *Star Trek:* "City on the Edge of Forever." McCoy accidentally injects himself with a huge dose, goes insane, and beams down to a planet where he, Kirk, and Spock enter a time-travel portal.

cormoline Naturally occurring. Rich deposits of this compound are found on the Kazon-Ogla homeworld; used for barter with the other Kazon sects.

Appeared in *Voyager:* "Caretaker."

cosmic string Naturally occurring. A string of particles with gravitational forces that have the strength of a black hole.

Appeared in *The Next Generation:* "The Loss." A flurry of energy-based entities surrounding the *Enterprise*-D were headed for a cosmic string, dragging the ship toward certain destruction. These creatures disabled counselor Troi's empathic powers for a time. The cosmic string was home to them.

De Broglie waves Naturally occurring in real life. In modern physics, a representation of ordinary matter as waves rather than particles. In *Star Trek,* artificially generated by aliens; a side effect of cloaking devices.

Appeared in classic *Star Trek:* "Balance of Terror." In James Blish's novel adaptation, the crew tracked the Romulan Warbird by sensing these waves. (In the aired episode, Spock used "motion sensors" to track the ship.)

deadly cheese Origin unknown. Cheese contaminated with a virus.

Appeared in *Voyager:* "Learning Curve." A contaminated piece of cheese threatened the entire *Voyager.*

dechyon Artificially generated by crew. In real life, dechyons are the class of particles that travel below the speed of light (i.e., the opposite of tachyons).

Appeared in *Voyager:* "Parallax." Used to open a fissure in an event horizon.

Appeared in *The Next Generation:* "Cause and Effect." The crew detected these particles as remnants of each "causality loop." Data used them to send a message into the next loop, which allowed them to break this most vicious cycle.

delta rays Naturally occurring. A type of radiation produced by older engines; exists in real life. Delta rays are moderate energy electrons that have been kicked off a nucleus by the passage of a nearby high energy charged particle.

Appeared in classic *Star Trek:* "The Menagerie, Part I." Delta rays were emitted from a broken piece of an old class-J starship. Christopher Pike, former captain of the Starship *Enterprise,* was overexposed in that accident leaving him in a "wheelchair."

Appeared in *Deep Space Nine:* "Visionary." O'Brien absorbed a heavy dose of delta radiation, which allowed the tetryon emissions from the Romulan Warbird to shift him through time.

deuterium Naturally occurring. Isotope of hydrogen, having twice the mass of ordinary hydrogen; also called "heavy hydrogen."

Appeared in *The Next Generation:* "Phantasms." Used to power the warp core. Deuterium and antideuterium are combined to provide energy.

dilithium Artificially generated by crew. Important in maintaining warp drives

Appeared in classic *Star Trek:* all episodes.

Appeared in *The Next Generation:* "Relics." La Forge tells an out-of-time Mr. Scott that they recrystallize the dilithium inside the reaction chamber.

displacement wave Artificially generated by aliens. Moves objects at high warp speed.

Appeared in *Voyager:* "The Caretaker." Used by caretaker to bring ship to Delta Quadrant.

disruptor beam Artificially generated by aliens. Klingon equivalent of a phaser. Accompanied by a shrill, echoing sound. The same beam is used by the Amenians. (Perhaps the Klingons once conquered Ameniar.)

Appeared in classic *Star Trek:* "Errand of Mercy," "Elaan of Troyius," others. Used by the Klingons to retaliate against the Organians for acts of sabotage by Kirk and Spock. The Klingons fired it at the *Enterprise* during an attack in "Elaan of Troyius." Kirk also used it to destroy suicide stations on Ameniar.

Eichner radiation Artificially generated by aliens.

Appeared in *The Next Generation:* "The Child." Caused genetically altered spores in a stasis cage to expand uncontrollably and threaten the *Enterprise.* Tracked to Iain, Troi's son.

electrophoretic energy In real life, electrophoresis is a process by which proteins are identified by putting them on a gel and running an electric current through the gel, then staining the gel and measuring how far the proteins moved in comparison to a group of standard proteins that were also put on the gel (bigger proteins generally move more slowly).

Appeared in *Voyager:* "The Elogium." The electrophoretic energy was generated by space-dwelling life forms, but caused Kes to prematurely enter the Elogium (puberty).

fistrium Naturally occurring. Refractory metal found in caves of Melona IV.

Appeared in *The Next Generation:* "Silicon Avatar." Data thought that the presence of fistrium and kelbonite prevented the Crystalline Entity from scanning the caves.

genesis wave Artificially generated by crew. An energy wave that has the effect of rapidly terraforming planets and nebular matter.

Appeared in the movies *The Wrath of Khan* and *The Search for Spock.* The Genesis Device, invented by Carol and David Marcus, was sought by Khan Singh as a weapon to be used to destroy Captain Kirk and the *Enterprise* NCC 1701. Ultimately, the device was activated, destroying the *Reliant,* killing Khan, and creating the Genesis Planet from matter in the Mutara Nebula. Because of the unusual properties of the planet, the body of Spock was brought back to life after he'd been killed saving the *Enterprise.*

gold-pressed latinum Origin unknown. A non-replicable material, typically pressed into bars (like gold).

Appeared in *Deep Space Nine.* The Ferengi use bars of gold-pressed latinum as their currency.

graviton Artificially generated by crew. Generated by *Voyager*. (A real particle, according to modern physics).

Appeared in *Voyager:* "The Caretaker." Used to try to escape the Caretaker's beam.

Appeared in *The Next Generation:* "The Best of Both Worlds." A "heavy graviton beam" was considered and rejected as a weapon against the Borg.

Appeared in *The Next Generation:* "Silicon Avatar." Used by the *Enterprise* crew to communicate with the Crystalline Entity. Used by a vengeful doctor to destroy the Entity.

Appeared in *The Next Generation:* "Hero Worship." Graviton waves destroyed the Veco when it was surveying a region of space. Reacted with all power output by ships and magnified it.

holomatter Artificially generated by crew. A simulation of matter using force field and holo-imaging technology within a chamber known as a "holodeck." Under certain circumstances, holomatter can take on all the recognized features of life forms; however, all holomatter disintegrates when removed from the holodeck.

Appeared in *The Next Generation:* Too numerous to list; also prominent in *Voyager*. Training, recreation and entertainment for the crew. Some medical applications. On board the *Voyager*, due to the death of the chief medical officer, a holomatter "doctor" has been designated as the de facto CMO.

hyperon Naturally occurring. Hyperons are a class of real particles whose name dates back to the days before quark structure was well known. Leptons (electrons, muons, tau, and their associated neutrinos) are "light," mesons are "medium," and baryons are "heavy." When more massive, short-lived par-

ticles heavier than the proton were produced, they were called hyperons. Some examples are the sigma lambda and cascade. After quark structure was understood, the first three names were kept, but the meaning was changed. Leptons are the same as originally, but are understood to be fundamental particles with no quark structure. Mesons are quark-antiquark pairs. Baryons are triplets of quarks. The term "hyperon" is still used, but not frequently.

Appeared in *The Next Generation:* "The Ensigns of Command." An obstacle preventing the use of transporters in the evacuation of a planet ceded to the Sheliak.

ilium 629 Naturally occurring. A by-product of the geological decay of dilithium.

Appeared in *The Next Generation:* "Pen Pals." Traces of ilium 629 were found on the planet Drema IV, leading to the discovery of unusual dilithium deposits in the planet's mantle. The dilithium transformed the planet's geological heat into mechanical stress, resulting in significant tectonic instabilities that nearly destroyed the planet. The geological instabilities were neutralized by the use of resonator probes launched from orbit.

infernite Origin unknown. When mixed with carbrodine, becomes explosive.

Appeared in *Deep Space Nine:* "In the Hands of the Prophets." Used by Neela to destroy Keiko's schoolroom.

invidium Origin unknown. Used in medical containment fields during the previous century. No longer used. Causes adverse reactions with equipment. If brought to 200 Celsius, it becomes inert.

Appeared in *The Next Generation:* "Hollow Pursuits." It spread into the ship due to a broken seal on the Michelaks' medical sample container. Laforge said, "Duffy and O'Brien picked up the broken canister and became contaminated." It affected the magnetic capacitors on the antimatter injector and an unnamed component in the transporter.

ionogenic particles Artificially generated by crew. Has a characteristic "magnetic flux density."

Appeared in *The Next Generation:* "Power Play." Used to create a containment field for the "spirits" of alien escapees of a penal colony when they attempted to possess the crew.

ion Naturally occurring. An atom or group of atoms that carries a positive or negative electric charge.

Appeared in classic *Star Trek:* "Spock's Brain." Used to propel the space ship that carried descendants of an advanced civilization who boarded the *Enterprise* and stole Spock's brain. Scotty marveled at its design at first sight, saying that "they could teach us a thing or two."

irillium Naturally occurring. A heavy element of the platinum group.

Appeared in classic *Star Trek:* "Requiem for Methuselah." The irillium rendered the ryetalyn inert and therefore unusable in combating an epidemic that the crew was trying to prevent on another planet (see ryetalyn).

jevonite Naturally occurring. Valuable gemstone found on Cardassia.

Appeared in *The Next Generation:* "Chain of Command, Part II." Ancient jevonite artifacts found on Cardassia were sold or stolen by the army to finance the war effort.

kinoplasmic radiation Origin unknown.

Appeared in *Voyager:* "Projections." Lt. Barclay tells the holodoc that his headaches are

due to "kinoplasmic radiation oxidizing your brain cells."

Krieger waves Artificially generated by aliens. Nature unknown. They eat holes in walls and decks and destroy a space station.

Appeared in *The Next Generation:* "A Matter of Perspective." An attempt is made to fashion a weapon out of a generator of these waves.

lepton Naturally occurring. Particle "activity" increased prior to the wormhole reappearing and shifting its position.

Appeared in *The Next Generation:* "The Price." Geordi's visor detected the "activity."

lucrovexitrin Origin unknown. Highly toxic; alters molecular structure when it comes in contact with glass. Exists in a nitrogen-oxygen atmosphere.

Appeared in *The Next Generation:* "Hollow Pursuits." Ruled out by Wesley Crusher as being the cause of the injectors failing, "selgninaem and lucrovexitrin are highly toxic."

magneton Artificially generated by crew. In real life, a quantum of the magnetic dipole moment of a particle. In short, it's a measurement (like inches or liters), not a particle, though the name is used for a particle in Star Trek.

Appeared in *Voyager:* "Cathexis." Used to scan the ship for the disembodied aliens and crew.

Merculite Artificially generated by aliens. An explosive material used in out-of-date rockets which are no match for Federation weaponry.

Appeared in *The Next Generation:* "Suddenly Human." Captain Endar threatened to use Merculite rockets against the *Enterprise* if

Picard did not release his adopted son, Jono. Riker remarked, "Shades of Gulliver."

Appeared in *The Next Generation:* "Heart of Glory." The Klingons who had stolen the ship "Batris" used Merculite rockets to destroy a pursuing Klingon ship.

meson Naturally occurring. Particle "activity" increased prior to the wormhole reappearing and shifting its position.

Appeared in *The Next Generation:* "The Price." Geordi's visor detected the "activity."

metrion Artificially generated by aliens. High levels of exposure can infect a humanoid with nitremia, a blood disease that causes its victims' cells to undergo fission.

Appeared in *Voyager:* "Jetrel." The Hakonians used a "Metrion Cascade" to conquer Rynax, a Talaxian moon.

muon Naturally occurring. Short-lived subatomic particle classified as a lepton.

Appeared in *The Next Generation:* "The Next Phase." The power feed to the Romulan vessel was altered by the Romulans to build up in the *Enterprise*'s engine core. This would lead to a catastrophic explosion that would destroy the *Enterprise*.

nadion Artificially generated by crew. Berman and Okuda's *The Next Generation Technical Manual* identifies "nadion" particles as the output produced by phasers.

Appeared in *Voyager:* "Time and Again"; *The Next Generation Technical Manual.* Janeway closes a "temporal rift" artificially generated by the crew by firing her phaser at it. (Torres identifies the "nadion particle feedback" as the reason why the fissure is closing.)

nanites Artificially generated by crew. Micro-robots that are bred for specific tasks; able in some instances to reproduce to collectively form a consciousness.

Appeared in *The Next Generation.* Part of Wesley's science experiment that got loose and eventually developed into an advanced civilization.

Appeared in *The Next Generation.* Beverly Crusher thought that a destructive breed could be introduced into the Borg collective.

neodilithium Naturally occurring. A different form of dilithium.

Appeared in *Voyager:* "Threshold." It was used to take Tom Paris to Warp 10, after which he turned into a giant salamander.

neutrino Artificially generated by crew. Real particle with no charge; thought until recently to have no mass.

Appeared in *The Next Generation:* "The Enemy." Used as a distress beacon.

Appeared in *The Next Generation:* "The Game." Wesley has to calibrate a sensing device that uses them. He ignores the device to flirt with the crew member who is helping him, at which point she says, "Your neutrinos are drifting."

Appeared in *Deep Space Nine:* All. "Increased neutrino emissions" is always said shortly before something comes through the wormhole.

Appeared in *The Next Generation:* "A Matter of Honor." Used to destroy hull-eating space bacteria endangering the *Enterprise* and a Klingon ship with Riker in crew.

Appeared in *Deep Space Nine:* "Rivals." The owner of the other bar/casino had machines to create good or bad luck. Dax traced all the bad luck happening everywhere on the station by noticing that the ratio between the two types of neutrino spins was not 1:1. The other casino/bar had 98% of all its neutrinos going in one spin, since it had the objects changing the probability.

neutron radiation Naturally occurring. Neutrons are neutral particles which, along with protons, are constituents of atomic nuclei. Neutrons not contained within a nucleus have a half-life of about 15 minutes.

Appeared in *Star Trek VI: The Undiscovered Country.* The improved Bird-of-Prey gave off a surge of neutron radiation just before it fired a photon torpedo.

neutronium Naturally occurring. Matter composed of densely-packed neutrons, held together by gravity. The material neutron stars are made of.

Appeared in classic *Star Trek:* "The Doomsday Machine." The Doomsday Machine's hull was composed of neutronium (which incidentally would have made it far too massive to ever be able to move).

Appeared in classic *Star Trek:* "Piece of the Action." One of the gangsters, upon being beamed up to the *Enterprise,* was mad enough to chew it.

nitrium Naturally occurring. A metal used in an important alloy commonly found in starships. The alloy is used for computers, replicators, stabilizers, ventilators, power transfer conduits, dilithium chamber walls, and life-support systems.

Appeared in *The Next Generation:* "Cost of Living." Nitrium parasites started feeding on the ship's systems after the *Enterprise* destroyed their nitrium-rich asteroid. The parasites digested much of the *Enterprise*'s nitrium into slime before Data lured them back onto the asteroids of the Pelloris Field.

nucleogenic Naturally occurring. Occurs in planetary atmospheres and is involved somehow in rain production.

Appeared in *Voyager:* "The Caretaker." The Ocampa homeworld's atmosphere didn't have any, which accounted for its desolate condition.

nucleonic particle Artificially generated by crew. Could refer to the nucleus of atoms?

Appeared in *Voyager:* "State of Flux." Used to detect damage to a Kazon ship at long range. The damage was later found to have been produced when a stolen Federation replicator exploded. Kim says something like, "I am reading nucleonic particle fluctuations from their ship."

nucleonic radiation Naturally occurring/artificially generated by crew. Something found in life forms.

Appeared in *Voyager:* "The Cloud." Used to make a suture to seal up the punctured nebula creature.

omicron Naturally occurring. Created by Space Nebula Creature, used in "circulatory" system.

Appeared in *Voyager:* "The Cloud." Thought to be a substitute for anti-matter for the warp drives, as well as fuel for the replicators.

Appeared in *Deep Space Nine:* "Shadow Play." Emitted by holographic generator. The projections/people were "made of" them.

phospholipid fibers Naturally occurring. In real life, phospholipids are fatty acids with phosphate groups attached. They are small and naturally occur only as liposomes and bilayer sheets, and as monolayer spheres called micelles. But they never form "fibers." Phospholipid bilayers are what cell membranes are mostly made of.

Appeared in *Voyager:* "The Cloud." Torres gave this as a possible identification for the blue material found on the hull.

photochronic Origin unknown.

Appeared in *The Next Generation:* "Descent." Used to fuse Borg nanocortical fibers.

photonic energy Naturally occurring. Emitted from the surface of a protostar. In real life, this would probably be called something along the lines of "light."

Appeared in *Voyager:* "Heroes and Demons." The life form that used the holodeck to kidnap crew members was made up of photonic energy.

plasma Naturally occurring. A very hot, ionized gas. The atoms in plasma have enough kinetic energy that the electrons are torn from their nuclei, ionizing the gas.

Appeared in *Star Trek VI: The Undiscovered Country.* Plasma emissions were used to detect a cloaked Klingon Bird-of-Prey.

polaric ion Artificially generated by aliens. Used as a power generation system.

Appeared in *Voyager:* "Time and Again." Used as a very unstable power generation system which the *Voyager* crew has to prevent from exploding.

polaron Artificially generated by crew. Exists in the real world. In condensed matter physics, a polaron is a type of mobile crystal defect consisting of an electron coupled to an induced lattice polarization.

Appeared in *Voyager:* "State of Flux." Used to detect a hidden Kazon ship.

Appeared in *Deep Space Nine:* "The Jem'Hadar." A phased polaron beam was used by the Jem'Hadar to penetrate the shields of the *U.S.S. Odyssey.*

Appeared in *Voyager:* "Non Sequitur." Harry Kim scanned the time stream with polarons, thus partially causing a distortion of the space-time continuum.

positron Naturally occurring. Real antimatter version of an electron.

Appeared in *The Next Generation:* "Encounter at Farpoint" through "All Good Things. . ." Data's brain is "positronic." Several readers have commented that "positronic" as initially used by Isaac Asimov didn't refer to the antimatter particle, but rather refers to a computer that uses atomic-scale components, so that might be what the show is referring to.

Appeared in *Deep Space Nine:* "Life Support." "Positronic" brain is used to prolong Vedek Bareil's life.

Appeared in *The Next Generation:* "Datalore." The Away Team mentions that Dr. Soong wanted to make Asimov's dream of a positronic brain a reality. Lore later confirms that this is the nature of his brain and Data's.

Appeared in *The Next Generation:* "The Nth Degree." When normal scans prove ineffective against the alien probe, Geordi tells Barclay to "try a positron scan."

preanimate matter Naturally occurring. Matter that is very, very, very, close to being classified as a form of life, but doesn't quite make the grade.

Appeared in *Star Trek II: The Wrath of Khan.* Chekov said this might be responsible for causing an energy flux in one dyno-scanner.

Promethean quartz Naturally occurring. Valuable mineral that glows with an internal light.

Appeared in *Deep Space Nine:* "Q-Less." Vash discovered a similar geode resembling Promethean quartz in the Gamma Quadrant and nearly destroyed the station with a graviton field.

protomatter Origin unknown. An unstable form of matter by David Marcus as a short cut in the construction of the Genesis Device.

Appeared in *Star Trek II: The Wrath of Khan* and *Star Trek III: The Search for Spock.*" Because of the instability of protomatter, the Genesis Planet began to age geologically at an accelerated rate. The resurrected Spock-child also began to age very rapidly, allowing Spock to regain his *katra* (soul) at about the same age as he was when he "died."

protoplasm Naturally occurring. Makes up the interior of cells in living matter.

Appeared in classic *Star Trek:* "The Immunity Syndrome." The giant amoeba had an interior consisting of protoplasm.

psilocynine Naturally occurring. A neurotransmitter involved in telepathy.

Appeared in *The Next Generation:* "Eye of the Beholder." Deanna Troi's levels of psilocynine were very high after having an empathically induced hallucination.

Appeared in *The Next Generation:* "Dark Page." Lwaxana Troi's levels of psilocynine were very high after her work with the Cairn.

quadrotriticale Artificially generated by crew. A "supervariant" of the hybrid grain known as triticale. Triticale is naturally occurring.

Appeared in classic *Star Trek:* "The Trouble with Tribbles." Kirk and crew were charged with protecting a shipment of quadrotriticale against Klingon sabotage. Matters were made worse when the tribbles found their way into the grain stores.

quantum filament Naturally occurring. An elongated subatomic object, hundreds of meters long, but possessing almost no mass.

Appeared in *The Next Generation:* "Disaster." Caused damage to the ship. Troi asked O'Brien if a quantum filament was a kind of cosmic string; O'Brien said it was something completely different.

retinex Artificially generated by crew. Used to improve eyesight.

Appeared in *Star Trek II: The Wrath of Khan.* In the beginning of the movie, McCoy gives Kirk a set of bifocals for his birthday since Kirk is allergic to retinex.

ryetalyn Naturally occurring. A mineral.

Appeared in classic *Star Trek:* "Requiem for Methuselah." The crew needed it to combat an epidemic on another planet.

saltzgadum Origin unknown. Can alter molecular structure when it comes into contact with glass and exists in a nitrogen-oxygen atmosphere.

Appeared in *The Next Generation:* "Hollow Pursuits." Saltzgadum was not the substance that caused the malfunctions aboard the *Enterprise.* LaForge said: ". . . yeah, we'd all be dead by now. That leaves saltzgadum and invidium."

selanogen Naturally occurring. A substance upon which a form of life is based, such as carbon.

Appeared in *The Next Generation:* "Schisms." Trans-dimensional creatures who were abducting members of the crew for medical experimentation were thought by Commander Data to be "selanogen based" and had to create "pockets" in our universe upon which to survive for short periods of time. These pockets can be detected by their emissions of tetryon particles.

selgninaem Origin unknown. Highly toxic; can alter molecular structure when it comes in contact with glass; exists in a nitrogen-oxygen atmosphere. (Try spelling it backwards! This was confirmed by one of the writers at a con.)

The Next Generation: "Hollow Pursuits." It was ruled out as the reason that the injectors were locked. LaForge said, ". . . yeah, we'd all be dead by now. That leaves saltzgadum and invidium."

soliton wave In real life, a wave whose energy doesn't diminish. (More complicated than that, but that's the basic idea.) In *Star Trek,* an artificially generated subspace effect capable of propelling vessels at warp speeds.

Appeared in *The Next Generation:* "New Ground." The *Enterprise* participates in a test of their use as a propulsion system.

sorium Origin unknown. An explosive compound.

Appeared in *Deep Space Nine:* "The Nagus." Used in Ferengi locator bomb intended to kill Quark.

static warp bubble Artificially generated by crew. An anomaly which replicates the universe and begins to make it shrink.

Appeared in *The Next Generation:* "Remember Me." Beverly was stuck in one and Wesley and the Traveler had to get her out.

synthehol Artificially generated by aliens. An alcohol substitute invented by the Ferengi that permits one to enjoy the intoxicating effects of alcoholic beverages without the deleterious effects.

Appeared in *The Next Generation:* "Relics." Mr. Scott found syntheholic scotch a poor substitute for the real thing.

tachyon Artificially generated by crew. A FTL (faster than light, or subspace) particle. (Postulated by some real physics theories.)

Appeared in *The Next Generation:* "Redemption, Part II." To detect cloaked Romulan ships.

Appeared in *The Next Generation:* "All Good Things. . ." An "inverse tachyon beam" was used to probe a space-time anomaly, and ultimately resulted in its creation.

Appeared in *The Next Generation:* "Face of the Enemy." When told by a disguised Troi to cross the Neutral Zone, Commander Toreth speculated that the Federation may have set up a tachyon net (similar to the one used in Redemption, Part II) to detect Romulan ships crossing the neutral zone.

Appeared in *Deep Space Nine:* "Explorers." Naturally occurring eddies of them propelled Sisko's Bajoran sailing ship into warp.

talgonite Artificially generated by aliens. A ceramic substance.

Appeared in *The Next Generation:* "The Inner Light." Used in the construction of the Kataan probe.

terminium Origin unknown. A metal alloy.

Appeared in *Star Trek III: The Search for Spock.* Used in casing of photon torpedoes.

terrion Artificially generated by aliens.

Appeared in *The Next Generation:* "Tapestry." A compressed terrion beam "mortally" wounded Picard at the beginning of the episode.

tetralubisol Origin unknown. Highly volatile lubricant used on starships.

Appeared in classic *Star Trek:* "The Conscience of the King." Lenore Karidian attempted to kill Kevin Riley by poisoning his milk with tetralubisol.

tetryon Artificially generated by aliens. Subspace particle; shouldn't be found in normal space.

Appeared in *The Next Generation:* "Schisms." Evidence of the alien abductions.

Appeared in *Deep Space Nine:* "Blood Oath." Klingon disruptor banks modulated to emit tetryon particles and deactivate the *Albino*'s phasers.

Appeared in *Deep Space Nine:* "Visionary." Sisko told the Romulan delegation that they had traced the tetryon emissions from an orbiting Warbird poised to attack the station.

Appeared in *Deep Space Nine:* "The Die is Cast." Commander Eddington sabotaged the tetryon compositor in the Defiant's cloaking device.

Appeared in *Voyager:* "Caretaker." A coherent tetryon beam was used by the Caretaker to scan *Voyager.*

thoron Naturally occurring. Radioactive isotope by-product from the decay of thorium. Thorium is also known as radon-220.

Appeared in *Deep Space Nine:* "If Wishes Were Horses." Elevated thoron emissions accompanied the appearance of aliens in the Denorios Belt.

transparent aluminum Artificially generated by crew. Just what the name implies: an invisible metal.

Appeared in *Star Trek IV: The Voyage Home.* Scotty showed a scientist how to make it, with the intent of using it to build a whale tank. (He used Plexiglas instead.)

trianium Artificially generated by aliens. Used in fusion-based power sources.

Appeared in *Voyager:* "The 37s." Kim and Chakotay located the alien stasis chamber by tracking down trianium readings.

triceron Origin unknown. An explosive compound.

Appeared in *The Next Generation:* "Reunion." Used in the bomb that exploded during the *Sonchi* ceremony.

trilithium Artificially generated by aliens.

Appeared in *Star Trek: Generations.* Used to collapse a star by dampening the energies in its core.

Appeared in *The Next Generation:* "Starship Mine." Terrorists attempted to steal a canister of trilithium resin to make a weapon.

trillium 323 Naturally occurring. A mineral substance.

Appeared in *The Next Generation:* "The Price." Used as a bargaining tool in the Chrysalian bid for the Bazaran wormhole.

trimagnesite Naturally occurring. A substance that reacts with trevium to produce non-visible, ultraviolet radiation.

Appeared in classic *Star Trek:* "Operation Annihilate!" Satellites containing trimagnesite and tritium were placed in orbit over the planet Deneva to destroy creatures that had taken over the bodies of the inhabitants. The ultraviolet radiation that they produced was found to be sufficient only after Spock was blinded by the full-spectrum radiation that McCoy was testing. Of course, Vulcans have an extra set of eyelids.

trinimbic turbulence Naturally occurring. An atmospheric phenomenon. Disruptive to transporter technology and Federation targeting systems, and apparently too "turbulent" for a shuttle.

Appeared in *Voyager:* "The 37s." Prevents beaming to site of in-stasis humans, and use of shuttles, so Janeway lands *Voyager* instead. Prevents *Voyager* from assisting in a small-arms battle by interfering with the targeting systems.

triolic wave Artificially generated by aliens. Byproduct of little-used energy production method. Harmful to most life.

Appeared in *The Next Generation:* "Time's Arrow, Part 1." Cave walls subjected to triolic waves, eventually pointing to inhabitants of Planet Davidia II.

triox Artificially generated by crew. Concentrated oxygen compound.

Appeared in classic *Star Trek:* "Amok Time." Dr. McCoy said he was going to give Kirk a shot of triox compound to make up for the low level of oxygen in Vulcan's atmosphere.

tritium Naturally occurring. A radioactive isotope of hydrogen with atoms of three times the mass of ordinary light hydrogen atoms

Appeared in classic *Star Trek:* "Operation Annihilate!" (See trimagnesite.)

Appeared in *Deep Space Nine:* "Q-Less." Used by Dax and O'Brien to trace the origins of the gravimetric disturbances.

ultritium Origin unknown. Chemical explosive almost undetectable by transporter scanners.

Appeared in *The Next Generation:* "Manhunt." Used by the Antidean delegates in an attempted assassination of everyone at the Pacifica Conference of 2365.

Appeared in *The Next Generation:* "The Enemy." Used by Romulans aboard the ship Pi to self-destruct at Galorndon Core.

verdion Naturally occurring. Generated in the cores or surfaces of White Dwarfs.

Appeared in *The Next Generation:* "Emergence." Made living organisms. Needed for the *Enterprise* to grow.

Appeared in *The Next Generation:* "The Pegasus." They used a wash of vertion particles to hide the Pegasus from a Romulan ship.

verteron Artificially generated by aliens. Somehow damaging to sub-space equipment (not the same as "vertion").

Appeared in *The Next Generation:* "Force of Nature." A generator of these, disguised as a buoy, is used by environmentalists to incapacitate several ships, including the *Enterprise.*

Appeared in *Deep Space Nine:* "Playing God." Threatened to destroy the proto-universe.

Appeared in *Voyager:* "Eye of the Needle." Captain Janeway pointed out that there were ". . . verteron emanations, tunneling secondary particles. It certainly looks like a wormhole . . ."

victurium alloy Artificially generated by crew. A very dense metal alloy.

Appeared in *The Next Generation:* "Hero Worship." Large amounts of it blocked the transporter.

virtual Naturally occurring.

Appeared in *The Next Generation:* "The Loss." Caught the *Enterprise* in their drift towards a "cosmic string." Deprived Counselor Troi of her empathic abilities.

warp particle Artificially generated by crew. Emitted by warp engines.

Appeared in *Voyager:* "Parallax." Evidence of the *Voyager's* path in the singularity.

warp shell Artificially generated by crew. A field generated by the *Enterprise's* engines to induce warp travel.

Appeared in *The Next Generation:* "All Good Things. . ." Picard used static warp shells to seal the temporal rifts in the three time instances.

wormholes Naturally occurring. A subspace bridge or tunnel between two points in "normal" time and space. Most wormholes are extremely unstable and their end points fluctuate widely across time and space. An improperly balanced warp drive system can create an artificial wormhole that can pose a serious danger to the ship and its crew.

Appeared in *Deep Space Nine*. The only known stable wormhole, leading to the Gamma Quadrant, is right next to the station, lending Deep Space Nine its strategic importance to the Federation.

Appeared in *The Next Generation:* "The Price." The *Enterprise*-D encountered one, and their mission was to study it.

Appeared in *Star Trek: The Motion Picture.* The *Enterprise* got caught in a wormhole due to a warp engine imbalance.

yominium sulfide Origin unknown.

Appeared in *Star Trek IV: The Voyage Home.* Spock recalls the chemical formula for yominium sulfide [$K_4Ym_3(SO_{73}Es_2)$] during a memory test during his re-education on Vulcan. The formula is inconsistent with that of a sulfide.

Z particle Artificially generated by aliens; also a real type of particle. Can mess up sensor and/or visual records. In real life: today's understanding puts particles into two basic categories, matter and exchange particles. Exchange particles are thrown like Frisbees between matter particles as the generators of forces. Photons mediate the electromagnetic force, gluons mediate the strong force, the graviton is proposed (not observed) to mediate the gravitational force. The weak force is mediated by the W+, W-, and Z particles.

Appeared in *The Next Generation:* "Devil's Due." Scientist on Ventax II station detected Z-particles coming from Ardra's ship.

Appeared in *The Next Generation:* "Identity Crisis." LaForge initiated a scan for "Z-particle emissions" on the video recording of the Tarchannen III mission.

zenite Naturally occurring. A raw mineral from which a potent compound is derived by the Federation for use in stopping botanical plagues.

Appeared in classic *Star Trek:* "Cloud Minders." Zenite in its naturally found state causes temporary mental impairment when its dust is breathed. Such an effect had profound social implications in separating the Troglyte miners from the Stratus city dwellers, an issue with which the crew of the *Enterprise* had to deal.

CHAPTER EIGHT

A Guide to UFP and Starfleet

The United Federation of Planets (UFP) was formed in 2161 to further peaceful coexistence of all beings. Member planets include Alpha III (Kericindal and Alpha), Alpha Centauri VII (Al Rijil and Alpha Centauri), Andor (Fesoan and Epsilon Indi), Betazed, Cait (Ferasa and 15 Lyncis), Binus, Delta, Earth (Earth and Sol), Izar (Izar and Epsilon Bootis), Mars (Mars and Sol), Tellar (Miracht and 61 Cygni), Vega IX (Kesir-Tosharra and Vega), and Vulcan (T'khasi and 40 Eridani).

The new federation quickly drafted a constitution for the protection of its citizens. Several earlier documents, including the Statutes of Alpha III, the Constitution of the United States of America, and the Fundamental Declarations of the Martian Colonies provided models for the new document. The preamble to the Articles of Federation clearly states the founding principles of the UFP.

Starfleet General Orders

Starfleet Command later issued General Orders, written by FASACorporation, as instructions for Starfleet Command. These were recommended by the Secretary of Starfleet and established through executive order by the Federation Council. They govern all Starfleet personnel. There are currently 32 General Orders for the proper conduct of Starfleet operations. The first six were established upon the founding of the United Federation of Planets.

Starfleet Ranks and Insignia

Starfleet created its own internal command structure to facilitate operations, including ranks, insignia, and uniforms. By the time of Captain Jean-Luc Picard, they used the following uniform colors to represent division:

Medical Corps and Sciences: Navy Blue
Security, Technical, and Engineering: Mustard Yellow
Command and Navigation: Wine Red

Insignia of rank (circles correspond to military "stars"):
Admiral: Two gold bars, one on each collar, each with three gold pips.
Vice Admiral: Gold rectangle with three circles.
Captain: Four solid gold circles.
Commander: Three solid gold circles.
Lieutenant Commander: Two solid gold circles and one empty gold circle.
Lieutenant: Two solid gold circles.
Lieutenant (Junior Grade): One solid gold circle and one empty gold circle.
Ensign: One solid gold circle.
Cadet (First Duty): Various black stripes depending on group assignment.

Starfleet Ships

Articles 52 through 54 of the Articles of Federation established Starfleet as the armed peace-keeping force of the United Federation of Planets. Starfleet now maintains a fleet of starships to carry out its mission to maintain interplanetary peace and security, and to conduct missions of scientific exploration.

Starfleet vessels use warp drive to achieve faster-than-light (FTL) speeds. Warp drive creates an asymmetric subspace field greater than 1 Cochrane in magnitude. The warp field creates a mobile pocket of normal space—a warp bubble. It moves by peristaltic control and can be considered an independent universe tightly coupled to our own universe.

All matter in the warp bubble moves with the bubble, making FTL possible.

Starfleet vessels depend on the phaser, a directed energy weapon. Phasers create rapid nadions liberating the strong nuclear force in a class of superconducting crystals.

The supplementary weapon system is the photon torpedo. They carry a variable-yield warhead of a maximum of 1.5 kg matter and 1.5 kg antimatter. Maximum yield of a photon torpedo is 64.6 megatons with a power output of approximately 5.4×10 terrawatts.

A micro warp drive sustainer system maintains the torpedo at warp speed when fired; it cannot propel the torpedo into warp, however.

Shields are produced by an intense subspace field in which an energetic graviton field is maintained. The frequency of the graviton field can be modulated to admit different wavelengths of energy or matter streams. The graviton and subspace fields govern matter interactions. The intense spatial distortion gives empty space a tensile strength greater than the strongest manufactured materials.

Table 8.1 Starfleet Vessels

Ship Name	Number	Notes	Episode
AMBASSADOR CLASS			
U.S.S. Adelphi	NCC-26849	Captain Darson	"Tin Man"
U.S.S. Enterprise	NCC-1701-C	Captain Rachel Garrett; Lieutenant Richard Castillo; destroyed in battle over Narendra III	"Yesterday's *Enterprise*"
U.S.S. Gandhi	NCC-26632		"Second Chances"
U.S.S. Horatio	NCC-10532	Captain Walker Keel; destroyed by possible saboteurs; debris found in Sector 63	"Conspiracy"
U.S.S. Valdemar	NCC-26198		*Deep Space Nine:* "Tribunal"
U.S.S. Zhukov	NCC-26136	Captain Gleason	"Data's Day," "Hollow Pursuits"
ANDROMEDA CLASS			
U.S.S. Prokofiev	NCC-68814		*Deep Space Nine:* "Tribunal"
ANTARES CLASS			
U.S.S. Hermes	NCC-10376		"Redemption II"
APOLLO CLASS			
U.S.S. Agamemnon	NCC-11638		"Descent"
U.S.S. Ajax	NCC-11574	Captain Narth (yr 2327)	"Where No One Has Gone Before," "Tapestry"
U.S.S. Clement	NCC-12537		"Lower Decks"
U.S.S. Gage	NCC-11672	Destroyed in Borg encounter at Wolf 359	
T'Pau	NSP-17938	Vulcan ship	"Unification: Part I"
BRADBURY CLASS			
U.S.S. Bradbury	NX-72307		"Menage a Troi"

Table 8.1   Starfleet Vessels *(continued)*

Ship Name	Number	Notes	Episode
CHALLENGER CLASS			
U.S.S. Buran	NCC-57580	Destroyed in Borg encounter at Wolf 359	
CHEYENNE CLASS			
U.S.S. Ahwahnee	NCC-71620	Destroyed in Borg encounter at Wolf 359	
CONSTELLATION CLASS			
U.S.S. Constellation	NCC-1974	Second ship with this name	
U.S.S. Gettysburg	NCC-3890	Captain Mark Jameson	"Too Short a Season"
U.S.S. Hathaway	NCC-2593	Commander William T. Riker; abandoned and later recovered	"Peak Performance"
U.S.S. Magellan	NCC-3069	Captain Conklin	"Starship Mine"
U.S.S. Stargazer	NCC-2893	Captain Jean-Luc Picard; recovered after its abandonment	"The Battle"
U.S.S. Victory	NCC-9754	Captain Zimbata	"Elementary, Dear Data"
CONSTITUTION CLASS			
U.S.S. Yorktown	NCC-1717	Recommissioned as *U.S.S. Enterprise* NCC-1701-A	
DAEDALUS CLASS			
U.S.S. Essex	NCC-173	Captain Bryce Shumar; presumed lost over 200 years ago, later found crashed on moon of Mab-Bu VI	"Power Play"
DANUBE CLASS RUNABOUT			
U.S.S. Ganges	NCC-72454		*Deep Space Nine:* "Armageddon Game"
U.S.S. Ganges	NCC-72454	Destroyed by T'Lani Cruiser	*Deep Space Nine:* "Emissary"
U.S.S. Mekong	NCC-72914		*Deep Space Nine:* "Whispers"
U.S.S. Orinoco	NCC-72905		*Deep Space Nine:* "The True Way"
U.S.S. Orinoco	NCC-72905		*Deep Space Nine:* "Our Man Bashir"
U.S.S. Orinoco	NCC-72905	Destroyed by warp core breach; sabotage by Cardassian separatist group	*Deep Space Nine:* "The Siege"
U.S.S. Rio Grande	NCC-72452		*Deep Space Nine:* "Emissary"
U.S.S. Rio Grande	NCC-72452		(visually verified registry in *Deep Space Nine:* "Paradise")
U.S.S. Rubicon			*Deep Space Nine:* "Family Business"
U.S.S. Yangtzee Kiang	NCC-79453		*Deep Space Nine:* "Battle Lines"
U.S.S. Yangtzee Kiang	NCC-79453	Crash landed on unnamed moon, Gamma Quadrant	*Deep Space Nine:* "Emissary"
U.S.S. Yukon			*Deep Space Nine:* "Sons of Mogh"

Table 8.1 Starfleet Vessels *(continued)*

Ship Name	Number	Notes	Episode
<Unnamed>		Destroyed by *U.S.S. Enterprise* power transfer beam	"Timescape"
<Unnamed>		Abandoned and presumed destroyed in Gamma Quadrant	*Deep Space Nine:* "The Die is Cast"
DEFIANT TYPE			
U.S.S. Defiant	NX-74205	Escort vessel/Warship prototype	*Deep Space Nine:* "The Search, Part I"
DENEVA CLASS			
U.S.S. Arcos	NCC-6237	Freighter, destroyed by warp core breach	"Legacy"
U.S.S. La Salle	NCC-6203		*The Next Generation:* "Reunion"
DY-500 CLASS			
S.S. Mariposa		Captain Walker Granger	"Up The Long Ladder"
EXCELSIOR CLASS			
U.S.S. Berlin	NCC-14232		"Angel One"
U.S.S. Cairo	NCC-42136	Captain Edward Jellico	"Chain of Command, Part I"
U.S.S. Charleston	NCC-42285		"The Neutral Zone"
U.S.S. Crazy Horse	NCC-50446		"Descent"
U.S.S. Crazy Horse	NCC-50446		(visually identified in *TNG* "The Pegasus")
U.S.S. Crockett	NCC-38955		*Deep Space Nine:* "Paradise"
U.S.S. Enterprise	NCC-1701-B	(identified by wall model in conference room)	
U.S.S. Fearless	NCC-14598		"Where No One Has Gone Before"
U.S.S. Gorkon	NCC-40521	Admiral Alynna Nechayev	"Descent"
U.S.S. Hood	NCC-42296	Captain Robert DeSoto	"Encounter at Farpoint," "Tin Man"
U.S.S. Intrepid	NCC-38907		"Family"
U.S.S. Livingston	NCC-34099		*Deep Space Nine:* "Invasive Procedures"
U.S.S. Melbourne	NCC-3184/3194 or NCC-62043		(visually identified type/registry in *Deep Space Nine:* "Emissary")
U.S.S. Melbourne	NCC-3184/3194 or NCC-62043	Destroyed in Borg encounter at Wolf 359	"11001001"
U.S.S. Potemkin	NCC-18253		"Legacy" (visually identified in "Ethics")
U.S.S. Repulse	NCC-2544	Captain Taggert	"The Child," "Unnatural Selection"
<Unnamed>			"The Offspring"
<Unnamed>			"The Drumhead"
<Unnamed>[2]			*Deep Space Nine:* "The Way of the Warrior"
EXCELSIOR CLASS (Refit)			
U.S.S. Enterprise	NCC-1701-B	Captain John Harriman	*Star Trek: Generations*

Table 8.1 Starfleet Vessels *(continued)*

Ship Name	Number	Notes	Episode
U.S.S. Lakota	NCC-42768 (?)	Captain Benteen	*Deep Space Nine:* "Homefront"
U.S.S. Lakota	NCC-42768 (?)		*Deep Space Nine:* "Paradise Lost"
FREEDOM CLASS			
U.S.S. Concorde	NCC-68711		"All Good Things . . ."
U.S.S. Firebrand	NCC-68723	Destroyed in Borg encounter at Wolf 359	
GALAXY CLASS			
U.S.S. Enterprise	NCC-1701-D	Captain Jean-Luc Picard / Destroyed by antimatter containment failure in independent timeline	"All Good Things . . ."
U.S.S. Enterprise	NCC-1701-D	Destroyed in alternate timeline	"Time Squared"
U.S.S. Enterprise	NCC-1701-D	Captain William T. Riker (field promotion)	"The Best of Both Worlds"
U.S.S. Enterprise	NCC-1701-D	William T. Riker (illusionary ship)	"Future Imperfect"
U.S.S. Enterprise	NCC-1701-D	Destroyed in collision with *U.S.S. Bozeman* in alternate timeline/loop	"Cause And Effect"
U.S.S. Enterprise	NCC-1701-D	Captain Edward Jellico	"Chain of Command, Part I"
U.S.S. Enterprise	NCC-1701-D	Captain Jean-Luc Picard	"Chain of Command, Part II"
U.S.S. Enterprise	NCC-1701-D	Captain Thomas Holloway (alternate timeline)	"Tapestry"
U.S.S. Enterprise	NCC-1701-D	Destroyed by energy feedback (alternate timeline)	"Timescape"
U.S.S. Enterprise	NCC-1701-D	Destroyed by antimatter containment failure in independent timeline	"All Good Things . . ."
U.S.S. Enterprise	NCC-1701-D	Destroyed: primary hull by warp core breach in orbit of Veridian III; saucer section crash landed on Veridian III	*Star Trek: Generations*
U.S.S. Enterprise	NCC-1701-D	Saucer section destroyed by shock wave from collapse of Veridian III star (alternate timeline)	*Star Trek: Generations*
U.S.S. Enterprise (285,000 +)	Parallel universe vessels	Captain William T. Riker (various); One Enterprise destroyed by Enterprise-proper	"Parallels"
U.S.S. Galaxy	NX-70637		
U.S.S. Odyssey	NCC-71832	Captain Keogh / Rammed and destroyed by Jem'Hadar vessel	*Deep Space Nine:* "The Jem'Hadar"
U.S.S. Venture	(presumed this class)		*Deep Space Nine:* "The Way of the Warrior"
U.S.S. Yamato	NCC-1305-E		"Where Silence Has Lease"
	NCC-71807	Captain Donald Varley; destroyed by computer virus from alien probe	"Contagion"

Table 8.1 Starfleet Vessels *(continued)*

Ship Name	Number	Notes	Episode
GALAXY CLASS (Refit)			
U.S.S. Enterprise	NCC-1701-D	Admiral William T. Riker (25 years after Stardate 47988)	"All Good Things . . ."
		Destroyed by antimatter containment failure in independent timeline	
HOPE CLASS (25 years after Stardate 47988)			
U.S.S. Pasteur	NCC-58928	Captain Beverly Picard; destroyed by warp core breach	"All Good Things . . ."
HOKULE'A CLASS			
U.S.S. Tripoli	NCC-19386	Decommissioned	"Datalore"
INTREPID CLASS			
U.S.S. Voyager	NCC-74656	Captain Kathryn Janeway	*Voyager* (all)
		Missing and presumed lost	
ISTANBUL CLASS			
U.S.S. Constantinople	NCC-34852	Transport ship	"The Schizoid Man"
U.S.S. Havana	NCC-34043		"Starship Mine"
KOROLEV CLASS			
U.S.S. Goddard	NCC-59621		"The Vengeance Factor"
MEDITERRANEAN CLASS			
U.S.S. Lalo	NCC-43837	Freight ship; missing after Borg encounter at Wolf 359; presumed lost	"We'll Always Have Paris," "The Best of Both Worlds, Part II"
MERCED CLASS			
U.S.S. Trieste	NCC-37124		"11001001"
<Unnamed>			*Star Trek: Generations*
<Unnamed>			*Deep Space Nine:* "The Way of the Warrior"
MIRANDA CLASS (Refit I)			
U.S.S. Brittain	NCC-21166	Found adrift in a Tychon's Rift	"Night Terrors"
U.S.S. Lantree	NCC-1837, Class 6 Supply	Captain L. Isao Telaka; destroyed by *U.S.S. Enterprise* to prevent spread of DNA virus	"Unnatural Selection"
MIRANDA CLASS (Refit II)			
U.S.S. Saratoga	NCC-31911	Destroyed in Borg encounter at Wolf 359	"Emissary"
U.S.S. Tian An Men	NCC-21382		"Redemption II"
NEBULA CLASS			
U.S.S. Bellerephon	NCC-62048	Destroyed in Borg encounter at Wolf 359	*Deep Space Nine:* "Emissary"
U.S.S. Endeavor	NCC-71805		"Redemption II"

Table 8.1 Starfleet Vessels *(continued)*

Ship Name	Number	Notes	Episode
U.S.S. Farragut	NCC-60597		*Star Trek: Generations*
U.S.S. Hera	NCC-62006	Captain Silva LaForge; missing; presumed lost	"Interface"
U.S.S. Lexington	NCC-14427		"Thine Own Self," *Deep Space Nine:* "Explorers"
U.S.S. Merrimac	NCC-61827		"Sarek"
U.S.S. Monitor	NCC-61826		"The Defector"
U.S.S. Phoenix	NCC-65420	Captain Benjamin Maxwell	"The Wounded"
U.S.S. Prometheus	NCC-71201	Host to Prof. Gideon Seyetik	*Deep Space Nine:* "Second Sight"
U.S.S. Sutherland	NCC-72015	Lt. Cmdr. Data (temporary)	"Redemption II"
<Unnamed>		Alternate reality ship	*Voyager:* "Non Sequitur"
NEW ORLEANS CLASS			
U.S.S. Kyushu	NCC-43837	Destroyed in Borg encounter at Wolf 359	"The Best of Both Worlds Part II"
U.S.S. Renegade	NCC-63102	Captain Tryla Scott; frigate	"Conspiracy"
U.S.S. Rutledge	NCC-57295	Captain Benjamin Maxwell (previous commander)	"The Wounded"
U.S.S. Thomas Paine	NCC-65530	Captain Rixx; frigate	"Conspiracy"
NIAGARA CLASS			
U.S.S. Princeton		Destroyed in Borg encounter at Wolf 359	
U.S.S. Wellington	NCC-28473		"11001001"
OBERTH CLASS			
U.S.S. Biko	NCC-50331	Supply ship	"A Fistful of Datas"
U.S.S. Bonestell	NCC-31600	Destroyed in Borg encounter at Wolf 359	
U.S.S. Cochrane	NCC-59318		*Deep Space Nine:* "Emissary"
U.S.S. Grissom	NCC-59314		"The Most Toys"
U.S.S. Pegasus	NCC-53847	Captain Erik Pressman; prototype phased-cloaking vessel; presumed destroyed by warp core breach; later located inside Asteroid Gamma 6-0-1 in the Devolin System	"The Pegasus"
U.S.S. Raman	NCC-59983	Science vessel	"Interface"
U.S.S. Tsiolkovsky	NCC-53911	Destroyed by exploding star fragment	"The Naked Now"
S.S. Vico	NAR-18834	Research vessel; non-Starfleet; destroyed in Black Cluster	"Hero Worship"
U.S.S. Yosemite	NCC-19002	Trapped in solar plasma stream	"Realm Of Fear"
<Unnamed>			"The Drumhead"
<Unnamed>			"The Game"
<Unnamed>		Destroyed in Borg encounter at Wolf 359	*Deep Space Nine:* "Emissary"
<Unnamed>			*Star Trek: Generations*

Table 8.1 Starfleet Vessels *(continued)*

Ship Name	Number	Notes	Episode
OLYMPIC CLASS			
U.S.S. Nobel	NCC-55012		"Interface"
PEREGRINE CLASS COURIER			
<Unnamed>			*Deep Space Nine:* "The Maquis, Part I"
<Unnamed>		Modified	*Deep Space Nine:* "The Maquis, Part I"
<Unnamed> (2)			*Deep Space Nine:* "The Maquis, Part II"
<Unnamed> (9)			"Preemptive Strike"
<Unnamed>		Ro Laren, pilot; abandoned; recovered by *U.S.S. Enterprise*	"Preemptive Strike"
<Unnamed>		Modified	*Deep Space Nine:* "Heart of Stone"
RENAISSANCE CLASS			
U.S.S. Aries		NCC-45167	"The Icarus Factor," "Identity Crisis"
U.S.S. Hokkaido		(Last of this class to be constructed [yr. 2337])	
U.S.S. Hornet	NCC-10532		"Redemption II"
RIGEL CLASS			
U.S.S. Akagi	NCC-62158		"Redemption II"
U.S.S. Tolstoy	NCC-62095	Destroyed in Borg encounter at Wolf 359	"The Best of Both Worlds, Part II"
SOYUZ CLASS			
U.S.S. Bozeman	NCC-1941	Captain Morgan Bateson; appeared from spacetime distortion (year 2278)	"Cause and Effect"
SPRINGFIELD CLASS			
U.S.S. Chekov	NCC-53702	Destroyed in Borg encounter at Wolf 359	
SURAK CLASS			
U.S.S. Zapata		NCC-33184	
SYDNEY CLASS			
U.S.S. Jenolen	NCC-2010	Transport ship; reported missing, then destroyed by *U.S.S. Enterprise* in Dyson sphere escape	"Relics"
<Unnamed>		Transport	*Deep Space Nine:* "Playing God"
<Unnamed>		Shuttle	*Deep Space Nine:* "Accession"
WAMBUNDU CLASS			
U.S.S. Drake	NCC-20381	Captain Paul Rice; light cruiser; destroyed by automated defence system on Minos	"The Arsenal of Freedom"
U.S.S. Fleming	NCC-20316	Medical transport; abandoned in Hekarus Corridor; presumed destroyed	"Force of Nature"

141

Table 8.1 Starfleet Vessels *(continued)*

Ship Name	Number	Notes	Episode
YELLOWSTONE CLASS RUNABOUT			
U.S.S. Yellowstone		Alternate reality prototype; tetryon-plasma warp nacelles; destroyed in warp core breach	*Voyager:* "Non Sequitur"
YORKSHIRE CLASS			
U.S.S. Denver	NCC-54927	Transport ship; struck gravitic mine; presumed abandoned	"Ethics"
ZODIAC CLASS			
U.S.S. Yorktown		(25 years after Stardate 47988)	"All Good Things . . ."
SHUTTLES			
<Unnamed>	#2		"Samaritan Snare"
<Unnamed>	#4		"The Next Phase"
<Unnamed>			"The Next Phase"
<Unnamed>		Crash landed and abandoned on moon of Mab-Bu VI	"Power Play"
<Unnamed>			"True Q"
<Unnamed>	RS-47	Shuttle from Communication Relay Station 47	"Aquiel"
PERSONNEL SHUTTLE TYPE 6			
Currie		"Stolen" by Cardassian agent	"Lower Decks"
Fermi			"True Q"
Feynman			"Chain of Command, Part I"
Goddard		Given to Captain Montgommery Scott	"Relics"
Justman	#3		"Suspicions"
Magellan	#15	Destroyed in null space pocket	"The Outcast"
Sakharov	#1		"Unnatural Selection"
<Unnamed>			"Genesis"
<Unnamed>		Extended body	*Star Trek: Generations*
PERSONNEL SHUTTLE TYPE 7			
Hawking			"The Host"
<Unnamed>	#5		"The Nth Degree"
<Unnamed>	#6		"Coming of Age"
<Unnamed>	#10	Shuttle from *U.S.S. Repulse*	"The Child"
<Unnamed>	#13	Crashed on Vegra II	"Skin of Evil"
<Unnamed>			"Q Who?"
<Unnamed>		Destroyed in Tiarchanon atmosphere	"Identity Crisis"
<Unnamed>			"The Best of Both Worlds, Part II"

Table 8.1 Starfleet Vessels *(continued)*

Ship Name	Number	Notes	Episode
PERSONNEL SHUTTLE TYPE 8			
Drake		Destroyed in hull breach in time stream	*Voyager:* "Non Sequitur"
<Unnamed>	71325		*Voyager:* "Caretaker"
<Unnamed>			*Voyager:* "Parallax"
<Unnamed>		Destroyed by Kazon warship under Jal Razik	*Voyager:* "Initiations"
<Unnamed>		Crash landed on planet "Hell"	*Voyager:* "Parturition"
<Unnamed>		Captured by Kazon Raider	*Voyager:* "Maneuvers"
<Unnamed>			*Voyager:* "Prototype"
<Unnamed>			*Voyager:* "Innocence"
SHUTTLEPOD TYPE 15			
Cousteau		Shuttle from *U.S.S. Aries*	"Identity Crisis"
El-Baz	#5		"Time Squared"
Onizuka	#5		"The Ensigns of Command"
<Unnamed>	#7		"The Mind's Eye"
Pike	#12	Destroyed	"The Most Toys"
Voltaire	#3	Destroyed in Mar Oscura nebula	"In Theory"
<Unnamed>	#9		"The Price"
TRAVEL PODS			
<Unnamed> (2)		Work Bee	*Star Trek: Generations*
DOCKING SLEDS			
<Unnamed>		Warp sled type	*Star Trek: Generations*
UNKNOWN			
Cochrane		Lt. Tom Paris, Pilot; experimental transwarp design	*Voyager:* "Threshold"
<Unnamed>		Shuttle from *U.S.S. Defiant*	*Deep Space Nine:* "The Search, Part I"
<Unnamed>		Shuttle from *U.S.S. Defiant;* new class design	*Deep Space Nine:* "Destiny"
U.S.S. Al-Batani			*Voyager:* "Caretaker"
U.S.S. Bozeman			*Star Trek: Generations*
U.S.S. Constellation			*Deep Space Nine:* "The Abandoned"
U.S.S. Kearsage			"Firstborn"
U.S.S. Okinawa		Captain Leyton	*Deep Space Nine:* "Paradise Lost"
U.S.S. Shika Maru		Captain Sylvester	"Darmok"
U.S.S. Ulysses		Captain Intebi	*Deep Space Nine:* "The Adversary"
<Unnamed>			"11001001"
<Unnamed>		Class IX Probe; modified with life support systems to carry Ambassador K'Ehleyrr	"The Emissary"
<Unnamed>		Commander Chakotay; destroyed by ramming Kazon warship	*Voyager:* "Caretaker"

Table 8.1   Starfleet Vessels *(continued)*

Ship Name	*Number*	*Notes*	*Episode*
OTHER CLASS/TYPE			
S.S. Artemis		Colony ship	"The Ensigns of Command"
U.S.S. Exeter		Alternate reality ship	*Voyager:* "Non Sequitur"
S.S. Odin	NGL-12535	Freighter; disabled and abandoned by crew	"Angel One"
U.S.S. Portland			*Deep Space Nine:* "The Die is Cast"
<Unnamed> (3)	Unmanned pods	Destroyed outside Mars Defense Perimeter	"The Best of Both Worlds, Part II"
<Unnamed> (5)		Nova Squadron; precision flying craft; destroyed in attempt of Kolvoord Starburst	"The First Duty"

CHAPTER NINE

The Cast and Crew

"The man has become so ingrained for me and such a lot of me has gone into him, and much of what he stands for and what he believes in represents my own beliefs and opinions. I'm an actor playing a role, but it is surprising though gratifying to find that the role influences aspects of everyday life in this particular way."

—Patrick Stewart

Patrick Stewart

Patrick Stewart began his keynote commencement address to the Pomona College Class of 1995 by saying, "This is only my second graduation ceremony ever, and when I say 'mine,' I don't mean 'mine,' because this is in fact the only one in which I've actually been a participant." He might have waited a long time for it, but Stewart was certainly doing his first graduation ceremony in style. The student body had mounted a massive letter-writing campaign to bring Stewart in as their commencement speaker, and College President Peter Stanley had just bestowed the degree of Doctor of Literature upon him.

"And to those of you who are at this moment reeling with shock," Stewart continued, "let me confirm that I never went to Starfleet Academy, that I never sat at the feet of the groundsperson Boothby, and I wouldn't know a space-time continuum or a warp core breach if they got into bed with me.

"That first graduation was when my son graduated three years ago from Cal Arts. It was a momentous day in my family when Daniel graduated. There he stood, Bachelor of Fine Arts, the first member of my family to receive a degree. I was tremendously proud and somewhat in awe of it. And not surprisingly I, his father, had completed my formal education at the age of 15 years and two days—the minimum age then required by the state of England at which schooling could cease."

"It's marvelous to rehearse Shakespeare, to stretch oneself in the company of such a mind. For I must acknowledge that, lacking higher education in the formal sense, education informally began for me the day that I joined the Royal Shakespeare Company."

Stewart had moved to America to assume the captain's chair on the *Enterprise.* He explained how life in America has changed him: "I have lived and worked in the United States for more than eight years now. This country has changed me in countless ways. It has transformed my career, it has given me material security; it made me a healthier person, and I think a nicer one. But perhaps more important than all these, it has given me more fun than in all the 45 years that have gone before. It will seem it has also changed the way I sound. After a recent interview with the BBC, the journalist, with an unmistakable sneer in his voice, commented upon my 'American accent.' Yes, I love this country, the United States, and its people. You are admirable, optimistic, enraging, funny, and infuriating. And at times, to a European, stunningly insecure and quite, quite lost."

In concluding, Stewart referred to his Picard persona: "About a month ago, one of your faculty suggested that I might take into theme those lines of Captain Jean-Luc Picard from the recent movie *Generations,* about how we can make a difference in the world in which we live. I know there are many *Star Trek* fans here, some of whom probably know the Prime

Directive better than me, and though fiction, I believe it is an admirable code for any society. Gene Roddenberry's vision of the 24th century was not merely utopianism. It can be a part of a blueprint for how we might live, how you might live today. Make a difference." And with that, he sent them on their way, where they had not gone before.

Stewart's long trek to the captain's chair began in Mirfield, West Yorkshire, England on July 13, 1940. He first acted in local drama groups at the age of 12, while suffering through a troubled childhood. He has few happy memories of those years. "Life was scary when I was growing up," Stewart told *TV Guide.* "I wasn't beaten, but there was violence in the house. My father would lose control, but recently I came across a photograph. I'm sitting on a beach, in a deck chair, and my father is tickling me. I am squirming with laughter. I must have been about six years old. I'd forgotten that my father made me laugh."

Stewart left school at 15 to work as a junior reporter on a local paper. That job didn't last long. He quit when the editor told him he was spending too much time at the theater. "At one point," Stewart told the *Los Angeles Times,* "I was rehearsing four plays simultaneously. This created problems since, as a journalist, you can be called on at any time to cover something without notice. So I'd have people covering for me on the job. I even went to the point of not attending city meetings and things that I was supposed to cover, then phoning somebody afterward to find out the particulars. I used to invent stuff. It all came to a head when I handed in copy one morning about a local council meeting I hadn't really attended, only to discover that a large weaving mill only 200 yards from where the meetings took place had burnt down and I hadn't covered it. So I was found out."

"That led to a meeting with the editor, who said 'Either you give up all your amateur acting or you give up the newspaper.' I went upstairs and told my colleague that our editor was a bastard and that I was leaving. So I took my typewriter, left that afternoon, and went home and told my parents that I was going to be an actor. They had no money, so I worked as a furniture salesman and then the county gave me a grant to study." He spent two years as a furniture salesman before attending the Bristol Old Vic Theatre.

Two more years passed, then, in 1959, Stewart made his professional debut at the Repertory in Lincoln. He never looked back. He spent the early 1960s working at the Manchester Library Theatre and touring worldwide with the Old Vic Company.

Stewart loves Shakespeare. "I was exposed to Shakespeare before I knew I was supposed to be frightened or intimidated or bored by it. I loved the sound of it," he told *Entertainment Weekly.* "When I was 17, my dreams were exclusively fixed on being a Shakespearean stage actor," Stewart recalled to *Cinescape.* "That's all I wanted to do-and when, finally in 1966, I was accepted into the Royal Shakespeare Company, I felt that there was nowhere

> *"Let me confirm that I never went to Starfleet Academy, that I never sat at the feet of the groundsperson Boothby, and I wouldn't know a space-time continuum or a warp core breach..."*

147

else I would ever want to be. At the end of the first season, I was offered a three-year contract to stay on. I can still remember that little phone booth where I called my [then] wife and said, 'It's happened. I'm just going to stay here forever.' There's not a single day of it I would change. I feel I've been extraordinarily blessed." Stewart's dream turned into a 27-year association with the prestigious Royal Shakespeare Company, but there were even bigger things in store.

Stewart began making movies in 1974 with *Churchill: The Gathering Storm,* and a role as Ejlert Loevborg in *Hennessy.* The next year, he acted alongside Glenda Jackson in *Hedda.* Stewart appeared in two TV movies in 1980: as Wilkins in *Little Lord Fauntleroy,* and as Claudius in *Hamlet, Prince of Denmark.* He had roles in two films as well, as Leondegrance in *Excalibur* (1981), and as the voice of the Major in the animated *The Plague Dogs* (1982).

Stewart's best work during this period was in three BBC TV miniseries: *I, Claudius* (1976); *Tinker, Tailor, Soldier, Spy* (1980); and *Smiley's People* (1982). All were acclaimed by viewing audiences when shown on public television in America. But Stewart later told *TV Guide,* "People who watch television seriously say how fabulous British television is and has always been, but it's changing, increasingly playing down to lower tastes and a popular market. *Star Trek* never underestimates the intelligence of its audience."

Stewart kept busy with the Royal National Theatre during the mid-1980s, and also made several films: *Gorky Park* (1983), *Dune* (1984), *Wild Geese II* (1985), *Lifeforce* (1985), *The Doctor and the Devils* (1985), *Code Name: Emerald* (1985), and *Lady Jane* (1986). His TV miniseries, *Playing Shakespeare* (1984), in which he appeared as himself, was a labor of love. Stewart performed two plays in 1986, in

the title role in Peter Shaffer's *Yonadab* at the National Theatre of Great Britain, and as George in *Who's Afraid of Virginia Woolf* at the Young Vic, for which he won the London Fringe Theatre Best Actor Award.

Stewart never became a fan of science fiction. "Gosh, no!" he told the *Los Angeles Times,* "Not at all. I have no enthusiasm for it whatsoever." His passion remains Shakespeare. He has contributed articles to Shakespeare publications and served as an associate director of the Santa Barbara–based Alliance for Creative Theatre, Education & Research, an organization that uses British actors to teach Shakespeare's plays as living scripts, "not as pieces of intimidating literature." He continues to lecture and teach "whenever possible." In fact, he was delivering dramatic readings to accompany a lecture at UCLA when he was spotted for *Star Trek: The Next Generation* by Robert Justman.

In 1986, Stewart moved to California to assume the role of Captain Jean-Luc Picard for the new syndicated TV series. The job lasted for seven years on television, and led to an ongoing series of movies. Some were surprised by his move from the Royal Shakespeare Company to a TV starship. Stewart told *TV Guide,* "My closet friends were delighted and astonished, perhaps a little envious. Later, Terry Hands, artistic director of the RSC, confessed to having been a fan of the original series and now of what I was doing. I only saw *Star Trek* on occasion, with my children, as they were growing up."

Stewart loved living in the U.S., and was especially taken with the roller coasters. He told the *Seattle Post-Intelligencer,* "The best [roller coaster] is in Blackpool, where I had my first roller coaster experience. There's also a great one at Magic Mountain! Also, of course, there's the one on Santa Cruz boardwalk. It's

an old wooden thing. Wooden! One of the things I love most about America is that it's a mecca of roller coasters."

His day hardly leaves time for play, though. "I wake up about 4:30 and listen to classical radio while I read and drink tea," Stewart told *TV Guide.* "To an Englishman, the day does not begin without a proper cup of tea—and the critical thing about tea-making is that the water be boiling as it hits the tea leaves. In America, they bring you water and a tea bag, outside the pot, which I shall never get used to.

"One of the things I love most about America is that it's a mecca of roller coasters."

"I read books. The hour before I go to work is for me. I don't want to be made angry by the newspapers. Later, I can cope with it. I've got to have one moment before I confront the reality of the world. Only after I shower and shave do I switch to words and voices."

Then it's off to work, to assume his role as Picard. Patrick Stewart told the *Orange County Register,* "I can no longer now discern a connection between Patrick Stewart leaving his dressing room and Jean-Luc Picard walking onto the set. The man has become so ingrained for me and such a lot of me has gone into him, and much of what he stands for and what he believes in represents my own beliefs and opinions. I'm an actor playing a role, but it is surprising though gratifying to find that the role influences aspects of everyday life in this particular way."

Few now distinguish the actor from the starship captain anywhere in the world. Stewart told *TV Guide,* "About a year ago, I was working with a film company in Croatia, and one night, my girlfriend and I went to a restaurant in the old town of Zagreb. We were ushered in by a very dignified and formal *maitre d',* shown to a table, given menus. When our salads arrived, sitting in the center of each—beautifully carved out of cucumber and green and red peppers—was a perfect little replica of the *Enterprise!* The other courses were served, and there was no change of any kind on this man's demeanor; we paid our bill and left without any other comment being made."

The role has changed the actor. "[Playing Captain Picard has] made me a little more thoughtful, a little less impulsive," Stewart told *TV Guide,* "I hope, more patient. I was very short on patience and tolerance once."

The Next Generation allowed Stewart to fulfill another dream: directing. He began with the fourth-season episode, "In Theory," then directed "Hero Worship" for the fifth season, "A Fistful of Datas" for the sixth season, and "Phantasms" and "The Good Fight" for the seventh season.

But even with most of his dreams coming true—world recognition, financial security, directing—Patrick Stewart missed the stage. "It's very important to me to be in front of a live audience," he told *TV Guide.* In 1992, during the fourth-season hiatus, Stewart took Tom Stoppard's play, *Every Good Boy Deserves Favour,* on the road. He not only starred in the production, but directed his Trek costars, Jonathan Frakes, Brent Spiner, Gates McFadden, and Colm Meaney, in a four-city tour that repeatedly opened to sold-out theaters and rave critical reviews.

Stewart kept busy. While working for *The Next Generation,* he also appeared in *L.A. Story* (1991), as King Richard in Mel Brooks' *Robin Hood: Men in Tights* (1993), and in

Alistair MacLean's *Death Train* (1993) for TV. He won the New York Theater Critics' Drama Desk Award for Best Solo Performance for his one-man play, *A Christmas Carol,* at the Broadhurst in 1993, then the Laurence Olivier Award for "Best Actor" and "Best Entertainment" for the same play at the Old Vic in 1994. He even won a Grammy nomination for the album version of *A Christmas Carol* in 1993. Stewart also hosted an evening of *Saturday Night Live* that ranked among the top five episodes of 1993. The good captain then appeared in *Star Trek: Generations* in 1994, after the TV series left the air.

The July 18, 1992, issue of *TV Guide* announced that a poll of readers voted Patrick Stewart the "Most Bodacious" male on TV with 54 percent of the votes, beating out Burt Reynolds, A. Martinez, John Corbett, and Luke Perry. He said he reacted to the news "With elegance, with grace, an overwhelming modesty, and huge numbers of locks on my door," and told *TV Guide,* "For a while I was in total denial, falling back on the persona of a deeply embarrassed Englishman. But as time went by, I began to confess, first to myself and then to others, that I enjoyed it very much."

A poll taken by *USA Today* asked what one person the reader would want to be stranded with on a desert island. Among celebrities, Patrick Stewart came in second only to Brad Pitt.

After *The Next Generation* TV series ended, Stewart took steps to protect his career. He was aware of the problems of stereotyping suffered by an earlier generation of Trek stars, and knew that he had appeared as Picard for more than twice as long as William Shatner had portrayed Kirk.

"For about a year or so," Stewart told the *Los Angeles Times,* "I've been talking to my agents about what I should do, and I kept say-ing that whatever that first piece of work is, it must shatter Jean-Luc Picard." His next film was *Jeffrey,* and it did just that. In it, Stewart plays Sterling, a razor-tongued gay interior decorator. The film opened the 10th London Lesbian and Gay Film Festival on March 21, 1996. "I had seen the play *Jeffrey* in Los Angeles," Stewart told the *Times,* "and I was sent the screenplay and was reading it while filming the last few days of the *Star Trek* movie. I just thought it was so brilliant and ultimately so moving that it felt as if I had no choice but to do it.

"We were filming on top of this finger of rock in the Nevada desert, shooting some violent sequences with Malcolm McDowell. It was 119 in the shade, and I was sitting there reading the script. Well, I completed it and found that I needed both wardrobe and makeup to help me because my face was streaming with tears and the tears dripped off onto my space suit."

When *Advocate* asked him if he was aware that the gay community generally believed he was homosexual or bisexual because he had prominently portrayed a gay man, Stewart replied, "I am entirely heterosexual. My only unease was that I would not be convincing as a gay man with a lover in New York. So I would say to Chris [Ashley, director] and Paul [Rudnick, writer/producer], who are both gay men, 'Please tell me if there's any moment that doesn't ring true or would appear to be a shallow approach to what we're doing.'"

He also added his varied talents to *500 Nations,* a TV series about the Amerindian nations, the animated *The Pagemaster,* and *Liberation,* a documentary about the Holocaust, alongside Whoopi Goldberg. He played a homeless ballroom-dance instructor with an American accent and a white wig for the romantic comedy *Let It Be Me,* a pesky spirit for the ABC TV movie *The Canterville Ghost,* and other very non-Trek roles in *Richard III* and *In Search of Dr. Seuss.*

But live theater always comes first for Stewart. He opened *The Tempest* in November of 1995 at New York's Shakespeare in the Park festival, playing Prospero, the former Duke of Milan who was washed ashore on a desert island after being unseated and exiled by his treacherous brother. But Trek followed him, even here. He told *Entertainment Weekly,* "One night, I made the mistake of tugging on the front of my doublet. There was an instantaneous burst of laughter. I was very careful never to do it again."

On August 6, 1995, his one-man show, *Uneasy Lies the Head,* opened at The Swan Theatre, Stratford-on-Avon, England. The prestigious benefit performance was attended by many RSC and ACTER actors and directors. Also in 1995, the industry trade journal, Variety, noted that of 29 Broadway productions in the past year, only four had made money. One of them was Patrick Stewart's *A Christmas Carol.*

In 1996, Stewart returned to the captain's chair for *Star Trek: First Contact.* While he wants to avoid becoming a one-role actor, he enjoys his involvement with the legendary *Star Trek.*

He does have one regret about the *Star Trek* years. He told *TV Guide,* "It separated me from my daughter for long periods of time, and I'll never get that back." To *Entertainment Weekly* he added, "I've been focused so entirely on my work for so many decades, I haven't paid attention as a father and a friend and a lover. I am now trying to pay attention." He had divorced his wife of 24 years, Sheila Falconer, in 1990. Stewart has two children, Daniel, an actor, and Sophie, a London boutique owner, from that marriage, and he wants

to devote more time to them. He is also said to be romantically involved with Wendy Neuss, a *Star Trek* producer living in Los Angeles.

Stewart values the friendships he has made with his castmates. He believes that they will all enjoy fine careers after Trek—with one exception. He told *TV Guide,* "Jonathan Frakes will have a marvelous career as a director. Brent Spiner is so multitalented that I would love to see him get a leading role in a musical or some dramatic play. In fact, one day I wish to see Brent play Stan Laurel; his likeness to Stan in his middle years is extraordinary. Within five years, Michael Dorn will be a leading member of either the Royal Shakespeare Company or the National Theatre of Great Britain. Marina Sirtis will have a movie career. LeVar Burton will be a significant movie producer or director. Whoopi Goldberg? Difficult to say. It's going to be a struggle for Whoopi when the series is over. All I can do is wish her luck. It's going to be really tough for her."

Jean-Luc Picard

In Labarre, France, Yvette Picard delivered a son to her husband, Maurice, on July 13, 2305. They named the boy Jean-Luc. The people of his hometown knew young Jean-Luc Picard as a hotheaded troublemaker who literally lost his heart in a knife fight (the heart was replaced with a bionic heart). He returned years later as a legendary Starfleet captain, tough but pragmatic, romantic but controlled and reserved, with a strong dedication to honor and duty. The undisciplined boy, who left school at the age of 15 because he was "not interested," had grown into a philosophical man with a keen interest in history and

151

archaeology. He was a lover of Shakespeare, horseback riding, Earl Grey tea, and old-fashioned books—especially 1940s hard-boiled detective novels by Dixon Hill.

Jean-Luc had an older brother named Robert. Robert was the "responsible" one, and he resented Jean-Luc for breaking the rules and getting away with it. When Jean-Luc left behind his traditional Luddite family to join Starfleet, Robert remained behind, married former schoolmate Marie, and had a son, René, with her. A rift grew between the brothers.

If Robert sometimes envied his brother's wild freedom of the spaceways, perhaps Jean-Luc, married only to his starship, often longed for the comfort and security of family, lifelong friends, and home. Both had made their choices while very young; now they must live with them.

Jean-Luc first applied to Starfleet Academy in 2322 at the age of 17, but he was rejected.

> **Jean-Luc first applied to Starfleet Academy in 2322 at the age of 17, but he was rejected.**

He reapplied and entered the Academy a year later, graduating in 2327.

Young Lieutenant Picard attended the wedding of Spock, the legendary half-Vulcan. Years later, while captain of the *Enterprise*, Jean-Luc mind-melded with Spock's Vulcan father, Sarek. When Sarek died, it fell to Picard to deliver the news to Spock. He told the disbelieving Spock that his father had expressed pride and love toward his son. Spock dismissed this as part of the "emotional disarray" caused by Sarek's illness, but Jean-Luc insisted that it was from the heart. Spock observed that Jean-Luc probably knew Sarek better than he did, for Spock and Sarek had never chosen to meld. "I offer you the choice to touch what he shared with me," said Jean-Luc. Then Spock and Jean-Luc melded, and Spock and Sarek were briefly united.

Starfleet first assigned Jean-Luc to command a deep-space-charting starship, *Stargazer,* in 2342. Jean-Luc held this command for 22 years, adding much to the knowledge of the galaxy.

Jean-Luc held the post aboard the *Stargazer* until the ship was badly damaged in a battle with the Ferengi. Starfleet then gave Jean-Luc command of the *Enterprise* NCC-1701-D in 2373. He resided in room 3601 on Deck 8 with his pet fish, Livingston. His serial number was SP-937-215. The *Enterprise* 1701-D, with its ship's complement of over a thousand crew and family, and its many strange adventures, offered more complex new challenges than young Jean-Luc imagined when he ran off to join Starfleet.

Jean-Luc appears to have engaged in a number of romances, but no enduring relationships. Among his paramours were Jenice Manheim, prior to her marriage to Dr. Manheim; Miranda Vigo, with whom he had a brief romance in his youth; and Dr. Beverly Crusher, to whom he confessed his love after her husband (Jean-Luc's best friend) died.

Perhaps the most profound experience in Jean-Luc's life occurred when the Borg took him to their ship and told him that humanity would be assimilated into the Borg culture. When Jean-Luc said that it was impossible, because his culture is based on freedom and self-determination, the Borg replied, "Freedom is irrelevant. Self-determination is irrelevant. You must comply." When he said they would rather die than be absorbed, the reply was, "Death is irrelevant." They then altered

Jean-Luc into a Borg and made him their spokesman, Locutus. Jean-Luc/Locutus was linked into the Borg consciousness via a transporter-like subspace field. "I am Locutus, of Borg. Resistance is futile. Your life as it has been is over. From this time forward, you will service us," the altered Jean-Luc told his former shipmates.

Riker ordered Data to use Locutus to plant a command into the Borg consciousness. Data could not plant a command to disarm or to power down, as all high-level commands were protected, but he put them to sleep and the untended Borg ship self-destructed. The destruction freed Jean-Luc, but he retained serious doubts about his own humanity.

Later, when Jean-Luc visited his brother Robert, whom he hadn't seen in 20 years, relations between them worsened. When the subject of Jean-Luc's recent problems with the Borg came up, Jean-Luc and Robert argued, brought up old jealousies, and got into a fist fight in the vineyard. Then both brothers laughed, and the openness allowed Jean-Luc to relate his anger and frustration at having been turned into Locutus by the Borg. Robert reassured him that he was still human, and Jean-Luc, heartened, returned to the *Enterprise*.

"Gene was so very non-Hollywood and quite paternal. One of the things he said to me was, 'You have a Machiavellian glint in your eye. Life is a bowl of cherries.' I think Gene felt that way, which is why he wrote the way he did. He's very positive, and Commander Riker will reflect that."

—Jonathan Frakes

Jonathan Frakes

"I gave myself a five-year limit," said Frakes of his 1974 move to New York City. "If I wasn't making a living at acting in five years, I would find something else to do. After a year and a half of being the worst waiter in New York, and screwing up my back as a furniture mover, I got a role in *Shenandoah* on Broadway and then landed a part in *The Doctors.*" It was that close; the man who played William Riker for seven years on *Star Trek: The Next Generation* for, then continued the role in feature films, almost returned to Pennsylvania instead.

Jonathan Frakes was born in Bethlehem, Pennsylvania, on August 19, 1952. He graduated from Penn State, then continued his education at Harvard, spending several seasons with the Loeb Drama Center. He then lived in New York for five years, working on and off Broadway, for regional theater productions, and appearing in small guest roles on *The Waltons* (as Ashley Longworth, Jr.) and on *Barnaby Jones,* before landing a regular part as a contract player for the daytime drama *The Doctors.*

Moving to Los Angeles in 1979 at the suggestion of his agent, he then began a steady stream of work. "I really have been very lucky. There's a cliché in this business that says the easy part of being an actor is doing the job. The hardest part is getting the job," Frakes later recalled to a convention audience. In the next few years, he played TV guest roles too small to have names, including parts for *Hart to Hart, The Dukes of Hazzard, It's a Living, Falcon Crest, The Fall Guy, Fantasy Island, Highway to Heaven, Hill Street Blues,* and *The Blue and the Gray.* Frakes also appeared in the TV movies *Beach Patrol* (1979) and *The Night the City Screamed* (1980). His character occasionally had a name: Adam Davis in *Beulah Land,* Marcus Marshall in *Bare Essence,* Lieutenant Gillespie in *Dream West,* and he played no less than Charles Lindbergh for *Voyagers.* Frakes has also appeared in *Charlie's Angels, Cybill, Five Mile Creek, Matlock, Lois & Clark: The New Adventures of Superman, Quincy, M.E., Remington Steele,* and *Wings* on TV, as well as the plays *The Common Glory, Henry VIII,* and *Li'l Abner.*

Frakes' role of Stanley Hazard for the 1985 TV miniseries *North and South* finally brought him more notice. He reprised the role for *North and South II* in 1986, and, much later, for *North and South III* in 1994—that final time alongside his new wife, Genie Francis. They began dating while filming *North and South* in Natchez, Mississippi, although they previously had worked together on *Bare Essence* in 1983. "We had our first date in New Orleans. This place has special meaning for us." Jonathan and Genie, who appears on *General Hospital,* reside in Los Angeles with their black Jeep Limited Edition.

Frakes appeared in the TV miniseries *Nutcracker: Money, Madness & Murder* in 1987, immediately before taking the job that would change his life: as Commander William Riker for *Star Trek: The Next Generation.* "I knew this was a real part, a big one, and I had to get it," Frakes said.

The actor credits Gene Roddenberry with giving him the needed insight into his character. "Gene was so very non-Hollywood and quite paternal. One of the things he said to me was, 'You have a Machiavellian glint in your eye. Life is a bowl of cherries.' I think Gene felt that way, which is why he wrote the way he did. He's very positive, and Commander Riker will reflect that."

Frakes sees Riker as "strong, centered, honorable, and somewhat driven. His job is to provide Captain Picard with the most efficiently run ship and the best-prepared crew he can. As a result, he maintains a more military bearing than the other characters, despite the fact that salutes and other military protocol no longer exist in the 24th century."

He told the Associated Press, "Gene once said he thought Picard and Riker and Wesley Crusher, a teen-age crewman, combined all the elements of Captain Horatio Hornblower at different ages." Hornblower was the main figure in a series of novels by C. S. Forester.

> "If I wasn't making a living at acting in five years, I would find something else to do."

Frakes started wearing a hairpiece after the first season, when he started getting "scalp-burn" from the hot lights on the set. He plays the trombone, but the cast hated scenes involving the trombone, because, as Marina Sirtis said, "[He] doesn't stop all day long with that bloody trombone!"

Frakes began directing with the third-season episode, "The Offspring." He later directed "Reunion" and "The Drumhead" for the fourth season, "Cause and Effect" for the fifth season, "The Quality of Life" and "The Chase" for the sixth season, and "Attached" for the seventh season. "It's really a split focus when you direct a show you're also acting in," Frakes told the *Charlotte Observer.* "Especially if your character is heavy in the show. That can be demanding, but other people far better than I have done it before. All I can tell you is, it's worth the challenge. I am proud and honored that episodes I've directed are well regarded. When one goes well, it usually means I get to do another." This proved true. He continues to direct *Star Trek: Deep Space Nine, Star Trek: Voyager,* and *University Hospital* for TV, and is now directing the feature film, *Star Trek: First Contact* (1996). Frakes appeared in this film, the earlier *Star Trek: Generations* (1994), and the newest Trek series, *Star Trek: Voyager.*

During the fourth season, Frakes toured with Patrick Stewart, Brent Spiner, Gates McFadden, and Colm Meaney, in a four-city tour of Tom Stoppard's drama, *Every Good Boy Deserves Favour.* While working for *TNG,* he also acted in *The New Twilight Zone* episode "But Can She Type" and the TV movie *The Cover Girl and the Cop* (1989). After *TNG,* he provided the voice of Xanatos for *Gargoyles,* hosted *Alien Autopsy: Fact or Fiction* (1995), and appeared in *Camp Nowhere* (1994).

Frakes wants to continue acting and directing. "That would be the logical route," he told the *Charlotte Observer.* "I'd be thrilled to continue directing. I'm hoping my work on *Star Trek* opens some doors. I'd love to direct some television, and I've got some scripts I'd like to do as films. Hopefully, knock on wood, it will all work out."

William Riker

First Officer of the starship *Enterprise* NCC-1701-D, William Riker has traveled a long way since he was born to Kyle and Elizabeth

155

Riker in Valdez, Alaska, in 2335. Riker's mother died when he was three years old. He deeply felt this loss, which began an emotional problem causing Riker to fear close relationships. Deanna Troi later became the first to break through this shell. He enjoys jazz, plays the trombone, is a master poker player, and enjoys cooking.

Riker entered Starfleet Academy in 2353 and graduated in 2357. His first assignment was on the Starship *Potemkin* as an ensign. Riker was quickly promoted to lieutenant, then later served on the *U.S.S. Yorktown* as lieutenant commander. Riker left that post because of his feelings for Deanna, who also served on the *Yorktown.*

He transferred to the post of First Officer on board the *U.S.S. Hood,* where he served until 2364. He left to join the crew of the *Enterprise* as first officer under the legendary Captain Picard, although he was also offered the command of the *U.S.S. Drake.* It would not be the last time he refused his own command, choosing instead to serve under Picard. Riker also turned down captaincies of the *Aries* and the *Melbourne.*

Riker joined the *Enterprise* crew when it picked him up at the Farpoint Station, which is where he first met Beverly and Wesley Crusher and Geordi LaForge. Riker normally commands Away Teams while Captain Picard remains aboard the *Enterprise.* Riker is also in charge of overseeing the condition of the vessel and the crew.

Riker enjoys women, but never lets it interfere with duty. Riker was surprised to find Troi aboard the *Enterprise.* He is uncomfortable with the situation, but each treats the other with respect, and they seem to have put their past relationship behind them.

"The sun is going to burn out eventually and we better be somewhere else as a race of people by the time that happens. I think that's why everybody digs *Star Trek,* because they know it's a part of all of our futures and represents a vision of home."

—Brent Jay Spiner

Brent Jay Spiner

Brent Spiner originally wanted to be a doctor. While interning, he took the blood pressure of a man awaiting a heart transplant. The man opened his eyes and asked, "Am I dead?" "Not yeeeet," Brent replied. They hustled him out and read him the riot act.

Fortunately, he was also an avid movie fan, having watched three films a day from age 11 until 15. "At 15 I was already a major film buff," Spiner recalled. "I could quote lines from movies, tell you who was in it and in what year it was made. I was also lucky enough to have a brilliant teacher in high school named Cecil Pickett, who was capable of seeing potential, nurturing it, and making me aware of it." Acting now exerted a siren call on the Houston native, and he followed it to New York after college.

Spiner drove a cab to support himself while looking for acting jobs. He once told an Infinite Visions Convention that he had 150 people in his cab in any one day, and three-quarters of them were legally insane.

He appeared in numerous off-Broadway plays. "The play that finally pushed me over into the serious-actor category was a Public Theater production of *The Seagull* for Joseph Papp," Spiner told a convention audience. Roles in the Broadway musical productions of *Sunday in the Park with George, The Three Musketeers,* and *Big River* followed.

He also played cameo roles in the movies *The Miss Firecracker Contest* and *Rent Control,* appeared in *The Dain Curse* TV miniseries, and guest-starred on *Cheers, Twilight Zone,* and *Hill Street Blues* for television. Spiner even played a "Fan in Lobby" for Woody Allen's *Stardust Memories* in 1980. He told the Infinite Visions Convention audience that "Woody Allen is great to work for. Woody is real loose with the dialogue; *Star Trek* demands you say everything exactly as written."

Spiner's winding road to stardom then led him to Los Angeles in 1984 for the Westwood Playhouse production of *Little Shop of Horrors.* He won greater attention in his role as Bob Wheeler for *Night Court* and appeared as Allard Lowenstein for the *Robert Kennedy & His Times* TV miniseries. He then made a string of TV movies, including *Crime of Innocence* in 1985, *Sunday in the Park with George* and *Manhunt* for Claude Dallas in 1986, and *Family Sins* in 1987, before assuming the role that would change his life.

"It was down to me and one other guy," Spiner told a Boston Con audience. "Actually, the first time I went in and read, I didn't know specifically whether they wanted me to play like a robot or closer to being a person. If the show ran for seven years, I thought it would get real tedious playing a robot. I was in the waiting room and [my agent] came out and said that they wanted this to be like a robot. I said, 'OK, well, thanks very much. I'm gonna leave then,' and she said, 'Well, why?' and I said, 'Because I don't want to do that.' She said, 'Well, let me go talk to them.' She came back out, and said, 'OK, you can

157

audition the way you want, but I want you to also consider the role of Riker,' and I said, 'Well, I don't want to play Riker. I want to play Data the way I want to, and hopefully they'll agree with me.' So I auditioned, and finally it was down to two people, me and Eric Menyuk, who later played The Traveler.

"Gene Roddenberry called that night, and said, 'Would you be willing to change your appearance to play Data?,' and I said, 'Sure!' thinking that it was gonna be ears or whatever. Then they called and said, 'Would you be willing to shave your head?' I said, 'No! I would mind shaving my head.' I wouldn't mind shaving my head if it was for a film, but this runs for seven years. Then they cast Patrick, and it became a moot point.

"When they cast Patrick, the executives at Paramount wanted him to wear hair, and he auditioned with a little wig on. Gene Roddenberry said, 'I don't want him to wear hair.' Gene said, 'By the 24th century, people won't be concerned with superficialities like that!' Thus was created the sexiest man in America [as chosen by *TV Guide*]. So they gave me the part, and then we did 35 different makeup tests, 35 different colors, ranging from bow-tie pink to battleship gray. That's the story in a nutshell."

> **"If the show ran for seven years, I thought it would get real tedious playing a robot."**

Spiner revealed the real reason he got the part when a young fan at another convention asked how Data flips up the top of his head. The actor replied, "There were hundreds of people auditioning for the part of Data, and I was the only one who could take the top of my head off."

Spiner, a life-long science fiction fan, was ready to step into his role as the spacefaring android Lieutenant Commander Data for *Star Trek: The Next Generation*. "I'm one of those people who believes that mankind will find all the answers out in space," he told the convention audience, "but the first step is to get off this planet. The sun is going to burn out eventually and we better be somewhere else as a race of people by the time that happens. I think that's why everybody digs *Star Trek,* because they know it's a part of all of our futures and represents a vision of home.

"As the series opens, we don't know much about Data, only that he was constructed by beings on a planet which no longer exists. He's the only thing left. His creators programmed him with a world of knowledge—he's virtually an encyclopedia—but only in terms of information, not behavior. He's totally innocent. However, he does possess a sense of question and wonder that allows him to evolve. His objective is to be as human as possible."

The actor identifies with his role, noting, "Marina [Sirtis] says of all the characters on the show, I'm the closest to my character. But I do think I'm innocent as Data. I think I'm as big a sap as Data is. I tend to believe everything that's told to me."

Spiner enjoys his role. He told the Canadian *TV Guide,* "The only parts of it that aren't fun are the makeup routine and, in direct contrast to what most actors tell you, learning the lines. That's usually the easy part, but the dialogue from Data has to flow; I don't have the luxury of being able to pause and look for the next line. And the dialogue usually consists of things that have never come out of my mouth in real life, so it isn't easy. But I am not complaining, *Star Trek* fans; I am absolutely not complaining!"

The infamous *Star Trek* technobabble proved challenging to the actor. Spiner told a

Grand Slam III audience, "Not only was technical dialogue difficult at the beginning, it was difficult at the end. Without question, the most difficult thing I had to do on the show was memorize large chunks of dialogue that meant absolutely nothing. At the end of a long day, I would open up the script, and my stomach would turn over at what I would have to talk about. I had to erase it from my head on a daily basis because there was a whole new block of it coming the next day. It was challenging, and ultimately an interesting aspect of the character."

The character grew over time. Spiner told the Canadian *TV Guide,* "Data's more 'human' now. Everything he experiences becomes a part of his programming, so human behavior becomes a part of his programming. He's constantly observing, adding this, adding that. His movements have therefore become more

Data Using Contractions

In "Datalore," Lore notes differences between himself and Data, including the ability to use contractions. In "The Offspring," Data himself states that he "hadn't quite mastered" contractions. Yet, despite Spiner's protestations, as the following shows illustrate, Data uses contractions.

Episode 1, "Encounter at Farpoint": At the beginning of the "post atomic-horror" courtroom, when Q enters, Data says, "At least we're acquainted with the judge, Captain." Also, when Data is asked by a very familiar "Admiral" if he is a Vulcan, Data replies, "No sir, I'm an android."

Episode 3, "The Naked Now": In the teaser, Data says, "Captain, what we've just heard is . . . impossible." Then, during Act One, while on the science vessel, Data says: "Correction, sir, that's blown out," instead of "that is." Then, after being examined by Dr. Crusher, Data says "I'm already listed in several biomechanical texts." Later, after Picard orders Yar to the sickbay, Yar asks "Did he say when?" Data replies, "I'm sure he meant now." In this same scene, "Chronological age, no. I'm afraid I am not. . . ."

Episode 4, "Code of Honor": Data says, "I've told 662 jokes." Data and Geordi have beamed down to the planet to examine the weapons to be used in the fight. Picard speculates as to the use of a number of metal lengths in the yard. Data answers at some length as to their possible uses and is cut off by Picard.

Picard: "Thank you, Data."

Data: "You're welcome, sir."

Back on board the *Enterprise,* Data is briefing Riker as to Picard's plan: "I'm here to brief you on what he wants."

Episode 5, "The Last Outpost": During the conversation with Sentry, Data clearly said, "I'm afraid not."

Episode 13, "Datalore": In the teaser, in response to Tasha's query about holding the memory of over 411 people, Data responds, "Actually, I'm quite efficient in some basic human information." Then in Act One, on the way to the place where he was found, in response to Tasha's query about the colonist's memories, Data replies, "I've always felt that it was done hurriedly, but I know little more." Next, in Act Two, in a conversation with Chief Argyle, Data says, "I've been most anxious to hear the Chief Engineer's opinion, Mr. Argyle." Then, in the final act, after the fight with Lore, Picard asks Data if he's okay, to which Data replies, "Yes Sir, I'm fine."

Episode 29, "Elementary, Dear Data": When Data and Geordi are about to confront Moriarty for the first time, Data notices scratches near Moriarty's secret entrance and he asks, "What's this?"

Episode 64, "The Offspring": In the Captain's quarters, after Picard answers Data's question about Admiral Halftel having children, Data replies, "I'm forced to wonder how much experience he had as a parent when his first child was born."

Episode 135, "The Quality of Life": Data clearly states, "The transporter controls are not malfunctioning. I've locked out the controls."

fluid over the years. The progress continues. The longer we go, the closer Data will become to being human without being human. Data likes to try on the clothes of other aspects of humanity. I've done Sherlock Holmes, Henry V, Friar Tuck, Scrooge. In one episode last year, I played the perfect mate, programming myself with all of the clichés and attributes of what Data would think would be the perfect male partner for a woman. Actually, Data could do very well at pickup bars."

Spiner has definite opinions as to which episodes worked best. "My favorite episodes featured Data," he told the Boston Con audience, "I loved a lot of the stuff early on. I loved 'Naked Now.' A lot of you didn't like it when it first came out because you didn't know the characters yet. But I think history has been kind to that. I liked 'The Offspring' a lot, for many reasons. I liked ''The Measure of a Man.' That was a great episode. I liked 'The Best of Both Worlds,' the two-part show. I think that was like the essence of *Star Trek*."

Spiner told the Grand Slam III audience that Jeri Taylor added to the high quality of the show. "Jeri is classy," he noted. "She's an incredibly smart and talented woman. She brought new life to the show when she came on. The sixth season, Jeri's debut season, when she literally produced our show, was the best season. She was very accessible to our suggestions. She wrote quite a few good scripts and she knew good writing when she read it. Ron [Moore] and Brannon [Braga] really shone that season, and Jeri had a lot to do with that."

Perhaps "A Fistful of Datas," in which he portrayed five characters, presented him with his greatest challenge. Spiner played three characters for "Brothers": Data, Data's evil twin Lore, and Noonian Soong, the man who created both androids. He told *TV Guide*,

"My initial impulse was to call upon the anger I once had toward my older brother, Ron. Ron had me convinced we'd had a middle brother he'd done away with. I was about five and Ron was about seven. My mother had just pulled out of the driveway to go somewhere, and he was telling me this story, with butcher knife in hand, about this older brother in a cave somewhere with a knife in his back. I swear my mother heard me screaming 10 miles away in her car."

Putting on and wearing the heavy makeup that transforms a very human actor into an alien android puts another burden on Spiner. "I was the first one to come to work, because of the makeup," he told the Boston Con audience. "My makeup took longer than Worf's did. I hated putting in those yellow contacts early in the morning because I couldn't take them out for the rest of the day. I kept them in the whole 16 hours or however long we were there because my hands were made up, and so I couldn't take them out at lunch and put them back in. They were as comfortable as could possibly be under the circumstances. They were soft, yellow prescription lenses that weren't my prescription."

He told the Canadian *TV Guide*, "It's a doubled-edged sword. It took about a year to get used to the contacts; for a long time it felt like I had Elvira's fingernails in my eyes. And it's a complete drag to sit in makeup for 75 minutes every morning. On the other hand, when you're in a scene with seven other cast members, viewers' eyes do tend to focus on the one who glows."

Spiner says he can't even scratch because his hands and face are covered with powder. Spiner uses a kerosene-based cleanser to remove the cosmetics. "I must swallow a gallon of kerosene a week. One day I suppose they'll find all my organs have been pickled." He also dyes his hair to maintain the look of his anemic-looking android character.

"The first day I [put on the makeup]," Spiner told the Boston Con audience, "it took one hour and fifteen minutes. The last day I did it, it was one hour and fifteen minutes. It never altered. Michael Westmore created the make-up, and he put it on me every single day. I would get there at 5:45 A.M., and spend an hour and fifteen minutes with Michael Westmore, which was great. He's a wonderful guy. It would just be the security guy and me and Michael in the Paramount lot in the morning. People would start filtering in at 7:00—Marina, then Gates would come in next. Dorn would come in to have his Worf stuff put on, and then Jonathan would come in five minutes before we rehearse, Patrick would come breezing in, and they would run a dry mop over his head."

Spiner's makeup hides the actor underneath. He's amused that the folks at *Entertainment Tonight* give his age wrong. "If you look at [*Entertainment Tonight*], they'll say 37 . . . I don't know where they got that number, but it's fine with me. I've had the benefit of being in this makeup and people trying to guess what I look like, how old I am, all that kind of stuff." (He was born February 2, 1949.)

"There's a pressure always—whether you're doing an interview or a talk show situation or on stage doing a convention—to be entertaining. I'm not sure that Brent at home alone is a very entertaining person," he told a convention audience.

Spiner told the *Orlando Sentinel*, "It's not a concern of mine that the fans know who I am because the me that I am, even at conventions or doing interviews or whatever, is not really me anyway."

Convention audiences often ask Spiner about Data's cat, Spot. Young viewers seem most interested. Spiner often gives less-than-serious answers, but then again, he always warns audiences, "I'm going to answer your questions as honestly as I can, but sometimes I'll be lying. There are two areas I'd like to stay away from: *Star Trek* and my personal life." A fan at the StarFest convention in Denver asked Spiner if Spot was really his cat. He replied, "No he's not. Spot isn't even a real cat. It's a small dog who plays the part brilliantly." He added that the first Spot had died and gone to Cat Heaven. "That cat couldn't act anyway. [The two new Spots] are two of the finest actors I have ever worked with."

He told the Grand Slam III audience, "Do I like cats as a species? I'm for them as domestic house pets, not as acting partners. As adorable as these cats are, they're not great actors, only because the writers write these cats as if they are human. They write lines like 'Data watches Spot sleep.' You can't say 'and action' and the cat lays down and goes to sleep. So any time the cat works, it's a long, long day. There are two of them. Brandy is the docile one and Monster the not-so-docile one. They are very nice cats. There has been only one line written in the entire history of the show that the cat was able to do on the first take, and that was 'Spot eats tuna from a bowl.'"

A fan at Boston Con insisted that Data sometimes used contractions, but Spiner

> *"I'm going to answer your questions as honestly as I can, but sometimes I'll be lying. There are two areas I'd like to stay away from: Star Trek and my personal life."*

denied it, insisting, "I can only think of one instance where Data used a contraction, and that was intentional. It was 'Datalore.' At the end, Captain Picard says, 'Are you all right, Data?' And Data was supposed to say, 'I am fine, Sir.' The director of that episode and I decided to play a little trick on the producers to see if they were watching the dailies, so I said, 'I'm fine,' thinking we'd fix it. They never noticed. At other times where you might think I'm using contractions, I'm actually not. It's just that I'm speaking quickly; it sounds like it, but that's the only real time I ever did that."

> "People have asked about being typecast in the role of Data; there just aren't that many good android parts out there."

While Spiner worked for *Star Trek: The Next Generation,* he also appeared as Preacher Mann in the film *Miss Firecracker,* in an uncredited role in *Crazy from the Heart,* as a computer system repair man in *Dream On,* and as Bob the agent in *Mad About You.* In 1990, he co-produced his first album, *Ol' Yellow Eyes is Back,* featuring popular classic standards—including one single, "It's a Sin to Tell a Lie"—with background vocals by "The Sunspots," made up of *TNG* co-stars Patrick Stewart, Jonathan Frakes, LeVar Burton, and Michael Dorn. In 1992, Spiner appeared with Patrick Stewart, Jonathan Frakes, Gates McFadden, and Colm Meaney in a four-city tour of the Tom Stoppard drama *Every Good Boy Deserves Favour.*

After the *Star Trek: The Next Generation* TV series ended in 1994, Spiner told the Grand Slam III audience, "I miss the people I worked with—not just the actors, who I continue to see, but the production people and the crew and the writers, and everybody on the show. I miss going onto the Paramount lot every day, which was a dream for me. Only Paramount and Disney still look like a movie studio. Walking on that lot in the morning past the dressing room buildings where Bing and Bob and all those guys were, and walking on the wood in the stage where *Rear Window* was shot.... We worked on Stages 8 and 9, and *Rear Window* was shot on Stage 9. *Duck Soup* by the Marx Brothers was shot on Stage 8. The stairway right behind my trailer was the stairway that William Holden came running down to meet Gloria Swanson in *Sunset Boulevard.* It was a dream come true, and I got chills every morning walking onto the lot.

"I miss it, but then again, we were working fourteen to seventeen hours a day for seven years and we were all exhausted. I was particularly exhausted. It's been nice to have a break, and come back every couple of years for a couple of months, instead of 10 months straight, although I miss a new show coming on every week."

The actors are friends off the set. They spend considerable time together. Spiner told Boston Con, "I had gone scuba diving during vacation, and I came back and said it was fantastic. Patrick [Stewart] said, 'I've always wanted to scuba dive,' so I said, 'Let's get certified together.' We started taking lessons together with all the equipment and all that, first in Patrick's pool. Patrick put on all the equipment and went down to the bottom of his pool first, then I came down with this knife... Since then, I never had opportunity. He's certified now, and I'm not."

Denying widely believed rumors, he also told them, "There were never practical jokes on the *Star Trek* set. People have said that, but it's not true. Everybody on the show was hilarious, but not with practical jokes. They were funny people. There were never any buckets of water over the turbo lift doors or anything like that." There were jokes off-set, though. He told the StarFest Denver audience that he impersonates co-star Denise's grandfather, Bing Crosby, when confronted with her accusation that he leaves weird messages on her answering machine.

Spiner told the Infinite Visions Convention that Patrick Stewart was slow to get into the silliness that pervaded the *Star Trek: The Next Generation* set (being a professional Shakespearean actor and all), but that when he came around he was among the silliest. When they filmed "Skin of Evil," in which Yar dies, they constructed a hillside set for Tasha's holographic good-bye. Stewart arrived first, and when the others followed, he stood on top of the hill bellowing, "The hills are alive with the sound of music . . ."

The Trek universe changed quickly. *Star Trek: Deep Space Nine* introduced new characters. *Star Trek: The Next Generation* left television to continue adventures of the *Enterprise* in feature films, beginning with *Star Trek: Generations* in 1994. *Voyager* introduced not only new characters and adventures, but a whole new space quadrant. Spiner told Grand Slam III, "I'm delighted *Voyager* is on. I think there's always going to be a *Star Trek* on the air. There's going to be a point when people stop talking about 'the spin-off' or 'Can lightning be captured in a bottle again?' It's the biggest epic in the history of show business, and I hope it goes on forever."

But is there life after *Star Trek: The Next Generation*? "What am I gonna do after *Star Trek: Generations*?" Spiner told Boston Con, "People have asked about being typecast in the role of Data; there just aren't that many good android parts out there. I feared on appoint-

ments I'd start to walk in the room and people would say, 'No, no, it's Data. He cannot do anything else.' That's not gonna happen because no producers or casting directors watched *Star Trek*. They'll say, 'So, what have you been doing? Tell us a little about yourself.' It's like I've been on vacation, which is better than being typecast. They don't have preconceived notions of me; I just do the audition, and get rejected."

He told Grand Slam III, "I much prefer to play comedy. It's too exhausting to play drama. You work yourself up into a state and you're in that state for the next few days. It's not worth it. I've told my agent, 'If it's not funny, I don't want to do it.' But I thought Data fit into that category. When I read the script initially, I saw Data as a comic character in the classical sense; he's not a tragic character."

Spiner also enjoys watching comedy in his free time. He told Boston Con, "I love Laurel and Hardy. As a matter of fact, I don't trust anyone who doesn't like Laurel and Hardy. I have a friend, a really close friend for years, who said to me, 'I don't get it.' Obviously we're not friends anymore. That was the best comedy there was, and I'm not the only one who has that opinion . . . Chaplin, and Laurel and Hardy. It never got better than that."

After the *Star Trek: The Next Generation* TV series ended in 1994, Spiner appeared as Witherspoon in *Corrina, Corrina* (1994), played a part in the *Deadly Games* TV series, had an uncredited role in the TV movie *Kingfish: A Story of Huey P. Long* (1995), and added the voice of Puck to the animated *Gargoyles*. Spiner's most recent non-Trek films are *Independence Day,* with Jeff Goldblum, and *Phenomenon,* with John Travolta. He joined Jeff Goldblum in dedicating one of Nevada's highways as the "Extraterrestrial Highway" when the state hoped to latch on to some of the UFO tourism market.

163

Spiner returned to the role of Data for *Star Trek: First Contact* (1996). He told *TV Guide* that he fears, "I'm getting too old for the part. He's a machine. How much can he age? Unfortunately, I'm getting older every day. They need a young android. Somebody they'll have a good 20 years with."

Lieutenant Commander NFN NMI Data

No one knows when Lieutenant Commander NFN NMI Data ("No First Name, No Middle Initial") was first activated, but the crew of the *U.S.S. Tripoli* found him at the destroyed Omicron Theta Colony. The android was near the site, deactivated, and programmed with all the knowledge and memories of the lost colonists—except for the memory of what killed them. At the time, Data had no memories of his own.

Data chose to emulate his rescuers and follow a career in Starfleet, entering Starfleet Academy in 2341 and graduating in 2345. He excelled in the entry tests and never received a mark against his performance. He has been second officer and chief of operations aboard the *Enterprise* 1701-D since 2363.

Data was created by Dr. Noonian Soong. Data's brain is so sophisticated that he is regarded as a sentient lifeform. He paints, plays the violin, acts, and cares for Spot, his cat. Data regretted his inability to feel emotion and understand jokes until he added an emotion chip made by Dr. Noonian Soong and recovered from Lore, Data's evil twin. His loyalty and actions toward others would qualify him as an exemplary human being. Data even had a brief intimate relationship with Tasha shortly after the Farpoint mission. Data's internal program updates itself. The more Data is around humans, the more he learns from them.

Data was built to look like a male human—except that he possesses superhuman strength and his head can be separated from his body. Data breathes air, but only to refrigerate his subsystems, and he can stop breathing for long periods of time. Data eats to lubricate his internal systems. Energy is generated by the decay of a small quantity of the radioactive isotope strontium 90, and is distributed through a direct flow of charged electrons in a nutrient fluid similar to human hemoglobin

Data's brain is a neural network composed of simple "nodes," roughly analogous to neurons. Nodes are arranged in layers, each with several inputs from other layers and outputs to other layers. Each input is an influence rather than a straightforward "yes" or "no." Inputs can differ. The sum of the inputs triggers action when they exceed a threshold. The output is combined with other node outputs to become the input to other nodes. A neural net learns by adjusting the thresholds of each node, and rerouting interconnections between nodes. Data has an ultimate storage capacity of 800 quadrillion bits. His total linear computational speed has been rated at 60 trillion operations per second.

Sensory inputs include sight, hearing, and touch, but not smell and taste, although he has some basic taste faculty. Data's eyes are superior to human eyes, and have the ability to magnify. Data also has a range of nonhuman sensors to monitor temperature, radiation, magnetic fields, etc. Information is stored in his brain.

"Playing Worf has been an incredible opportunity for me as an actor. The challenge has been having to overcome the makeup and physical barriers of this role, to develop a strong and forthright character."

—Michael Dorn

Michael Dorn

Michael Dorn was born to play a role in *Star Trek*. Perhaps he was destined to be a Klingon. Born in Luling, Texas, on December 9, 1952, Dorn was already a "Trekkie" by the time he graduated from high school in Pasadena, California. Eventually, the TV series would consume his professional life more than it did that of any other actor in any Trek series.

Dorn performed in a rock band during high school and college. He moved to San Francisco in 1973, worked at a variety of jobs, and soon returned to L.A. where he continued to play in rock bands. Shortly after his return, his friend's father, an assistant director of *The Mary Tyler Moore Show*, suggested he switch to acting. He first appeared on TV in the background, as a newswriter in episodes of *The Mary Tyler Moore Show*. "I had done a little modeling by this time and had studied drama and TV producing in college," Dorn later recalled. "Once I started, I caught the bug."

He then guest-starred on *W.E.B.,* a show based on the hit film *Network*. The producer introduced him to an agent, and Dorn began studying with Charles Conrad. Six months later, he landed a job as Officer Turner in *CHIPs,* a role he played for three years (1980–1982). "I love doing cop roles, and as a highway patrolman I got to drive fast and never got hurt," Dorn said. He also appeared in bit parts for the films *Demon Seed* (1977) and *Rocky II* (1979).

Dorn resumed acting classes after *CHIPs* ended. Small parts kept him working—*Room 227, Amanda and the Alien, Charles in Charge, Falcon Crest, Getting By, Hotel, Hunter, Knots Landing, Parker Lewis Can't Lose,* and *Webster* on television, and as Dan Hislan in the film *Jagged Edge* (1985). Dorn said, "I worked very hard; the jobs started coming and the roles got meatier." He played recurring roles in *Days of Our Lives* and *Capitol.*

Star Trek: The Next Generation followed in 1987. The part of the *Enterprise*'s Klingon, Lieutenant Worf, first won Dorn public recognition. "[The role] was a dream come true," Dorn recalled. "First, because I'm a Trekkie, and second, I'm playing a Klingon, a character so totally different from the nice-guy roles I'd done in the past. Worf is the only Klingon aboard the *Enterprise.* That makes him an outsider, but that's okay by me because Worf knows he's superior to these weak humans. But he never lets the other crew members see that, because he's a soldier first and second."

Dorn praised series creator Gene Roddenberry for having the "genius and vision" to depict an optimistic future in which a peaceful alliance could be struck between Earth and the Klingon Empire. "Gene believed there is good in everybody—even Klingons!"

Dorn said, "Playing Worf has been an incredible opportunity for me as an actor. The challenge has been having to overcome the makeup and physical barriers of this role, to develop a strong and forthright character." The producers gave him freedom to evolve the

165

Worf character. He said most of the Worf you see now is his.

He only had one major complaint about his seven Trek years, he told the Grand Slam III convention audience. "I really hated it when I heard the writers and producers using sentences that started with 'wouldn't it be cute if?' For example, 'Wouldn't it be cute if we put Worf up to his neck in a mud bath?' or 'Wouldn't it be cute if we dunked Worf in the ocean?'"

Dorn pursued a dream during the show's first-season hiatus: he took flying lessons and earned his pilot's license. Since then, he has flown with the Blue Angels and participated in the flight maneuvers of an F-16 with the USAF Precision Flight team. He currently owns several aircraft.

Dorn spoke before the Oklahoma City chapter meeting of the Tuskegee Airmen. He later told AP he couldn't understand the discrimination that kept black fighter pilots on the ground for half of World War II. "I've been through a bit of racism," Dorn noted, "but nothing like this, where you put yourself in a position to take all of that abuse." Forced to admit blacks in 1941, the Army Air Corps formed the all-black fighter-pilot squads but never intended to let them fly. When the pilots finally got a chance in 1943, they turned out to be the best the Army produced. Dorn praised the airmen, who got their name because they trained near Tuskegee Institute in Alabama. Dorn added, "This group gives people a sense of what the country was like, what the human spirit can do."

After completing production on the fourth season of *Star Trek: The Next Generation*, Dorn donned another Klingon guise, that of Lt. Worf's grandfather, a "Klingon Defense Attorney" in the film *Star Trek VI: The Undiscovered Country* (1991). The role made him the first *Star Trek: The Next Generation* cast member to work with the original series cast in a *Star Trek* feature.

Dorn designed a new Worf hairdo for the sixth season of *Star Trek: The Next Generation*. He called it "funky and interesting." During that season, he also guest-starred opposite Thelma Hopkins and Cindy Williams in ABC's *Getting By.* Dorn grew a beard for season seven so he wouldn't have to glue one on every day; Klingons are proud of their beards.

Dorn wasn't ready to leave his role as Worf when *Star Trek: The Next Generation* ended in 1994 after season seven. "When the show was ending, I was 'Mr. Denial'," he told Grand Slam III, "I was going around saying, 'It's just a job. I'm moving on.' During the poker game scene at the very end of 'All Good Things,' we all spontaneously held hands and just looked at each other saying, 'Oh no, it's the last shot.' When the director, Rick Kolbe, hugged me good-bye, I just started crying with the full Klingon makeup on."

At first, he looked for other roles, telling the *Charlotte Observer,* "I'm not sure if it's a matter of life after Trek or life after any series that ran seven years. I just wanted to get back out there quickly and show my face . . . show that I could play more than a Klingon." That proved harder than he had expected. He supplied a voice for the animated *Gargoyles* and met a kid who sells Trek toys as a guest on *Parker Lewis Can't Lose.* The kid tries to sell

> **Dorn was already a "Trekkie" by the time he graduated from high school in Pasadena.**

him an "original" model of the *Enterprise,* but Dorn asks the kid, "But how do I know it has the original photon torpedoes?" Of the entire *Star Trek: The Next Generation* cast, Dorn is the only one who hasn't done theater.

Dorn returned to the role of Worf for *Star Trek: Generations* immediately after the television series left the air, but he was unhappy with the result. He told the *Charlotte Observer,* "It wasn't what I'd call a *Next Generation* movie, because it didn't involve the crew as we'd come to know them. Worf had nothing to do, and the sequence where he gets promoted was a gag. It was really about Kirk and Picard meeting, and that was tough to accept." Less than one year later, Dorn joined the cast of the weekly television series *Star Trek: Deep Space Nine*—the only ongoing member of the *Enterprise* crew to do so. Paramount sent out the following press release:

MICHAEL DORN JOINS DEEP SPACE NINE

The Klingons Are Back!

In an unprecedented move, Michael Dorn of Star Trek: The Next Generation *will reprise his Klingon role as Lieutenant Commander Worf on* Star Trek: Deep Space Nine *as a member of the ensemble cast. The two-hour fourth season premiere of* Star Trek: Deep Space Nine *marks the introduction of Worf to the top-rated, first-run syndicated series. The show begins production on Tuesday, July 11, 1995.*

As the Dominion threat to the Alpha Quadrant increases, the peace treaty between the Klingon Empire and the Federation is in jeopardy. Captain Sisko (Avery Brooks) has requested that Lieutenant Commander Worf come to act as a diplomatic liaison with the Klingons.

Under the headline, "WORF EMBARKS ON 'DEEP SPACE' VOYAGE," the industry trade paper *Variety* reported, "Dorn is pleased Worf will be taking center stage on *Star Trek: Deep Space Nine.* His screen time in the *Generations* movie was limited, and on the *Next Generation* series, he got only a few episodes a season in which to shine. With *Star Trek: Deep Space Nine*'s Klingon story line, he'll be an integral part of each show. 'As an actor, even with all the makeup, something like that is hard to pass up,' he says.'"

Berman had told *Variety,* "We got the feeling in the last year that *The Next Generation* viewers had stopped watching *Star Trek: Deep Space Nine.* We needed to get viewers to resample the show, and we thought having the Klingons back would do the trick." In addition to the TV series, Dorn returned Worf to the *Star Trek: The Next Generation* team for the film *Star Trek: First Contact* (1996).

Dorn performed a few other roles as well, appearing as himself to host *The Future Is Now: The Sci-Fi Channel Preview;* as the enigmatic Chairman, creator of a powerful virtual-reality game, co-starring with Duncan Regehr and Pat Morita in the film *Timemaster* (1995); as Vint, a police detective in search of an alien, in Showtime's *Amanda & the Alien* (1995); and as an astronaut who lands on Mars in "The Voyage Home" episode of Showtime's *The Outer Limits.*

Dorn hopes eventually to direct, but for now, he said, "I want to take one step at a time and do the best work I can do." He's still interested in rock music, plays in a band, does studio work as a bass player, and writes music in his spare time. Mostly, though, Dorn continues to bring his Klingon Worf to life. Dorn once told the *Baltimore Evening Sun,* "I looked around at all these people [the original *Star*

167

Trek cast] and said, 'They've been doing this 25 years.' And then I thought, 'Twenty-five years as Worf? It's going to be a little rough.'"

Lieutenant Commander Worf

Lieutenant Commander Worf, Chief of Security of *Enterprise* NCC-1701-D since 2364, is the only Klingon officer to serve on a Starfleet ship. Worf was born on December 9, 2340, in the city of Qo'noS on the Klingon homeworld, and graduated from Starfleet Academy in 2361. He was named after his grandfather.

A Romulan attack on the Klingon outpost of Khitomer killed Worf's family, including his father, Mogh, soon after the alliance between the Federation and the Klingon empire was formed. Sergey and Helena Rozhenko, Slavic humans from the planet Gault, raised Worf. Sergey had been a member of the *U.S.S. Intrepid*'s rescue team. Sergey and Helena have another son, Simon.

Worf grew up under the shadow of the belief that his father, Mogh, had betrayed Khitomer. The traitor was in fact, however, a member of the powerful Duras family; the Klingon High Council had avoided disruption by altering the records and blaming Worf's father. They did not believe that Worf kept Klingon ways or would learn of this dishonor. They were also unaware that he had a younger brother, *Enterprise* exchange officer Commander Kurn, who had been adopted by a family friend when Worf and his parents went to Khitomer.

Kurn eventually learned of his true heritage and of his father's dishonor, and told Worf that he must challenge the Klingon High Council's accusation. In the ensuing clash of wills with K'mpec, the chair of the High

Council, Worf accepted "discommodation" (being cast out) to save Kurn's life, in hopes that Kurn or his children would eventually restore Mogh's honor.

Later, Captain Picard was called in to arbitrate a leadership dispute; Duras was vying

Guinan

The left-handed hostess of the Ten-Forward Lounge offers more questions than answers. Borg destroyed her homeworld, scattering a few survivors around the galaxy. Her people normally had very long lifespans, and she is believed to be over 700 years old.

Her father taught her to learn from the great thinkers of 19th-century Earth. Guinan avoided racial prejudice by living in San Francisco, where she entertained many great thinkers of the time and gained a firsthand education from legendary wordsmiths such as Samuel Clemens. Some say she worked as an actress and comedienne in the late 20th century.

She returned home to bond with a female friend, Delcara, whose planet had been destroyed by Borg. When the Borg killed her second family, Delcara went mad with revenge until a monstrous combination of Ferengi and Borg killed her. Her spirit lived on without her body, caught in an infinite time-loop.

Guinan is a mother. One son has found trouble near Bajoran space.

Guinan didn't know Picard before boarding the *Enterprise*, but she had met him 500 years before in San Francisco, as a result of a time-travel experience he had. In one episode, Picard got Guinan out of serious trouble, bonding them for life. He invited her to serve as hostess on the *Enterprise*.

Most crew members see Guinan as the 24th-century equivalent of a classic bartender. She not only serves the right variety of synthehol, but also lends a caring ear and humane wisdom when it is needed.

with outsider Gowron for the throne of K'm-pec, who was dying. In the ensuing skirmish, Duras killed Worf's former lover, K'Ehleyr, and Worf killed Duras in revenge.

Later, Worf learned of a secret Romulan prison camp where Klingons were being held. The Klingons told him that they had been knocked unconscious and never given the opportunity to die. The Klingon High Council would not acknowledge their existence, so they stayed in the prison camp rather than dishonor their families. Worf began educating the children of the camp, teaching meditation exercises, explaining old artifacts, and telling Klingon legends. He ultimately left the camp with some of the children on a Romulan supply ship and reunited with the *Enterprise*.

At one point, Worf's foster parents visited him on the *Enterprise*. They discussed concerns about Worf with Guinan, who told them they had done a wonderful job, and that he really does care for them. Sergey and Helena told Worf that, despite his discommendation, he is not alone, and that they are proud of him and love him.

Although raised by humans, and third in command aboard a Federation starship, Worf remains very much a Klingon. He wears a beard because Klingons are proud of beards.

He is aggressive by nature, and wants to confront menaces head on, but he has learned to control his anger even when provoked. He practices a form of *Tai Chi*. Worf takes honor and duty seriously, and once asked Commander Riker to help him commit suicide after a debilitating accident.

Worf rarely talks about himself or his culture. Riker persuaded Worf to talk about Klingon sexual attitudes once when Worf failed to enjoy the pleasures offered by the sybaritic Edo. Worf explained that only Klingon women could survive sex with a Klingon man.

> *Worf grew up under the shadow of the belief that his father, Mogh, had betrayed Khitomer.*

Klingons do not feel comfortable with humans, and often a faction advocates improved relations with Romulans. Though Klingons hate Romulans, they understand them better than humans. Worf occupies a unique position between the two cultures. As the only Klingon in Starfleet, he may one day be a key factor in Klingon-Federation relations.

169

"It's always told to me that Crusher is a mother and this is the way it is, and I always say, 'Wait a minute, Jane Seymour is a mother, and she is beautiful.' I wish that the character could occasionally loosen up outside of the operating room."

—Cheryl Gates McFadden

Cheryl Gates McFadden

A mystery surrounds the birth date of Cheryl Gates McFadden ("Gates" is her mother's maiden name). Although "officially" listed as born August 26, 1953, the *Star Trek* guide gives her birth date as August 28, 1953; Gunthers Internet home page on Gates McFadden reports it as being March 2, 1953; while the *Official Star Trek: The Next Generation Poster Magazine* Issue 27 claims that it is August 28, 1949. As it turns out, when someone first asked her for her date of birth, she wasn't keen on people knowing, so she made one up. March 2 is the date she confirmed at the *Star Trek: Generations* Convention in Sydney in March of 1995. Jessica Levine at Brandeis University believes that 1949 is the correct year based on her graduation date. The best guess, then, would be March 2, 1949.

McFadden grew up in Cuyahoga Falls, Ohio, but she says that that her hometown is different now than it was then. "Even the physical layout of the town is different. The school I went to is no longer a high school; it's an elementary school. The elementary school I went to was a private school and now it's a city school. Silverlake Village, where I spent a lot of time, is very much the same. The lake's still there, and I'm sure they still have a Strawberry Festival in August, or whenever it was. There's all sorts of budding prepubescent love going on, holding hands. I remember all that. But the town's different. Shopping malls have changed a lot of this country. Everything's so generic."

When she lived in the Cuyahoga Falls of memory, McFadden trained to be a dancer. She recalled, "I had extraordinary teachers; one was primarily a ballerina and the other had been in a circus. I grew up thinking most ballerinas knew how to ride the unicycle, tap dance, and do handsprings. Consequently, I was an oddball to other dancers."

She told a Trekon audience in Kansas City, "I began performing as a young child. I started dancing school when I was about two and a half or three years old. We would have a little recital. I took that very seriously. I would do that for hours every day after school. When I was eight, I started taking acting lessons with the local theater, the Coachhouse Theater. I played a couple of parts. I never got the lead parts or supporting roles, but I got the comic supporting roles. It's okay if you don't get the lead gal roles, so long as you get the comedy roles. That's really what happened for me. I got a lot of those roles and did a lot of things, majored in [acting] in school, and there you are . . . I am still looking for a job.

"When I was ten, my brother and I attended back-to-back Shakespeare for eight days in a musty, nearly empty theater. There were 12 actors who played all the parts. I couldn't get over it—the same people in costumes every day, but playing new characters. It was like visiting somewhere but never wanting to leave."

McFadden earned her B.A. *cum laude* in Theatre Arts from Brandeis University, then studied with Jacques LeCoq in Paris. "I attended his first workshop in the United States," she said. "His theatrical vision and the breadth of its scope were astonishing. I left for Paris as soon as possible to continue to study acting with LeCoq at his school. We worked constantly in juxtapositions. We once explored immobility in order to better understand movement. We explored silence in order to better understand sound and language. It was theatrical research involving many mediums.

"Just living in a foreign country, where you have to speak and think in another language, cracks your head open. It was both terrifying and freeing. Suddenly I was taking more risks in my acting. Learning to think in another language allows you to see your own culture in a better viewpoint. The whole experience of going away, not having much money, having to make my way in this new world that was so beautiful and had so much history, was quite profound. Any time you spend time in another culture, it's not just a matter of visiting the museums, taking a quick week vacation or something—that can be wonderful too—but to actually communicate, spend the time, that can be quite wonderful.

"The people who were in my classes were from all over the world. There were many, many languages and all of us spoke French in order to communicate. I had learned French in school, but I was dumbfounded when I first got there. I got off the plane and they all spoke so fast, and it was so different! But after two months, I was doing great. You just need to calm down and not panic. I kept doing things like asking for an undertaker, but other than that I made it along. It was really a big deal when I came back. People in my hometown didn't know what a croissant was. You just didn't hear about them."

The New York–based stage, mime, dance, and improvisation veteran played lead roles in many New York productions, including Mary Gallagher's *How to Say Good-bye* and Caryl Churchill's *Cloud 9*. She also appeared at California's La Jolla Playhouse in *The Matchmaker* with Linda Hunt and in *The Emerald City* by David Williamson.

Her first feature film role was in *The Muppets Take Manhattan,* as Mr. Price's secretary. She continued to work with Jim Henson for several years. McFadden assisted Gavin Miller in staging fantasy sequences, and served as choreographer for *Dreamchild* (1985), then as choreographer and director of puppet movement for *Labyrinth* (1986). "Those films were my baptism-by-fire into the world of special effects and computerized props," she later recalled.

McFadden made guest appearances in the TV series *Another World, All My Children,* and *The Wizard,* and played roles in the films *When Nature Calls* (1985) and *Rustlers' Rhapsody* (1985), before moving on to *Star Trek: The Next Generation.* She stayed with *TNG* for six of its seven years, 1987 to 1988, then 1989 to 1994. McFadden played Dr. Beverly Crusher, a troubled but very important role. "I have often felt straight-jacketed," she once told a Trekon audience. "They say, 'Go ahead and make it more yourself,' but the minute any behavior's really tried, it's like no hair can be out of place. Certainly, with the tap-dancing thing, I tried to

> *"I grew up thinking most ballerinas knew how to ride the unicycle, tap dance, and do handsprings."*

get some of that in. It's always told to me that Crusher is a mother and this is the way it is, and I always say, 'Wait a minute, Jane Seymour is a mother, and she is beautiful.' I wish that the character could occasionally loosen up outside of the operating room.

"There are wonderful things about the character that I have tried to develop, and I can just hope that that part comes across. I like the humanism. Health care is very difficult. Having been in a hospital myself, in an emergency room after a skiing accident—with the tubes and thinking you are going to die and in horrible pain—somebody who treats you nicely and compassionately makes all the difference. I have at least tried to make her do that, to be somebody that puts a hand on the patient. I tried to get away from just doing a hypospray.

"I had modeled my character after the man who wrote *Awakenings*. He's written a lot of books, including *The Man Who Mistook His Wife for a Hat*. I had read all of his books published up to that point. I brought all of his material into the producer's office the first day. I said, 'This is the guy. He is a neurologist, a humanist; he's funny.' I even showed them *Awakenings*."

Television viewers react to McFadden's character, Dr. Crusher, in very different ways. She told *TV Guide* that some see the *Enterprise*'s doctor as a role model. A doctor getting ready to start her own practice considered Dr. Crusher so inspirational that she wrote and requested a picture to hang in her office. Other viewers take a more prurient interest. McFadden receives correspondence from convicts, asking, "Please send me a picture, but not the one of you in your uniform. Do you have any 8x10s of you in your panties?"

Some episodes are harder to perform than others. McFadden told the Trekon audience,

"'The Host' was real interesting because I was hugely pregnant. It was right before I gave birth, and that was the first love episode I had. They shot it so you could not tell how huge I was, because I was big. Trust me. There were a lot of scenes of me behind furniture. A lot of close-ups of me in big, big lab coats. 'Remember Me' was difficult because I had very little time to learn the script, and it was only me shooting for a whole day.

"Some of the more difficult things are when I have operations and I have a lot of props and complicated sets. There are a couple that I can think of. 'Cause and Effect' was hard to do because the lines were slightly different, and you shoot all of those four scenes, one after another. We were wild by the time that poker game was done. There was a lot of pressure on that one because it was a hand-held camera. Jonathan is a great guy, and a great director. He is my favorite director. The operation in 'Ethics' was difficult because there are many people in the room and it is shot in a very strange way. I make up most of the 'business' on the way.

> *"Just living in a foreign country, where you have to speak and think in another language, cracks your head open."*

"In a theater production, you can have a week to work on props. LeVar and I have the props. He and I do the prop acting on our show. Some things were difficult to work with. I always felt it was kinda weird being on the Away Team and having this medical kit that if I happen to lose my grip the whole kit would fall out on the planet. I did have some input in the design of the new one, though it did not happen the way I had envisioned. The props are very expensive. I am usually given tremendous choice in what instrument I want to use."

McFadden left *Star Trek: The Next Generation* after the first season. When asked at Trekon, "What were you doing while Dr. Pulaski was replacing your part?" McFadden replied, "Replacing me? You mean trying to replace me? I was in New York City, doing a play—playing an Australian. I also did *The Hunt for Red October* [she played Caroline Ryan, the wife of the main character, a part that was later cut]. I taught a third-year graduate seminar at New York University."

She returned to *Star Trek: The Next Generation* at the start of the third season, wearing a wig so she wouldn't have to fuss with her hair each morning, but stopped wearing it midway through season six. During the third season, she also played in *Beyond the Groove*, a British television production written by and starring the late actor David Rappaport; the film *Taking Care of Business* (1991), as Diane, alongside John deLancie, Charles Grodin, and Jim Belushi; and the world premiere in Los Angeles of Derek Walcott's play, *Viva Detroit*. "I would love to do movies," McFadden told Trekon. "I got a movie and the producers were terrific about letting me off to do other things. They let me off and it was all set and then the movie company changed the shooting date, and Paramount could not accommodate that because that was [during an] episode I was heavy in. So I lost the movie. It was disappointing. Then I did *Taking Care of Business*. That was very funny because I did not know John deLancie was in the movie as my underling until the first day of shooting. We had a great time. We are good friends. He's got a terrific family, a terrific little boy. He is a great family man."

During the sixth season of *Star Trek: The Next Generation*, she went on tour with fellow *TNG* cast members Patrick Stewart, Jonathan Frakes, Brent Spiner, and Colm Meaney in Tom Stoppard's *Every Good Boy Deserves Favour*. She also acted in HBO's *Dream On*, and as the narrator for Saint-Saens' *Carnival des Animaux*, with Katia and Marielle Labeque and the Cleveland Symphony Orchestra under the direction of Leonard Slatkin.

McFadden became the second woman director in *Star Trek* history with "Genesis." "We have had only one woman director on our show, and that is pretty unusual," she told Trekon. "Most shows now have many women directors. *L.A. Law* has an enormous amount of women directors. The show I did, *Dream On*, is predominantly women directors. So it is very unusual that there has only been one woman director."

She told *Sci-Fi/Fantasy*, "I'm wildly excited. It was seven years ago—at the start of the first season—that I asked if I could direct, and it's finally happening. The possibilities are tremendous. Every night in bed, I keep seeing these shots I want to do."

McFadden's experience under the tutelage of Jim Henson served her well, although there were unexpected complications. Those who labored under her direction felt the earth move. "The [Los Angeles] earthquake hit right in the middle of [production]," McFadden told the *Charlotte Observer*. "I was getting ready for work when it happened. I was fortunate, but many people on the crew weren't. There was a tremendous amount of loss for some people. I hope the episode is successful and that people respond to it. It's absolutely the culmination of my *Star Trek* experience."

Star Trek: Deep Space Nine hit the airwaves before *Star Trek: The Next Generation* left television to become a series of films. The producers planned for it to inherit the mantle. McFadden said, "All I have are positive things to say about *Deep Space Nine,* unless it starts to affect us in a bad way. The energy is very much 'over there.' I like all of the people I have met in the show. I think they are great. I did not get to watch the pilot; I was in Europe. I think it makes a lot of sense that they wanted to have a spin-off series. If I were a producer, I would probably want to do the same thing."

The *Star Trek: The Next Generation* television series ended in 1994, at the height of its popularity. *Star Trek: Generations* (1994) appeared in theaters soon after. *Star Trek: First Contact* follows in 1996. McFadden reprised Dr. Beverly Crusher for both films. During this time, McFadden also appeared in Stravinsky's *L'Histoire du Soldat,* playing the devil under the direction of Kent Nagano at the La Jolla Chamber Music Festival; in her *Marker* TV series on the United Paramount Network (dropped after one season); and as a semi-regular, the boss of the male lead character, in *Mad About You.* She performed for an audiobook of *Star Trek: The Next Generation: Reunion* and *Star Trek: The Next Generation: The Devil's Heart,* and even had a piece of music named after her: "Lady McFadden," track 14 on *Star Trek: The Next Generation Soundtrack Volume 3.*

It keeps her busy. She likes that. The workaholic still lives in New York City and drives a Capri station wagon. She wants to continue directing, perhaps for *Star Trek: Deep Space Nine* or *Star Trek: Voyager,* freelances as an interior designer (though not for the money), and is an avid gardener. She also dabbles in drawing and sculpture, likes theater, admires the work of Vanessa Redgrave, and is a fan of old movies and continental cinema, particularly *Les Enfants de Paradis.* She will

probably teach again, having already served on the faculties of New York University Graduate School of the Arts, Brandeis University, and the University of Pittsburgh.

"Years ago, I did not want to do television," McFadden told Trekon, "because it was impossible to do films if you were doing television. I don't think that is true now. I know that my greatest love is theater; it probably always will be. I also know that there are a million other things that I would like to study and do in my life. I feel like it just turned out this way, and acting is such an extraordinary profession and craft. I would also like to study painting more, and I would love to be able to write and would love to be able to draw houses and be an architect. I would love to be a poet. My grandmother was a poet. There are a million things.

"I absolutely know I am going to teach again. I miss teaching very much. It is something that gave me a great deal of satisfaction. I learned every day. My students were so good that they taught me every single day. I feel that education is in such sad condition in our country, we really need to turn our attention to that and health care. I know, being a person who is paid better than the average person, that my tax rate is going to go up. That's the way it has to be, so be it. I have seen what can happen when children are given the love and attention and are excited about learning. They don't have to have high SAT scores. If they are excited about learning, they will do well in the world. And that is important and it has to come first from the home. It has to come first from the parents. Since I am a parent now, it is amazing how much I worry about protecting my son.

"When I was young, it was very exciting to have a thought that we can change the world if we all collaborate. We all have responsibilities to different things, whatever we choose in our lives. I feel responsible to my family and also many other things and people in my life. You start to think, how much do I want to do as an individual? How are you going to live your life? I don't have a short answer. That thought informs the way I live my life. What is my responsibility as a citizen, as an actress, as a mother, and on and on? I don't do nearly as much as I could. It's very hard.

"Life is so fast these days, and we're exposed to so much information. Television makes us a witness to such misery. Also you're a witness if you're driving in certain areas, walking in certain areas. It can be next door. It's hard to actually take action. It's much easier to talk about it. I have done a lot of talking about it and not much action, so I feel remiss in that. My responsibilities to my job and to my family take just about all of the time available.

"I have the greatest little boy. He's fabulous. I would love to have a little girl someday. I think children are great. He's the greatest thing in our lives. His name is James Cleveland McFadden Talbert. We call him 'Jack.' Don't ask why. We don't know. There is no reason. Nobody can figure it out. The kid is probably going to call himself Randolph or something. He's growing up so fast."

Dr. Beverly Crusher

Beverly was married to Jack Crusher in 2348, and their son, Wesley, was born one year later. Jack perished in 2354 while serving under Captain Picard aboard the *U.S.S. Stargazer.* Jack died saving Picard's life. Picard accompanied the body back to the officer's widow on Earth, to show his respect for the man. Beverly knew that it wasn't logical to blame Picard, but still associated him with her loss.

In 2364, Beverly and Wesley joined the crew of the *Enterprise* at Farpoint Station. Picard offered to have her transferred, but she declined; she had requested the position serving with him. Initial misgivings gave way to mutual respect, and she continues to hold the rank of Commander and the rating of Chief Medical Officer. A starship's chief medical officer is the only force capable of removing a starship captain from his or her post other than a court martial.

Beverly was born on August 28, 2323 in Copernicus City, Luna, the daughter of Paul and Isabel Howard. She grew up there and on Aveda Three, where her grandmother lived. Beverly entered Starfleet Medical School in 2342, and graduated from Starfleet Academy in 2350. She was first assigned to the *U.S.S. Hood* as chief medical officer before joining the *Enterprise* crew. Beverly later served as head of Starfleet Medical for one year before returning to the *Enterprise.*

Beverly has a talent for healing, a thorough medical education, and years of experience. Her most difficult moments involve her son, Wesley, such as when he was sentenced to death but saved by Picard. Wesley also narrowly escaped death in a training exercise off Saturn, but another cadet died. Wesley later

> *Beverly knew that it wasn't logical to blame Picard, but still associated him with her loss.*

admitted participating in a cover-up, was humiliated in front of his Starfleet Academy peers, and was forced to repeat his final year.

Beverly has faced other crises. She recently found romance with a humanoid alien, only to have it shattered by bizarre secrets. Another entity possessed her mind and caused Beverly to resign from Starfleet and live on a colony. And, while passing through an energy cloud, an intelligence took over Worf, Beverly, Assistant Chief Engineer Singh, and Captain Picard.

Beverly is now interested in Picard, no longer harboring resentment over her husband's death. She hasn't escaped the notice of Captain Picard, but they both know the problems that arise when key personnel become involved with each other.

"While I was looking at the script, director Cory Allen came in and said, 'you have something personally that the character should have—an empathy—so use it.' I love being able to play someone who is so deep, with that kind of insight into people, particularly since I get cast as the hard 1980s type."

—Marina Sirtis

Marina Sirtis

Marina Sirtis' new husband, rock musician Michael Lamper, hates the scenes in which Troi has a romantic encounter. He tells her, "You're too good. That looks real!" Her strict Greek immigrant parents would agree. Her tailor father and dressmaker mother had difficulty accepting her desire to become an actress, although her mother recalled that when she was three, "[Marina] used to stand up on the seat of the bus and sing to the other passengers."

Sirtis was born on March 29, 1959, in East London, England, but grew up with her younger brother in North London. Her quick wit and winning personality made her "the leader of the pack" despite her looking "on the plain side." She first appeared on stage in a student production at age sixteen, then studied at the Guild Hall School of Music and Drama for three years. She immersed herself in the London theater scene and became a member of the Worthing Repertory Theatre. Sirtis portrayed Ophelia in *Hamlet* shortly after graduation, among other classical roles. She appeared on British television, and toured with musical theater and repertory companies throughout England and Europe, including the *Rocky Horror Show* European tour.

> "[Marina] used to stand up on the seat of the bus and sing to the other passengers."

Sirtis' first film was a TV movie, *The Thief of Baghdad* (1978). In that movie, there was a scene in which Rodney McDowell said to her, "Feed me a kumquat." Sirtis had no idea what a kumquat was. The only edible-looking thing she could find was a grape, so she handed him a grape. He said, "That's a grape, stupid!" She asked, "Well, okay, what's a kumquat?"

Sirtis continued to work in films, including a part as Jackson's Girl in *The Wicked Lady* (1983) with Faye Dunaway. "Working with Dunaway was like working with the Queen of England," Sirtis remembered. She also played a hooker in *Blind Date* (1984) and the part of Maria in *Death Wish 3* (1985), alongside Charles Bronson, before moving to Los Angeles in November of 1986. She found her first job as Lucrezia in *The Return of Sherlock Holmes* TV series within a week, then signed on for the role of Counselor Deanna Troi in *Star Trek: The Next Generation* six months later. She later said, "It's taken me years to become an overnight success. I had a six-month visa, which was quickly running out. In fact, I got the call telling me I had the part only hours before I was to leave for the airport to return home."

Sirtis first auditioned for the role of Tasha Yar, the *Enterprise*'s Security Chief. "After my third audition for Tasha, I was literally walking out the door when they called me back to read for Deanna," she said. "While I was looking at the script, director Cory Allen came in and said, 'You have something personally that the character should have—an empathy—so use it.' I love being able to play someone who is so deep, with that kind of insight into people, particularly since I get cast as the hard 1980s type." Despite her role, Marina has never had a class in psychology. She did subscribe to *Psychology Today,* however.

"Deanna is a very wise person with extensive knowledge of philosophy, psychology, and different religions, and is called on to advise Captain Picard in a variety of situations," Sirtis said. She calls Troi's original hairdo the "Country and Western hairdo," and personally created the distinctive accent. "In the 24th century, geographical or nationalistic barriers are not so evident. The Earth as a planet is your country, your nationality. I didn't want anyone to be able to pin down my accent to any particular country, and being good at accents, the producers trusted me to come up with something appropriate."

She was a little scared after the pilot episode, wondering, "Why do I still have a job?" Sirtis later became more content with her work. "My favorite episode is 'Face of the Enemy' because it was not a 'girlie' episode," she recalled. "Any one of the crew could have been transformed into a Romulan. Troi was chosen because she was an empath, not because she was female." It was also the season's highest-rated episode.

Her favorite character on the show is Data. She feels her best episode is "The Child," and her favorites are "The Face of the Enemy" and "A Fistful of Datas." "My regret is when they made me captain for a day, I was disappointed that [Troi] didn't know what she was doing. She is supposed to be a lieutenant commander who went to the Academy. Where was she during the technical classes?"

Sirtis told a Creation Con audience that she did her own stunts for "Power Play," saying, "When they asked me if I wanted to do my own stunt, I asked what I had to do. They told her all she had to do was fall over. I said, 'Okay, I'll do it.' So, the time came and I noticed all the stunt men around me. All the other actors had decided not to do this stunt and were having a coffee." So she yelled across the entire set at them, "You bunch of girls should be ashamed of yourselves." They then began to film the sequence.

"On the first try everything went fine; the storm came up and we fell down. I fell back like we were taught, fell back and rolled onto a softer portion of my body. The director came up to me and said it was great, but thought that since I was actually doing my own stunt, the audience should see that it is me. The second time I fell straight back. The director shouted it was a good take and for me to get up. I just lay there in pain. I landed right on my tailbone. I ended up walking [half bent over] for a week, and Jonathan and the guys never let me forget it! Then, when I saw the tape, I was as tiny as a pin on the screen. You could have put Worf in my uniform and you wouldn't have known the difference."

Sirtis tells stories about her dog, a Toy Yorkie called Skilagie. As she doesn't have children, she thinks of her dog as her only child. She brings Skilagie on the set. "He's very well trained on the set," she told Creation Con, "only one time he got a little bit confused. In 'Sub Rosa' we were shooting on planet hell—that's what we call any foreign planet—and he thought he was outside at the graveyard scene. So he went and christened all the tombstones .... [and a] big whoopsie right on the spot where [Beverly] was to stand."

One day Sirtis had to run off and leave him in 'uncle Brent's trailer.' Sirtis said, "When I got back to the trailer, I opened it up and found Brent stuffing Skilagie into the microwave! It's true. If you ask him if he did it, Brent will deny it." He does, insisting, "I don't know why Marina tells that story. It was a trash compactor."

Another time on the set, she said, "I was doing my part and Jonathan was watching Skilagie. He was being unusually nice about it too." A few minutes later, she heard Michael Dorn yelling, "Take it long," and saw Jonathan holding Skilagie like a football. "I think it has something to do with male hormones and football that men act like that!"

Sirtis said the crew still sees one another quite often, and she sees Dorn almost daily. She loves working with Majel Barrett Roddenberry, and makes fun of the extravagant costumes Lwaxana wears. ("Majel, are you doing an episode this season?" "Yes, Marina, I am." "Okay, that's why I didn't get a raise this year.") Sirtis recalled, "The cast is normally a pretty rowdy bunch, but they decided that they would be really good the first time Majel guest-starred. However, about halfway through, they discovered that Majel was even nuttier than the rest of them!"

She returned to England during the third season, to shoot *One Last Chance* for the BBC on location in London and Windsor. During the fifth season, Sirtis appeared in other productions while working for *The Next Genera-*

> *"The cast is normally a pretty rowdy bunch, but they decided that they would be really good the first time Majel guest-starred."*

tion, including a cameo role for the film *Wax-work II: Lost in Time* (1992) and voice work for the animated film *Gargoyle: The Heroes Awaken* (1994), as well as for the TV series *Gargoyles.* Sirtis enjoys playing the voice of evil Demona. Jonathan Frakes provides the voice of an evil human for the same series. She told Creation Con, "He likes to tell everyone that I'm his sidekick in the show. Now, I ask you, what is the title of the show? *Gargoyles.* So I'm the head evil person and he's my sidekick!"

Sirtis resides in Hollywood with her husband. When they married in a traditional Greek ceremony, he cried all the way through the service while she was all smiles. They honeymooned in Cabo San Lucas. He surfs; she doesn't. He tried to teach her twice, and both times she ended up on the beach, completely covered with sand, with her bikini around her ankles.

She now drives a white Chrysler Le Baron convertible, delights in listening to *Les Miserables* and Bon Jovi, watches "far too much MTV," and keeps track of her local London soccer team, Tottenham Hotspur, in which she owns a few shares. Her brother is a professional soccer player. The *New Haven Register* reported that she "never appears in character outside the show. She also refuses to demonstrate the alien accent; she speaks to her fans in her own cockney accent."

Her American stage debut was in the comedy/mystery *Loot,* at Hartford Stage in Hartford, Connecticut, in which she played Fay, "a pious, much-married woman with a secret dark side." Her husband, Michael Lamper, urged her to take the part. "He said, 'I want to see you act for longer than a minute and a half.'" One of her long-term goals is to work for the National Shakespeare Company in England, not the Royal Shakespeare Company. Another is to do a Broadway play. She

179

has a space on her mantle for "the Oscar that one day I'm gonna win."

Meanwhile, Sirtis returned to her role as Counselor Deanna Troi for *Star Trek: Generations* in 1994 and *Star Trek: First Contact* in 1996. She enjoys playing in science fiction because she has always been interested in the stars and space exploration, and believes she once saw a UFO. "I was working with a repertory company in Worthing, a seaside town in England. One night as I was walking down the street, I saw this huge orange thing in the sky. At first I thought it must be the moon, but it was very off color. It was very close, but too high to be a balloon. Apparently a lot of other people saw it, too."

Deanna Troi

Half-Betazoid empath Deanna Troi wanted to be a part of Starfleet. She realized that the success of a starship depends on human relationships, and that the counselor becomes critical when a starship encounters alien life forms. Psychiatry had become a field of applied science, as hard evidence replaced guesswork. Starfleet Command now respected and made use of counselors, particularly with the added complexities of families and children aboard ship.

Most Betazoids develop full telepathic abilities during adolescence, but Deanna could read only feelings and sensations, not coherent thoughts. She realized that if she studied human and alien psychology, her natural talents would make her a valuable addition to a starship crew.

Deanna entered Starfleet Academy in 2355 and graduated in 2359. She also studied psychology at the University of Betazed in 2357. Upon graduation, she served aboard the *U.S.S. Yorktown* before joining the *Enterprise* NCC-1701-D crew in 2364 with the rank of Lieutenant Commander and a rating as Ship's Counselor.

Deanna was born on Betazed on March 29, 2336. She is the daughter of a human father, Ian Andrew Troi, a Starfleet officer who lived on Betazed, and aristocratic, eccentric Lwaxana, the daughter of the fifth house and holder of the sacred chalice of Riix. Her mother later proved an acute embarrassment on the *Enterprise* by chasing Picard—who she said has great legs.

Deanna had an elder sister, Kestra, who died in 2337 after falling into Lake Elnar. Lwaxana never forgave herself or buried the memories. When Deanna's father died in 2343, Lwaxana's dominating personality emerged out of a fear of losing her remaining daughter.

Deanna is single, but a glowing white sphere entered the *Enterprise* and caused her to become pregnant with an alien child. The human-emulating infant soon reverted to its original glowing spherical state. She also once had a Betazoid cat.

Deanna is often selected as an Away Team member because she can sense moods and attitudes toward Federation representatives. She also provides important insights into motives and feelings of beings they encounter.

> *Deanna is often selected as an Away Team member because she can sense moods and attitudes toward Federation representatives.*

Her abilities don't always work, though. Some races intentionally block their minds, while Ferengi prove resistant due to peculiarities of brain structure. She could detect nothing from the Traveler, as if he wasn't there.

Serving aboard the *Enterprise* has brought Deanna many strange new experiences. An alien race once took her over. Another time, spirits of cadet prisoners possessed her, O'Brien, and Data. A visiting mediator used Deanna to pass on his negative emo-tions, while a Romulan used her to help in a defection.

She was once *Imzadi* (Betazoid term for "beloved") to Riker when they served on the *U.S.S. Yorktown* before being assigned to the *Enterprise*. Deanna doesn't feel that she can become deeply involved with him again, but found the previous affair meaningful and pleasant. Each now feels honor-bound to maintain a disciplined and professional dis-tance while aboard the ship.

"Gene's vision of the future always included minorities—not just blacks, but Asians and Hispanics as well. I think that by projecting that image, we're actually creating reality for today."

—LeVar Burton

LeVar Burton

LeVar Burton grew up a *Star Trek* fan. He told a convention audience that he "appreciated Gene Roddenberry's approach to science fiction. Gene's vision of the future always included minorities—not just blacks, but Asians and Hispanics as well. I think that by projecting that image, we're actually creating reality for today." Burton remembered looking to Nichelle Nichols as a role model in his youth, watching her character, Uhura, and being reassured that "there was a place for me in the future" as a black man. Other influences included Sidney Poitier, "one of the main reasons I'm an actor," and Arthur C. Clarke, his favorite science fiction author.

Burton was born in Landstuhl, West Germany, on February 16, 1957, where the Signal Corps, Third Armored Division, had stationed his photographer father. His mother worked as an educator, and later as a social worker. Burton's parents taught strong values and vision as well as a sense of duty. He entered Catholic seminary at 13 with the goal of becoming a priest. Then he discovered Lao-Tzu, Kierkegaard, and Nietzsche, and an interest in existentialism grew. By age 15, "I began to wonder how I fit into the grand scheme of things. The more I thought about it, the less sense it made that the dogma of Catholicism was the be-all, end-all, of the universe."

He then decided to pursue an acting career. "What attracted me to the priesthood," Burton recalled, "was the opportunity to move people, to provide something essen-

tial. I was drawn by the elements of history and magic. As a priest, you live beyond the boundaries of the normal existence. It's like joining an elite club. You see, it's not that different from acting; even the Mass is a play, combining these elements of mystery and spectacle." He won a scholarship to USC in drama and fine arts.

The contrast between a sedate, small-town seminary and the USC campus proved startling. "I'd never had so much freedom," Burton said, "and it was difficult to concentrate the first year." Burton appears to have had an almost effortless career. He played in the film *Almos' a Man* (1976) and hosted *Rebop* for TV as soon as he arrived in Los Angeles. No pumping gas or waiting tables for this young actor.

The pivotal role of young Kunta Kinte in the award-winning TV miniseries, *Roots,* followed a year later. Some actors wait a lifetime for such an opportunity. The chance came during his sophomore year. He was 19. "I think the producers had exhausted all the normal means of finding professional talents and were beating the bushes at the drama schools," Burton recalled.

He won an Emmy nomination for *Roots,* then a steady stream of acting roles prevented his return to college. Burton played Cap Jackson in the film *Looking for Mr. Goodbar* (1977) and had roles in several TV movies, including Billy Peoples in *Billy: Portrait of a Street Kid* (1977), Ron LeFlore in *One in a Million: The Ron LeFlore Story* (1978), Richard in *Guyana Tragedy: The Story of Jim Jones* (1980), Tommy Price in *The Hunter* (1980), and Rodney in *The Acorn People* (1981), as well as parts in *Grambling's White Tiger* (1981) and *Emergency Room* (1983). He won an Emmy nomination for *Dummy* in 1979.

Burton began hosting *PBS's Reading Rainbow* from its inception in 1983. The series received eight daytime Emmy award nominations. The NAACP presented Burton with an Image award for outstanding performance in an educational series.

The string of TV movies continued. Burton appeared in *The Jesse Owens Story* (1984), *The Midnight Hour* (1985), *Liberty* (1986), and *A Special Friendship* (1986). A lifelong dream came true when he played alongside childhood idol and former *Enterprise* crew member Nichelle Nichols in *The Supernaturals* (1986). His own service aboard an *Enterprise* began a year later when he stepped into the Starfleet uniform of Lieutenant Geordi LaForge for *Star Trek: The Next Generation*. Burton referred to Roddenberry as "a giant in his field," and said that he will always remember Roddenberry's comment to him after his first audition: "Thanks for making my words come alive."

Burton told a Creation Con audience in Boston that the characters were formed about 85 percent through the efforts of the actors and only 15 percent by the writers, although the writers had more to say about the stories. Burton added, "These days, we [actors] know the characters best." Burton described his Geordi LaForge, saying, "He's been blind since birth, but 'sees' through the use of the VISOR [Visual Input Sensory Optical Reflector] he wears over his eyes. In fact, I am told that my character is named after a disabled *Star Trek* fan who passed away. It's nearly impossible [to see with the VISOR on]. I used to bump into things a lot in the beginning. The irony is that the VISOR gives Geordi the

ability to see, but LeVar sees nothing. It's a tremendous challenge for me to perform without the expressiveness that eyes can lend. I think I'm a better actor now than I was five years ago." The buttons on the sides of Geordi's head, called "blinkies," mark the spots where fiber optic cables were surgically connected to bring signals from the VISOR to his brain.

Trek fan Burton enjoys working with Classic Trek veterans and has the "utmost respect" for James Doohan, his favorite co-star. Burton recalled that the cast felt "very nervous" before shooting the *Star Trek: The Next Generation* episodes featuring Leonard Nimoy as Spock, explaining, "We have our own way of working . . . a certain energy" that they weren't sure Nimoy would understand. However, Burton and the rest of the cast were "surprised and delighted" that Nimoy proved to be "very loose, not stuffy or uptight," and that "he fit."

> *"Gene's vision of the future always included minorities—not just blacks, but Asians and Hispanics as well."*

Burton made his directorial debut with the sixth-season episode "Second Chances," then continued with "The Pegasus" for the seventh season. He also directed for the related *Star Trek: Deep Space Nine* series. "I loved directing," he told the *Charlotte Observer*. His fellow actors "were pretty helpful, especially Jonathan. I couldn't have done it without him."

The year after he began *Star Trek: The Next Generation*, Burton returned to his other

183

famous role, Kunta Kinte, for *Roots: The Gift* (1988). He also provided the voices of Khwami for the animated *Captain Planet and the Planeteers* series and Hayden Sloane for *Batman: The Animated Series,* as well as appearing in two TV movies, *Firestorm: 72 Hours in Oakland* and ABC's *Mather.*

After *Star Trek: The Next Generation* ended its TV run, Burton played his Geordi La Forge for the film, *Star Trek: Generations* (1994). He also appeared in the *Christy* TV series as Daniel Scott and as Dr. Franklin Carter in Showtime's *Parallel Lives* (1994). *Parallel Lives,* a follow-up project to *Chantilly Lace,* was produced and directed by Linda Yellen; it premiered at the Sundance Film Festival before being entered in jury competition at the Cannes Film Festival. Burton then guest-starred in *Deadly Games,* before returning to the role of LaForge for *Star Trek: First Contact* (1996). Burton also directed a *Star Trek: Voyager* episode, and will be directing *Stairway to Heaven,* an independent romantic comedy film.

> *"I think that by projecting that image, we're actually creating reality for today."*

Despite his fame for *Reading Rainbow, Roots,* and *Star Trek: The Next Generation,* LeVar Burton sometimes gets a dose of reality. Cops once stopped his black BMW because he looked like a gang leader. He now wears glasses or contact lenses that he didn't wear before *TNG* began.

Burton wants to continue directing other types of projects. As a filmmaker, he would like to "tell stories that make a difference," and to use the Internet that links the world together as a tremendous tool for "spreading light and consciousness." He launched Eagle Nation Films to develop projects for film and television, some of which he will direct. He also wants to spend more time with his 11-year-old child.

Fifteen-hundred of America's top CEOs invited LeVar Burton to emcee the National Business Hall of Fame induction on April 20, 1996, co-sponsored by *Fortune Magazine* and Junior Achievement. *Star Trek* has assured Burton that there is a place for him in the future.

Geordi LaForge

Both Geordi LaForge's mother, a starship command officer, and his exobiologist father served Starfleet before him. His father worked in the Modine system, while his mother, Silva, disappeared with her ship, the *U.S.S. Hera.* Geordi later risked his life in a futile attempt to rescue her. He followed the family tradition, entering Starfleet Academy in 2353, graduating in 2357, then accepting a posting as Ensign aboard the *U.S.S. Victory* in 2362. He was promoted to Lieutenant before joining the crew of the *Enterprise* NCC-1701-D as a Lieutenant Commander in 2364. He later became the Chief Engineer.

Geordi was born blind due to a non-correctable birth defect on February 16, 2335, in the African Confederation of Earth. He received a VISOR when he was five. It enables him to see the entire electromagnetic spectrum. Riker later gave him sight when he served aboard the *Enterprise,* but he rejected the gift. He also turned down Dr. Pulaski when she suggested an operation to restore his sight.

Geordi has trouble forming romantic relationships because he lacks self-confidence, despite being a genius in the engine room. He has saved his ship many times. Even the legendary Montgomery Scott admired his work. Geordi gets along with everyone, although Data is his only close friend.

Serving aboard the *Enterprise* brought Geordi many unusual experiences. Both Lore and an alien race have held him captive. Romulans once kidnapped him and turned him into a killing machine, while another time he was stranded with a Romulan on a storm-ravaged planet. A parasite once possessed him and another Starfleet member and began transforming them into alien creatures, and Geordi and Ro were presumed dead after a transporter accident. He even grew enamored of a mysterious Starfleet lieutenant who was accused of murder. No doubt, many equally strange adventures await him in the future.

185

"Tasha meant a lot to a lot of people and I'm grateful for that. There was a sort of diamond-in-the-rough street kid element that people just related to."

—Denise Crosby

Denise Crosby

"My grandfather was a Hollywood legend. Growing up with that wasn't exactly normal." said Denise Crosby. "There is, appropriately, a music studio dedicated to [Bing Crosby] on the Paramount lot," she told a convention in Adelaide, South Australia. "We were in the studio, in an area dedicated for away missions, called 'planet hell,' and that wasn't an understatement, with all the smoke, mist, and dog's and cat's 'visits.' It was really late and we were on a break. Everybody clearly just wanted to wrap up the scene and go home. I was on my way out, when I turned, out of impulse, and shouted very angrily, 'Hey! My grandfather built this studio!!' You could hear a pin drop in that resulting silence. Everybody just looked at me as if to say, 'I think we should call the asylum,' except for Jonathan, who was struggling not to laugh; only he caught the joke! So whenever he and I are together at a convention or whatever, Jonathan will always say, 'Hey watch it, her grandfather built this studio!'"

Crosby was raised in Los Angeles, where she still lives. Everything about her, including her boyfriend, screenwriter Ken Sylk, seems connected with the film industry. Oddly, her first career was started a continent away, and her acting began almost by accident. "European runway model thing. I hated modeling, but I was taken to Europe by three California designers who were trying to launch their fashions there. I loved London, so I just stayed on," Crosby recalled. She returned home for the Christmas holidays. "Toni Howard was casting a movie called *Diary of a Teenage Hitchhiker* and had seen my picture in a magazine. I looked wild. My hair was about a quarter of an inch all the way around. I wore army fatigues and no makeup." She didn't land the role, but Toni Howard encouraged her to enroll in acting classes, and roles soon followed in *Days of Our Lives* for television, *Trail of the Pink Panther* (1982), *48 HRS.* (1982), *The Man Who Loved Women* (1983), *Curse of the Pink Panther* (1983), *Desert Hearts* (1985), and *Eliminators* (1986) for film, and three TV movies, *Cocaine: One Man's Seduction* (1983), *Stark* (1985), and *Malice in Wonderland* (1985).

The part of security officer Natasha "Tasha" Yar in *Star Trek: The Next Generation* in 1987 should have guaranteed her career, with a five-year contract and a regular berth on the starship *Enterprise*. But it only lasted one year. Crosby liked the role at first, saying of Tasha, "She comes from an incredibly violent and aggressive Earth colony where life was a constant battle for survival. She can fight and she knows her job, but she has no family, is emotionally insecure, and somehow feels that she doesn't quite belong on this ship of seemingly perfect people," she told the Adelaide convention audience. "Originally the counselor was envisioned to be just like me, and the security officer was to be dark, stocky, short, and a fighter. One day, the producer just said, 'Switch your roles around,' and it was done. Simple as that."

She had fun working with the *Star Trek: The Next Generation* cast, telling the convention,

"All of us were given a bathrobe to wear while we had our makeup put on, removed, or 'touched up.' Jonathan [Frakes] had been given, temporarily, a pink bathrobe to wear—which was a lady's bathrobe and three sizes too small. It wouldn't even fit around his waist. But he kept wearing it. He would parade it around in front of the cast and crew.

"One morning, he and I were getting ready for the day. I was touching up on makeup and Jonathan was in his pink bathrobe shaving, with shaving cream all over his face. And then there was an earthquake—and we started running! We weren't sure where we were running to, but we were running! It stopped just as soon as it started, but suddenly there were reporters from *Entertainment Tonight* everywhere. They came up to me and said, 'Hi! We're from *ET,* and we know you're Denise Crosby from *Star Trek: The Next Generation.* Tell us about the earthquake, where were you and how did you feel.' Well, I just pointed a finger at Jonathan, who still was dressed in that pink undersized robe and still had shaving cream all over his face, and I said, 'You know, why don't you ask him.' And as the reporters rushed over to him, I thought, 'There goes your career, Frakes,' but Jonathan chatted away happily with the reporters with shaving cream dripping from his face!"

But, by the end of the first season, Crosby asked to be freed from her contract because she felt that her character was underused. Roddenberry agreed, and told her that Tasha would be killed; there could be no going back. "I just figured, 'That's it, I'm dead,'" she told the *Charlotte Observer.* Tasha met her violent, meaningless end in "Skin of Evil."

"I would like to make it clear that it was my decision," Crosby told the convention. "It didn't offer what I needed as an actor at that time in my life. I wanted to get out there and

really act. It usually takes a new show about a season to get itself together, and I soon realized that it didn't really offer what I had been looking for at the time. Since the show didn't generally share episodes between characters, I felt it wasn't satisfying what I wanted out of acting. I do not look back on that decision with regret."

If not regret, then nostalgia. Years later, Crosby waxed nostalgic, telling the *Charlotte Observer,* "Tasha meant a lot to a lot of people and I'm grateful for that. There was a sort of diamond-in-the-rough street kid element that people just related to."

> "My grandfather was a Hollywood legend. Growing up with that wasn't exactly normal."

Crosby wasn't through with *Star Trek: The Next Generation,* though. An alternate-time-line Tasha returned in the third season's "Yesterday's Enterprise," generally considered the best *Star Trek: The Next Generation* episode. This, she told the *Charlotte Observer* "gave Tasha the chance to die with a sense of meaning. It was a beautiful episode—moving, exciting and with a real emotional payoff."

Crosby portrayed Tasha a final time in "All Good Things. . . ," the concluding television episode of *Star Trek: The Next Generation.* This was Tasha in another time-travel adventure, before "Encounter at Farpoint."

After her year on *Star Trek: The Next Generation,* Crosby appeared in the films *Crime Zone* (1988), *Arizona Heat* (1988), *Tennessee Nights* (1989), *Skin Deep* (1989), *Pet Sematary* (1989), *Miracle Mile* (1989), *Blackwater*

(1989), *High Strung* (1991), *Dolly Dearest* (1992), *Desperate Crimes* (1993), *Relative Fear* (1994), *Max* (1994); the TV movies *O'Hara* and *Red Shoe Diaries 2: Double Dare* (1992); TV guest appearances on *L.A. Law, The Flash, Diagnosis: Murder, Lois & Clark: The New Adventures of Superman,* and *Sisters;* and as Chaucy, a regular in the TV series *Key West.*

Crosby also portrayed Sela, Tasha's villainous half-human/half-Romulan daughter, for the fourth-season concluding cliffhanger of *Star Trek: The Next Generation,* "Redemption I," and the fifth season's "Redemption II." She was also in both parts of "Unification," when she appeared with Leonard Nimoy's Ambassador Spock. Crosby told the *Charlotte Observer,* "I watched *Star Trek* as a kid, and there I was on *Star Trek: The Next Generation* with Leonard. It was exciting to be back, to see everyone, to work with Leonard, and to play my character's daughter."

Perhaps Sela will still return for *DS9* or *Voyager.* She fondly recalls playing the character. "There is a lot of life left in Sela yet," she told the Adelaide convention. "I have been in communication with Rick Berman. I expressed an interest for Sela to return, but we keep missing each other, keep putting off meetings. I've been doing these conventions all over the world. I feel like a rock star!"

Tasha Yar

The very human Tasha Yar was born on a savage world of feudal ganglords, Turkana IV, in 2337. Natasha was of Ukrainian descent. Her sister, Ishara, was born in 2342, the year crossfire killed their parents. Five-year-old Tasha raised her sister, spending her nights and days foraging for food and avoiding roving rape gangs.

When Tasha escaped to Earth in 2352, Ishara chose to stay behind. Tasha entered Starfleet Academy in 2356 and graduated in 2360. She loved the order and safety of Starfleet, the opposite of the terrors of her childhood. Tasha dedicated herself to preserving this order, and became Security Chief of the *Enterprise* in 2364. She served as part of all initial contact teams, always protecting her commanding officers. Having visited Turkana IV, Captain Picard understood her obsession and became her mentor.

> *She loved the order and safety of Starfleet, the opposite of the terrors of her childhood.*

The muscular but feminine beauty proved to be an exciting sensual and intellectual challenge to men. She even seduced emotionless Data. Data cherished her memory, and kept a holographic snapshot of her among his most cherished possessions after Armus murdered Tasha on Vagra II later that year.

In an independent timeline, Tasha became the consort of a Romulan general to save the lives of the time-traveling crew of the *Enterprise*-C. She had a Romulan daughter, Sela, in 2345. This Tasha was executed in 2349, after trying to escape Romulus.

Sela became a Romulan commander and encountered Picard's *Enterprise*-D. She doesn't miss her mother, whom she believes deserved her fate.

"I try to play an omnipotent being who is too stupid to know it. An all-powerful being with feet of clay. It's the feet of clay that I play, not the omnipotent seer or the powerfulness."

—John deLancie

John deLancie

"I usually have small roles in big movies," John deLancie told *Cinescape*, "playing the obligatory asshole." DeLancie was born on March 20, 1948, and his acting career began at the age of 14 when he played Henry V at his Philadelphia private school. They told his parents to encourage him because he had a "flair" for performing, but deLancie resisted acting as a career and went to college instead of acting school. He still performed in plays, however. "Then, at age 36," he told *Starlog*, "I found myself with no other talent—experience, I should say—than acting. I made a full commitment to the task [in 1984]."

Before then, he had appeared in only three films, *Legacy* (1975), *The Onion Field*, (1979), and *Loving Couples* (1980), and four TV movies, *SST – Death Flight* (1977), *Little Women* (1978), *Nightside* (1980), and *The Miracle of Kathy Miller* (1981). DeLancie had most actively pursued TV miniseries, having appeared in six: *Captains and the Kings* (1976), *Testimony of Two Men* (1977), *Black Beauty* (1978), *The Bastard* (1978), *Scruples* (1980), and *The Thorn Birds* (1983). This work covered more than a 10-year period. He had done no other television except three years of *Days of Our Lives,* and no work other than *The Thorn Birds* between 1981 and 1986. He played in the film *Houston: The Legend of Texas* in 1986, then made his first appearance as Q in the first episode of *Star Trek: The Next Generation* in 1987. Q is, beyond a doubt, his most memorable creation.

"In creating a new show, I think Gene [Roddenberry] looked back and extracted the things that seemed the most successful," deLancie told *Entertainment Weekly's Special Star Trek Collector's Edition,* "so the qualities of that character [Trelane from 'The Squire of Gothos' in the original series], whether consciously or unconsciously, became the foundation of the character. I thought 'Q' stood for question or questioner, only to discover that Gene had written a letter to a lady in Scotland saying, 'I'm writing *Star Trek: The Next Generation* and I'm going to name a character after you.' And her name is Janet Quarton. It just shows that you can add great meaning or give it no meaning."

He told *Cinescape*, "I wanted to know who Q was before we saw him. We're really talking about a race of gods here—minds that grasp far more than the human mind is able to. In a wonderful way, he's got a kind of amorality to him. He's not there to promote his point of view. He's out there to figure out what you're about, and as long as what you're about is okay, then everything else is okay. If it isn't, God help you. You see, that's the fun of a good script. A good script allows you to think. There are lots of scripts that are so bad that they have no possibility of discussion, whereas you and I can sit down over a drink and talk about all sorts of possibilities relating to Q."

He further clarified his view of the character in Internet's Mr. Showbiz Celebrity Lounge, saying, "I try to play an omnipotent being who is too stupid to know it. An all-powerful being

189

with feet of clay. It's the feet of clay that I play, not the omnipotent seer or the powerfulness.

"You can't improvise. There are lots of shows that accept improvisation. Then there are shows like this one. There are good reasons why one doesn't improvise, not the least of which is that you don't want to be bringing 1996 idiomatic phrases into what's supposed to be in the future."

DeLancie likes *Star Trek,* and believes that they did a good job on the first episode of *The Next Generation,* "Encounter At Farpoint." "How can I help but look back at the show affectionately?" deLancie told *Cinescape.* "It kind of burned the idea of the character into the minds of the audience, which was gratifying." He told *Starlog,* "I was on the set the day after the pilot aired, and everybody was flushed with the general feeling of having done a good job. They have a sense that they're on the right track. You have a group that works hard and is gaining in success as they begin to see what they have.

> **DeLancie resisted acting as a career and went to college instead of acting school.**

The people on *Star Trek: The Next Generation* approach their work very seriously, but they're still fun and relaxed. When I go there, I know I'm really going to work and it will be an enjoyable experience.

"*Star Trek* was light years ahead. But you have to understand that it's still working in the same medium, with the same restrictions, the same time allotment and all that other stuff. The roles that I've played on stage are not too dissimilar to the type of range that I play in Q. Q was never played tongue-in-cheek. I keep thinking of Q in terms of what it would be like to be with the other Qs. One of the makeup guys and I had a wonderful thought, that if you would ever pull away Q's face, it would reveal the universe. That's the area that I keep in mind. Hopefully, I'll come back enough times and create a full-fledged character—an archetype character in the minds of people watching the show. I will take as many opportunities as I'm given to make this character, Q, a part of the fabric of *Star Trek.*"

He did just that, reappearing in several episodes of *Star Trek: The Next Generation* DeLancie commented to *Cinescape* on the episodes in which he appeared:

- "Hide and Q": "I didn't like that one too much. It didn't go anywhere. I did like the idea, though, of Q being whisked away by someone even more powerful than he was."

- "Q Who?": "I thought that it was really neat to introduce another very popular concept, the Borg. It wasn't so much a morality play as it was closer to straight science fiction. I also loved the idea that the Borg are not unlike the criminal element of today that will come into your house and take anything that's plugged in."

- "Deja Q": "A lot of people say this is their favorite. It was a somewhat restrained Q that audiences saw, and I think it was the first time that you felt some sympathy for him. A lot of fun to do."

- "Q-Pid": "My memory of it is that it was a little underdriven plot-wise. You just don't know what to play in an episode like that. I enjoyed the costumes and the people, but not really the episode."

- "True Q": "Q baby-sits? It just seems an odd kind of story to write for this character. Again, a little disappointing."

- "Tapestry": "Kind of like *It's a Wonderful Life* in space. A great episode, and I think the best scenes for me were the ones in heaven. I loved those lines: 'Welcome to the afterlife, Jean-Luc. You're dead and I'm God.' I thought the issues being dealt with were wonderful and the writing was excellent."

- "All Good Things . . .": "I loved the episode, though I thought it was a little confusing toward the end with all the anomalies. But I thought it was doing what *Star Trek* does very well, which is make a statement rather than just entertain."

He also showed up for "Q-Less" on *Star Trek: Deep Space Nine*. DeLancie told *Cinescape* that this was "Another episode I wasn't crazy about. Chasing Vash to *Deep Space Nine*? Does anyone really care? It pales in comparison to some of the other episodes, because, again, there's no real purpose to having Q there."

"I have tried to organize my career by being somewhat anonymous," deLancie told *Starlog*. "When I've had opportunities to become exceedingly popular, especially by being on a soap opera, I chose not to go that route, only because it makes doing other work more difficult." During this time, deLancie became much more active outside of *Star Trek*, as well. He performed the voice of Eagleton for *Batman: The Animated Series* and appeared as Bob Adams for the *Trial and Error* TV series. He appeared in TV movies, playing in *Get Smart, Again!* (1989), *Christine Cromwell: Things That Go Bump in the Night* (1989), *Angel of Death* (1990), *The Fisher King* (1991), *Arcade* (1993), and *Without Warning* (1994). He also played in films, including, *On Fire* (1987), *Blood Red* (1989), *Bad Influence* (1990), *Taking Care of Business* (1991), *The Hand That Rocks the Cradle* (1991), *Fearless* (1993), *Deep Red* (1994), and *Schemes* (1995).

In 1995, Q entered the Delta Quadrant to appear on the newest Star Trek, *Voyager.* The episode "Death Wish" offers not one, but two members of the Q Continuum. The episode brings about many changes in how we perceive Q. "This is an episode where discussions are of a larger philosophical nature," deLancie said in the Mr. Showbiz Celebrity Lounge. "Janeway discovers things about the Q Continuum that have never been known before." He told the *Charlotte Observer*, "It answers so many questions about Q, but it raises several new issues. I bring in all sorts of people to testify that I've had a positive impact on some people's lives, including Riker, Isaac Newton, and a hippie from Woodstock. Q is one big stew that keeps on boiling."

DeLancie noted that the role of Q has changed and grown. "The character has moved from being perceived as a villain to more of a messenger of what might not be considered good news, but news that one needs to hear," he told Mr. Showbiz Celebrity Lounge. "There was discussion that the exploration was not without but within, which is interesting—that Q would be delivering the 'pop psychology' of the '90s."

Many believe that deLancie is now too closely identified with Q. He informed Mr. Showbiz Celebrity Lounge, "Typecasting is a natural punitive result of having done a good job. You are penalized by the public for having done something that stands out in their minds. All you can do is continue working."

DeLancie briefly starred in his own series, *Legend,* in 1995 on the United Paramount Network, the same network on which *Voyager* appears. He played Janos Bartok, but despite a fan base, the show ended after six episodes. He blamed it on the network, telling the *Charlotte*

191

Observer, "It was on UPN, which just didn't have a delivery system that was ideal for it to be widely seen. It was a show that asked of the audience a level of attention to script and detail which has become a rather nostalgic notion." UPN has also had difficulty delivering audiences to other series, including *Star Trek: Voyager.*

DeLancie keeps busy as a husband and father to two sons, acting in *Evolver* on the Sci-Fi Channel, and in the film, *Multiplicity,* as the "jerk" who causes problems for Michael Keaton. The *Charlotte Observer* reported that he also has a secret project with Leonard Nimoy, the actor best known for playing Spock. DeLancie would only reveal, "It has to do with our shared interest in classic science fiction and the reasons why such stories strike a chord with people."

Q

Q, an immensely powerful extradimensional entity, exhibits a childlike petulance and playfulness, similar to that of Trelane, the squire of Gothos. The *Enterprise*-D first made contact with Q in 2364, when Q detained the ship and enacted a courtroom drama by putting the crew on trial for the crimes of humanity.

Q returned to offer William Riker supernatural powers. Riker fought against the impulse to dominate his colleagues, and someone more powerful took Q away.

On his third visit, Picard rejected Q's request to join the *Enterprise* crew, but Q retaliated by sending the *Enterprise* 7,000 light years beyond Federation space to System J-25, where they met the Borg, providing the Federation with an early warning of oncoming danger.

The Q Continuum took away Q's powers in 2366, and sentenced him to live as a mortal human. Q sought refuge on the *Enterprise.* Unfortunately, one of Q's many enemies, the Calamarain, came hunting him. Data saved Q. Surprised by Data's selfless action, Q tried to save the *Enterprise* by leaving. The Continuum restored his powers for this altruistic act.

Q interrupted a symposium of the Federation Archaeology Council aboard the *Enterprise* in 2367 to help Picard pursue his romantic interest, Vash, with a Robin Hood reprise. Q later vanished, taking Vash with him as his new partner.

He returned in 2369 to instruct and evaluate *Enterprise* intern Amanda Rogers, whose biological parents were members of the Q Continuum who took human form. The Continuum felt a moral obligation not to allow members of their kind to abuse their powers with inferior beings.

Vash left Q after they explored the Gamma Quadrant together. She returned in the Starfleet runabout *U.S.S. Ganges* through the Bajoran wormhole. Q followed to station Deep Space Nine, unsuccessfully trying to win her back. He provoked Benjamin Sisko into a 19th-century-style fist fight, and Sisko knocked him to the floor.

Later that year, Q returned to the *Enterprise* while Picard lay dying in sickbay. Q gave him the opportunity to alter his past by reliving the three days leading up to his boyhood injury in a knife fight at the Bonestall Recreation Facility in 2327. This time Picard avoided the fight that cost him his heart, but also discovered that his rash youth had molded the future starship captain.

A more sober Q later appeared aboard the starship *Voyager* in the Delta Quadrant. The familiar Q had abandoned his prankster ways, but later reclaimed them.

APPENDIX A

Episode Guide

FIRST SEASON

Season Notes

Changes made between the pilot, "Encounter at Farpoint," and the opening of the first season:

- Opening credits changed from actor's name only to actor and character name.
- Troi's outfit was changed from a blue "miniskirt" to a nonuniform dress with rank pips removed.
- Troi's hair is tied into a tight bun.

Opening Credits (first and second season):
During the opening sequence, the graphics show a departure from the Sol system, beginning with Earth with the sun in the background, and featuring fly-bys of Jupiter and Saturn. During this sequence, the camera pans right, and we see sunlight off the left side of Earth and Jupiter and the right side of Saturn, indicating that Saturn is backlit.

Season Credits

Starring:
Patrick Stewart as Captain Jean-Luc Picard
Jonathan Frakes as Commander William Riker
Also Starring:
LeVar Burton as Lieutenant Junior Grade Geordi LaForge
Denise Crosby as Lieutenant Natasha Tasha Yar
Michael Dorn as Lieutenant Junior Grade Worf
Gates McFadden as Doctor (Commander) Beverly Crusher
Marina Sirtis as Counselor (Lieutenant Commander) Deanna Troi
Brent Spiner as Lieutenant Commander Data
Wil Wheaton as Wesley "Wes" Crusher

Creator and Executive Producer: Gene Roddenberry
Supervising Producer: Rick Berman
Supervising Producer: Robert H. Justman
Producer: Maurice Hurley
Co-Producer: Robert Lewin
Co-Producer: Herbert Wright
Associate Producer: Peter Lauritson
Story Editor: Johnny Dawkins
Music: Dennis McCarthy
Main Title Theme: Jerry Goldsmith and Alexander Courage
Editor: Tom Benko
Production Designer: Herman Zimmerman
Director of Photography: Edward R. Brown, A.S.C.

Episodes 1 and 2: "Encounter at Farpoint"

Stardate: 41153.7
Air date: September 26, 1987
Writers: D. C. Fontana and Gene Roddenberry
Director: Corey Allen
Guest Stars: John deLancie: Q; Michael Bell: Bandi Groppler Zorn; DeForest Kelley: Dr. Leonard McCoy; Colm Meaney: Battle Bridge Conn; Cary Hiroyuki: Mandarin Bailiff; Timothy Dang: Main Bridge Security; David Erskine: Bandi Shopkeeper; Evelyn Guerrero: Young Female Ensign; Chuck Hicks: Military Officer; Jimmy Ortega: Torres.

The crew of the *Enterprise* is put on trial by a mysterious Q for all the crimes of mankind.

Roddenberry taped two stories together to make the two-hour premiere, adding Q to D. C. Fontana's story. It didn't work.

Notes

The production code for "Encounter at Farpoint" is 721 for the two-hour version, and 101 and 102 for the two-part version.

In Jokes

"Kill all the lawyers!" comes from Shakespeare's *Henry VI*.

DeForest Kelley makes an appearance as an unnamed admiral who hates transporters and notices that Data, with all that knowledge, doesn't have pointed ears.

The military uniform Q wears is that of a Marine Corps lieutenant colonel. And if you look closely, you can see that his rank, ribbons, and badges are all identical to those worn by Lt. Col. Oliver North when he testified during the Iran-Contra hearings in 1986–87, just before the episode went into production.

SNAFUs

The computer tells Riker to meet Data in the holodeck through the next door on the right, but Riker turns left and walks into the holodeck.

Picard Surrenders

Picard says, "Transmit the following in all languages and in all frequencies: 'We surrender.'"

Saucer Separation

While Worf takes the saucer section to Farpoint Station, Picard takes the warp drive section to meet up with the Q entity.

Episode 3: The Naked Now

Production Number: 103
Stardate: 41209.2
Air date: October 3, 1987
Teleplay: J. Michael Bingham
Story: John D. F. Black and J. Michael Bingham
Director: Paul Lynch
Guest Stars: Brooke Bundy: Lt. Cmdr. Sarah MacDougal; Benjamin W. S. Lum: Asst. Chief Engineer Jim Shimoda; Michael Rider: Transporter Chief; David Renan: Conn; Skip Stellrecht: Engineering Crewman; Kenny Koch: Kissing Crewman.

Romance, danger, and chaos result when a mysterious contaminant renders the crew of the *Enterprise* intoxicated.

A bad remake of the original series' "The Naked Time."

Insider's Story

The records from the original *Enterprise* ("The Naked Time") were used to combat a microbe that caused people to act drunk.

This episode and "Haven" were the only ones in which William Riker was called "Bill."

The second starship in *Star Trek: The Next Generation,* the *U.S.S. Tsiolkovsky,* appeared. The bridge dedication plaque read: "Earth is the cradle of the mind, but one cannot remain in the cradle forever."

In Jokes

Data says, "When you prick me, do I not . . . leak?" which is paraphrased from Shakespeare's *The Merchant of Venice.*

The dedication plaque for the *Horatio* showed that it was built by Yoyodyne, and the dedication read: "Damn the torpedoes, full speed ahead!"

During the scan of records, we see a parrot wearing a Starfleet shirt, complete with insignia and nacelles, an obvious reference to Gene Roddenberry, "The Great Bird of the Galaxy." This same screen also reappears in "Conspiracy."

Data quotes a limerick: "There was once a lady from Venus, whose body was shaped like a . . ." The limerick was written by David Gerrold while he was still working with *Star Trek: The Next Generation* in its early days. The complete version of the limerick appeared in the third book of his "War Against the Chtorr" series, *A Rage for Revenge.* (The limerick appears on a page opposite another dirty limerick which seems to be about Gene Roddenberry.)

SNAFUs

When Troi finds Tasha in her quarters, affected by the intoxication disease and trying on Troi's scarves, she and Tasha grab hands as Tasha tries to take a scarf from Troi. The camera switches views between Troi and Tasha as they face each other. When the camera is facing Troi, Troi is holding Tasha's right hand with her right hand. When the camera is facing Tasha, Troi is holding Tasha's right hand with her left hand. Also, in one of the views they are holding a scarf, but not in the other.

Wesley Saves the Day:

Wesley modifies a tractor beam into a repulser beam to push the *Enterprise* away in order to give Data the extra time needed to reinsert the chips.

Episode 4: Code of Honor

Production number: 104
Stardate: 41235.25
Air date: October 10, 1987
Writers: Katharyn Powers and Michael Baron
Director: Russ Mayberry
Guest Stars: Jessie Lawrence Ferguson: Lutan; Karole Selmon: Yareena; James Louis Watkins: Hagon; Michael Rider: Transporter Chief.

The Ligonian leader, Lutan, kidnaps Tasha. His wife, Yareena, challenges Tasha to a duel to the death, which she must accept. Yar wins the duel, killing Yareena. They both then beam up to the ship, Beverly revives Yareena, and Yareena's marriage to Lutan is dissolved.

SNAFUs

In the group shots, Deanna's arms are at her sides, while in the close-ups, her arms are behind her back.

During the fight with Yareena, Yar's weapon is in her left hand. However, when Yar beams up with Yareena, the weapon moves to her right hand.

Episode 5: The Last Outpost

Production number: 107
Stardate: 41386.4
Air date: October 18, 1987
Teleplay: Herbert Wright
Story: Richard Krzemien
Director: Richard Colla
Guest Stars: Armin Shimerman: Letek; Jake Dengel: Mordoc; Tracey Walter: Kayron; Darryl Henriques: Portal; Mike Gomez: DaiMon Tarr.

Held captive over an unknown planet, the Away Teams of the *Enterprise* and a Ferengi starship must pass an important inquisition by a mysterious life form known as Portal.

Borrowing its plot from "The Arena," this episode introduced the Ferengi into the Star Trek universe.

Picard Surrenders

The crew assumes that the Ferengi have them immobilized and attempt to surrender, but the Ferengi surrender first, believing that the *Enterprise* has them immobilized.

Episode 6: Where No One Has Gone Before

Production number: 106
Stardate: 41263.1
Air date: October 24, 1987
Working Title: "Where None Have Gone Before"
Writers: Diane Duane and Michael Reaves
Director: Rob Bowman
Guest Stars: Stanley Kamel: Lt. j.g. Kosinski; Eric Menyuk: Assistant (aka Traveler); Herta Ware: Maman Picard; Biff Yeager: Lt. Cmdr. Argyle; Charles Dayton: Crewmember; Victoria Dillard: Ballerina.

Teenager Wesley Crusher and a dying alien are the crew's only hope for escape from a bizarre galaxy where thoughts become real.

Wesley first meets the Traveler, a powerful alien in a story that will not conclude until season seven's "Journey's End."

Note
The Paramount press release shows the title as "Where None Have Gone Before," the working title, but the actual title aired with the episode was "Where No One Has Gone Before."

Wesley Saves the Day
Wesley is the only one to notice that the Traveler is phasing.

Enterprise Exceeds Warp Speed Limits
During a warp field experiment with the Traveler, Wesley's distraction causes the Traveler to phase in and out, which causes the *Enterprise* to travel 2.7 million light-years in a few seconds.

Episode 7: Lonely Among Us

Production number: 108
Stardate: 41249.3
Air date: October 31, 1987
Teleplay: D. C. Fontana
Story: Michael Halperin
Director: Cliff Bole
Guest Stars: John Durbin: Ssestar; Colm Meaney: First Security Guard; Kavi Raz: Lt. j.g. Singh.

Passing through a series of complex energy patterns, the *Enterprise* crew find themselves trying to solve the mystery surrounding the murder of Assistant Chief Engineer Singh and the altered personalities of Lt. Worf, Dr. Crusher, and the Captain.

Note
The Paramount press release has John Durbin listed as "Joan Durbin."

Insider's Story
When they needed to redo a scene to reshoot the back of Mr. Singh's head after they'd dismissed the actor, they put a wig similar to his real hair on a chair.

Episode 8: Justice

Production number: 109
Stardate: 41255.6
Air date: November 7, 1987
Teleplay: Worley Thorne
Story: Ralph Wills and Worley Thorne
Director: James L. Conway
Guest Stars: Brenda Bakke: Rivan; Jay Louden: Liator; Josh Clark: Conn; David Q. Combs: First Mediator; Richard Lavin: Second Mediator; Judith Jones: Edo Girl; Eric Matthew: First Edo Boy; Brad Zerbst: Medical Technician; David Michael Graves: Second Edo Boy.

When Wesley is sentenced to death for innocently violating a foreign planet's customs, Captain Picard is forced to choose between negotiating for Wesley's life and adhering to the Federation's Prime Directive, which prohibits interfering with another civilization's way of life.

Wesley Screws Up
Wesley trips over a barrier, and nearly loses his life when he steps on the grass.

Picard Violates the Prime Directive
In order to save Wesley from the death penalty for (accidentally) violating one of the Edo laws, Picard goes against the punishment mandated for disobeying the Prime Directive.

Episode 9: The Battle

Production number: 110
Stardate: 41723.9
Air date: November 14, 1987
Teleplay: Herbert Wright
Story: Larry Forrester
Director: Rob Bowman
Guest Stars: Frank Corsentino: DaiMon Bok; Doug Warhit: Kazago; Robert Towers: Rata.

A thought-altering device, controlled by a Ferengi Captain seeking revenge on Picard for his son's death, threatens the life of the Captain and the safety of the *Enterprise*.

Adds background about the time when Picard was captain of the *Stargazer*.

In Jokes
The widget used by Dr. Crusher to put Captain Picard to sleep is a Macross fighter part from the Japanese animation series.

SNAFUs
The Ferengi DaiMon raises the shields on the *Stargazer*, which should prevent transport, yet, right after raising shields, the DaiMon beams off the *Stargazer*.

Wesley Saves the Day
Wesley discovers the Ferengi transmissions that are affecting Picard.

Episode 10: Hide and Q

Production number: 111
Stardate: 41590.5
Air date: November 21, 1987
Teleplay: C. J. Holland and Gene Roddenberry
Story: C. J. Holland
Director: Cliff Bole

Guest Stars: John deLancie: Q; Elaine Nalee: female Klingon; William A. Wallace: adult Wesley Crusher.

The *Enterprise* is once again challenged by Q, who offers Riker god-like powers.

SNAFUs
Data's rank insignia are wrong shortly after Riker and the bridge crew are teleported to the planet by Q. He's suddenly a Lt. j.g. for about three minutes.

The Walking (Near) Dead
Worf and Wesley get impaled by soldiers.

Episode 11: Haven

Production number: 105
Stardate: 41294.5
Air date: November 28, 1987
Working Title: "Love Beyond Time and Space"
Teleplay: Tracy Tormé
Story: Tracy Tormé and Lan O'Kun
Director: Richard Compton
Guest Stars: Majel Barrett: Lwaxana Troi; Rob Knepper: Wyatt Miller; Nan Martin: Victoria Miller; Robert Ellenstein: Steven Miller; Carel Struycken: Mr. Homn; Anna Katarina: Valeda Innis; Raye Birk: Wrenn; Danitza Kingsley: Ariana; Michael Rider: Transporter Chief.

Deanna Troi is caught between her feelings for Riker and her devotion to family customs when she faces a prearranged marriage.

Introduces Lwaxana Troi, Deanna's mother.

Insider's Story
The "Deck 11 Dorsal Lounge" used for the banquet reappeared as the lounge in "Outrageous Okona."

Gene Roddenberry died as the crew was filming "Hero Worship."

"Hero Worship" and "Haven" are the only episodes in which William Riker was called Bill.

Episode 12: The Big Good-bye

Production number: 113
Stardate: 41997.7
Air date: January 9, 1988
Writer: Tracy Tormé
Director: Joseph L. Scanlan
Guest Stars: Lawrence Tierney: Cyrus Redblock; Harvey Jason: Felix Leech; William Boyett: Lt. Dan Bell; David Selburg: Lit-Historian Whalen; Gary Armagnac: Lt. McNary; Mike Genovese: Desk Sergeant; Dick Miller: Vendor; Carolyn Allport: Jessica Bradley; Rhonda Aldrich: Secretary; Erik Cord: Thug.

This is the first major holodeck story. When the holodecks malfunction, the Captain and two crew members become trapped in San Francisco in 1941, where they are held hostage by murderous gangsters.

Note
The promotion included a special notice:

> *The following legal restriction applies to the promotion of this episode: There is a scene in which characters are seen at a newsstand in 1941 San Francisco. One of the characters picks up a copy of* Time *magazine and the front and back cover is shown. Please do not use this cover in any advertising, promotion or publicity of this episode. None of the materials provided to you contain this scene. If you produce your own promos for any reason, please be sure to avoid using it.*

Wesley Saves the Day
Wesley fixes the holodeck because his mother is inside.

Episode 13: Datalore

Production number: 114
Stardate: 41242.4
Air date: January 16, 1988
Teleplay: Robert Lewin and Gene Roddenberry
Story: Robert Lewin and Maurice Hurley
Director: Rob Bowman
Guest Star: Biff Yeager: Engineer Argyle.

Data's android look-alike formulates an evil master plan that could destroy the *Enterprise*.
   Introduces Lore, and reveals Data's real origins.

SNAFUs
Upon beaming down to the planet's surface, Commander Riker gives the stardate as 4124.5. A little later, Captain Picard gives it as 41242.45.
   The glass of champagne that Lore pours for Data goes flat immediately before Data picks it up because of the time that passed between the filming of the scenes. It is visible during the traveling wipe.

Wesley Saves the Day
Wesley realizes that Lore is impersonating Data.

Episode 14: Angel One

Production number: 115
Stardate: 41636.9
Air date: January 23, 1988
Writer: Patrick Barry
Director: Michael Rhodes
Guest Stars: Karen Montgomery: Beata; Sam Hennings: Ramsey; Patricia McPherson: Ariel; Leonard John Crofoot: Trent.

While the Away Team struggles to save male fugitives on a planet run by women, the *Enterprise* is ravaged by a highly infectious virus.

Picard Violates the Prime Directive

The crew barely managed to save the survivors of a Federation ship from death for trying to change the society of Angel One.

Episode 15: 11001001

Production number: 116
Stardate: 41365.9
Air date: January 30, 1988
Working Title: "Unconditional Return"
Writers: Maurice Hurley and Robert Lewin
Director: Paul Lynch
Guest Stars: Carolyn McCormick: Minuet; Gene Dynarski: Commander Quinteros; Katy Boyer: Zero One; Alexandra Johnson: One Zero; Iva Lane: Zero Zero; Kelli Ann McNally: One One; Jack Sheldon: Piano Player; Abdul Salaam El Razzac: Bass Player; Ron Brown: Drummer.

The *Enterprise* is hijacked by an alien species who need the ship's computer to regenerate their own.

Cast Favorites: Jonathan Frakes' Favorite

". . . because I got to play music in New Orleans."

Note

The Paramount press release shows Katy Boyer listed as "Kathy Boyer."

Insider's Story

The translation of the French, after Riker introduces Minuet and Picard:

Riker: (indicating) "Minuet. Minuet, Captain Jean-Luc Picard."

Minuet: *Enchantée, comme c'est merveilleux de vous voir ici.* (It's wonderful to meet you.)

Picard: *Incroyable! Vous êtes Parisienne?* (Amazing! You are from Paris?)

Minuet: *Au fond, c'est vrai nous sommes toutes Parisienne.* (Deep down we're all from Paris.)

Picard: *Ah, oui, au fond nous sommes tous Parisiens.* (Ah yes, deep down we're all from Paris.)

In Jokes

"11001001" is a binary number that equals 201 in our base-10 system, or C9 in the hexadecimal system. Using the Z-80 microprocessor series (as did the TRS-80 Model I, III, and IV, and the Sega Genesis for sound processing), the C9 is known in assembly language as "Unconditional Return." In addition, in another machine language, 201 corresponds to no valid machine instruction at all, or a NOP (No Operation for two machine cycles). In other words, the title can mean: no meaning.

Attempts at Self-Destruct

Picard and Riker try to destroy their own ship to prevent the *Enterprise* from falling into enemy hands.

Episode 16: Too Short a Season

Production number: 112
Stardate: 41309.5
Air date: February 6, 1988
Teleplay: Michael Michaelian and D. C. Fontana
Story: Michael Michaelian
Director: Rob Bowman
Guest Stars: Clayton Rohner: Admiral Mark Jameson; Marsha Hunt: Anne Jameson; Michael Pataki: Karnas.

The *Enterprise* escorts a Federation admiral to a planet to negotiate the release of hostages, but the planet governor wants to kill him in revenge for a previous hostage crisis that ended in tragedy.

Episode 17: When the Bough Breaks

Production number: 118
Stardate: 41509.1
Air date: February 13, 1988
Writer: Hannah Louise Shearer
Director: Kim Manners
Guest Stars: Jerry Hardin: Radue; Brenda Strong: Rashella; Jandi Swanson: Katie; Paul Lambert: Melian; Ivy Bethune: Duana; Dierk Torsek: Dr. Lt. Bernard; Michele Marsh: Leda; Dan Mason: Accolan; Philip N. Waller: Harry Bernard; Connie Danese: Toya; Jessica and Vanessa Bova: Alexandra.

Wesley and several children from the *Enterprise* are kidnapped by a sterile civilization which hopes to use them to rebuild their race.

Note

The opening and closing theme music is not in full stereo. The stereo separation was greatly reduced. The sound effects during the opening are also in mono. The reason for the mix change is unknown.

Enterprise Exceeds Warp Speed Limits

When Captain Picard insists that the Aldean people return the children kidnapped from the *Enterprise*, the *Enterprise* is hit with a bolt of energy that causes it to travel a distance that requires three days at Warp 9 to travel back to Aldea.

Episode 18: Home Soil

Production number: 117
Stardate: 41463.9
Air date: February 20, 1988
Teleplay: Robert Sabaroff
Story: Karl Geurs, Ralph Sanchez, and Robert Sabaroff

Director: Corey Allen
Guest Stars: Walter Gotell: Kurt Mandl; Elizabeth Lindsey: Louisa Kim; Gerard Prendergast: Bjorn Benson; Mario Roccuzzo: Arthur Malencon; Carolyne Barry: Female Engineer.

A powerful microscopic life form declares war on humans, takes over the *Enterprise*'s lab and computers, and threatens to destroy the ship.

Note

As in the previous episode, the opening and closing theme music is not in full stereo. The stereo separation was greatly reduced. The sound effects during the opening are also in mono. The reason for the mix change is unknown.

Episode 19: Coming of Age

Production number: 119
Stardate: 41416.2
Air date: March 12, 1988
Writer: Sandy Fries
Director: Mike Vejar
Guest Stars: Ward Costello: Admiral Gregory Quinn; Robert Schenkkan: Lt. Cmdr. Dexter Remmick; John Putch: Mordock; Robert Ito: Tac Officer Chang; Stephen Gregory: Jake Kurland; Tasia Valenza: T'Shanik; Estee Chandler: Oliana Mirren; Brendan McKane: Technician #1; Wyatt Knight: Technician #2; Daniel Riordan: Rondon.

While Wesley endures the grueling Starfleet Academy entrance exam, Captain Picard faces an investigation into his competence as a commander.

Episode 20: Heart of Glory

Production number: 120
Stardate: 41503.7

Air date: March 19, 1988
Teleplay: Maurice Hurley
Story: Maurice Hurley, Herbert Wright, and D.C. Fontana
Director: Rob Bowman
Guest Stars: Vaughn Armstrong: Korris; Charles H. Hyman: Konmel; David Froman: K'nera; Robert Bauer: Kunivas; Brad Zerbst: Nurse; Dennis Madalone: Ramos.

When two Klingon fugitives take over the ship, Lt. Worf is torn between his loyalty to the *Enterprise* and his fierce Klingon heritage.

Worf character episode.

Note

The Paramount press release lists Charles H. Hyman as "Charles B. Hyman."

Insider's Story

The Klingon ship was footage from *Star Trek: The Motion Picture.*

Episode 21: The Arsenal of Freedom

Production number: 121
Stardate: 41798.2
Air date: April 9, 1988
Teleplay: Richard Manning and Hans Beimler
Story: Maurice Hurley and Robert Lewin
Director: Les Landau
Guest Stars: Vincent Schiavelli: The Peddler; Marco Rodriguez: Captain Paul Rice; Vyto Ruginis: Chief Engineer Logan; Julia Nickson: Ensign Lian T'Su; George De La Pe-a: Lt. j.g. Orfil Solis.

Picard and the Away Team fight for their lives on a planet run by a computerized weapons system.

Note

The arrangement for the closing theme music changed slightly. The normal arrangement was

45 seconds long, while this arrangement is one minute long.

The Paramount press release has the Ensign T'Su character listed as Lt. T'Su.

Saucer Separation

Geordi takes the Warp Drive section in order to destroy the defense device on Minos, while Chief Engineer Logan takes the saucer section to safety.

Command Offered to Commander Riker

It is mentioned that Riker was offered the command of the *U.S.S. Drake* before he joined the *Enterprise.*

Episode 22: Symbiosis

Production number: 123
Stardate: Unknown
Air date: April 16, 1988
Teleplay: Robert Lewin, Richard Manning, and Hans Beimler
Story: Robert Lewin
Director: Win Phelps
Guest Stars: Judson Scott: Sobi; Merritt Butrick: T'Jon; Richard Lineback: Romas; Kimberly Farr: Langor.

The *Enterprise* is caught in the middle when two alien races wage a bitter battle over cargo which one of them needs for survival.

Note

The Paramount press release has Merritt Butrick listed as "Merrit Butrick."

Insider's Story

Merritt Butrick appeared as Kirk's son, David Marcus, in *Star Trek II: The Wrath of Khan* and *Star Trek III: The Search For Spock.* After his appearance in *TNG*, Merritt Butrick died due to complications from AIDS.

Denise Crosby (Lt. Tasha Yar) waved good-bye as Picard and Crusher left the cargo bay. This would prove ironic.

Episode 23: Skin of Evil

Production number: 122
Stardate: 41601.3
Air date: April 23, 1988
Working Title: "The Shroud"
Teleplay: Joseph Steven and Hannah Louise Shearer
Story: Joseph Stefano
Director: Joseph L. Scanlan
Guest Stars: Mart McChesney: Armus; Ron Gans: Voice of Armus; Walker Boone: Lt. Cmdr. Leland T. Lynch; Brad Zerbst: Nurse; Raymond Forchion: Ben Prieto.

A rescue mission turns to tragedy when Tasha Yar is killed by an evil alien.

In Jokes
The graph showing the energy level of Armus is labeled: "Mean Field Intensity," a commentary on the oil slick.

SNAFUs
When Riker is being pulled into Armus, the Away Team runs towards Armus, and Geordi drops his phaser into Armus. When Captain Picard beams onto the planet, the Away Team is standing around calmly, and Geordi's phaser is back in his pocket.

The computer-generated picture that Worf is looking at within the first minutes is the very same one that appears twice later: It already contains the graph of Armus' energy-level with the peaks and valleys which Troi causes much later in the show.

Episode 24: We'll Always Have Paris

Production number: 124
Stardate: 41697.9

Air date: April 30, 1988
Writers: Deborah Dean Davis and Hannah Louise Shearer
Director: Robert Becker
Guest Stars: Michelle Phillips: Jenice Manheim; Rod Loomis: Dr. Paul Manheim; Co-Stars Isabel Lorca: Gabrielle; Dan Kern: Lt. Dean; Jean-Paul Vignon: Edourd; Kelly Ashmore: Francine; Lance Spellerberg: Transporter Chief Herbert.

Captain Picard is unexpectedly reunited with his first love in the midst of an investigation into lethal time-warp experiments.

Note
Although the deceased Lt. Yar (Denise Crosby) is still listed in the credits, the Paramount press release does not have her listed.

The closing theme music is not in full stereo. The stereo separation was greatly reduced.

In Jokes
The Café des Artistes had strange items on the menu, including Croissant Dilithium, Targ Klingon à la mode, Tribble Blanket, and John Cougar Mellencamp.

SNAFUs
The Eiffel Tower moved around the holodeck.

Time Travel
Dr. Paul Manheim's experiment causes small loops to occur in time.

Episode 25: Conspiracy

Production number: 125
Stardate: 41775.5
Air date: May 7, 1988
Teleplay: Tracy Tormé
Story: Robert Sabaroff
Director: Cliff Bole
Guest Stars: Henry Darrow: Admiral Savar; Ward

Costello: Admiral Quinn; Robert Schenkkan: Lt. Commander Dexter Remmick; Ray Reinhardt: Admiral Aaron; Jonathan Farwell: Captain Walker Keel; Michael Berryman: Captain Rixx; Ursaline Bryant: Captain Tryla Scott.

Captain Picard and Commander Riker travel to Earth to investigate a conspiracy in the highest ranks of Starfleet command.

Introduces alien parasites and their plot to control the Federation.

Note

The credits still list Lt. Yar (Denise Crosby), but the Paramount press release does not.

Insider's Story

Paramount and the *TNG* Production Office were aware of the change in the way *Star Trek* was presented (the new inclusion of gory scenes), but went with it so that the franchise would not fall into a rut. The idea was to do something different. Paramount recommended a "Parental Guidance" message before the episode, which was ignored by virtually every station. None was provided with the satellite feed.

The Iconion gizmo that Captain Varley plays with was originally a weapon when the Iconions were warlike. When they changed, so did the gizmo.

In Jokes

The topographical map of the planetary surface was a "very shaky" drawing of Kei and Yuri. Yuri is on the right side, and Kei is upside down.

The planet Digitalis is clearly named after a medicine for heart patients.

SNAFUs

At the beginning of the episode, while Picard is asleep, Riker tells LaForge to increase speed to Warp 6. LaForge replies, "Aye Sir, full impulse."

Episode 26: The Neutral Zone

Production number: 126
Stardate: 41986.0
Air date: May 14, 1988
Television Story and Teleplay: Maurice Hurley
Story: Deborah McIntyre and Mona Clee
Director: James L. Conway
Guest Stars: Marc Alaimo: Commander Tebok; Anthony James: Sub-Commander Thei; Leon Rippy: L.Q. Sonny Clemens; Gracie Harrison: Clare Raymond; Peter Mark Richman: Ralph Offenhouse.

While traveling to a meeting with hostile Romulans, the crew discovers a ship containing three frozen Americans from the 20th century.

Note

Although Lt. Yar (Denise Crosby) is listed in the credits, the Paramount press release does not have her listed.

The closing theme music is not in full stereo. The stereo separation was greatly reduced.

Lieutenant Commander Data gave the year as 2364.

In Jokes

References to various shows, including W. Hartnell m. P. Troughton, J. Pertwee m. T. Baker, P. Davison m. C. Baker (from *Doctor Who*), and J-L. Picard m. W. Riker are on the family tree of Clare Raymond recalled by Troi. Other references include *Gilligan's Island* and *M*A*S*H*.

The face pictured on the screen belongs to Peter Lauritson, one of the producers of *TNG*.

One of the life support canisters contained Rick Sternbach.

SECOND SEASON

Season Notes

The start of the second season was delayed until late November due to a writer's strike that lasted from March 7, 1988, to August 7, 1988.

Changes from first to second season:

- Wesley Crusher changes from shirt with rainbow stripe to all-gray uniform.

- Wesley Crusher is made Acting Ensign.

- Worf is made permanent Security Chief (from red to gold uniform).

- Geordi LaForge is made permanent Chief of Engineering (from red to gold uniform).

- Geordi and Worf are both promoted to (full) Lieutenant.

- Ten-Forward is made as a permanent set.

- Guinan (Whoopi Goldberg) is added to the crew as a recurring special guest star.

- Dr. Beverly Crusher (Gates McFadden) is transferred to Starfleet Medical, and is replaced by Dr. Katerine Pulaski (Diana Muldaur).

- Commander Riker has grown a beard.

- The Con and Ops chair were changed from couch-style chairs to regular chairs.

- Worf wears a new aluminum-like sash instead of the old foil-like sash.

- The stardates now advance in a more logical manner during a season, instead of being somewhat random as they had been during the original *Star Trek* and the first season of *TNG*.

- The opening and closing theme music is re-done for the second season.

- The opening credits are 5.8 seconds shorter than the first season. They were edited after the third speeding *Enterprise* fly-by. The star-field appears to jump.

Season Credits

Starring:
Patrick Stewart as Captain Jean-Luc Picard
Jonathan Frakes as Commander William Riker

Also Starring:
LeVar Burton as Lieutenant Geordi LaForge
Michael Dorn as Lieutenant Junior Grade Worf
Marina Sirtis as Counselor Deanna Troi
Brent Spiner as Lieutenant Commander Data
Wil Wheaton as Wesley "Wes" Crusher

Creator and Executive Producer: Gene Roddenberry
Co-Executive Producer: Maurice Hurley
Co-Executive Producer: Rick Berman
Line Producer: David Livingston
Producer: Burton Armus
Producers: John Mason and Mike Gray
Associate Producer: Peter Lauritson

Episode 27: The Child

Production number: 127
Stardate: 42073.1
Air date: November 19, 1988
Writers: Jaron Summers, Jon Povill, and Maurice Hurley
Director: Rob Bowman
Guest Stars: Diana Muldaur: Doctor Comdr. Katherine "Kate" Pulaski; Seymour Cassel: Hester Dealt; Whoopi Goldberg: Guinan; R.J. Williams: Ian; Colm Meaney: Transporter Chief; Dawn Arnemann: Miss Gladstone; Zachary Benjamin: Young Ian; Dore Keller: Crewman.

While the crew prepares to transport a deadly plague virus to a research lab, Counselor Troi gives birth.

Note
Troi's rank of Lt. Cmdr. is shown.

Insider's Story
This story was originally developed for an unaired *Star Trek* TV series called *Star Trek II*, planned before *TNG*. Jon Povill and Jaron Summers wrote the original script of the same title.

In Jokes
Doctor Pulaski refers to "Cyano Acrylates," the active ingredients for SuperGlue, as a possible source of the Eichner radiation that was causing the plague samples to grow.

Episode 28: Where Silence Has Lease

Production number: 128
Stardate: 42193.6
Air date: November 26, 1988
Writer: Jack B. Sowards
Director: Winrich Kolbe
Guest Stars: Diana Muldaur: Doctor Comdr. Katherine "Kate" Pulaski; Earl Boen: Nagilum; Charles Douglas: Ensign Haskell; Colm Meaney: Transporter Chief .

The crew is held hostage in a mysterious void by a being who wishes to observe the many ways in which humans die.

In Jokes
The *U.S.S. Yamato* (NCC-1305-E) is mentioned in the story. This was a Japanese battleship during WWII. The name is used in the Japanese animation television series *Space Cruiser Yamato*, or *Star Blazers* in the United States.

Attempts at Self-Destruct
Picard tries to self-destruct for Nagilum.

Episode 29: Elementary, Dear Data

Production number: 129
Stardate: 42286.3
Air date: December 3, 1988
Writer: Brian Alan Lane
Director: Rob Bowman
Guest Stars: Diana Muldaur: Doctor Comdr. Katherine "Kate" Pulaski; Daniel Davis: Moriarty; Alan Shearman: Lestrade; Biff Manard: Ruffian; Diz White: Prostitute; Anne Elizabeth Ramsay: Assistant Engineer Clancy; Richard Merson: Pie Man.

Pretending to be Sherlock Holmes, Data uses the holodeck to solve a mystery that threatens Dr. Pulaski's life.
Sequel to "The Big Good-bye."

Cast Favorites: LeVar Burton's Favorite
"After wearing our 'space suits' day in and day out and being so serious so much of the time, it was always fun to put on those great costumes and play!"

SNAFUs
Geordi asks, "What's wrong, Data?" Data gives him the page. Geordi says, "Data, this is impossible," and he flips the paper over so that it faces the camera. At this point the drawing is right-side-up, which means that Geordi was looking at it upside down.

Episode 30: The Outrageous Okona

Production number: 130
Stardate: 42402.7
Air date: December 10, 1988
Teleplay: Burton Armus
Story: Les Menchen, Lance Dickson, and David Landsberg

Director: Robert Becker
Guest Stars: William O. Campbell: Captain Thaduin
Okona; Douglas Rowe: Debin; Albert Stratton:
Kushell; Rosalind Ingledew: Yanar; Kieran Mulroney:
Benzan; Joe Piscopo: the Comic; Whoopi Goldberg:
Guinan.

While the *Enterprise* crew play host to a witty
renegade captain, Data struggles to acquire a
sense of humor.

Insider's Story
The lounge originally appeared as the Deck
11 Dorsal Lounge in "Haven."

Picard Surrenders
Picard drops shields "In case we decide to surrender to them."

Episode 31: Loud as a Whisper

Production number: 132
Stardate: 42477.2
Air date: January 7, 1989
Writer: Jacqueline Zambrano
Director: Larry Shaw
Guest Stars: Diana Muldaur: Doctor Comdr. Katherine
"Kate" Pulaski; Marnie Mosiman: Woman; Thomas
Oglesby: Scholar; Leo Damian: Warrior/Andonis;
Howie Seago: Riva; Colm Meaney: Transporter Chief;
Richard Lavin: Warrior #1; Chip Heller: Warrior #2;
John Garrett: Lieutenant.

The future of a warring planet depends on a
deaf mediator, who suddenly loses his ability
to communicate.

Insider's Story
Marnie Mosiman, the actress who played one
third of Riva's Chorus, is John (Q) deLancie's
wife. They called their baby, "R."

In Jokes
One handsign made to Data is the Vulcan
greeting turned sideways.

The conference table, "made to resemble
indigenous rock," had various markings, including "Kei" and "Yuri."

SNAFUs
Data has learned sign language and interprets
what the mediator signs, but Data quotes the
mediator as signing, "My friends have died"
before it is signed.

Episode 32: The Schizoid Man

Production number: 131
Stardate: 42437.5
Air date: January 21, 1989
Teleplay: Tracy Tormé
Story: Richard Manning and Hans Beimler
Director: Les Landau
Guest Stars: Diana Muldaur: Doctor Comdr. Katherine
"Kate" Pulaski; W. Morgan Sheppard: Ira Graves; Suzie
Plakson: Lt. Selar; Barbara Alyn Woods: Kareen Brianon.

A brilliant but terminally ill scientist seeks eter-
nal life by transferring his mind into Data's body.

In Jokes
The psycho-analyzer used on Data is a
Macross fighter part from the Japanese anima-
tion series.

Episode 33: Unnatural Selection

Production number: 133
Stardate: 42494.8
Air date: January 28, 1889
Writer: John Mason and Mike Gray
Director: Paul Lynch

Guest Stars: Diana Muldaur: Doctor Comdr. Katherine "Kate" Pulaski; Patricia Smith: Dr. Sara Kingsley; Colm Meaney: Transporter Chief; J. Patrick McNamara: Capt. Taggert; Scott Trost: Ensign.

The crew grapples with a mysterious disease that accelerates the aging process, causing humans to die of old age within a matter of days.

Episode 34: A Matter of Honor

Production number: 134
Stardate: 42506.5
Air date: February 4, 1989
Teleplay: Burton Armus
Story: Wanda M. Haight, Gregory Amos, and Burton Armus
Director: Rob Bowman
Guest Stars: Diana Muldaur: Doctor Comdr. Katherine "Kate" Pulaski; John Putch: Ensign Mendon; Christopher Collins: Captain Kargan; Brian Thompson: Klag; Colm Meaney: Chief O'Brien; Peter Parros: Tactics Officer; Laura Drake: Vekma.

Riker's loyalties are put to the test when he is assigned to a Klingon vessel which plans to attack the *Enterprise*.

Picard Surrenders
Picard surrenders to Riker on the *Pagh*.

Riker Commands a Ship
Riker commands Klingon Ship *Pagh*.

Episode 35: The Measure of a Man

Production number: 135
Stardate: 42523.7
Air date: February 11, 1989
Writer: Melinda M. Snodgrass
Director: Robert Scheerer

Guest Stars: Diana Muldaur: Doctor Comdr. Katherine "Kate" Pulaski; Amanda McBroom: Captain Phillipa Louvois; Clyde Kusatsu: Admiral Nakamura; Brian Brophy: Commander Bruce Maddox;Whoopi Goldberg: Guinan; Colm Meaney: Chief O'Brien.

When Data refuses to be disassembled for research purposes, Picard is enlisted to defend his rights in court.

Note
Data said that he has an ultimate storage capacity of 800 quadrillion bits and has been rated at 16 trillion operations per second.

Insider's Story
Data's arm was made up of whatever happened to be lying on Rick's desk at the time: Exacto knives, model parts, a little R2-D2, etc.

In Jokes
When Riker is showing off Data's arm to the JAG representative, there is a pad on her desk which lists Data's parts, including "Nausicaan Valve" and "Totoro Interface." Data is made of something called "Yurium." These are all references to Japanese animation.

Picard inscribed a quotation from one of Shakespeare's sonnets inside the cover of an antique book he gave to Data:

"When in disgrace with fortune in men's eyes, I all alone beweep my outcast state."

SNAFUs
In the first third, the *Enterprise* circles the spinning space station, but then, when Picard meets this woman the first time, they stay at the window and the *Enterprise* moves in front of motionless stars.

Data is shown bending a metal bar. However, the metal bar that Riker places on the JAG officer's desk is not bent in the same manner. In addition, the speed at which the bar is bent should have produced excess heat.

Episode 36: The Dauphin

Production number: 136
Stardate: 42568.8
Air date: February 18, 1989
Writers: Scott Rubenstein and Leonard Mlodinow
Director: Rob Bowman
Guest Stars: Diana Muldaur: Doctor Comdr. Katherine "Kate" Pulaski; Paddi Edwards: Anya; Jaime Hubbard: Salia;Whoopi Goldberg: Guinan; Colm Meaney: Chief O'Brien; Peter Neptune: Aron; Mädchen Amick: Teenage Girl; Cindy Sorenson: Furry Animal; Jennifer Barlow: Ensign Gibson.

Wesley finds romance with the beautiful young ruler of Daled IV, whose secret power could destroy the *Enterprise* and her crew.

Note
The ending theme music was changed, giving it a new length of 1:03 (including the Paramount logo at the end).

Insider's Story
The title, "The Dauphin," comes from the French term "Le Dauphin," used to designate the male heir to the French throne.

In Jokes
Daled Four is a planet's name. Daled is also the fourth letter in the Hebrew alphabet, and thus has the numeric value of four.

SNAFUs
The appearance of the aliens became monstrous in one scene. The nanny changed to attack Wesley, then the girl changed. After a cut, both monsters appeared in a side view. The girl-monster stood in front of a mirror, but cast no image. The monsters changed back to their human forms but still had no mirror images. After another cut to a similar view of the room, the mirror showed an image of the girl. When they composited the monsters into the film, they overlooked the mirror.

Episode 37: Contagion

Production number: 137
Stardate: 42609.1
Air date: March 18, 1989
Writers: Steve Gerber and Beth Woods
Director: Joseph L. Scanlan
Guest Stars: Diana Muldaur: Doctor Comdr. Katherine "Kate" Pulaski; Thalmus Rasulala: Donald Varley; Carolyn Seymour: Taris; Dana Sparks: Tactician; Colm Meaney: Chief O'Brien; Folkert Schmidt: Doctor.

The *Enterprise*'s computer system falls prey to a mysterious electronic virus which programs the ship to self destruct.

Reintroduces the Romulans.

Insider's Story
Views as seen through the portal include Toronto's City Hall, Nathan Phillips Square (depicting the arches over the reflecting pool/skating rink), and Toronto's City Council Chambers.

In Jokes
The Iconian artifact says "Kei and Yuri," "Dirty Pair," "Gundam," and "Totoro" on the flip side.

Another Galaxy Class Starship is mentioned: the *U.S.S. Yamato*. This was the name of the flagship of the Japanese fleet that fought in World War II at both the Coral Sea and Midway before it was sunk by Torpedo Bombers from an American carrier. Many years later, a Japanese animation series reconfigured a battleship into a starship to recover something called the "Cosmo DNA." This series was called *Starship Yamato,* or *Star Blazers* in the United States.

The Romulan ship that attacked the *Enterprise* was named the *Harkonnen,* the name of the family that attacked the Atriedes family in Frank Herbert's *Dune* series.

Episode 38: The Royale

Production number: 138
Stardate: 42625.4
Air date: March 25, 1989
Writer: Keith Mills
Director: Cliff Bole
Guest Stars: Diana Muldaur: Doctor Comdr. Katherine "Kate" Pulaski; Sam Anderson: Assistant Manager; Jill Jacobson: Vanessa; Leo Garcia: The Bell Boy; Nobel Willingham: Texas; Colm Meaney: Chief O'Brien; Gregory Beecroft: Mickey D.

Investigating the discovery of a piece of metal bearing a United States Air Force insignia, the Away Team finds itself trapped in the world of The Hotel Royale, a novel come to life.

SNAFUs

They scan the atmosphere to see if it's safe to breathe after beaming down.

Episode 39: Time Squared

Production number: 139
Stardate: 42679.2
Air date: April 1, 1989
Working Title: "Time to the Second"
Teleplay: Maurice Hurley
Story: Kurt Michael Bensmiller
Director: Joseph L. Scanlon
Guest Stars: Diana Muldaur: Doctor Comdr. Katherine "Kate" Pulaski; Colm Meaney: Chief O'Brien.

The *Enterprise* discovers a Federation shuttle containing an exact double of Captain Picard from six hours in the future.

Note

The 2/14/89 Paramount air schedule listed this episode as "Time to the Second," the working title.

Insider's Story

The shuttle was named after NASA geologist, Boston University Professor Farouk El-Baz. When the episode was shown, Prof. El-Baz was at home with his children. The kids' response: "Dad, it's us!!" Of course, Mike Okuda got a call from Boston University the next morning.

Time Travel

Due to a strange energy vortex, a duplicate Picard from the future arrives on a shuttlecraft.

The Walking (Near) Dead

The *Enterprise* is seen being destroyed.

Episode 40: The Icarus Factor

Production number: 140
Stardate: 42686.4
Air date: April 22, 1989
Teleplay: David Assael and Robert L. McCullough
Story: David Assael
Director: Robert Iscove
Guest Stars: Diana Muldaur: Doctor Comdr. Katherine "Kate" Pulaski; Colm Meaney: Chief O'Brien; Mitchell Ryan: Kyle Riker; Lance Spellerberg: Ensign Herbert.

Riker's long-lost father reappears on the eve of his departure to become captain on a new starship.

Insider's Story

Marina Sirtis said that her husband, Michael Lamper, started to cry a bit when he saw the episode. As Riker was about to leave the *Enterprise,* and said good-bye to Deanna, and Marina also started to cry a little.

In Jokes

The mat has the Chinese character of *sei,* or "star," as in "starry sky." The two scrolls hanging on the walls say, in Japanese *hiragana* syllabic characters, *urusei yatsura,* a pun for *ususai yatsura* ("noisy neighbors" or "annoying neighbors," a Japanese animation). Other markings include *Kei, Yuri, Akira, Tonari No Totoro, Ataru, Lum,* and *Uresai Yatsura.*

Riker's father says, "*youroshiku onegaishimasu,*" in a terrible accent. Literally, it means, "Please do me the favor of being kind to me," but with the same usage as the English phrase, "Pleased to meet you."

Command Offered to Commander Riker

U.S.S. Aries.

Episode 41: Pen Pals

Production number: 141
Stardate: 42695.3
Air date: April 29, 1989
Teleplay: Melinda M. Snodgrass
Story: Hannah Louise Shearer
Director: Winrich Kolbe
Guest Stars: Diana Muldaur: Doctor Comdr. Katherine "Kate" Pulaski; Nicholas Cascone: Davies; Nikki Cox: Sarjenka; Ann H. Gillespie: Hildebrant; Colm Meaney: Chief O'Brien; Whitney Rydbeck: Alans.

Data races against time to save the life a little alien girl on a planet doomed for destruction.

Picard Violates the Prime Directive

Helping a girl whose planet was slowly self-destructing.

Episode 42: Q Who?

Production number: 142
Stardate: 42761.3
Air date: May 6, 1989
Writer: Maurice Hurley
Director: Rob Bowman
Guest Stars: Diana Muldaur: Doctor Comdr. Katherine "Kate" Pulaski; John de Lancie: Q; Lycia Naff: Ensign Sonya Gomez; Colm Meaney: Chief O'Brien; Whoopi Goldberg: Guinan.

The crew is hurled into the future by the malevolent Q, who sets them up for destruction by a race of half-human, half-robot aliens.

Introduces the Borg.

Insider's Story

Borgs include 5¼-inch floppy drive doors.

The model of the *Enterprise* seen as the Borg were slicing the "core" sample out was an exercise in forced perspective. From the angle of the camera, the saucer section appears to go on forever, which is the intended effect. From the top, however, you would see a grossly distorted piece of the saucer section, with the areas closest to the camera being large, and the areas farthest being small. It made the NCC-1701-D logo look strange. Among the fine detail work done on the core section are portions of a ship's cabin, including tables, chairs, walls, and a "space toilet."

The Borg ship was constructed with the damaged sections built in. Additional pieces of the model could be inserted over the damaged sections to hide them for shots when the Borg ship was to be shown in its undamaged state. Each damaged section had magnets that were the same color as the background. Brass rings were added and hidden around the magnets to act as guides, so that the undamaged sections could be held securely and would always be placed in the same position when installed. This prevented the undamaged pieces from "jumping" as they went from shot to shot on the Borg ship.

The Borg ship is a large model. Since the base cube is six feet per side, an incredible amount of models, tubes, and other stuff went into this cube, including toy soldiers, R2-D2s, parts from airplanes, and miscellaneous tubing. The logo for the company (SFPX) appears eight times in various places on the model.

At the time of the filming, there were two visual supervisors, Dan Curry and Rob Legato. They each had their own specifications for the design of the Borg ship: Rob Legato said that the Borg ship should be a ball with a trench of detail around the middle. Dan Curry said that the Borg ship should be a cube that looked smooth at a distance; as you got closer and closer, more detail would be revealed. Dan had hired Special Effects for this job. Rob's team had problems, so Special Effects got the job and built the Borg ship Dan's way. It took fourteen model-makers two weeks to finish the job. Special Effects supplied a Borg ship that was finished on all sides.

SNAFUs

Q snaps his fingers to send the *Enterprise* back to the starting point. The ship then turns around to the left, but the stars on the screen move from right to left—the wrong direction. Worf shoots Borg #1, who falls to the ground, his left arm sprawled over his head and his right leg bent in an awkward position. The camera switches to wide-angle, and in that instant the dead Borg changes his position.

Enterprise Exceeds Warp Speed Limits

Q sends the *Enterprise* 7,000 light years away for their first encounter with the Borg. Also, when the *Enterprise* is being chased by the Borg, LaForge reads the speed off as Warp 9.65.

Episode 43: Samaritan Snare

Production number: 143
Stardate: 42779.1
Air date: May 13, 1989
Writer: Robert L. McCullough
Director: Les Landau
Guest Stars: Diana Muldaur: Doctor Comdr. Katherine "Kate" Pulaski; Christopher Collins: Grebnedlog; Leslie Morris: Reginod; Daniel Benzali: Surgeon; Lycia Naff: Ensign Sonya Gomez; Tzi Ma: Biomolecular Specialist.

While Picard fights for his life in surgery, Geordi is held hostage by the leaders of an alien race.

In Jokes

When Picard and Wesley arrive at the Starbase, a directory lists departments and personnel. Filming stopped when this directory was installed while everyone looked to see where they appeared. This Starbase was staffed by the crew of *TNG*.

Picard mentions "Nausicaans" in a conversation with Wesley on the shuttlecraft.

SNAFUs

Wesley opens a communications channel and says that Shuttle #2 is ready for take-off. However, in the following scene, when the shuttle is seen powering up, there is a "01" on the outside of the shuttle.

Episode 44: Up the Long Ladder

Production number: 144
Stardate: 42823.2
Air date: May 20, 1989
Working Title: "Send in the Clones"
Writer: Melinda M. Snodgrass
Director: Winrich Kolbe
Guest Stars: Diana Muldaur: Doctor Comdr. Katherine

"Kate" Pulaski; Barrie Ingham: Danilo O'Dell; Jon De Vries: Granger; Rosalyn Landor: Brenna O'Dell; Colm Meaney: Chief O'Brien.

The crew's rescue of a missing earth colony leads to the discovery of a civilization composed entirely of clones.

Note
The Paramount air schedule originally listed the story as "Send in the Clones," the working title.

In Jokes
When Picard looked for *Mariposa* on the list of ships, the list included *Buckaroo Banzai*, captained by John Whorfin and built by the red Lectroids, and Hathaway, built by Yoyodyne Propulsion Systems of Grover's Mill, NJ, where Orson Welles' *War of the Worlds* radio play took place.

SNAFUs
When Riker and his team are overpowered in the clone Prime Minister's office, Riker is rendered unconscious by a phaser set to stun. As he is being dragged off-scene, he looks up at the camera.

Picard Violates the Prime Directive
Picard forced a clone race to live and breed with the Bringloidi, despite the strong resistance of the clone race and the fact that this would completely destroy their non-sexual nature.

Episode 45: Manhunt

Production number: 145
Stardate: 42859.2
Air date: June 17, 1989
Writer: Terry Devereaux
Director: Rob Bowman
Guest Stars: Diana Muldaur: Doctor Comdr. Katherine "Kate" Pulaski; Majel Barrett: Lwaxana Troi; Robert Costanzo: Slade Bender; Carel Struycken: Mr. Homn;

Rod Arrants: Rex; Colm Meaney: Chief O'Brien; Robert O'Reilly: Second Hoodlum (Scarface); Rhonda Aldrich: Madeline; Mick Fleetwood: Antidean Dignitary; Wren T. Brown: Transporter Pilot.

Troi's mother beams aboard the *Enterprise* and sets her sights on Captain Picard in her search for the perfect mate.

Episode 46: The Emissary

Production number: 146
Stardate: 42901.3
Air date: June 24, 1989
Television Story and Teleplay: Richard Manning and Hans Beimler. Based on an unpublished story by Thomas H. Calder
Director: Cliff Bole
Guest Stars: Diana Muldaur: Doctor Comdr. Katherine "Kate" Pulaski; Suzie Plakson: K'Ehleyr; Lance Le Gault: K'Temoc; Georgann Johnson: Admiral Gromek; Colm Meaney: Chief O'Brien; Anne Elizabeth Ramsey: Ensign Clancy; Dietrich Bader: Tactical Crewman.

An official mission becomes a personal matter when Worf's former love is sent to the *Enterprise* to mediate a dispute between Klingons and the Federation.

Note
Anne Elizabeth Ramsey's name is spelled differently here than in "Elementary, Dear Data," where her name was spelled "Ramsay."

Insider's Story
K'Ehleyr's specially modified probe was a redress of a photon torpedo tube from *Star Trek: The Search For Spock*, which was a redress of Spock's coffin from *Star Trek: The Wrath of Khan*.

SNAFUs
The episode begins with Data playing poker with the bridge crew. The stakes are raised as

they go around the table. Geordi folds, and Dr. Pulanski sees and raises by pushing a stack of coins onto the pot, yet a long shot shows a small pot with no stacks, while the close-up shows a pot with three stacks of coins. Number One sees and moves another stack into the pot, but again a long shot shows a small pot with no stacks. Worf wins with three aces.

Episode 47: Peak Performance

Production number: 147
Stardate: 42923.4
Air date: July 8, 1989
Writer: David Kemper
Director: Robert Scheerer
Guest Stars: Diana Muldaur: Doctor Comdr. Katherine "Kate" Pulaski; Roy Brocksmith: Sirna Kolrami; Armin Shimerman: Bractor; David L. Lander: Tactician; Leslie Neale: Ensign Nagel; Glenn Morshower: Ensign Burke.

A simulated war game turns deadly when the crew is ambushed by a Ferengi battleship.

Insider's Story
Blue candle wax made great antimatter.

Wesley Saves the Day
Wesley's experiment is beamed onto Riker's ship, giving the ship the necessary power to "save the day."

Picard Surrenders
Riker asks Picard, "Would you care to surrender now?" even before the war games begin. Later, the Ferengi drop by and demand the surrender of the Hathaway.

Riker Commands a Ship
U.S.S. Hathaway.

Episode 48: Shades of Gray

Production number: 148
Stardate: 42976.1
Air date: July 15, 1989
Teleplay: Maurice Hurley, Richard Manning, and Hans Beimler
Story: Maurice Hurley
Director: Rob Bowman
Guest Stars: Diana Muldaur: Doctor Comdr. Katherine "Kate" Pulaski; Colm Meaney: Transporter Chief.

Commander Riker is struck down by a deadly microbe that invades his central nervous system and attacks his brain.

THIRD SEASON
Season Notes

Changes from second to third season:

- In the first portion of the opening title sequence, the planets have been replaced by various views of the galaxy.
- Dr. Katherine Pulaski (Diana Muldaur) was mysteriously replaced by Dr. Beverly Crusher (Gates McFadden).
- The one-piece collarless uniforms were replaced by looser two-piece uniforms with collars.
- Geordi LaForge is promoted to Lt. Commander.
- The opening credit sequence and theme music were changed for the third season.

Season Credits

Starring:
Patrick Stewart as Captain Jean-Luc Picard
Jonathan Frakes as Commander William Riker

Also Starring:

LeVar Burton as Lieutenant Commander
Geordi LaForge
Michael Dorn as Lieutenant Worf
Gates McFadden as Dr. Beverly Crusher
Marina Sirtis as Counselor Deanna Troi
Brent Spiner as Lieutenant Commander Data
Wil Wheaton as Wesley "Wes" Crusher

Creator and Executive Producer: Gene
Roddenberry
Executive Producer: Rick Berman
Line Producer: David Livingston
Co-Producers: Hans Beimler and Richard
Manning
Co-Producer: Peter Lauritson
Executive Script Consultant: Melinda M.
Snodgrass

Episode 49: Evolution

Production number: 150
Stardate: 43125.8
Air date: September 23, 1989
Teleplay: Michael Piller
Story: Michael Piller and Michael Wagner
Director: Winrich Kolbe
Guest Stars: Ken Jenkins: Dr. Paul Stubbs; Whoopi
Goldberg: Guinan; Mary McCusker: Nurse; Randal
Patrick: Crewman #1; Scott Grimes: Eric; Amy O'Neill:
Annette.

The crew fights for survival when a mysterious
force attacks the ship's life support systems.

Insider's Story
The length of the final scene with Wesley and
his friends was cut.

In Jokes
The front of the Egg is based on Nanmo, the
Dirty Pair's robot's green eye.

Wesley Screws Up
Wesley, while pulling an all-nighter, leaves a
container open, causing some nanites to
escape and wreck havoc on the ship.

Episode 50: The Ensigns of Command

Production number: 149
Stardate: Unknown
Air date: September 30, 1989
Writer: Melinda M. Snodgrass
Director: Cliff Bole
Guest Stars: Eileen Seeley: Ard'rian; Mark L. Taylor:
Haritath; Richard Allen: Kentor; Colm Meaney: Trans-
porter Chief O'Brien; Grainger Hines: Gosheven; Mart
McChesney: Sheliak.

Data races against time to save a human
colony that's been marked for death by aliens.

Insider's Story
Grainger Hines, who played the lead colonist,
received no credit because after filming was
completed, they decided that his voice "sounded
too much like John Wayne" and dubbed in
another voice. Hines then asked that his name
not be credited.

The shuttle *Onizuka* was named in tribute
to one of the astronauts of the Space Shuttle
Challenger.

Picard Violates the Prime Directive
The *Enterprise* delayed a Sheliak vessel from
destroying a Federation colony on Tau Cygna
V, even though the planet was part of the Sheliak Corporate.

Episode 51: The Survivors

Production number: 151
Stardate: 43152.4

Air date: October 7, 1989
Writer: Michael Wagner
Director: Les Landau
Guest Stars: John Anderson: Kevin Uxbridge; Anne Haney: Rishon Uxbridge.

The crew travels to Rana IV, a remote colony where just two of the former 11,000 inhabitants have miraculously survived a devastating attack.

Episode 52: Who Watches the Watchers?

Production number: 152
Stardate: 43173.5
Air date: October 14, 1989
Writers: Richard Manning and Hans Beimler
Director: Robert Wiemer
Guest Stars: Kathryn Leigh Scott: Nuria; Ray Wise: Liko; James Greene: Dr. Barron; Pamela Segall: Oji; John McLiam: Fento; James McIntire: Hali; Lois Hall: Mary Warren.

Mistakenly believing Captain Picard to be a god, the members of a primitive culture seize Troi and prepare to sacrifice her to him.

Insider's Story
The present that Picard received at the end of this episode reappeared on the back of Picard's chair in "Sarek."

This episode was filmed almost entirely on location at Vasquez Rocks. Marina Sirtis had a hard time with the heat (over 100 degrees), and snakes, scorpions, and bees prevented using deodorant or perfume.

The fusion reactor reappeared slightly redressed in "The Vengeance Factor."

The "Snoop Scope" used by the observation post was based on the video cameras used by the TMA-1 team from *2001: A Space Odyssey.*

Picard Violates the Prime Directive
The *Enterprise* treats a Mintakan person for serious injuries received as a result of the failure of a Federation observation post's cloaking device, ending with the Mintakans believing Picard is a god.

Episode 53: The Bonding

Production number: 153
Stardate: 43198.7
Air date: October 21, 1989
Writer: Ronald D. Moore
Director: Winrich Kolbe
Guest Stars: Susan Powell: Marla Aster; Gabriel Damon: Jeremy Aster; Colm Meaney: O'Brien; Raymond D. Turner: Teacher.

When the ship's archeologist is killed on a mission led by Worf, the Klingon feels responsible for the son she left behind.

Insider's Story
"The Bonding" and "The Defector" were both written by Ronald D. Moore, a fan and first-time writer. Paramount bought and filmed "The Bonding," then bought and filmed "The Defector," before hiring him as series story editor.

Episode 54: Booby Trap

Production number: 154
Stardate: 43205.6
Air date: October 28, 1989
Teleplay: Ron Roman, Michael Piller, and Richard Danus
Story: Michael Wagner and Ron Roman
Director: Gabrielle Beaumont
Guest Stars: Susan Gibney: Leah Brahms; Colm Meaney: O'Brien; Whoopi Goldberg: Guinan; Albert Hall: Galek Dar; Julie Warner: Christy Henshaw.

The *Enterprise* is caught in a booby trap that captures the ship and converts its energy into lethal levels of radiation.

Insider's Story

The original holographic scientist was to be Leah Daistrum, the grand-grand-grand-daughter of Dr. Daistrum from the original *Star Trek*. After they cast Susan Gibney for the part, they realized that she is not African-American and changed her last name to Brahms. They still made references to The Daistrum Institute.

The original model in the holodeck was supposed to be a mock-up of the inside of a warp engine. Time constraints forced more modesty. The sliding panels idea was ultimately used for Geordi's model.

Episode 55: The Enemy

Production number: 155
Stardate: 43349.2
Air date: November 4, 1989
Writers: David Kemper and Michael Piller
Director: David Carson
Guest Stars: John Snyder: Centurian Bochra; Andreas Katsulas: Commander Tomalak; Colm Meaney: O'Brien; Steve Rankin: Patahk.

After Geordi is stranded on a storm-ravaged planet, the crew's attempts to rescue him are hindered by an aggressive Romulan warship.

Insider's Story

Flashlights far too bright to run on batteries required power cords going through the actors' sleeves and down their pant legs to a power source. At one point, Jonathan Frakes stretched a little too far and received a shock.

SNAFUs

Picard tells Tomaluk that he will escort the Romulan ship to the Neutral Zone. Yet in the closing shot, the *Enterprise* and the Romulan Ship take off in two different directions.

Episode 56: The Price

Production number: 156
Stardate: 43385.6
Air date: November 11, 1989
Writer: Hannah Louise Shearer
Director: Robert Scheerer
Guest Stars: Matt McCoy: Devinoni Ral; Elizabeth Hoffman: Premier Bhavani; Castulo Guerra: Dr. Seth Mendoza; Scott Thomson: DaiMon Goss; Dan Shor: Dr. Arridor; Kevin Peter Hall: Leyor; Colm Meaney: O'Brien.

Counselor Troi is swept off her feet by a dashing delegate who uses unethical methods to conduct his business on board the *Enterprise*.

The Ferengi return.

Insider's Story

A Ferengi stretches his hands out while hitting on a female crewmember. She says "no way," and leaves. The original concept included Ferengi being endowed "not unlike a horse," which explains that exchange.

SNAFUs

When the Ferengi DaiMon talks to Picard about putting photon torpedoes through the worm hole, he says, "Casualties of war, Captain." However, his mouth looks as if he is saying "Picard."

When Troi and someone share dinner, at one point one of them lifts a fork and takes a bite, without anything on the fork.

Episode 57: The Vengeance Factor

Production number: 157
Stardate: 43421.9
Air date: November 18, 1989
Writer: Sam Rolfe
Director: Timothy Bond
Guest Stars: Lisa Wilcox: Yuta; Joey Aresco: Brull;

Nancy Parsons: Marouk; Stephen Lee: Chorgan; Marc Lawrence: Volnath; Elkanah J. Burns: Temarek.

The crew's attempts to mediate a violent dispute between warring clans is sabotaged by a mysterious assassin.

Note

The press release lists the character Volnath as "Volnoth."

Insider's Story

The fusion reactor originally appeared in "Who Watches the Watchers?"

Gene Roddenberry did not want the woman summarily executed. However, he was in D.C. at the time. The first time Riker fired, it was for standard human stun. The second time, it would have taken out an elephant. The third shot, setting sixteen, would have taken out a bulkhead.

Episode 58: The Defector

Production number: 158
Stardate: 43462.5
Air date: December 30, 1989
Writer: Ronald D. Moore
Director: Robert Scheerer
Guest Stars: James Sloyan: Setal/Jarok; Andreas Katsulas: Tomalak; John Hancock: Admiral Haden; S.A. Templeman: John Bates; Patrick Stewart: Michael Williams.

A Romulan defector leads the crew into a showdown that could erupt into a full-scale war.

Note

The Paramount press release lists Stack Pierce, not John Hancock, as playing the part of Admiral Haden.

Insider's Story

"The Defector" and "The Bonding" were both written by Ronald D. Moore, a fan and first-time writer. Paramount bought and filmed "The Bonding," then bought and filmed "The Defector," before hiring him as series story editor.

The Romulan Scout has a nose which can detach from the rest of the ship. The separated nose can serve as a lifeboat.

At the beginning of the episode, Data performs a scene from *Henry V* on the holodeck, in which the King mingles with his troops shortly before the Battle of Agincourt. Some lines were cut out. Originally written for the King and three soldiers (Court, Williams, and Bates), the author of the episode combined Court and Williams into one role, represented here as Williams. Williams, incidentally, was played by Shakespearean actor Patrick Stewart. Later in the episode, Picard quotes from Williams' speech.

Episode 59: The Hunted

Production number: 159
Stardate: 43489.2
Air date: January 6, 1990
Writer: Robin Bernheim
Director: Cliff Bole
Guest Stars: Jeff McCarthy: Roga Danar; James Cromwell: Nayrok; Colm Meaney: O'Brien; J. Michael Flynn: Zayner; Andrew Bicknell: Wagnor.

The *Enterprise* is bombarded by a soldier who is the victim of government mind control which turned him into a violent killer.

Insider's Story

Frakes got cute in one take of the scene in which Riker and Worf were about to leave the turbolift and they see a guy about to fire on them. Worf was supposed to push Riker out of the way, but Frakes set all of his weight against Dorn, and Dorn couldn't move him.

When Riker said "Set phasers on maximum stun," he was originally supposed to say "Set phasers on kill," but Roddenberry vetoed it.

SNAFUs

At the end, when the prisoners show up, Danar tells the leader to shoot. Danar blasts a hole in the wall, but later scenes show an undamaged wall.

Episode 60: The High Ground

Production number: 160
Stardate: 43510.7
Air date: January 27, 1990
Writer: Melinda M. Snodgrass
Director: Gabrielle Beaumont
Guest Stars: Kerrie Keane: Alexana Devos; Richard Cox: Kyril Finn; Marc Buckland: Waiter; Fred G. Smith: Policeman; Christopher Pettiet: Boy.

Doctor Crusher's abduction by a radical terrorist group thrusts the crew into an explosive civil war on Rutia IV.

Wesley Saves the Day

Wesley comes up with a way to track the dimensional shift of the terrorists.

Picard Violates the Prime Directive

The *Enterprise* engages in a commando raid to rescue Captain Picard and Beverly Crusher on a warring world.

Episode 61: Deja Q

Production number: 161
Stardate: 43539.1
Air date: February 3, 1990
Writer: Richard Danus
Director: Les Landau

Guest Stars: John deLancie: Q; Corbin Bernsen: Q2; Whoopi Goldberg: Guinan; Richard Cansino: Dr. Garin; Betty Muramoto: Bre'el Scientist.

The crew is surprised by the appearance of their mischievous nemesis, a now-exiled and powerless Q.

Q enables Data to understand humor, although this was not followed up on.

Insider's Story

They had problems filming John deLancie's nude scene. The director had him in a jockstrap, but couldn't film around the indentations it made in his skin because of the camera's perspective. Finally, the director told everyone who was offended by nudity to leave the set, dropped the jock strap, and got the scene in one take. That scene was filmed at 7:00 A.M., and the mariachi band scene at midnight.

Episode 62: A Matter of Perspective

Production number: 162
Stardate: 43610.4
Air date: February 10, 1990
Writer: Ed Zuckerman
Director: Cliff Bole
Guest Stars: Craig Richard Nelson: Krag; Gina Hecht: Manua Apgar; Mark Margolis: Dr. Nel Apgar; Colm Meaney: O'Brien; Juli Donald: Tayna.

Riker is suspected of murdering a respected scientist who had accused the *Enterprise* officer of seducing his wife.

Episode 63: Yesterday's *Enterprise*

Production number: 163
Stardate: 43625.2

Air date: February 17, 1990
Teleplay: Ira Steven Behr, Richard Manning, Hans Beimler, and Ronald D. Moore
Story: Trent Christopher Ganino and Eric A. Stillwell
Director: David Carson
Guest Stars: Denise Crosby: Tasha Yar; Christopher McDonald: Lt. Richard Castillo; Tricia O'Neil: Captain Rachel Garrett; Whoopi Goldberg: Guinan.

The course of history is altered when a time rift brings a starship *Enterprise* from the past into the present with a crew that includes Tasha Yar.

Note
The stardate is given as "Military log, combat date."

SNAFUs
Wesley Crusher wore a regulation Ensign's uniform.

At the end of the episode, Geordi talks with Guinan while wearing an open-neck uniform with black cuffs from the alternate timeline.

Time Travel
A wormhole is created, causing the *Enterprise-C* to travel through time.

Episode 64: The Offspring

Production number: 164
Stardate: 43657.0
Air date: March 10, 1990
Writer: René Echevarria
Director: Jonathan Frakes
Guest Stars: Hallie Todd: Lal; Nicolas Coster: Admiral Haftel; Leonard John Crofoot: Robot; Whoopi Goldberg: Guinan; Judyann Elder: Lt. Ballard; Diane Moser: Ten-Forward Crew; Hayne Bayle: Ten-Forward Crew; Maria Leone: Ten-Forward Crew; James G. Becker: Ten-Forward Crew.

Data becomes a father when he creates an android using a transfer of his own neural programming.

Cast Favorites: Patrick Stewart's Favorite
". . . because it represents all of the things that we have always tried to do on *Star Trek: The Next Generation*. Also, it has another brilliant performance from Brent Spiner matched by an equally fine performance by Hallie Todd, and because it marked the first opportunity given by the studio for one of us to direct an episode, which Jonathan Frakes did outstandingly."

Cast Favorites: Jonathan Frakes' Favorite
"For obvious reasons."

Insider's Story
Jonathan Frakes directed this episode.

Episode 65: Sins of the Father

Production number: 165
Stardate: 43685.2
Air date: March 17, 1990
Teleplay: Ronald D. Moore and W. Reed Moran
Story: Drew Deighan
Director: Les Landau
Guest Stars: Charles Cooper: K'mpec; Tony Todd: Kurn; Patrick Massett: Duras; Thelma Lee: Kahlest; Teddy Davis: Transporter Tech.; B.J. Davis: Assassin; Chris Doyle: Assassin.

When his long-lost brother appears on the *Enterprise*, Worf is thrust into a life-and-death battle for his family's honor.

Reveals much about Klingons.

Insider's Story
The title comes from *The Merchant of Venice*.

SNAFUs

The sound effects people must have fallen asleep every time someone got slapped.

Episode 66: Allegiance

Production number: 166
Stardate: 43714.1
Air date: March 24, 1990
Writer: Richard Manning and Hans Beimler
Director: Winrich Kolbe
Guest Stars: Stephen Markle: Kova Tholl; Reiner Schöne: Esoqq; Joycelyn O'Brien: Cadet Mitena Haro; Jerry Rector: Alien #1; Jeff Rector: Alien #2.

Without the crew's knowledge, Captain Picard is kidnapped and replaced by an evil impostor.

Episode 67: Captain's Holiday

Production number: 167
Stardate: 43745.2
Air date: March 31, 1990
Writer: Ira Steven Behr
Director: Chip Chalmers
Guest Stars: Jennifer Hetrick: Vash; Karen Landry: Ajur; Michael Champion: Boratus; Michael Grodenchik: Sovak; Deirdre Imershein: Joval.

While on vacation, Picard becomes entangled in the search for a missing weapon from the future.

Insider's Story

The basic design of the pack used by Picard came from *Robinson Crusoe on Mars*.

The name "Risa" came from the German word "Reise," which means trip or journey.

SNAFUs

Picard gave Vash the shovel with the handle pointing toward himself, but a far shot showed the handle pointing toward Vash.

Time Travel

Two Vorgons travel from the 27th century to get the Tox Uthat.

Episode 68: Tin Man

Production number: 168
Stardate: 43779.3
Air date: April 21, 1990
Writer: Dennis Putman Bailey and David Bischoff
Director: Robert Scheerer
Guest Stars: Michael Cavanaugh: Capt Robert DeSoto; Peter Vogt: Romulan Commander; Colm Meaney: O'Brien; and; Harry Groener: Tam Elbrun.

The crew is thrust into a deadly showdown with the Romulans over a newly discovered lifeform in a remote star system.

Insider's Story

This episode was based on the writers' own book, *Tin Woodman* (ACE/Doubleday and Co, Inc., 1979), and the lifeform borrowed from the "Wild Card" book series.

The model maker added wood knots, for some reason, making the final product look like a pine cone and feel like tree bark.

SNAFUs

The *Enterprise* and the Romulan ship were thrown far away by Tin Man. Wesley said they had been thrown "3.8 billion kilometers away." The sun went nova seconds later as they watched on the viewscreen, yet, unless the viewscreen had a sensor mechanism that relayed events faster than the speed of light, they couldn't view the star going nova for another three and a half hours.

Episode 69: Hollow Pursuits

Production number: 169
Stardate: 43807.4

Air date: April 28, 1990
Writer: Sally Caves
Director: Cliff Bole
Guest Stars: Dwight Schultz: Barclay; Charley Lang: Duffy; Colm Meaney: O'Brien; Whoopi Goldberg: Guinan.

The crew struggles to help a young engineer who is obsessed with a holodeck fantasy world that endangers the ship.

Insider's Story

The Transporter Test Object used by O'Brien to show that the transporter isn't working is actually a Navy Sonar Buoy Transport Case.

In Jokes

The anti-gravity units contain a flux capacitor, an essential part of the DeLorean/Time Machine in *Back to the Future.*

Episode 70: The Most Toys

Production number: 170
Stardate: 43872.2
Air date: May 5, 1990
Writer: Shari Goodhartz
Director: Timothy Bond
Guest Stars: Nehemiah Persoff: Palor Toff; Jane Daly: Varria; Colm Meaney: O'Brien; Saul Rubinek: Kivas Fajo.

The crew leave Data for dead when his shuttle craft explodes during a dangerous mission.

In Jokes

A quote from Shakespeare's *Hamlet,* bookmarked by Data, catches Picard's eye when the volume is returned to him after the android is presumed lost.

The Ferengi Security code begins with "Kei E Yuri," and the Ferengi access code is "Kei Yuri Dirty Pair," obvious references to the Japanese animation series. Unfortunately, the commander was cut off before he reached the

last word, and used the Japanese pronunciation. People who haven't seen the series in the original Japanese language are at a disadvantage.

SNAFUs

When Data talked to the *Enterprise* at the start of the episode, he said, "Level 1 precautions for incoming material remain in effect," but when Geordi and Wesley later played back the tapes, it appeared that Data had said, "Level 1 precautions remain in effect."

The Walking (Near) Dead

Data is believed to be dead by the crew.

Episode 71: Sarek

Production number: 171
Stardate: 43917.4
Air date: May 12, 1990
Television Story and Teleplay: Peter S. Beagle
Story: Mark Cushman and Jake Jacobs
Director: Les Landau
Guest Stars: Mark Lenard: Sarek; Joanna Miles: Perrin; William Denis: Ki Mendrossen; Rocco Sisto: Sakkath; Colm Meaney: O'Brien; John H. Francis: Science Crewman.

The *Enterprise* is plagued by an outbreak of violence when it is visited by the renowned Vulcan ambassador.

Insider's Story

Mark Lenard makes an appearance as Sarek, Spock's father from Classic Trek.

SNAFUs

The music recital in this episode contained several errors. First, the quartet seating was towards the audience, not toward each other. Classical music was originally developed with the performers facing each other in order to watch visual cues. Performing in front of an audience began much later. Second, the Allegro is by Brahms, not Mozart. Third, the Allegro is a sextet, not a quartet.

Geordi and Wesley set up a pool, and Wesley said that the temperature was 150 degrees Celsius, which is 302 degrees Fahrenheit. However, there was no obvious radiant heat when Geordi and Wesley stood close to the pool and peered inside.

Episode 72: Ménage à Troi

Production number: 172
Stardate: 43930.7
Air date: May 26, 1990
Writers: Fred Bronson and Susan Sackett
Director: Robert Legato
Guest Stars: Majel Barrett: Lwaxana Troi; Frank Corsentino: DaiMon Tog; Ethan Phillips: Dr. Farek; Peter Slutsker: Nibor; Rudolph Willrich: Reittan Grax; Carel Struycken: Mr. Homn

The *Enterprise* is thrown into chaos when Counselor Troi and her mother are kidnapped by the Ferengi.

In Jokes
The Ferengi Security code begins with "Kei Yuri."

Picard sets about wooing Lwaxana Troi back from DaiMon Tog. In the process, he delivers a Shakespearean mish-mash from *Sonnets* 147, 141, 18, 116, and *Othello* V.ii.13–15.

Wesley Saves the Day
Wesley identifies a sound as resembling a Betazoid gong, helping to save Lwaxana Troi, Deanna Troi, and Riker from the Ferengi ship.

Episode 73: Transfigurations

Production number: 173
Stardate: 43957.2

Air date: June 2, 1990
Writer: René Echevarria
Director: Tom Benko
Guest Stars: Mark LaMura: John Doe; Charles Dennis: Commander Sunad; Julie Warner: Christy Henshaw; Colm Meaney: O'Brien; Patti Tippo: Nurse Temple.

The *Enterprise* rescues a mysterious humanoid whose remarkable powers effect the entire crew.

Insider's Story
The new design for the Medical Tricorder is first seen in this episode as Beverly Crusher holds it in every other shot.

In Jokes
An outline of the top portion of a TARDIS is shown upside down against the wall in the sick bay. This is from the British science fiction series *Doctor Who*. Also, three roundals can be seen against the wall. They show up again in several episodes after this one.

The Walking (Near) Dead
Worf falls down in the shuttle bay, only to be saved by John Doe.

Episode 74: The Best of Both Worlds, Part I

Production number: 174
Stardate: 43989.1
Air date: June 16, 1990
Writer: Michael Piller
Director: Cliff Bole
Guest Stars: Elizabeth Dennehy: Lt. Commander Shelby; George Murdock: Admiral J.P. Hanson; Colm Meaney: O'Brien; Whoopi Goldberg: Guinan.

The evil Borg capture Picard in an attempt to conquer the human race.

Picard becomes a Borg named Locutus.

Insider's Story

Commander Shelby (Elizabeth Dennehy) is actor Brian Dennehy's daughter.

Command Offered to Commander Riker

U.S.S. Melbourne.

FOURTH SEASON

Season Notes

Changes from third to fourth season:

- Wesley was made full Ensign before going to Starfleet Academy. ("Ménage à Troi")
- *Star Trek* is now broadcast in Dolby Surround Sound.

Season Credits

Starring:
Patrick Stewart as Captain Jean-Luc Picard
Jonathan Frakes as Commander William Riker
Also Starring:
LeVar Burton as Lieutenant Commander
  Geordi LaForge
Michael Dorn as Lieutenant Worf
Gates McFadden as Dr. Beverly Crusher
Marina Sirtis as Counselor Deanna Troi
Brent Spiner as Lieutenant Commander Data
Wil Wheaton as Wesley "Wes" Crusher

Creator and Executive Producer: Gene
  Roddenberry
Executive Producer: Rick Berman
Executive Producer: Michael Piller
Co-Producer: Peter Lauritson
Producer: David Livingston
Producer: Lee Sheldon
Associate Producer: Wendy Neuss
Executive Story Editor: Ronald D. Moore
Executive Story Editor: Joe Menosky

Episode 75: The Best of Both Worlds, Part II

Production number: 175
Stardate: 44001.4
Air date: September 22, 1990
Writer: Michael Piller
Director: Cliff Bole
Guest Stars: Elizabeth Dennehy: Lt. Commander Shelby;
  George Murdock: Admiral J.P. Hanson; Colm Meaney:
  O'Brien; Whoopi Goldberg: Guinan; Todd Merrill:
  Gleason.

Riker must choose between saving Picard and saving humanity when the Borg use the kidnapped captain as part of their plan to destroy Earth.

Insider's Story

When shooting began, LeVar Burton was in the hospital for emergency surgery. Colm Meaney was used instead for several scenes, but LeVar appeared in close-ups. He was absent for several episodes after this.

SNAFUs

When the Away Team is on the Borg ship, Beverly notices Picard/Locutus behind six Borg soldiers, yet when Worf rushes to rescue Picard, the soldiers have disappeared.

As the Borg ship warps toward Saturn, the planet is lit from the right; the Borg ship arrives from the right, indicating that the ship is coming from the same direction as the sun—a roundabout way to get to the Earth.

Saucer Separation

In order to retrieve Locutus/Picard, the *Enterprise* separates into two sections, with Riker in charge of the warp drive section, and Commander Shelby in charge of the saucer section. While the Borg attack the warp drive section, the rescue shuttle with Worf and Data aboard launches from the saucer section.

Riker Commands a Ship
U.S.S. Enterprise NCC-1701-D

Episode 76: Family

Production number: 178
Stardate: 44012.3
Air date: September 29, 1990
Writer: Ronald D. Moore
Director: Les Landau
Based in part on a premise by Susanne Lambdin and
  Bryan Stewart
Guest Stars: Jeremy Kemp: Robert Picard; Samantha Eggar:
  Marie Picard; Theodore Bikel: Sergey Rozhenko; Georgia
  Brown: Helena Rozhenko; Dennis Creaghan: Louis; Colm
  Meaney: O'Brien; Whoopi Goldberg: Guinan; David Tris-
  tan Birkin: René Picard; Doug Wert: Jack R. Crusher.

While the *Enterprise* undergoes repairs on Earth,
crew members reunite with family. Picard comes
face to face with his brother.

Note
O'Brien's full name is Miles Edward O'Brien.
  "Family" and "Liaisons" are the only episodes in Classic Trek, the movies, or *TNG* that
have no scenes filmed on the bridge.

SNAFUs
Jack Crusher is not wearing a communicator
pin, then, magically, he is.
  At the end of the episode, Picard's young
nephew, René, sits under a tree gazing up at the
stars, presumably imagining following in his
uncle's footsteps. The constellation Orion clearly
appears in the middle of the sky, but the episode
is set in the summer, while Orion is visible only
in the early evenings in the dead of winter.

Episode 77: Brothers

Production number: 177
Stardate: 44085.7

Air date: October 6, 1990
Writer: Rick Berman
Director: Rob Bowman
Guest Stars: Cory Danziger: Jake Potts; Colm Meaney:
  O'Brien; Adam Ryen: Willie Potts; James Lashly:
  Ensign Kopf; Brent Spiner: Lore/Dr. Noonian Soong.

Data clashes with his evil brother, Lore, after
being summoned home by his elderly creator.

SNAFUs
The spoken code Data gives to lock the *Enterprise* computer system differs from the version
displayed on the screen.

Attempts at Self-Destruct
Picard attempts to engage the self-destruct sequence in order to regain control of the *Enterprise,* but fails.

Episode 78: Suddenly Human

Production number: 176
Stardate: 44143.7
Air date: October 13, 1990
Teleplay: John Whelpley and Jeri Taylor
Story: Ralph Phillips
Director: Gabrielle Beaumont
Guest Stars: Sherman Howard: Captain Endar; Chad
  Allen: Jono; Barbara Townsend: Admiral Connaught
  Rossa.

Picard risks war when he refuses to return a
human boy to the alien father who raised him.

SNAFUs
When Jeremiah sits down in Ten-Forward to
have a banana split, he is on Wesley's left. Then,
when Wesley gets hit by the ice cream, it comes
from Wesley's right.
  Near the end, when Picard brings Jeremiah
onto the bridge, the usual sound of the turbolift doors opening is missing.

Episode 79: Remember Me

Production number: 179
Stardate: 44161.2
Air date: October 20, 1990
Writer: Lee Sheldon
Director: Cliff Bole
Guest Stars: Eric Menyuk: Traveller; Bill Erwin: Commander Dalen Quaice, M.D.; Colm Meaney: O'Brien.

Wesley's experiments with warp fields result in the mysterious disappearance of the crew.

Insider's Story

Gates McFadden's stunts in "Remember Me" were done when she was pregnant, but she did not know about it until days later.

In Jokes

The title is from *Hamlet*.

SNAFUs

Beverly asks the computer to show her "the Universe." The computer outputs a drawing of the *Enterprise* with the portion of the saucer section with the bridge cropped off.

In the final act, when Wesley and the Traveler are entering the equations into the computer, Wesley closes his eyes, and then places his hand on the case, about three inches below the entry pad. While he is making his entries, his hand starts moving up, while the sound effects people keep making the sounds in time.

In the last act, Dr. Crusher enters the turbolift and asks to go to engineering. The computer refuses, so she then asks to go anywhere on Deck 36, and the turbolift does. The lights of the turbolift then go down, indicating that the lift went up from the bridge. When everyone has disappeared and Bev comes off the turbolift and down onto the bridge, the cameraman and equipment can be seen in the reflective glass to the left of the lift.

Wesley Screws Up

Wesley's experiment causes his mother to be trapped in a warp bubble.

Episode 80: Legacy

Production number: 180
Stardate: 44215.2
Air date: October 27 90
Working Title: "Beyond Tomorrow"
Writer: Joe Menosky
Director: Robert Scheerer
Guest Stars: Beth Toussaint: Ishara Yar; Don Mirault: Hayne; Colm Meaney: O'Brien; Vladimir Velasco: Tan Tsu; Christopher Michael: Man #1, Coalition lieutenant.

A rescue mission leads the crew to the birthplace of their late comrade, Tasha Yar, where they encounter her sister.

Insider's Story

A label on a nuclear reactor reads, "Remember, you can never add TOO MUCH water to a Nuclear Reactor," and other rules.

SNAFUs

During the card trick with Data, Riker's hand changes position whenever the camera switches.

Picard Violates the Prime Directive

The commando raid might have radically changed the balance of power on the planet.

Enterprise Exceeds Warp Speed Limits

In the teaser, the *Enterprise* flies Warp 9.6 to Tasha Yar's birthplace.

Episode 81: Reunion

Production number: 181
Stardate: 44246.3
Air date: November 3, 1990
Working Title: "When Honor is Lost"

Teleplay: Thomas Perry, Jo Perry, Ronald D. Moore, and Brannon Braga
Story: Drew Deighan, Thomas Perry, and Jo Perry
Director: Jonathan Frakes
Guest Stars: Suzie Plakson: K'Ehleyr; Robert O'Reilly: Gowron; Patrick Massett: Duras; Charles Cooper: K'm-pec; Jon Steuer: Alexander; Michael Rider: Security Guard; April Grace: Transporter Technician; Basil Wallace: Klingon Guard #1, Duras aide; Mirron Edward Willis: Klingon Guard #2, Vorn.

When Picard is chosen to mediate a Klingon power struggle, Worf confronts the Klingon who disgraced him.

Introduces Worf's son, Alexander.

Insider's Story
Jonathan Frakes directs.

SNAFUs
After K'Ehleyr dies, Alexander runs away and Worf lets out his primal scream. Her body is lowered to the floor. As she finally settles, her eyes flutter open and closed several times. Her head faces toward her left. However, when her body is shown full-on from the perspective of her feet, her head faces slightly toward her right and remains that way for the rest of the scene.

Dr. Crusher and her aide come from the bedroom, not from the corridor.

When Worf kills Gowron near the end of the episode, the camera shows Gowron's dead body with red blood flowing from it, in conflict with *Star Trek VI*, in which the Klingons had lavender blood.

Episode 82: Future Imperfect

Production number: 182
Stardate: 44286.5
Air date: November 10, 1990
Writers: J. Larry Carroll and David Bennett Carren
Director: Les Landau

Guest Stars: Andreas Katsulas: "Ambassador" Tomalak; Chris Demetral: Jean-Luc/Ethan; Carolyn McCormick: Minuet; Patti Yasutake: Nurse; Todd Merrill: Ensign Gleason; April Grace: Transporter Chief Hubbell; George O'Hanlon, Jr.: N.D. Transporter Chief; Dana Tjowander: Barash.

After an Away Team mission fails, Riker awakens in sickbay to discover that 16 years have passed and he now commands the *Enterprise.*

Episode 83: Final Mission

Production number: 183
Stardate: 44307.3
Air date: November 17, 1990
Teleplay: Kasey Arnold-Ince and Jeri Taylor
Story: Kasey Arnold-Ince
Director: Corey Allen
Guest Stars: Nick Tate: Dirgo; Kim Hamilton: Chairman Songi; Mary Kohnert: Ensign Tess Allenby.

After being accepted into Starfleet Academy, Wesley accompanies Picard on a final mission, only to find himself struggling to keep the captain alive.

Wesley Saves the Day
Wesley is able to get past the guardian of the well and get water for Captain Picard.

Episode 84: The Loss

Production number: 184
Stardate: 44356.9
Air date: December 29, 1990
Teleplay: Hilary J. Bader, Alan J. Adler, and Vanessa Greene
Story: Hilary J. Bader
Director: Chip Chalmers
Guest Stars: Kim Braden: Ensign Janet Brooks; Mary Kohnert: Ensign Tess Allenby; Whoopi Goldberg: Guinan.

Counselor Troi resigns her post after experiencing a mysterious loss of her empathic powers.

Note
The opening title sequence was edited because of the departure of Wil Wheaton. Instead of redoing the actors' names, and keeping the length of the title sequence the same, a quick-and-dirty two-second edit was done. The two-second interval when Wil's name used to appear was cut. The star field abruptly changes, and the music runs shorter.

Insider's Story
The originally planned ending scene of Troi and Riker kissing in Ten-Forward viewed from outside the ship was hard to achieve, due to the need to have reliable reflection of space, and was cut.

Episode 85: Data's Day

Production number: 185
Stardate: 44390.1
Air date: January 5, 1991
Teleplay: Harold Apter and Ronald D. Moore
Story: Harold Apter
Director: Robert Wiemer
Guest Stars: Rosalind Chao: Keiko Ishikawa; Colm Meaney: O'Brien; Sierra Pecheur: Ambassador T'Pel (Sub-Commander Selok); Alan Scarfe: Commander Mendak; Shelly Desai: V'Sal; April Grace: Transporter Technician.

A friend's impending wedding compounds Data's confusion about the nuances of human feelings.

Episode 86: The Wounded

Production number: 186
Stardate: 44429.6
Air date: January 26, 1991

Teleplay: Jeri Taylor
Story: Stuart Charno, Sara Charno, and Cy Chermak
Director: Chip Chalmers
Guest Stars: Bob Gunton: Captain Benjamin Maxwell; Rosalind Chao: Keiko Ishikawa O'Brien; Marc Alaimo: Gul Macet; Colm Meaney: O'Brien; Marco Rodriguez: Glin Telle; Time Winters: Glin Daro; John Hancock: Admiral Haden.

Picard must stop a renegade Federation starship that is making unprovoked attacks on a former enemy's ship.

This episode introduced the Cardassians.

Insider's Story
The Cardassian ships were designed with an Egyptian theme. They come complete with a sacrificial temple on top and pyramid running lights along the side.

Colm Meaney serves Keiko steak and potatoes for dinner. The potatoes had to get from the spoon to the plate easily, while he continued with the dialogue, moved around, served himself, etc. After about a zillion takes, it finally worked, except that one small piece of potato bounced off the plate and onto the table. So, Colm improvised, and quickly popped it in his mouth. "Cut!" "What was wrong with that?" "Well, you popped that potato in your mouth." "Yeah, so?" "Well, you can't do that—see, this is a self-cleaning ship." "I got to it first!"

Episode 87: Devil's Due

Production number: 187
Stardate: 44474.5
Air date: February 2, 1991
Teleplay: Philip Lazebnik
Story: Philip Lazebnik and William Douglas Lansford
Director: Tom Benko
Guest Stars: Marta Dubois: Ardra; Paul Lambert: Dr. Clarke; Marcello Tubert: Jared; Thad Lamey: Devil Monster; Tom Magee: Klingon Monster; William Glover: Marley.

Picard fights to save a terrorized planet from a powerful woman who claims to be the devil.

Insider's Story
Originally a script for the proposed *Star Trek: Phase II* television series. The series idea was scrapped, and sets were used for the shooting of *Star Trek: The Motion Picture.*

SNAFUs
In the Classic Trek episode, "Day of the Dove," Captain Kang explicitly remarks that the Klingons have no devil. However, in "Devil's Due," Ardra adopts the guise of the Klingon devil, Fekhlar, a creature that consumes the souls of cowards.

Episode 88: Clues

Production number: 188
Stardate: 44502.7
Air date: February 9, 1991
Teleplay: Bruce D. Arthurs and Joe Menosky
Story: Bruce D. Arthurs
Director: Les Landau
Guest Stars: Colm Meaney: O'Brien; Pamela Winslow: Ensign McKnight; Rhonda Aldrich: Madeline; Whoopi Goldberg: Guinan; Patti Yasutake: Nurse; Thomas Knickerbocker: Gunman.

Picard and the crew are shocked to discover that Data is lying to them.

SNAFUs
Guinan's cigarette in a holder changes length with each camera cut.

Episode 89: First Contact

Production number: 189
Stardate: Unknown
Air date: February 16, 1991
Teleplay: Dennis Russell Bailey, David Bischoff, Joe Menosky, Ronald D. Moore, and Michael Piller

Story: Marc Scott Zicree
Director: Cliff Bole
Guest Stars: George Coe: Chancellor Avill Durken; Carolyn Seymour: Mirasta; George Hearn: Berel; Michael Ensign: Krola; Steven Anderson: Nilrem; Sachi Parker: Dr. Tava; Bebe Neuwirth: Lanel.

Riker is mistaken for a hostile alien after being critically wounded during a first contact mission.

Picard Violates the Prime Directive
The *Enterprise* contacts a planet in order to rescue Commander Riker.

Episode 90: Galaxy's Child

Production number: 190
Stardate: 44614.6
Air date: March 9, 1991
Teleplay: Maurice Hurley
Story: Thomas Kortozian
Director: Winrich Kolbe
Guest Stars: Susan Gibney: Dr. Leah Brahms; Lanei Chapman: Ensign Rager; Jana Marie Hupp: Ensign Pavlik; Whoopi Goldberg: Guinan; April Grace: Transporter Technician.

The *Enterprise* becomes surrogate mother to a huge alien creature after Picard is forced to destroy its real mother.

Episode 91: Night Terrors

Production number: 191
Stardate: 44631.2
Air date: March 16, 1991
Teleplay: Pamela Douglas and Jeri Taylor
Story: Shari Goodhartz
Director: Les Landau
Guest Stars: Rosalind Chao: Keiko Ishikawa O'Brien; John Vickery: Andrus Hagan; Duke Moosekian: Ensign Gillespie; Craig Hurley: Ensign Peeples; Brian Tochi: Ensign Kenny Lin; Lanei Chapman: Ensign Rager; Colm

229

Meaney: O'Brien; Whoopi Goldberg: Guinan; Deborah Taylor: Captain Chantel R. Zaheva.

Unexplained paranoia and hallucinations plague the crew of the *Enterprise* after they are trapped by a rift in space.

SNAFUs

Brittain's visual log shows the ship as *U.S.S. Brattain*, even though the saucer decal reads *U.S.S. Brittain*.

Episode 92: Identity Crisis

Production number: 192
Stardate: 44664.5
Air date: March 23, 1991
Teleplay: Brannon Braga
Story: Timothy de Haas
Director: Winrich Kolbe
Guest Stars: Maryann Plunkett: Lieutenant Commander Susanna Leijten; Patti Yasutake: Nurse Alyssa Ogawa; Amick Byram: Lieutenant Hickman; Dennis Madalone: Transporter Technician Chief Hedrick; Mona Grudt: Ensign Graham; Paul Tompkins: Breville.

Dr. Crusher races against time to locate a parasite that threatens to transform Geordi into an alien creature.

Note

Mona Grudt, Miss Universe 1990, hails from Norway.

Episode 93: The Nth Degree

Production number: 194 [AU: not 193?]
Stardate: 44704.2
Air date: March 30, 1991
Working Title: "To the Nth Degree"
Writer: Joe Menosky
Director: Robert Legato

Guest Stars: Jim Norton: Einstein; Kay E. Kuter: Cytherian; Saxon Trainor: Lt. Linda Larson; Page Leong: Ensign April Anaya; Dwight Schultz: Barclay; David Coburn: Ensign Brower.

An alien probe endows a crew member with superhuman intelligence and threatens the Enterprise.

Note

The four-second bumper used for the second through fifth commercial breaks changed. While the length remained the same—four seconds and fifteen frames—the music changed. The new music started when the logo first appeared. The ten frames that contained the star field were removed, while ten extra black frames were added to the tail of the bumper. The new music extended into the new black area. The new bumper was even added to repeats of episodes shown after this episode (184 through 192).

SNAFUs

In the holodeck scene, when Troi attempts to talk Barclay out of the neural net device he has concocted, the holodeck doors don't close properly. A section of light at waist level remains visible for a minute.

Enterprise Exceeds Warp Speed Limits

Barclay, using knowledge gained from an alien probe, creates a space distortion that causes the *Enterprise* to travel halfway across the galaxy.

Episode 94: Qpid

Production number: 193
Stardate: 44741.9
Air date: April 20, 1991
Teleplay: Ira Steven Behr
Story: Randee Russell and Ira Steven Behr

Director: Cliff Bole

Guest Stars: Jennifer Hetrick: Vash; Clive Revill: Sir Guy; John deLancie: Q; Joi Staton: Servant.

The mischievous Q turns Picard into Robin Hood and sends him on a quest designed to force him to prove his love for an old flame.

Cast Favorites: LeVar Burton's Favorite

"All in all, I would have to say the holodeck shows. After wearing our 'space suits' day in and day out and being so serious so much of the time, it was always fun to put on those great costumes and play!"

Insider's Story

When Q joins Maid Marion and Sir Guy at a dining table, Q uncharacteristically hugs and kisses a maid. This maid was John deLancie's real-life wife, Marnie Mosiman. She also did a guest shot on *TNG* in season two, "Loud as a Whisper," as the woman in Riva's chorus.

The 24th century characters assumed "Robin Hood" roles as follows:

Picard:	Robin Hood
Riker:	Little John
Data:	Friar Tuck
Worf:	Will Scarlet
LaForge:	Alan-a-Dale
Vash:	Maid Marian
Q:	The Sheriff

In Jokes

The scene in which Worf smashes Geordi's lute, then says "Sorry," is reminiscent of a toga party scene in *Animal House*.

During the sword fight, when Picard/Robin Hood says, "There is something you should know . . . I'm not from Nottingham," it recalls a sword fight in *Princess Bride* when similar dialog is uttered.

Episode 95: The Drumhead

Production number: 195
Stardate: 44769.2
Air date: April 27, 1991
Working Title: "It Can't Happen Here"
Writer: Jeri Taylor
Director: Jonathan Frakes
Guest Stars: Bruce French: Sabin; Spencer Garrett: Simon Tarses; Henry Woronicz: J'Ddan; Earl Billings: Admiral Thomas Henry; Jean Simmons: Admiral Norah Satie; Ann Shea: Nellen.

A search for a spy aboard the *Enterprise* turns into a witch hunt after Picard is implicated as a traitor.

Cast Favorites: Michael Dorn's Favorite

"A good courtroom drama."

SNAFUs

After the first hearing, Worf and J'Ddan leave the room. The doors open, but as they are walking though the doorway, the doors start to close, hesitate, then open back up and then close after they leave the doorway.

Satie says that Captain Picard took command of the *Enterprise* on Stardate 41162. It was 41152.

Episode 96: Half a Life

Production number: 196
Stardate: 44805.2
Air date: May 4, 1991
Working Title: "Civil Wars"
Teleplay: Peter Allen Fields
Story: Ted Roberts and Peter Allen Fields
Director: Les Landau
Guest Stars: Majel Barrett: Lwaxana Troi; Michelle Forbes: Dara; Terrence E. McNally: B'Tardat; Colm Meaney: O'Brien; Carel Struycken: Mr. Homn; David Ogden Stiers: Dr. Timicin.

Picard risks war when he offers asylum to a visiting scientist who wishes to escape the ritual suicide mandated by his society.

In Jokes

A display shows the number "4077," a reference to the television series *M*A*S*H*.

SNAFUs

Near the end of the episode, when Lwaxana Troi talks to Deanna, Deanna's reflection appears in the mirror. When Lwaxana walks toward Deanna, the microphone boom can be clearly seen in the mirror.

Episode 97: The Host

Production number: 197
Stardate: 44821.3
Air date: May 11, 1991
Working Title: "Paradise"
Writer: Michael Horvat
Director: Marvin V. Rush
Guest Stars: Barbara Tarbuck: Governor Leka Trion; Nicole Orth-Pallavicini: Kareel; William Newman: Kalin Trose; Patti Yasutake: Nurse Ogawa; Robert Harper: Lathal; Franc Luz: Odan.

Dr. Crusher falls in love with an alien who survives by occupying different "host bodies." Introduces the Trill.

Cast Favorites: Gates McFadden's Favorite

". . . because it introduced a very different species and asked the question 'what is love?' in a very different way."

Episode 98: The Mind's Eye

Production number: 198
Stardate: 44885.5

Air date: May 25, 1991
Teleplay: René Echevarria
Story: Ken Schafer and René Echevarria
Director: David Livingston
Guest Stars: Larry Dobkin: Ambassador Kell; John Fleck: Taibak; Colm Meaney: O'Brien; Edward Wiley: Governor Vagh; Majel Barrett: Computer Voice.

Romulan forces kidnap Geordi and turn him into a killing machine.

Episode 99: In Theory

Production number: 199
Stardate: 44932.3
Air date: June 1, 1991
Working Title: "Breaking Up Is Hard To Do"
Teleplay: Ronald D. Moore and Joe Menosky
Director: Patrick Stewart
Guest Stars: Michele Scarabelli: Ensign Jenna D'Sora; Rosalind Chao: Keiko Ishikawa O'Brien; Colm Meaney: O'Brien; Pamela Winslow: Ensign McKnight; Whoopi Goldberg: Guinan; Majel Barrett: Computer Voice.

Data experiments with love by pursuing a romantic relationship with a fellow crew member.

Insider's Story

Patrick Stewart directs.

In Jokes

Picard says, "Now would be a good time," recalling a line used by Kirk during the Classic Trek episode, "The Doomsday Machine," which, in turn, was also heard in *Star Trek IV: The Voyage Home.*

SNAFUs

In the teaser, Data told Jenna the reasons why she broke up with Jeff. She and Data then appear close to the photon torpedo before she moves to a control panel. A black, hand-sized object rests on top of the torpedo. Data stands up, holding a sensor in his left hand. Then, as Data walks toward Jenna, the sensor mysteriously jumps into his right hand, and Jenna suddenly holds the device she had left on top of the torpedo.

Episode 100: Redemption, Part I

Production number: 200
Stardate: 44995.3
Air date: June 15, 1991
Writer: Ronald D. Moore
Director: Cliff Bole
Guest Stars: Robert O'Reilly: Gowron; Tony Todd: Commander Kurn; Barbara March: Lursa; Gwynyth Walsh: B'Etor; Ben Slack: K'Tal; Nicholas Kepros: General Movar; J.D. Cullum: Toral; Denise Crosby: Commander Sela; Whoopi Goldberg: Guinan; Tom Ormeny: Klingon 1st Officer; Clifton Jones: Helmsman; Majel Barrett: Computer Voice.

Worf's loyalties are torn between the Federation and his people when civil war threatens the Klingon Empire.

SNAFUs

Worf says he will be serving on the *Bortas,* but instead serves on the *Hectar,* with no explanation about the transfer.

Picard tells Guinan that Yar died a year prior to Guinan joining the crew. However, "Skin of Evil" was the fourth-to-last story of the first season, and Guinan was first seen in the second season premiere, "The Child," suggesting only a three- to four-month gap between the two stories.

Picard tells Sela that the battle on Narendra III took place 24 years before, but tells Guinan that it was 23 years before.

FIFTH SEASON

Season Notes

During the fifth season, a 30-second ad during one of the show's 10 national ad slots in a first-run episode cost $200,000.

Changes from fourth to fifth season:

- The title sequence was slightly rearranged, with the *Star Trek: The Next Generation* logo coming out of a video-tunnel-like effect.

- Captain Picard occasionally wears a blue-gray uniform with a red jacket. This was Stewart's request because he was getting bored with his regular uniform. He helped design the jacket. The jacket is made out of very soft suede with leather shoulders, and cost about $3,000 to make.

- In the conference room, the wall relief containing the *Enterprise* lineage has been changed to another pattern.

- The *Enterprise*'s commissioning plaque is starting to tarnish.

Season Credits

Starring:
Patrick Stewart as Captain Jean-Luc Picard
Jonathan Frakes as Commander William Riker
Also Starring:
LeVar Burton as Lieutenant Commander Geordi LaForge
Michael Dorn as Lieutenant Worf
Gates McFadden as Dr. Beverly Crusher
Marina Sirtis as Counselor Deanna Troi
Brent Spiner as Lt. Commander Data

Creator and Executive Producer: Gene Roddenberry
Executive Producer: Rick Berman

Executive Producer: Michael Piller
Supervising Producer: Jeri Taylor
Co-Producer: Joe Menosky
Co-Producer: Ronald D. Moore
Co-Producer: Peter Lauritson
Producer: David Livingston
Associate Producer: Wendy Neuss

Episode 101: Redemption, Part II

Production number: 201
Stardate: 45020.4
Air date: September 21, 1991
Writer: Ronald D. Moore
Director: David Carson
Guest Stars: Denise Crosby: Commander Sela; Tony Todd: Commander Kurn; Barbara March: Lursa; Gwynyth Walsh: B'Etor; J.D. Cullum: Toral; Robert O'Reilly: Gowron; Michael G. Hagerty: Captain Larg; Fran Bennett: Admiral Shanthi; Nicholas Kepros: General Movar; Colm Meaney: O'Brien; Timothy Carhart: Lieutenant Commander Christopher Hobson; Jordan Lund: Kluge; Stephen James Carver: Hegh'ta Helmsman; Clifton Jones: Ensign Craig; Majel Barrett: Computer Voice.

Picard risks all-out war with the Romulans when he involves Starfleet in the Klingon civil war.

SNAFUs
When Worf is given back his family name, the blood on the knife is red, not lavender as in *Star Trek VI*.

Riker Commands a Ship
U.S.S. Excalibur.

Episode 102: Darmok

Production number: 202
Stardate: 45047.2
Air date: September 28, 1991

Teleplay: Joe Menosky
Story: Philip Lazebnik and Joe Menosky
Director: Winrich Kolbe
Guest Stars: Richard Allen: Tamarian 1st Officer; Colm Meaney: O'Brien; Paul Winfield: Captain Dathon; Ashley Judd: Ensign Robin Lefler; Majel Barrett: Computer Voice.

The *Enterprise* crew is rendered helpless when Picard is kidnapped and forced to go to war with an alien captain.

Insider's Story
The writers played with words. DARMOK read backwards forms KOMRAD (comrade), while JILARD scrambled forms most of JLpIcARD.

Gilgamesh is based upon the Gilgamesh of Sumerian lore, a character described as combining the traits of Solomon, Ulysses, and Hercules. One of the important factors is that Gilgamesh feared death after his friend died, leading to his quest for immortality. He comes very close, but always misses.

SNAFUs
The very last shot, from outside the ship, shows Picard looking through the windows of his ready room on the port side of the ship. The window shows a reflection of moving stars, but they move straight toward the window. The stars should have moved left to right.

Due to a post-production error, the phasers shot out of the photon torpedo tubes.

Episode 103: Ensign Ro

Production number: 203
Stardate: 45076.3
Air date: October 5, 1991
Teleplay: Michael Piller

Story: Richard Berman and Michael Piller
Director: Les Landau
Guest Stars: Michelle Forbes: Ensign Ro Laren; Scott Marlowe: Keeve Falor; Frank Collison: Gul Dolak; Jeffrey Hayenga: Orta; Harley Venton: Collins; Ken Thorley: Barber Mot; Cliff Potts: Admiral Kennelly; Majel Barrett: Computer Voice.

Picard suspects a high-level Federation conspiracy when the crew is ordered to locate the terrorist leader of a renegade race.

Introduces the Bajoran ensign, Ro.

SNAFUs

Ensign Ro takes off her jacket with the communicator still attached. However, when she hands the jacket to the little girl, her communicator appears on her uniform.

When Ro talks with the girl, we sometimes see shots taken from behind the girl, showing Ro less crouched than in shots taken from behind her.

Episode 104: Silicon Avatar

Production number: 204
Stardate: 45122.3
Air date: October 12, 1991
Teleplay: Jeri Taylor
Story: Lawrence V. Conley
Director: Cliff Bole
Guest Stars: Ellen Geer: Dr. Kila Marr; Susan Diol: Carmen Davila.

Picard struggles to communicate with a mysterious, destructive force before a visiting scientist can destroy it.

SNAFUs

Dr. Marr holds a tricorder while talking to Data in the second act. The tricorder is open. She closes it, then reopens it, but always holds it upside down.

Episode 105: Disaster

Production number: 205
Stardate: 45156.1
Air date: October 19, 1991
Teleplay: Ronald D. Moore
Story: Ron Jarvis and Philip A. Scorza
Director: Gabrielle Beaumont
Guest Stars: Rosalind Chao: Keiko Ishikawa O'Brien; Colm Meaney: O'Brien; Michelle Forbes: Ensign Ro Laren; Erika Flores: Marissa; John Christian Graas: Jay Gordon; Max Supera: Paterson; Cameron Arnett: Ensign Mandel; Jana Marie Hupp: Ensign Monroe.

Troi holds the lives of the *Enterprise* crew in her hands when a natural disaster forces her to take over as captain of the seriously damaged ship.

SNAFUs

Dr. Crusher and Geordi evacuate all the air from the cargo bay. Then Geordi hits the button for the cargo bay, causing the door to audibly close, even though sound doesn't travel in a vacuum.

The scene cuts to Ten-Forward when the ship begins shaking. The stars shake along with the ship.

When Picard gives the two pips to the girl in the turbolift, her collar already has two small holes.

In the last scene, Picard leaves the bridge heading to his ready room, but the door closes too early, and the sound comes too late.

Episode 106: The Game

Production number: 206
Stardate: 45208.2
Air date: October 26, 1991
Teleplay: Brannon Braga
Story: Susan Sackett, Fred Bronson, and Brannon Braga
Director: Corey Allen

Guest Stars: Ashley Judd: Ensign Robin Lefler; Katherine Moffat: Etana Jol; Colm Meaney: O'Brien; Patti Yasutake: Nurse Alyssa Ogawa; Wil Wheaton: Wesley Crusher; Diane M. Hurley: Woman; Majel Barrett: Computer Voice.

The fate of the Federation lies in Wesley Crusher's hands when he returns to find the crew of the *Enterprise* addicted to a dangerous new game.

SNAFUs

The crew force Wesley to play the game, but Wesley blinks while Riker holds his eyes open.

Wesley Saves the Day

Wesley realizes the true purpose of the game and repairs Data in time to awaken everyone from hypnosis.

Episode 107: Unification, Part I

Production number: 208
Stardate: 45233.1
Air date: November 2, 1991
Story: Rick Berman and Michael Piller
Teleplay: Jeri Taylor
Director: Les Landau
Guest Stars: Leonard Nimoy: Spock; Joanna Miles: Perrin; Stephen D. Root: Captain K'Vada; Graham Jarvis: Klim Dokachin; Malachi Throne: Senator Pardek; Norman Large: Proconsul Neral; Daniel Roebuck: Romulan #1 (Jaron); Erick Avari: B'ljik; Karen Hensel: Admiral Brackett; Mimi Cozzens: Soup Woman; Majel Barrett: Computer Voice; Mark Lenard: Sarek.

Picard and Data travel to Romulus to investigate an unauthorized mission undertaken by the Federation's legendary Mr. Spock.

Note

This episode included a ten-second tribute to Gene Roddenberry.

Insider's Story

Leonard Nimoy makes an appearance as Spock and Mark Lenard as Sarek.

Malachi Throne, who plays Romulan Senator Pardek in "Unification," appeared in Classic Trek's "The Menagerie" as Commodore José Mendez.

SNAFUs

When Dr. Crusher examines Data to prepare him for Romulus, she asks if Data's ears are detachable. Data replies that they are not, yet, in "Datalore," Data's brother, Lore, was shown without ears.

Episode 108: Unification, Part II

Production number: 207
Stardate: 45245.8
Air date: November 9, 1991
Teleplay: Michael Piller
Story: Rick Berman and Michael Piller
Director: Cliff Bole
Guest Stars: Leonard Nimoy: Spock; Stephen D. Root: Captain K'Vada; Malachi Throne: Senator Pardek; Norman Large: Proconsul Neral; Daniel Roebuck: Romulan #1 (Jaron); William Bastiani: Omag; Susan Fallender: Romulan #2; Denise Crosby: Commander Sela; Vidal Peterson: D'Tan; Harriet Leider: Amarie.

Picard and Mr. Spock clash over a proposed reunification of the Romulans and the Vulcans.

Sarek dies. Tasha Yar's daughter, Sela, appears.

Note

This episode included a ten-second tribute to Gene Roddenberry.

Insider's Story

When Riker went into the bar on Quaylor II to talk to the four-handed piano player, the actress' real voice had a Brooklyn accent, so they got a different actress to read the part, and then edited it in over the original actress' voice. They also did that for log entries. In the "before" clip, it was another voice reading the First Officer's Log entry, while in the "after" clip, it was Frakes' voice. The woman who re-voiced the four-handed piano player is the actress who does the voice of the computer in *Deep Space Nine*.

The junkyard consisted mostly of ships dragged out from wherever Mike Okuda could find them. Some models came from the unmade *Star Trek: Phase II* series. Some models were designed by Greg Jein or Robert McCall.

SNAFUs

After Spock, Picard, and Data knock out the Romulan guards, Spock holds Sela at gun-point, but Picard has no gun in his hand. After a camera switch, Picard holds a Romulan "disrupter pistol." A minute later, after a scene with the *Enterprise,* Picard has a Romulan "disrupter rifle."

After Data gives Sela the neck pinch, when Picard, Data, and Spock leave the room the glass pyramid in Sela's office shows a reflection of a cameraman chewing gum.

Episode 109: A Matter of Time

Production number: 209
Stardate: 45349.1
Air date: November 16, 1991
Writer: Rick Berman
Director: Paul Lynch
Guest Stars: Stefan Gierasch: Dr. Hal Moseley; Matt

Frewer: Berlingoff Rasmussen; Sheila Franklin: Ensign Felton; Shay Garner: Female Scientist.

Picard's quest to save an endangered planet leads him to violate the Prime Directive when he seeks the advice of a visitor from the future.

Insider's Story

This episode was written because Robin Williams, a fan of the show, wanted to appear. However, when the script was ready for shooting, Robin was unavailable, so Matt Frewer was cast instead.

Time Travel

Berlinghoff Rasmussen, in the 22nd century, steals a time machine from a visiting time traveler from the 26th century, and uses it to visit the *Enterprise* and steal devices to later "invent."

Episode 110: New Ground

Production number: 210
Stardate: 45376.3
Air date: January 4, 1992
Working Title: "Barriers"
Teleplay: Grant Rosenberg
Story: Sara Charno and Stuart Charno
Director: Robert Scheerer
Guest Stars: Georgia Brown: Helena Rozhenko; Brian Bonsall: Alexander; Richard McGonagle: Dr. Ja'Dar; Jennifer Edwards: Kyle; Sheila Franklin: Ensign Felton; Majel Barrett: Computer Voice.

Worf learns painful lessons about parenting when his son Alexander arrives to join him on the *Enterprise*.

SNAFUs

Alexander states that he was born on stardate 42305, making him only two and a half years old.

Riker saves what is obviously a hand puppet from the lab.

Episode 111: Hero Worship

Production number: 211
Stardate: 45397.3
Air date: January 25, 1992
Teleplay: Joe Menosky
Story: Hilary J. Bader
Director: Patrick Stewart
Guest Stars: Joshua Harris: Timothy; Harley Venton: Transporter Chief; Sheila Franklin: Ensign Felton; Steven Einspahr: Teacher.

A young boy, the sole survivor of a devastated ship, becomes obsessed with copying Data.

Insider's Story

Patrick Stewart directs.

Gene Roddenberry died during filming.

"Hero Worship" and "Haven" are the only episodes in which William Riker was called "Bill."

Episode 112: Violations

Production number: 212
Stardate: 45429.3
Air date: February 1, 1992
Teleplay: Pamela Gray and Jeri Taylor
Story: Shari Goodhartz, T. Michael, and Pamela Gray
Director: Robert Wiemer
Guest Stars: Rosalind Chao: Keiko Ishikawa O'Brien; Ben Lemon: Jev; David Sage: Tarmin; Rick Fitts: Dr. Martin; Eve Brenner: Inad; Craig Benton: Crewman Davis; Doug Wert: Lieutenant Commander Jack Crusher; Majel Barrett: Computer Voice.

Troi, Riker, and Dr. Crusher fall into unexplained comas while the *Enterprise* plays host to an alien race.

SNAFUs

Troi and Tarmin enter the turbolift on Deck 3. Troi orders it to go to Deck 8, but when she gets off, the doors close just in front of the camera, clearly showing Deck 3.

Episode 113: The Masterpiece Society

Production number: 213
Stardate: 45470.1
Air date: February 8, 1992
Teleplay: Adam Belanoff and Michael Piller
Story: James Kahn and Adam Belanoff
Director: Winrich Kolbe
Guest Stars: John Synder: Aaron Conor; Dey Young: Hannah Bates; Ron Canada: Marcus Benbeck; Sheila Franklin: Ensign Felton.

Picard's efforts to save a genetically engineered society from a natural disaster threaten to destroy it.

SNAFUs

Geordi states that his VISOR covers the range from 1 Hertz to 1 Terahertz. While this covers radio, microwave, and far infrared frequencies, it does not cover near infrared, visible, ultraviolet, x-rays, or gamma rays.

Episode 114: Conundrum

Production number: 214
Stardate: 45492.2
Air date: February 15, 1992
Teleplay: Barry Schkolnick
Story: Paul Schiffer
Director: Les Landau
Guest Stars: Erich Anderson: Commander Keiran MacDuff; Michelle Forbes: Ensign Ro Laren; Liz Vassey: Kristin; Erick Weiss: Crewman; Majel Barrett: Computer Voice.

While suffering an unexplained case of amnesia, the crew find themselves fighting a war they do not remember or understand.

SNAFUs

A record search shows Deanna's father listed as "Alex," but, in "The Child," she named her child "Ian," after him.

When MacDuff talked to Picard in Picard's ready room, and Picard went to the window, it only showed the reflection of Picard and the room behind him, not the stars outside. Then, as MacDuff appeared in the reflection, leaving the room behind Picard, when the door opened, no reflection of the bridge appeared, as only the stars were visible.

After Riker's first love scene, a wide-angle-view-pan-to-close-up on the bridge appeared at the very top of the screen, in the brightly lit area. Shortly afterward, in the same scene, MacDuff walked around then up to the tactical station from his chair, and his legs appeared next to Worf's. The camera cut to Worf, and MacDuff approaching Worf.

The crew manifest listed Beverly Crusher as a Lt. Cmdr., but her actual rank is Commander.

Episode 115: Power Play

Production number: 215
Stardate: 45571.2
Air date: February 22, 1992
Working Title: "Terror In Ten-Forward"
Teleplay: René Balcer, Herbert J. Wright, and Brannon Braga
Story: Paul Ruben and Maurice Hurley
Director: David Livingston
Guest Stars: Rosalind Chao: Keiko Ishikawa O'Brien; Colm Meaney: O'Brien; Michelle Forbes: Ensign Ro Laren; Ryan Reid: Transporter Technician; Majel Barrett: Computer Voice.

Possessed by alien spirits, Data and Troi take over the *Enterprise.*

Episode 116: Ethics

Production number: 216
Stardate: 45587.3
Air date: February 29, 1992
Teleplay: Ronald D. Moore
Story: Sara Charno and Stuart Charno
Director: Chip Chalmers
Guest Stars: Caroline Kava: Dr. Toby Russell; Brian Bonsall: Alexander; Patti Yasutake: Nurse Alyssa Ogawa.

Loyalty and ethics clash when a paralyzed Worf asks Riker to help him commit suicide.

SNAFUs

When the barrel falls on Worf, a second barrel also falls. Its lid pops off, yet when Geordi runs over to Worf, the lid is back on the barrel.

The Walking (Near) Dead

After a barrel crashes on Worf's back, Worf dies during experimental surgery.

Episode 117: The Outcast

Production number: 217
Stardate: 45614.6
Air date: March 14, 1992
Writer: Jeri Taylor
Director: Robert Scheerer
Guest Stars: Melinda Culea: Soren; Callan White: Krite; Megan Cole: Noor.

A rescue mission leads to a dangerous romance between Riker and a rebellious member of an androgynous race.

Insider's Story

Piller wanted to present the issue of sexual intolerance, not a "gay story." Berman said they tried not to let perceptions of what the public would find acceptable "influence us too much . . . but having Riker engaged in passionate kisses with a male actor might have been a little unpalatable to viewers."

In Jokes

Technical phrases included, "Reverse the polarity of the neutron flow," a common utterance of the third Doctor Who, played by Jon Pertwee.

Episode 118: Cause and Effect

Production number: 218
Stardate: 45652.1
Air date: March 21, 1992
Writer: Brannon Braga
Director: Jonathan Frakes
Guest Stars: Michelle Forbes: Ensign Ro Laren; Patti Yasutake: Nurse Alyssa Ogawa; Kelsey Grammer: Captain Morgan Bateson.

The *Enterprise* is trapped in a time warp that forces the crew to endlessly repeat the same experiences.

Insider's Story

Jonathan Frakes directs.

SNAFUs

When Picard talks to Geordi and Dr. Crusher in the sickbay, his clothing mysteriously switches from gray to standard, then back to gray.

Time Travel

The *Enterprise* and the *Bozeman* get caught in a time loop.

The Walking (Near) Dead

A collision with a starship causes the *Enterprise* to explode, killing everyone on board.

Episode 119: The First Duty

Production number: 219
Stardate: 45703.9
Air date: March 28, 1992
Co-Producer: Joe Menosky
Writer: Ronald D. Moore and Naren Shankar
Director: Paul Lynch,
Guest Stars: Walker Brandt: Cadet Second Class Jean Hajar; Shannon Fill: Cadet Second Class Sito; Richard Rothenberg: Cadet; Ray Walston: Boothby; Robert Duncan McNeill: Cadet First Class Nicholas Locarno; Ed Lauter: Lt. Commander Albert; Richard Fancy: Captain Satelk; Jacqueline Brooks: Superintendant Admiral Brand; Wil Wheaton: Cadet Third Class Wesley Crusher.

Caught between loyalty to his friends and the need to tell the truth, Wesley becomes involved in a cover-up when his Starfleet Academy squadron suffers a deadly collision.

SNAFUs

Wes opens a door with his left hand, but the close-up shows the door being opened with his right hand.

Later Wes talks to someone in his quarters. From behind, his hands are in one position, but a front view shows them in a different position.

Wesley Screws Up

Wesley's flight team performs an extremely dangerous maneuver which results in a serious accident and causes the death of a fellow team member. The resulting cover-up forces Wesley to repeat a year at the Academy.

Episode 120: Cost of Living

Production number: 220
Stardate: 45733.6
Air date: April 18, 1992
Writer: Peter Allan Fields
Director: Winrich Kolbe
Guest Stars: Majel Barrett: Lwaxana Troi; Brian Bonsall: Alexander; Tony Jay: Campio; Carel Struycken: Mr. Homn; David Oliver: Young Man; Albie Selznick: Juggler; Patrick Cronn: Erko; Tracy D'Arcy: Young Woman; George Ede: Poet; Christopher Halsted: 1st Learner; Majel Barrett: Computer Voice.

Troi's free-thinking mother causes trouble between Worf and his son while she prepares for her wedding aboard the *Enterprise*.

SNAFUs

When Picard and Data are trapped in the turbolift due to metal parasites, Picard wears only three pips.

After being told that the inertial dampers have failed, Picard orders the *Enterprise* out of warp. If the inertial dampers had failed, they would have been splattered all over the bridge.

When Lwaxana and Alexander are in the mud bath, Alexander holds an edible glass with a bite missing. First the bite points to the right, then to the left.

Episode 121: The Perfect Mate

Production number: 221
Stardate: 45761.3
Air date: April 25, 1992
Teleplay: Gary Perconte and Michael Piller
Story: René Echevarria and Gary Perconte
Director: Cliff Bole
Guest Stars: Famke Janssen: Kamala; Tim O'Connor: Briam; Max Grodenchik: Par Lenor; Mickey Cottrell: Alrik; Michael Snyder: Qol; David Paul Needles: Miner #1; Roger Rignack: Miner #2; Charles Gunning: Miner #3; April Grace: Transporter Officer; Majel Barrett: Computer Voice.

A beautiful woman, chosen by her people to serve as a peace offering to end a centuries-long war, falls in love with Picard.

Episode 122: Imaginary Friend

Production number: 222
Stardate: 45852.1
Air date: May 2, 1992
Teleplay: Edithe Swensen and Brannon Braga
Story: Jean Lousie Matthias, Ronald Wilderson, and Richard Fliegel
Director: Gabrielle Beaumont
Guest Stars: Noley Thorton: Clara Sutter; Shay Astar: Isabella; Jeff Allin: Ensign Daniel Sutter; Brian Bonsall: Alexander; Patti Yasutake: Nurse Alyssa Ogawa; Sheila Franklin: Ensign Felton.

A little girl's imaginary friend becomes a frightening reality for the crew when she threatens to destroy the *Enterprise*.

SNAFUs

Data says something about a lower strand density to the starboard side, and Picard tells him to move toward it. Then the *Enterprise* turns left.

Episode 123: I, Borg

Production number: 223
Stardate: 45854.2
Air date: May 9, 1992
Writer: René Echevarria

Director: Robert Lederman
Guest Star: Jonathan Del Arco: Hugh Borg.

Picard and the crew suffer from conflicting emotions when the *Enterprise* rescues a critically injured Borg.

Introduces Hugh.

SNAFUs

During the first scene in the lab, Three of Five asks, "Do I have a name?" saying "I," instead of the "we" normal for Borg.

Episode 124: The Next Phase

Production number: 224
Stardate: 45927.5
Air date: May 16, 1992
Writer: Ronald D. Moore
Director: David Carson
Guest Stars: Michelle Forbes: Ensign Ro Laren; Thomas Kopache: Mirok; Susanna Thompson: Varel; Shelby Leverington: Transporter Chief Brossmer; Brian Cousins: Parem; Kenneth Meseroll: Ensign McDowell.

Geordi and Ro are pronounced dead after a transporting maneuver from a distressed Romulan ship goes awry.

In Jokes

One of the control panels on the Romulan Ship looks like the control console of the TARDIS from *Doctor Who*.

SNAFUs

Geordi and Ro breathed and walked on floors despite being phased, and thus intangible, although Geordi's hand passed through a table. A phased Romulan sat in a chair that rocked when he got up.

When the Romulan fought Ro, and LaForge shoved him through the bulkhead, the Romulan exited the *Enterprise* right-side up, but drifted away facing the wrong way as he rotated.

Riker started playing the trombone before his lips reached the mouthpiece.

Episode 125: The Inner Light

Production number: 225
Stardate: 45944.1
Air date: May 30, 1992
Teleplay: Morgan Gendel and Peter Allan Fields
Story: Morgan Gendel
Director: Peter Lauritson
Guest Stars: Margot Rose: Eline; Richard Riehle: Batai; Scott Jaeck: Administrator; Jennifer Nash: Meribor; Patti Yasutake: Nurse Alyssa Ogawa; Daniel Stewart: Young Batai.

After a mysterious accident, Picard lives the life of another person on a faraway planet.

Episode 126: Time's Arrow, Part I

Production number: 226
Stardate: 45959.1
Air date: June 13, 1992
Teleplay: Joe Menosky and Michael Piller
Story: Joe Menosky
Director: Les Landau
Guest Stars: Jerry Hardin: Samuel Clemens; Michael Aron: Bellboy; Barry Kivel: Doorman; Ken Thorley: Seaman; Sheldon Peters Wolfchild: Joe Falling Hawk; Jack Murdock: Beggar; Marc Alaimo: Gambler/Fredrick La Rouque; Milt Tarver: Sc entist; Michael Hungerford: Roughneck.

After Data learns of his own death in late-19th-century San Francisco, a freak accident transports him back to that period.

In Jokes

The paper Data picks up is the San Francisco *Register,* the same newspaper Kirk and company saw being taken out of the vending machine.

The translation:

Data (in English): "I am a Frenchman."

Poker Player: *"Ah, mes parents sont originaires de Boubonnais. Je suis né en New Orleans."* / "Ah, my parents are from Boubonnais. I was born in New Orleans."

Data: *"Alors nous sommes presque frères. Je suis heureux de vous connaître."* / "Then, we are almost brothers. I am pleased to meet you."

Poker Player (in English): "Please sir . . ."

SNAFUs

The newspaper was dated "Sunday, August 11, 1893," but August 11, 1893 was a Friday.

Time Travel

Data constructs a phase inverter, and, in the process, travels to 1893. Picard, Riker, Troi, Dr. Crusher, and Geordi walk into the time vortex, and end up in the 19th century.

SIXTH SEASON

Season Notes

Changes from fifth to sixth season:

• The title sequence was changed, with the *Star Trek: The Next Generation* logo returning to the original effect seen in the first four seasons.

• The painting of the *Enterprise* in Picard's ready room (signed by Andy Probert and Rick Sternbach) has been replaced by a piece of sculpture.

• A new Jefferies tube set has been constructed. This set is three stories tall, and has ladders, sliding doors, and lots of grating.

• Chief O'Brien now wears a hollow circle (Ensign Junior Grade?).

Season Credits

Starring:
Patrick Stewart as Captain Jean-Luc Picard
Jonathan Frakes as Commander William Riker
Also Starring:
LeVar Burton as Lieutenant Commander Geordi LaForge
Michael Dorn as Lieutenant Worf
Gates McFadden as Dr. Beverly Crusher
Marina Sirtis as Counselor Deanna Troi
Brent Spiner as Lieutenant Commander Data

Created By: Gene Roddenberry
Executive Producer: Michael Piller
Executive Producer: Rick Berman
Co-Executive Producer: Jeri Taylor
Supervising Producer: David Livingston
Supervising Producer: Frank Abatemarco
Co-Producer: Ronald D. Moore
Co-Producer: Wendy Neuss
Line Producer: Merri D. Howard
Producer: Peter Lauritson
Story Editor: Brannon Braga
Story Editor: René Echevarria

Episode 127: Time's Arrow, Part II

Production number: 227
Stardate: 46001.3
Air date: September 19, 1992
Teleplay: Jeri Taylor
Story: Joe Menosky

Director: Les Landau

Guest Stars: Jerry Hardin: Samuel Clemens; Pamela Kosh: Mrs. Carmichael; William Boyett: Policeman; Michael Aron: Bellboy, Jack London; James Gleason: Dr. Appollinaire; Mary Stein: Alien Nurse; Alexander Enberg: Young Reporter; Bill Cho Lee: Male Patient; Majel Barrett: Computer Voice.

The *Enterprise* crew travels between the 19th and 24th centuries in an attempt to prevent Data's death in 19th-century San Francisco.

Insider's Story

Samuel Clemens mispronounces Halley's Comet. The pronunciation he uses comes from the 1950s, when "Bill Hailey and the Comets," best known for "Rock Around the Clock," was popular.

Episode 128: Realm of Fear

Production number: 228

Stardate: 46041.1

Air date: September 26, 1992

Writer: Brannon Braga

Director: Cliff Bole

Guest Stars: Colm Meaney: O'Brien; Patti Yasutake: Nurse Ogawa; Dwight Schultz: Barclay; Renata Scott: Admiral; Thomas Belgrey: Crewmember; Majel Barrett: Computer Voice.

A young *Enterprise* engineer is forced to confront his paralyzing fear of being transported—then reports seeing something inside the beam.

SNAFUs

O'Brien's two normal pips were suddenly replaced by a single hollow pip. Other pip-problems included Lt. Barclay's single and hollow pips swapping position, as well as his having two solid pips when in Troi's office.

Episode 129: Man of the People

Production number: 229

Stardate: 46071.6

Air date: October 3, 1992

Writer: Frank Abatemarco

Director: Winrich Kolbe

Guest Stars: Chip Lucia: Ambassador Ramid Ves Alkar; Patti Yasutake: Nurse Ogawa; George D. Wallace: Admiral; Lucy Boryer: Ensign Janeway; Susan French: Ramid Sev Maylor; Rick Scarry: Jarth; Stephanie Erb: Liva; J.P. Hubbell: Ensign; Majel Barrett: Computer Voice.

Troi is drastically transformed when a visiting ambassador secretly uses her to achieve his aims.

Insider's Story

Mike Westmore asked Marina Sirtis to get her face waxed. Unfortunately, the glue for the make-up burned her face, and she was in agony for two days.

SNAFUs

In engineering, Geordi wears two hollow pips and one solid, instead of two solid and one hollow.

When Riker and Troi walk out of Ten-Forward, they step right into a turbolift. The sign on the lift's door reads "08 Turbolift," indicating that they are on Deck 8, instead of Deck 10, the deck of Ten-Forward.

Near the end, when Beverly revives Deanna in sickbay, Deanna's eyes flutter open a couple of times, then remain shut. It is obvious that Marina isn't wearing her black contacts.

Picard refers to Transporter Room 3 twice while beaming out the ambassador's aide, yet tells Room 2 to be ready. Transporter Room 2 is referred to throughout the episode.

Amazingly, dead hair follicles change color from gray to brown when Troi de-ages.

The Walking (Near) Dead

Deanna is killed in order to stop an ambassador from passing his evil emotions to another empathic person.

Episode 130: Relics

Production number: 230
Stardate: 46125.3
Air date: October 10, 1992
Writer: Ronald D. Moore
Director: Alexander Singer
Guest Stars: Lanei Chapman: Ensign Rager; Erick Weiss: Ensign Kane; James Doohan: as Scotty; Stacie Foster: Engineer Bartel; Ernie Mirich: Waiter; Majel Barrett: Computer Voice.

Trapped in limbo for 75 years, Scotty reawakens in the 24th Century.

Insider's Story

Several scenes were cut, including a scene in which Troi stops in to see Scotty after a big argument with Geordi, which is also cut.

It was impossible to re-use the original bridge, partly because it was broken up and destroyed after the original series. Instead, they used a captain's chair and helm/navigation console build by a *Star Trek* fan named Steve Horch. The only other part that was built was from about a foot to the left of the turbolift to the end of Scotty's engineering station, as well as the railing that separates that from the center of the bridge. Also, the Con and Ops chairs were look-alikes, and are tilted back more than the real ones. The rest was a still from "This Side of Paradise."

The Aldeberan Whiskey was actually Hi-C Ecto Cooler.

In Jokes

With Scotty on board, there are plenty of references to the old series. For instance, the "miracle worker" bit comes from *Star Trek III.* The "It is green" bit comes from "By Any Other Name."

Episode 131: Schisms

Production number: 231
Stardate: 46154.2
Air date: October 17, 1992
Teleplay: Brannon Braga
Story: Jean Lousie Matthias and Ron Wilkerson
Director: Robert Wiemer
Guest Stars: Lanei Chapman: Ensign Rager; Ken Thorley: Mott; Angelina Fiordellisi: Kaminer; Scott T. Trost: Lt. Shipley; Angelo McCabe: Crewman; John Nelson: Medical Technician; Majel Barrett: Computer Voice.

The *Enterprise* crew suffers bizarre consequences following a secret, unwelcome alien visit.

SNAFUs

When Riker sits down at Conn, when the ensign has trouble navigating, his hands are over the console, the display for Ops.

The experimenters had homed in on the *Enterprise* because Geordi modified the sensors. Yet Riker experiences chronic insomnia days before Geordi makes his modifications.

Worf notes that Lt. Haggerl returned to Deck 9, Section 17, but, seconds later, Dr. Crusher wants a device brought to Deck 9, Section 19.

Episode 132: True Q

Production number: 232
Stardate: 46192.3
Air date: October 24, 1992
Working Titles: "Q and I," "Q-Me."

Writer: René Echevarria
Director: Robert Scheererr
Guest Stars: Olivia d'Abo: Amanda Rogers; John P. Connolly: ?; John deLancie: Q.

The *Enterprise* picks up relief supplies and Amanda Rogers, an honor student who then interns on board. Strange occurrences center around Amanda until Q reveals that he has been testing Amanda's powers, for she is the offspring of two Q.

Episode 133: Rascals

Production number: 233
Stardate: 46235.7
Air date: October 31, 1992
Teleplay: Alison Hock
Story: Ward Botsford, Diana Dru Botsford, and Michael Piller
Director: Adam Nimoy
Guest Stars: Colm Meaney: O'Brien; Rosalind Chao: Keiko; Michelle Forbes: Ensign Ro; David Tristan Birkin: Young Picard; Megan Parlen: Young Ro; Caroline Junko King: Young Keiko; Isis J. Jones: Young Guinan; Mike Gomez: Lurin; Tracey Walter: Berik; Michael Snyder: Morta; Brian Bonsall: Alexander; Whoopi Goldberg: Guinan; Morgan Nagler: Kid #1; Hana Hatae: Molly; Majel Barrett: Computer Voice.

A bizarre transporter mishap transforms Picard and three other staff members into children just as Ferengi invade and disable the ship.

SNAFUs
The computer display in the classroom clearly shows "Classroom Seven" on the screen. Yet, when Picard meets Riker, he refers to Classroom Eight.

When Keiko gets coffee, she picks it up in her left hand, yet it then appears in her right hand.

Clothing shrinks, but not proportionally, while Guinan's hat and Ro's headband remain unchanged.

When Riker dives to avoid a phaser blast, we hear the phaser, but do not see it.

Episode 134: A Fistful of Datas

Production number: 234
Stardate: 46271.5
Air date: November 7, 1992
Teleplay: Robert Hewitt Wolfe and Brannon Braga
Story: Robert Hewitt Wolfe
Director: Patrick Stewart
Guest Stars: Brian Bonsall: Alexander; John Pyper-Ferguson: Eli Hollander; Joy Garrett: Annie; Jorge Cervera, Jr.: Bandito; Majel Barrett: Computer Voice.

A holodeck fantasy goes awry, sending Worf and his son into a Wild West showdown with a villain who's a dead ringer for Data.

Insider's Story
Directed by Patrick Stewart.

SNAFUs
When Data is connected to the computer, the edge of the gold makeup is visible on his neck.

When Pa Hollinder speaks to young Hollinder and Pa turns, his hand gets "cut off" by the video wipe.

While Pa talks with Worf and Troi, a mannequin visibly fills in for young Hollinder.

Episode 135: The Quality of Life

Production number: 235
Stardate: 46307.2
Air date: November 14, 1992
Writer: Naren Shankar

Director: Jonathan Frakes
Guest Stars: Ellen Bry: Dr. Farallon; J. Downing: Transporter Chief; Majel Barrett: Computer Voice.

Data risks Picard and Geordi's lives to protect another "living" machine.

Insider's Story
Jonathan Frakes directs.

Episode 136: Chain of Command, Part I

Production number: 236
Stardate: 46357.4
Air date: December 12, 1992
Teleplay: Ronald D. Moore
Story: Frank Abatemarco
Director: Robert Scheerer
Guest Stars: Ronny Cox: Captain Edward Jellico; Natalija Nogulich: Vice Admiral Elena Nechayev; John Durbin: Gul Lemec; Lou Wagner: DaiMon Solok; David Warner: Gul Madred; Majel Barrett: Computer Voice.

After resigning his command to participate in a dangerous secret mission, Captain Picard is taken hostage by the Cardassians.

Insider's Story
The thing inside the eggs that Picard and the Cardassian eat are dead squid with little machines under them to make them move.

Patrick Stewart watched tapes from Amnesty International to prepare for the episode. These tapes included statements of those who had been tortured, and a long interview with a torturer who talked about what it was like to inflict pain.

SNAFUs
The tunnels are underground; they never use a flashlight, but there is light.

When Worf opens the magnetically sealed door, it opens inward like a normal door. But when they start to run out, the door slides closed.

Episode 137: Chain of Command, Part II

Production number: 237
Stardate: 46360.8
Air date: December 19, 1992
Writer: Frank Abatemarco
Director: Les Landau
Guest Stars: Ronny Cox: Captain Edward Jellico; John Durbin: Gul Lemec; David Warner: Gul Madred; Heather Lauren Olson: Jil Orra; Majel Barrett: Computer Voice.

The *Enterprise* attempts to rescue Picard from the Cardassians while under the command of an unfeeling new captain.

Episode 138: Ship in a Bottle

Production number: 238
Stardate: 46424.1
Air date: January 23, 1993
Writer: René Echevarria
Director: Alexander Singer
Guest Stars: Daniel Davis: Moriarty; Stephanie Beacham: Countess Regina Bartholomew; Dwight Schultz: Barclay; Clement von Franckenstein: Gentleman; Majel Barrett: Computer Voice.

A calculating Sherlock Holmesian character traps Picard and others in a holodeck simulation.
Sequel to "Elementary, Dear Data."

SNAFUs
When the book is tossed out of the holodeck, it gets zapped immediately. This conflicts with "The Big Good-bye," in which the gangsters

de-rezz slowly after they walk out of the holodeck, and "Elementary, Dear Data," in which a sheet of paper does not de-rez when Picard takes it out of the holodeck.

Picard wears an open coat with a blue shirt when he walks into the holodeck, but he wears his one-piece red shirt when he walks out.

After Moriarty tells Picard that he has taken over the ship, they cut to a commercial and the screen fades as Picard begins to say something.

The command, "Computer, freeze program," fails to stop flames in a fireplace from flickering, or a clock from ticking, in a holodeck simulation.

Episode 139: Aquiel

Production number: 239
Stardate: 46461.3
Air date: January 30, 1993
Teleplay: Brannon Braga and Ronald D. Moore
Story: Jeri Taylor
Director: Cliff Bole
Guest Stars: Renee Jones: Lt. Acquiel Uhnari; Wayne Grace: Governor Torak; Reg E. Cathey: Morag; Majel Barrett: Computer Voice.

Geordi is enamored of a beautiful and mysterious Starfleet lieutenant accused of murder.

SNAFUs

The name of the Klingon battle cruiser that meets with the *Enterprise* is the *Qu'vatlh* (proper spelling, badly pronounced by Picard). This is listed in the Klingon Dictionary.

Episode 140: Face of the Enemy

Production number: 240
Stardate: 46519.1
Air date: February 6, 1993
Teleplay: Naren Shankar

Story: René Echevarria
Director: Gabrielle Beaumont
Guest Stars: Scott MacDonald: N'Vek; Carolyn Seymour: Commander Toreth; Barry Lynch: DeSeve; Robertson Dean: Pilot, Co-Star; Majel Barrett: Computer Voice; Pamela Winslow: Ensign McKnight.

Forced to impersonate a Romulan Intelligence officer, Counselor Troi becomes a pivotal part of an elaborate defection scheme.

Cast Favorites: Marina Sirtis' Favorite

". . . because it was not a 'girlie' episode. Any one of the crew could have been transformed into a Romulan. Troi was chosen because she was an empath, not because she was female."

SNAFUs

When the defector ensign boarded the *Enterprise*, he asked Riker to meet with Captain Picard, yet when Picard walked to that ensign's quarters, the defector addressed him as "Commander," as if Picard were a Romulan CO.

Troi was surgically altered to look like a Romulan, including the short hair style, but when Crusher altered her back, she already had long hair.

Episode 141: Tapestry

Production number: 241
Stardate: Unknown
Air date: February 13, 1993
Writer: Ronald D. Moore
Director: Les Landau
Guest Stars: Ned Vaughn: Corey; J.C. Brandy: Marta; Clint Carmichael: Nausicaan #1; Rae Norman: Penny; John deLancie: Q; Clive Church: Maurice Picard; Marcus Nash: Young Picard; Majel Barrett: Computer Voice.

After Picard loses his life in a surprise attack, Q gives him the chance to change his destiny.

Time Travel

Q takes Picard back to his days after graduating from the Academy.

Episode 142: Birthright, Part I

Production number: 242
Stardate: 46578.4
Air date: February 20, 1993
Writer: Brannon Braga
Director: Winrich Kolbe
Guest Stars: Siddig El Fadil: Dr. Julian Bashir; James Cromwell: Shrek; Cristine Rose: Gi'ral; Jennifer Gatti: Ba'el; Richard Herd: L'Kor.

Worf and Data embark on unusual journeys to seek out their fathers.
Worf visits Deep Space Nine.

SNAFUs

Data's furious little brushstrokes make an audible sound against the canvas even after he stops painting and steps back to view his work.

Episode 143: Birthright, Part II

Production number: 243
Stardate: 46595.2
Air date: February 27, 1993
Writer: René Echevarria
Director: Dan Curry
Guest Stars: Cristine Rose: Gi'ral; James Cromwell: Shrek; Sterling Macer, Jr.: Toq; Alan Scarfe: Tokath; Jennifer Gatti: Ba'el; Richard Herd: L'Kor.

Imprisoned in a society of peaceful Klingons and Romulans, Worf risks his life to show the younger Klingons their lost heritage and inspire them to claim their honor.

SNAFUs

Worf states that Kahless caused the oceans to overflow with his tears, yet in *Star Trek VI*, Spock stated that Klingons have no tear ducts.

Episode 144: Starship Mine

Production number: 244
Stardate: 46682.4
Air date: March 27, 1993
Writer: Morgan Gendel
Director: Cliff Bole
Guest Stars: David Spielberg: Hutchinson; Marie Marshall: Kelsey; Tim Russ: Devor; Glenn Morshower: Orton; Tom Nibley: Neil; Tim deZarn: Satler; Patricia Tallman: Kiros; Arlee Reed: Waiter; Alan Altshuld: Pomet; Majel Barrett: Computer Voice.

Picard is trapped on board the *Enterprise* with a band of interstellar thieves while it is bombarded with lethal rays.

Insider's Story

Robin Curtis was originally slated to play the female terrorist, but a conflicting shooting schedule prevented her from playing the part. Instead she appeared in "Gambit" as a Romulan.

Episode 145: Lessons

Production number: 245
Stardate: 46693.1
Air date: April 3, 1993
Writer: Ronald Wilkerson and Jean Louise Matthias
Director: Robert Wiemer
Guest Stars: Wendy Hughes: Lt. Cmdr. Nella Darren; Majel Barrett: Computer Voice.

Picard is torn between love and duty when he is forced to send the woman he loves on a potentially deadly mission.

Episode 146: The Chase

Production number: 246
Stardate: 46731.5
Air date: April 24, 1993
Teleplay: Joe Menosky
Story: Joe Menosky and Ronald D. Moore
Director: Jonathan Frakes
Guest Stars: Salome Jens: Humanoid; Jogn Cothran, Jr.: Nu'Daq; Maurice Ro'ves: Romulan Captain; Linda Thorson: Gul Ocett; Special Appearance by Norman Lloyd: Professor Galen; Majel Barrett: Computer Voice.

Picard finds himself in a race with Cardassians, Klingons, and Romulans to solve a four-billion-year-old genetic puzzle.

Explains why there are so many humanoid races.

Episode 147: Frame of Mind

Production number: 247
Stardate: 46778.1
Air date: May 1, 1993
Writer: Brannon Braga
Director: James L. Conway
Guest Stars: David Selburg: Doctor Syrus; Andrew Prine: Administrator; Gary Werntz: Mavek; Susanna Thompson: Inmate; Allan Dean Moore: Wounded Crewmember.

Trapped in an alien mental hospital, with little memory of the past, Riker is convinced that he is going insane.

Episode 148: Suspicions

Production number: 248
Stardate: 46830.1
Air date: May 8, 1993
Writers: Joe Menosky and Naren Shankar
Director: Cliff Bole
Guest Stars: Patti Yasutake: Nurse Ogawa; Tricia O'Neil: Kurak; Peter Slutsker: Dr. Reyga; James Horan: Jo'Bril; John S. Ragin: Dr. Chrostopher; Joan Stuart Morris: T'Pan; Majel Barrett: Computer Voice.

Beverly risks her career to prove that a pioneering Ferengi scientist was murdered.

Episode 149: Rightful Heir

Production number: 249
Stardate: 46852.2
Air date: May 15, 1993
Teleplay: Ronald D. Moore
Story: James E. Brooks
Director: Winrich Kolbe
Guest Stars: Alan Oppenheimer: Koroth; Robert O'Reilly: Gowron; Norman Snow: Torin; Charles Esten: Divok; Kevin Conway: Kahless; Majel Barrett: Computer Voice.

Worf finds his faith sorely tested when it appears that the greatest Klingon warrior of all time has returned from the dead to reclaim the Empire.

SNAFUs

It is stated that there has not been a Klingon Emperor for over 300 years. However, in "Sins of the Father," Worf's nanny says that Worf's father was loyal to the Emperor.

Episode 150: Second Chances

Production number: 250
Stardate: 46915.2
Air date: May 22, 1993
Teleplay: René Echevarria
Story: Michael A. Medlock
Director: LeVar Burton
Guest Star: Dr. Mae Jemison: Ensign Palmer.

Returning to the site of an eight-year-old mission, Riker encounters an identical double of himself, who tries to rekindle a relationship with Troi.

Introduces Thomas Riker.

Insider's Story
LeVar Burton directs.

SNAFUs
Near the end of the episode, Commander Riker rescues Lieutenant Riker on the edge of the cliff. In a long shot, the stunt double dressed as Lieutenant Riker wears a *DS9* gold and black uniform tunic, not a *TNG* tunic. Then, in close-up, Lieutenant Riker is back in a *TNG* gold tunic.

Episode 151: Timescape

Production number: 251
Stardate: 46944.2
Air date: June 12, 1993
Writer: Brannon Braga
Director: Adam Nimoy
Guest Stars: Michael Bofshever: Romulan/Alien; John DeMita: Romulan; Joel Fredericks: Engineer.

The *Enterprise* is frozen in time on the brink of total annihilation, as Picard must figure out how to rescue the ship without destroying it.

A friendly encounter with a Romulan ship.

Insider's Story
Leonard's son, Adam Nimoy, directs.

SNAFUs
As Troi enters sickbay for the first time, she scoots past two security officers in mid-stride just before they enter sickbay. Later, as she yanks Beverly out of the way and draws on the Romulan, no security guards had entered the room, even though they were scant feet from entering and in mid-stride.

When Data, Troi, and Picard return to the *Enterprise* and set time in motion again, Picard is on the bridge. When time starts forward again, Picard tells Riker that he'll find Geordi on the Romulan ship and to beam him directly to sickbay, yet the Romulan ship is no longer around.

The runabout crew has just suffered a port engine shutdown, due to the effect of the time discontinuity bubbles. Picard tells Data that he is going to check the fuel consumption logs and then proceeds to go to another part of the craft.

We see a plate of aged fruit as Picard walks in. Notice his right hand as he enters. His fingers are curled inward, shielding his nails from our view. When he sits down at the control panel, he begins to touch the controls with the pads of his fingers. His extra-long nails are already clearly visible, moments before he ever reaches for the fruit.

Time Travel
An alien creature on a Romulan ship causes time to stand still in order to save its young.

Episode 152: Descent, Part I

Production number: 252
Stardate: 46982.1
Air date: June 19, 1993
Teleplay: Ronald D. More
Story: Jeri Taylor
Director: Alexander Singer
Guest Stars: John Neville: Isaac Newton; Jim Norton: Albert Einstein; Natalija Nogulich: Admiral Nechayev; Brian J. Cousins: Crosis; Richard Gilbert-Hill: Bosus; Stephen James Carver: Tayar; Professor Stephen Hawking as himself.

When the Borg, under Lore's leadership, return to battle with the Federation, Data joins them.

Cast Favorites: Brent Spiner's Favorite

"My most memorable moment was sitting across the table from Stephen Hawking in the episode."

Insider's Story

At the start of the show, the android creates a poker game in the holodeck between himself and computer-generated recreations of Stephen Hawking, Albert Einstein, and Isaac Newton. In his dramatic television appearance, Hawking, who is confined to a wheelchair and cannot speak, plays himself, although Newton and Einstein do not.

Enterprise Exceeds Warp Speed Limits

The *Enterprise* uses a transwarp conduit while chasing the Borg and tracking down Data.

SEVENTH SEASON

Season Credits

Starring:
Patrick Stewart as Captain Jean-Luc Picard
Jonathan Frakes as Commander William Riker
Also Starring:
LeVar Burton as Lieutenant Commander Geordi LaForge
Michael Dorn as Lieutenant Worf
Gates McFadden as Dr. Beverly Crusher
Marina Sirtis as Counselor Deanna Troi
Brent Spiner as Lieutenant Commander Data

Created By: Gene Roddenberry
Executive Producer: Jeri Taylor
Executive Producer: Michael Piller
Executive Producer: Rick Berman
Co-Executive Producer: Jeri Taylor
Supervising Producer: David Livingston

Supervising Producer: Frank Abatemarco
Co-Producer: Ronald D. Moore
Co-Producer: Wendy Neuss
Co-Producer: Brannon Braga
Line Producer: Merri D. Howard
Producer: Peter Lauritson
Executive Story Editor: René Echevarria
Story Editor: Brannon Braga
Story Editor: René Echevarria
Story Editor: Naren Shankar

Episode 153: Descent, Part II

Production number: 253
Stardate: 47025.4
Air date: September 18, 1993
Writer: René Echevarria
Director: Alexander Singer
Guest Stars: Jonathan Del Arco: Hugh; Alex Datcher: Taitt; James Horan: Barnaby; Brian Cousins: Crosis; Benito Martinez: Salazar;Michael Reilly Burke: Goval.

Picard, Troi, and Geordi are held prisoner by Data, who has left the *Enterprise* to join his evil brother Lore as leaders of the Borg.

Episode 154: Liaisons

Production number: 254
Stardate: Unknown
Air date: September 25, 1993
Teleplay: Jeanne Carrigan Fauci and Lisa Rich
Story: Roger Eschbacher and Jaq Greenspon
Director: Cliff Bole
Guest Stars: Barbara Williams: Anna; Eric Pierpoint: Voval; Paul Eiding: Loquel; Michael Harris: Byleth; Ricky D'shon Collins: Boy.

While the crew plays host to ambassadors from an alien race, Picard is stranded on a barren planet with a woman who falls desperately in love with him.

Insider's Story

"Family" and "Liaisons" are the only episodes in Classic Trek, the movies, and *TNG* which have no scenes filmed on the bridge.

SNAFUs

In the poker scene, when the Ambassador "steals" some of Worf's chips, Worf states that he saw him steal two of his chips, but the cutaway shot clearly shows him taking three.

Episode 155: Interface

Production number: 255
Stardate: 47215.5
Air date: October 2, 1993
Writer: Joe Menosky
Director: Robert Wiemer
Guest Stars: Madge Sinclair: Captain Silva LaForge; Warren Munson: Admiral Holt; Ben Vereen: Doctor LaForge.

Geordi defies Picard's commands and risks his life in what appears to be a futile attempt to rescue his missing mother.

Introduces Geordi's parents, and kills off his mother.

Episode 156: Gambit, Part I

Production number: 256
Stardate: 47135.2
Air date: October 9, 1993
Teleplay: Naren Shankar
Story: Christopher Hatton and Naren Shankar
Director: Peter Lauritson
Guest Stars: Richard Lynch: Baran; Robin Curtis: Tallera; Caitlin Brown: Vekor; Cameron Thor: Narik; Alan Altshuld: Yranac; Bruce Gray: Admiral Chekote; Sabrina LeBeauf: Ensign Giusti; Stephen Lee: Bartender; Derek Webster: Lt. Sanders.

Riker is shocked to find Picard, who has been missing and presumed dead, posing as a mercenary on an alien ship.

Reveals something new about Romulans.

The Walking (Near) Dead

Captain Picard is believed to be dead.

Episode 157: Gambit, Part II

Production number: 257
Stardate: 47160.1
Air date: October 16, 1993
Teleplay: Ronald D. Moore
Story: Naren Shankar
Director: Alexander Singer
Guest Stars: Richard Lynch: Baran; Robin Curtis: Tallera; Caitlin Brown: Vekor; Cameron Thor: Narik; James Worthy: Koral; Sabrina LeBeauf: Ensign Giusti; Martin Goslins: Setok.

Picard and Riker masquerade as mercenaries in order to retrieve a potentially lethal Vulcan artifact.

SNAFUs

Worf reports a hit on the port nacelle, but the phaser blast struck the starboard nacelle.

Episode 158: Phantasms

Production number: 258
Stardate: 47225.7
Air date: October 23, 1993
Writer: Brannon Braga
Director: Patrick Stewart
Guest Stars: Gina Ravarra: Ensign Tyler; Bernard Kates: Sigmund Freud; Clyde Kusatsu: Admiral Nakamura; David L. Crowley: Workman.

Data's first bad dream turns into a real-life nightmare for the rest of the *Enterprise* crew.

Episode 159: Dark Page

Production number: 259
Stardate: 47254.1
Air date: October 30, 1993
Writer: Hilary J. Bader
Director: Les Landau
Guest Stars: Majel Barrett: Lwaxana Troi; Norman Large: Maques; Kirsten Dunst: Hedril; Amick Byram: Mr. Troi; Andreana Weiner: Kestra.

Troi must probe her mother's psyche when a traumatic secret causes a psychic breakdown that threatens Lwaxana's life.

Episode 160: Attached

Production number: 260
Stardate: 47304.2
Air date: November 6, 1993
Writer: Nicholas Sagan
Director: Jonathan Frakes
Guest Stars: Robin Gammell: Mauric; Lenore Kasdorf: Lorin; J.C. Stevens: Kes Aide.

Imprisoned and telepathically joined by an alien race, Picard and Beverly are forced to face the feelings they have always had for each other.

SNAFUs
The same painting hung in both Dr. Crusher's quarters and Captain Picard's quarters.

Episode 161: Force of Nature

Production number: 261
Stardate: 47310.2
Air date: November 13, 1993
Writer: Naren Shankar
Director: Robert Lederman

Guest Stars: Michael Corbett: Rabal; Margaret Reed: Serova; Lee Arenberg: Prak; Majel Barrett: Computer Voice.

An alien brother and sister resort to desperate measures to prove their theory that warp drive is destroying the universe.

SNAFUs
Data's cat, Spot, was usually referred to as a "he," but, in this episode, is referred to as a "she," and, in "Genesis," had kittens before turning, temporarily, into an Iguana.

Episode 162: Inheritance

Production number: 262
Stardate: 47410.2
Air date: November 20, 1993
Teleplay: Dan Koeppel and René Echevarria
Story: Dan Koeppel
Director: Robert Scheerer
Guest Stars: Fionnula Flanagan: Juliana Tainer; William Lithgow: Pran.

A routine mission to save an endangered planet brings Data face to face with a woman who claims to be his mother.

SNAFUs
Juliana stepped onto the transporter pads wearing heels, and arrived on the planet wearing flats.

Episode 163: Parallels

Production number: 263
Stardate: 47391.2
Air date: November 27, 1993
Writer: Brannon Braga
Director: Robert Wiemer

Guest Stars: Wil Wheaton: Lieutenant Wesley Crusher; Patti Yasutake: Doctor Alyssa Ogawa; Mark Bramhall: Gul Nador; Majel Barrett: Computer Voice.

Returning to the *Enterprise* from a competition, Worf finds reality changing, and is troubled when no one else seems to notice.

SNAFUs

In several scenes, Data has blue eyes instead of the yellowish-gray eyes.

Time Travel

Worf passes through a time eddy, and traverses several timelines.

Episode 164: The Pegasus

Production number: 264
Stardate: 47457.1
Air date: January 8, 1994
Writer: Ronald D. Moore
Director: LeVar Burton
Guest Stars: Nancy Vawter: Admiral Blackwell; Terry O'Quinn: Admiral Pressman; Michael Mack: Sirol.

Riker is torn when his former commander, now an admiral, orders him to hide the real purpose of a risky mission from Picard.
　　Adds background for Riker.

Episode 165: Homeward

Production number: 265
Stardate: 47423.9
Air date: January 15, 1994
Teleplay: Naren Shankar
Story: Spike Steingasser
Director: Alexander Singer
Guest Stars: Penny Johnson: Dobara; Brian Markinson: Vorin; Edward Penn: Kateras; Paul Sorvino: Nikolai;

Susan Christy: Tarrana; Majel Barrett: Computer Voice.

Worf's foster brother violates the Prime Directive in an effort to save a doomed alien race.

Episode 166: Sub Rosa

Production number: 266
Stardate: Unknown
Air date: January 29, 1994
Teleplay: Brannon Braga
Story: Jeri Taylor
Director: Jonathan Frakes
Guest Stars: Michael Keenan: Maturin; Shay Duffin: Ned Quint; Duncan Regehr: Ronin; Ellen Albertini Dow: Felisa.

Shortly after her grandmother's death, Beverly falls under the spell of a ghost lover who has been in her family for generations.

Insider's Story

Directed by Jonathan Frakes.

SNAFUs

In the cemetery, Beverly asks Deanna to go with her to the house. Deanna agrees and they walk out of the cemetery. Then Picard begins a discussion with the Governor of the colony. Toward the end of the discussion, when the Governor is explaining about visiting the castle, Deanna walks across the cemetery in the background. The next scene shows Beverly and Deanna entering the house.

Episode 167: Lower Decks

Production number: 267
Stardate: Unknown
Air date: February 5, 1994

Teleplay: René Echevarria
Story: Ronald Wilkerson and Jean Louise Matthias
Director: Gabrielle Beaumont
Guest Stars: Dan Gauthier: Lavelle; Shannon Fill: Sito; Alexander Enberg: Torak; Bruce Beatty: Ben; Patti Yasutake: Ogawa; Don Reilly: Joret.

While enduring the *Enterprise*'s promotion evaluation process, four junior officers find themselves involved in a top-secret mission.

Episode 168: Thy Known Self

Production number: 268
Stardate: 47611.2
Air date: February 12, 1994
Teleplay: Ronald D. Moore
Story: Christopher Hatton
Director: Winrich Kolbe
Consulting Producer: Peter Lauritson;
Guest Stars: Ronnie Claire Edwards: Talur; Michael Rothhaar: Garvin; Kimberly Cullum: Gia; Michael G. Hagerty: Skoran; Andy Kossin: Apprentice; Richard Ortega-Mir: Rainer; Majel Barrett: Computer Voice.

Having completely lost his memory, Data is stranded on a primitive planet where the inhabitants fear he is carrying a deadly plague.

Note
This episode was nominated for an Emmy for Outstanding Individual Achievement in Art Direction for a Series.

Episode 169: Masks

Production number: 269
Stardate: 47618.4
Air date: February 19, 1994
Writer: Joe Menosky
Director: Robert Wiemer
GuestStar: Rickey D'shon Collins: Eric.

Data is taken over by several different personalities from an extinct civilization.

Episode 170: Eye of the Beholder

Production number: 270
Stardate: 47622.1
Air date: February 26, 1994
Teleplay: René Echevarria
 Story: Brannon Braga
 Director: Cliff Bole
Guest Stars: Mark Rolston: Walter Pierce; Nancy Harewood: Lt. Nara; Tim Lounibos: Lt. Kwan; Johanna McCloy: Calloway; Nora Leonhardt: Woman; Dugan Savoye: Man; Majel Barrett: Computer Voice.

While experiencing empathic visions after an officer's mysterious suicide, Troi becomes romantically involved with Worf.

Episode 171: Genesis

Production number: 271
Stardate: 47653.2
Air date: March 19, 1994
Writer: Brannon Braga
Director: Gates McFadden
Guest Stars: Patti Yasutake: Ogawa; Dwight Schultz: Barclay; Carlos Ferro: Ensign Dern; Majel Barrett: Computer Voice.

Picard and Data return to the *Enterprise* to discover that the entire crew has devolved into prehistoric beings.

Note
This episode was nominated for Emmy awards for Outstanding Individual Achievement in Makeup for a Series, Outstanding Individual Achievement in Sound Editing for a Series,

and Outstanding Individual Achievement in Sound Mixing for a Series.

Cast Favorites: Gates McFadden's Favorite

"The most fun I've ever had was directing, and I loved any moment that I was able to do comedy."

Episode 172: Journey's End

Production number: 272
Stardate: 47751.2
Air date: March 26, 1994 3
Writer: Ronald D. Moore
Director: Corey Allen
Guest Stars: Wil Wheaton: Wesley Crusher; Tom Jackson: Lakanta; Natalija Nogulich: Admiral Necheyev; Ned Romero: Anthwara; George Aguilar: Wakasa; Richard Poe: Gul Evek; Eric Menyuk: Traveller; Doug Wert: Jack Crusher.

While Picard is forced to relocate a group of American Indians from a planet they have settled, Wesley and the Traveler leave to explore the universe. Sequel to "Where No One Has Gone Before."

Wesley Screws Up

Wesley warns the colonists that the Federation may beam them up, endangering the Away Team.

Note

One of *Star Trek: Voyager*'s main characters, Chakotay, comes from the world introduced in this episode.

Episode 173: Firstborn

Production number: 273
Stardate: 47779.4
Air date: April 23, 1994
Teleplay: René Echevarria

Story: Mark Kalbfeld
Director: Jonathan West
Guest Stars: James Sloyan: K'mtar; Brian Bonsall: Alexander; Gwynyth Walsh: B'etor; Barbara March: Lursa; Joel Swetow: Yog; Colin Mitchell: Gorta; Armin Shimerman: Quark; Michael Danek: Singer; John Kenton Shull: Molor; Rickey D'Shon Collins: Eric; Majel Barrett: Computer Voice.

A mysterious family friend arrives to help transform Worf's reluctant son Alexander into a warrior.

Note

This episode was nominated for an Emmy for Outstanding Individual Achievement in Hairstyling for a Series

Cast Favorites: Michael Dorn's Favorite

". . . because in it I was able to do everything I ever wanted to as Worf. The episode has drama, danger, and sensitivity."

Time Travel

Alexander from the future comes to the present to change his own personal history.

Episode 174: Bloodlines

Production number: 274
Stardate: 47829.1
Air date: April 30, 1994
Writer: Nicholas Sagan
Director: Les Landau
Guest Stars: Ken Olandt: Jason; Lee Arenberg: Bok; Peter Slutsker: Birta; Amy Pietz: Lt. Rhodes; Michelan Sisti: Tol; Majel Barrett: Computer Voice.

Picard learns that he has a son, and that the young man has been targeted for murder by an old enemy in search of revenge.
Sequel to "The Battle."

Episode 175: Emergence

Production number: 275
Stardate: 47869.2
Air date: May 7, 1994
Teleplay: Joe Menosky
Story: Brannon Braga
Director: Cliff Bole
Guest Stars: David Huddleston: Conductor; Vinny Argiro: Hitman; Thomas Kopache: Engineer; Arlee Reed: Hayseed.

The lives of the *Enterprise* crew are endangered when the ship suddenly develops its own intelligence.

Episode 176: Preemptive Strike

Production number: 276
Stardate: 47941.7
Air date: May 14, 1994
Working Title: "The Good Fight"
Teleplay: René Echevarria
Story: Naren Shankar
Director: Patrick Stewart
Guest Stars: Michelle Forbes: Ro Laren; John Franklyn-Robbins: Macias; Natalija Nogulich: Admiral Necheyev; William Thomas, Jr.: Santos; Shannon Cochran: Kalita; Richard Poe: Gul Evek.

Ro Laren is forced to choose between her loyalty to Picard and her hatred toward Cardassia when she accepts an assignment to infiltrate the Maquis.

Insider's Story
Patrick Stewart directs.

Episode 177: All Good Things...

Production number: 277
Stardate: 47988.1
Air date: May 23, 1994

Writer: Ronald D. Moore and Brannon Braga
Director: Winrich Kolbe
Guest Stars: John deLancie: Q; Andreas Katsulas: Tomalak; Clyde Kusatsu: Admiral Nakamura; Patti Yasutake: Ogawa; Denise Crosby: Tasha Yar; Colm Meaney: O'Brien; Pamela Kosh: Jessel; Tim Kelleher: Lt. Gaines; Alison Brooks: Ensign Chilton; Stephen Matthew Garvin: Ensign; Majel Barrett: Computer Voice.

Picard finds himself traveling between the past, present, and future while attempting to prevent the destruction of humanity.

Shows a possible future. Tasha Yar appears. TV finale.

Note
This episode was nominated for Emmys for Outstanding Individual Achievement in Costume Design for a Series, Outstanding Individual Achievement in Editing for a Series: Single Camera Production, and Outstanding Individual Achievement in Music Composition for a Series.

SNAFUs
It was stated that all three *Enterprise*s fired the tachyon beams. However, it was the *Pasteur* that fired the initial beam.

Time Travel
Q keeps Picard jumping from the present, to seven years previous, to twenty years in the future.

Additional Notes
The Art Department crew kept an anime program running in the Trek production office at all times. The writers, unaware of the anime connection, independently came up with the ship name for the *U.S.S. Yamato*. Rick Sternbach was as surprised as anyone when he found out.

A standing list contains names that writers can use for alien planets/races/etc., including several from anime. "Nausicaans" came from that list.

The main holodeck entrance/control panel has six lines of default choices for "adventures." Number three says: "Tomobiki Simulator." Rick Sternbach's comment after pointing it out was, "Be sure to wear insulated clothing!"

The *Stargazer* original in Picard's office has a Macross fighter cockpit on the top, and a Shogun Warriors robot on the bottom.

Many in jokes were written in Japanese, so they might be taken for YAAS (Yet Another Alien Script).

Unseen in jokes in the series include: Shuttlecraft "Pontiac" and "Indiana Jones" on operations board, and crew quarters for Lt. Luke Skywalker. The race, Bolians, to which Mott the barber belongs, is mentioned. They are named after Cliff Bole, a frequent director of *TNG* and *DS9*.

Frequent *TNG* in jokes primarily reference:

- *Doctor Who,* the most popular science fiction series in British television history, which ran on BBC from November 23, 1963 to December, 1989. The series now appears in a series of made-for-TV movies from America's Fox Television, a part of Australian Rupert Murdoch's Worldwide Media. The title character is known only as "The Doctor," a time lord who travels through time and space in a TARDIS (Time And Relative Dimensions In Space). The TARDIS is bigger on the inside than on the outside, and can change outward appearance. The Doctor's TARDIS, being a broken down Type-40, is stuck in the shape of a blue British Police Call Box. The Doctor himself can, at point of death, regenerate into a totally different body and personality.

- *Lovely Angels/Dirty Pair,* a Japanese anime series. The two main characters, "Kei" and "Yuri," are members of World Welfare Foundation. Their job is to take care of problems. However, they usually leave things in worse shape than when they arrived, although it's usually not their fault. The series has included Classic Trek in jokes.

Trek Quotes

"Seize the time, Meribor. Live now; make now always the most precious time. Now will never come again."
—Picard ("The Inner Light")

"Shields up! Rrrrred alert!"
—Riker (practically every episode)

"Eaten any good books lately?"
—Q (to Worf)

Picard: "What is it?" (about Nagillum)
Data: "There's nothing out there; absolutely nothing."
Geordi (aside to Worf): "Well it's a damn ugly nothing!"
("Where Silence Has Lease")

Nagillum: "Masculine and feminine. I understand."
Picard: "Yes. That is how we propagate our species."
Nagillum: "Please demonstrate."
Dr. Pulaski: "Not likely!"
("Where Silence Has Lease")

"With the first link, the chain is forged. The first speech censured, the first thought forbidden, the first freedom denied chains us all irrevocably."
—Picard (quoting Judge Aaron Satie) ("The Drumhead")

"Fate protects fools, little children, and ships named *Enterprise.*"
—Riker ("Contagion")

More Trek Quotes

"Let's make sure that history never forgets the name . . . *Enterprise*."

—Picard ("Yesterday's *Enterprise*")

"If there's nothing wrong with me . . . maybe there's something wrong with the universe!"

—Dr. Crusher ("Remember Me")

"The universe is a spheroid region, 705 meters in diameter."

—The Computer ("Remember Me")

"Nice legs . . . for a human."

—Worf ("Qpid")

"Jean-Luc! It's so good to see you again. How about a big hug?"

—Q ("Qpid")

"I am NOT a merry man!!!"

—Worf ("Qpid")

Picard: "Well, it seems Mrs. Troi is our acting ambassador of good will for today."

Lwaxana Troi: "You just think of me as your entertainment director."

("Half a Life")

"If you can't take a little bloody nose, maybe you oughtta go back home and crawl under your bed. It's not safe out here. It's wondrous, with treasures to satiate desires both subtle and gross; but it's not for the timid."

—Q ("Q Who?")

"Spot. This is down. Down is good."

—Data ("Force of Nature")

"Please Mrs. Troi . . . and it's 'Worf,' not 'Wolf.'"

—Worf ("Half a Life")

"All good things come to an end . . ."

—Q ("All Good Things . . .")

A song sung by Chief O'Brien in "The Wounded":

A minstrel boy to the war has gone,
In the ranks of death ye will find him.
His father's sword he hath girded on,
With his wild harp slung behind him.
"Land of song," said the warrior bard,
"The war the world betrays thee.
One sword at least thy rights shall guard,
One faithful harp shall praise thee."

"Besides, you look good in a dress."

—Riker, to Worf ("Liaisons")

Data: "But I have no sexual desire."

Sigmund Freud: "Ah! Impotence on top of everything!"

("Phantasms")

"Sometimes a cigar is just a cigar!"

—Sigmund Freud ("Phantasms")

Data: "You must talk to him; tell him that he is a good cat, and a pretty cat, and . . ."

Worf: "I will feed him."

("Phantasms")

"Some of the colonists objected to having an anatomically correct android running around without any clothes on."

—Juliana Soong ("Inheritance")

"Captain, we're receiving two hundred and eighty-five thousand hails!"

—Lt. Wesley Crusher ("Parallels")

Riker: "They were just sucked into space."

Data: "Blown, sir."

Riker: "Sorry, Data."

Data: "Common mistake, sir."

("The Naked Now")

Dr. Crusher: "He got turned into a spider and now he has a disease named after him."

(referring to Lt. Barclay)

Troi: "I'd better clear my calendar for the next few weeks."

("Genesis")

"I will just have to trust that you will not let Admiral Pressman put the *Enterprise* in unnecessary risk, and if I find that that trust has been misplaced, I will have to re-evaluate the command structure of this ship. Dismissed."

—Picard ("The Pegasus")

Taya: "Father said she went to a beautiful place, where everything is peaceful, and everyone loves each other, and no one ever gets sick. Do you think there's really a place like that?"

Data: "Yes . . . I do."

("Thine Own Self")

"Rock, fire, sky, and water are the four basic elements of the universe."

—Talur ("Thine Own Self")

"Synthetic Scotch, synthetic Commanders . . ."

—Captain Scotty ("Relics")

More Trek Quotes

"... and get that fish out of my ready room!"
—Captain Jellico ("Chain of Command, Part I")

"Policemen—I'd recognize them in any century."
—Professor Moriarty ("Ship in a Bottle")

"You're dead, this is the afterlife—and I'm God."
—Q ("Tapestry")

"Yes, absolutely, I do indeed concur, wholeheartedly!"
—Riker ("Where Silence Has Lease")

"Well, he did make a pass at me ... and it was a good one!"
—Troi, referring to Lt. Barclay ("The Nth Degree")

"We must anticipate, and not make the same mistake once."
—Picard ("Time Squared")

Star Trek: Generations

"Oh, shit!!!"
—Data

"I was out saving the galaxy when your grandfather was in diapers."
—Kirk

"I have an appointment with eternity and I don't want to be late."
—Dr. Soran

Kirk: "You say history considers me dead. Who am I to argue with history?"
Picard: "You have a duty! You're a Starfleet officer!"

"Lifeforms .... You tiny little lifeforms.... You precious little lifeforms ... Where are you?"
—Data, singing and playing the control panel like a musical instrument

Picard: "Come back! Make a difference!"
Kirk: "I take it the odds are against us and the situation's grim."
Picard: "You could say that."
Kirk: "If Spock were here, he'd say that I was an irrational, illogical human being for going on this mission... Sounds like fun!"

Geordi: "Data ... I made that joke seven years ago."
Data: "I know.... I just got it!"

"Time is the fire in which we burn ..."
—Dr. Soran

Data: "I hate this! I really hate this!"
Guinan: "More?"
Data: "Please."

"Yes!!!!!!!"
—Data

APPENDIX B

Lists of Cast and Characters

Cast Members: The Next Generation

LeVar Burton:
Lt. Commander Geordi LaForge (Chief Engineer) (Season 1: Lieutenant Junior Grade; Season 2: Lieutenant)
Also directed "Second Chances," "The Pegasus."

Denise Crosby:
Lieutenant Natasha "Tasha" Yar (Security Chief) (Died in Action on "Skin of Evil")
Lieutenant Tasha Yar ("Yesterday's *Enterprise*," "All Good Things...")
Voice of Romulan Commander in shadows ("The Minds Eye"; uncredited)
Romulan Commander in shadows ("Redemption"; uncredited)
Sela ("Redemption II," "Unification")

Michael Dorn:
Lieutenant Worf (Security Chief) (Season 1 and 2: Lieutenant Junior Grade)

Jonathan Frakes:
Commander William Thomas Riker (First Officer)
Lieutenant Thomas Riker (Second Chances)
Odan (The Host)
Also directed "The Offspring," "Reunion," "The Drumhead," "Cause and Effect," "The Quality of Life," "The Chase," "Sub Rosa."

Whoopi Goldberg:
Guinan (Manager, Ten-Forward Lounge)

Cheryl Gates McFadden:
Commander Beverly Crusher (Chief Medical Officer) (Seasons 1, 3, and subsequent; Crusher was in Starfleet Medical during Season 2)
Also Choreographed "Data's Day" and directed "Genesis."

Marina Sirtis:
Counselor Deanna Troi

Brent Spiner:
Lieutenant Commander Data (Second Officer)
Lore ("Datalore," "Brothers," "Descent")
Dr. Noonian Soong ("Brothers," "Birthright: Part I," "Inheritance")
Jayden ("Thy Known Self")

Patrick Stewart:
Captain Jean-Luc Picard
Michael Williams ("The Defector")
Locutus of Borg ("The Best of Both Worlds")
Also directed "In Theory," "Hero Worship," "A Fistful of Datas," "Phantasms," "Preemptive Strike."

Guest Stars

Marc Alaimo:
Subcommander Tebok ("The Neutral Zone")
Gul Macet ("The Wounded")
Gambler ("Time's Arrow I")

Chad Allen:
Jono ("Suddenly Human")

Majel Barrett(-Roddenberry):
Lwaxana Troi ("Haven," "Manhunt," "Ménage à Troi," "Half a Life," "Cost of Living")
Computer (*The Next Generation*)

Stephanie Beacham:
Countess Regina Bartholomew ("Ship in a Bottle")

Corbin Bernsen:
Q2 ("Deja Q," uncredited)

Theodore Bikel:
Sergey Rozhenko ("Family")

David Tristan Birkin:
Rene Picard ("Family")
Jean-Luc Picard ("Rascals")

Brian Bonsall:
Alexander ("New Ground," "Ethics," "Cost of Living," "Imaginary Friend," "Rascals")

Caitlin Brown:
Vekor ("Gambit")

Georgia Brown:
Helena Rozhenko ("Family," "New Ground")

Merritt Butrick:
T'Jon ("Symbiosis")

Cat II:
Spot ("A Fistful of Datas")

William O. Campbell:
Okona ("The Outrageous Okona")

Rosalind Chao:
Keiko Ishikawa/O'Brien (civilian) ("Data's Day," "The Wounded," "Night Terrors," "In Theory," "Disaster," "Violations," "Rascals")

Kevin Conway:
Kahless ("Rightful Heir")

Charles Cooper:
K'mpec ("Sins of the Father," "Reunion")

Nicholas Coster:
Admiral Haftel ("The Offspring")

James Cromwell:
Jaglom Shrek ("Birthright, Parts I & II")

Ronny Cox:
Captain Edward Jellico ("Chains of Command")

Robin Curtis:
Tallera ("Gambit")

Olivia D'Abo:
Amanda Rogers ("True Q")

Daniel Davis:
Professor James Moriarty ("Elementary, Dear Data," "Ship in a Bottle")

John deLancie:
Q ("Encounter at Farpoint," "Hide and Q," "Q Who?" "Deja Q," "Qpid," "True Q," "Tapestry," "All Good Things. . .")

Jonathan Del Arco:
Hugh ("I, Borg," "Descent Part II")

Elizabeth Dennehy:
Commander Shelby ("The Best of Both Worlds")

James Doohan:
Captain Montgomery "Scotty" Scott ("Relics")

Samantha Eggar:
Marie Picard ("Family")

Siddig El Fadil:
Dr. Julian Bashir ("Birthright, Part I")

Shannon Fill:
Sito ("The First Duty," "Lower Decks")

Mick Fleetwood:
Antedian dignitary ("Manhunt")

Michelle Forbes:
Lieutenant Ro Laren
(Ensign in "Ensign Ro," "Rascals")
Dara ("Half a Life")

Matt Frewer:
Berlingoff Rasmussen ("A Matter of Time")

Susan Gibney:
Leah Brahms ("Booby Trap," "Galaxy's Child")

Kelsey Grammer:
Captain Morgan Bateson ("Cause and Effect")

Max Grodenchik:
Sovak ("Captain's Holiday")
Par Linor ("The Perfect Mate")

Jerry Hardin:
Radue ("When the Bough Breaks")
Samuel "Mark Twain" Clemens ("Time's Arrow Parts I & II")

Teri Hatcher:
Transporter Chief ("The Outrageous Okona")

Dr. Stephen Hawking:
Himself ("Descent")

Jennifer Hetrick:
Vash ("Captain's Holiday," "Qpid")

Wendy Hughes:
Nella Daren ("Lessons")

Ashley Judd:
Ensign Robin Lefler ("Darmok," "The Game")

Andreas Katsulas:
Tomalak ("The Enemy," "The Defector," "Future Imperfect," "All Good Things...")

DeForest Kelley:
"Admiral" ("Encounter at Farpoint")

Jeremy Kemp:
Robert Picard ("Family")

Mark Lenard:
Sarek ("Sarek," "Unification I")

Liberty:
Spot (Data's Cat: "Data's Day," "In Theory")

Norman Lloyd:
Professor Galen ("The Chase")

Patrick Massett:
Duras ("Sins of the Father," "Reunion")

Carolyn McCormick:
Minuet ("11001001," "Future Imperfect")

Robert Duncan McNeill:
Nicholas Locarno ("The First Duty")

Colm Meaney:
Battle Bridge Conn ("Encounter at Farpoint")
Security Guard ("Lonely Among Us")
Transporter Chief Miles Edward O'Brien (Season 2 through 6; we first learn of him in "Unnatural Selection")

Eric Menyuk:
The Traveler ("Where No One Has Gone Before," "Remember Me," "Journey's End")

Joanna Miles:
Perrin ("Sarek," "Unification I")

Jim Morton:
Albert Einstein ("The Nth Degree," "Descent Part I")

Diana Muldaur:
Commander Katerine "Kate" Pulaski, Chief Medical Officer
(Special Appearances in Season 2)

George Murdock:
Admiral J.P. Hanson ("The Best of Both Worlds")

Lycia Naff:
Ensign Sonya Gomez ("Q Who?" "Samaritan Snare")

Bebe Neuwirth:
Lanel ("First Contact")

John Neville:
Sir Isaac Newton ("Descent Part I")

Julia Nickson:
Ensign Tsu ("Arsenal of Freedom")

Leonard Nimoy:
Ambassador Spock ("Unification")

Tim O' Connor:
Ambassador Bre'em ("The Perfect Mate")

Tricia O'Neil:
Captain Rachael Garrett ("Yesterday's *Enterprise*")
Kurak ("Suspicions")

Robert O'Reilly:
"Scarface" ("Manhunt")
Gowron ("Reunion," "Redemption I & II," "Rightful Heir")

Michael Pataki:
Governor Karnas ("Too Short a Season")

Ethan Phillips:
Dr. Farek ("Menage a Troi")

Michelle Phillips:
Jenice Manheim ("We'll Always Have Paris")

Eric Pierpoint:
Voval ("Liaisons")

Joe Piscopo:
The Comic ("The Outrageous Okona")

Suzie Plakson:
Dr. Selar ("The Schizoid Man")
K'Ehleyr ("The Emissary," "Reunion")

Saul Rubinek:
Kivas Fajo ("The Most Toys")

Tim Russ:
Pel Orton ("Starship Mine")

Michele Scarabelli:
Ensign Jenna D'Sora ("In Theory")

Robert Schenkkan:
Lieutenant Commander Dexter Remmick
   ("Coming of Age," "Conspiracy")

Dwight Schultz:
Lieutenant Reginald "Reg" "Broccoli" Barclay
   ("Hollow Pursuits," "The Nth Degree,"
   "Realm of Fear," "Ship in a Bottle," "Genesis")

Judson Scott:
Sobi ("Symbiosis")

Carolyn Seymour:
Sub-Commander Taris ("Contagion")
Mirasta Yale ("First Contact")
Toreth ("Face of the Enemy")

W. Morgan Sheppard:
Dr. Ira Graves ("The Schizoid Man")

Armin Shimerman:
Letek ("The Last Outpost")

The Box ("Haven")
DaiMon Bractor ("Peak Performance")
Quark ("Firstborn")

Jean Simmons:
Admiral Norah Satie ("The Drumhead")

Madge Sinclair:
Captain Silva La Forge ("Interface")

John Snyder:
Bochra ("The Enemy")
Aaron Conor ("The Masterpiece Society")

Jon Steuer:
Alexander ("Reunion")

Daniel Stewart:
Young Batai ("The Inner Light")
(Yes, he's Patrick Stewart's son)

David Ogden Stiers:
Timicin ("Half A Life," "Ceremonial Death")

Carel Struycken:
Mr. Homm ("Haven," "Manhunt," "Menage
   a Troi," "Half A Life," "Cost of Living")

Patrica Tallman:
   Kiros ("Starship Mine")
   Romulan ("Timescape")

Nick Tate:
   Dirgo ("Final Mission")

John Tesh:
Holodeck Klingon ("The Icarus Factor"; non-
   speaking, uncredited)

Malachi Throne:
Pardek ("Unification")

Hallie Todd:
Lal ("The Offspring")

Tony Todd:
Commander Kurn ("Sins of the Father,"
   "Redemption")
Captain Kurn ("Redemption")

Beth Toussaint:
Ishara Yar ("Legacy")

Ben Vereen:
Dr. LaForge ("Interface")

William A. Wallace:
Wesley Crusher, age 25 ("Hide and Q")

Ray Walston:
Boothby ("First Duty")

Herta Ware:
Maman Picard ("Where No One Has Gone
  Before")

David Warner:
Gul Madred ("Chain of Command")

Julie Warner:
Christy ("Booby Trap," "Transfigurations")

Doug Wert:
Lt. Cmdr. Jack R. Crusher ("Family" [holo-
  gram], "Violations" [flashback],"Journey's
  End" [vision])

Wil Wheaton:
Ensign Wesley Crusher ("Final Mission")
Season 1: Civilian
Seasons 1-3: Acting Ensign
Seasons 4-7: in Starfleet Academy
Seasons 7: resigned from Academy
Wesley Crusher ("The Game," "The First
  Duty," "Parallels," "Journey's End")

Nobel Willingham:
Texas ("The Royale")

Paul Winfield:
Tamarian Captain Dathon ("Darmok")

Ray Wise:
Liko ("Who Watches The Watchers?")

James Worthy:
Koral ("Gambit, Part II")

Table B.1 Crossover Actors

Actor/Actress	Original Star Trek	The Next Generation	Deep Space Nine	Voyager
Marc Alaimo		The Neutral Zone; The Wounded; Time's Arrow, Pt I	recurring role	
Michael Ansara	Day of the Dove		Blood Oath	
Lee Arenberg		Force of Nature; Blood-lines	The Nagus	
Vaughn Armstrong		Heart of Glory	Past Prologue	Eye of the Needle
Majel Barrett	regular 66-69, ST:TMP; STIV:TVH; computer voice in all incarnations of Star Trek	Haven; Manhunt; Ménage à Troi; Half a Life; Cost of Living; Dark Page	The Forsaken	
Michael Bell		Encounter at Farpoint	The Homecoming; The Maquis, Pt II	
Michael Berryman	STIV:TVH	Conspiracy		
Michael Bofshever		Timescape	Progress	
Caitlin Brown		Gambit, Part I & II	The Passenger	
Michael Reilly Burke		Descent, Part II	Profit and Loss	
Merritt Butrick	STII:TWoK; STIII:TSfS	Symbiosis		
William Campbell	The Squire of Gothos; The Trouble with Tribbles		Blood Oath	
Stephen James Carver		Redemption, Part II; Descent	A Man Alone	
Nicholas Cascone		Pen Pals	Equilibrium	
Jefrey Alan Chandler			Facets	Emanations
Rosalind Chao		recurring role	recurring role	
Josh Clark		Justice		Caretaker; Parallax; Prime Factors
Shannon Cochran		Preemptive Strike	Defiant	
John Colicos	Errand of Mercy		Blood Oath; The Sword of Kahless	
Christopher Collins		A Matter of Honor; Samaritan Snare	The Passenger; Blood Oath	
Charles Cooper	ST V: TFF	Sins of the Father; Reunion		
John Cothran Jr.		The Chase	Crossover	
Robin Curtis	STIII:TSfS; STIV:TVH	Gambit, Part I & II		

Table B.1 Crossover Actors *(continued)*

Actor/Actress	Original Star Trek	The Next Generation	Deep Space Nine	Voyager
John de Lancie		recurring role	Q-Less	
Tim deZarn		Starship Mine		Initiations
Thomas [Alexander] Dekker		*Star Trek: Generations*		Learning Curve
James Doohan	regular 66-69; ST:TMP; STII:TWoK; STIII:TSfS; STIV:TVH; STV:TFF; STVI:TUC	Relics	regular 95-??	
Michael Dorn	STVI:TUC	regular 87-94		
Judi Durand	STIII:TSfS		Emissary; A Man Alone	
Gene Dynarski	Mudd's Women; The Mark of Gideon	11001001		
Siddig El Fadil		Birthright, Part I	regular Jan. 93-??	
Robert Ellenstein	STIV:TVH	Haven		
Van Epperson		Time's Arrow, Part II	Q-Less	
Fionnula Flanagan		Inheritance	Dax	
Jonathan Frakes		regular 87-94	Defiant	
Bruce French		The Drumhead		Caretaker
Jennifer Gatti		Birthright, Pt I & II		Non Sequitur
Mike Genovese		The Big Goodbye	The Circle	
Ann Gillespie		Pen Pals	Babel; The Wire	
April Grace		Reunion; Future Imperfect; Data's Day; Galaxy's Child; The Perfect Mate	Emissary	
Bruce Gray		Gambit, Part I	The Circle	
Max Grodenchik		The Perfect Mate	recurring role	
Martha Hackett			The Search, Part I & II	Parallax; Phage; Prime Factors; Maneuvers
Anne Haney		The Survivors	Dax	
Jerry Hardin		When the Bough Breaks; Time's Arrow, Part I & II		Emanations
Hana Hatae		Rascals	recurring role	
Karen Hensel		Unification, Part I	Cardassians	
Jennifer Hetrick		Captain's Holiday; Qpid	Q-Less	

Table B.1 Crossover Actors *(continued)*

Actor/Actress	Original Star Trek	The Next Generation	Deep Space Nine	Voyager
Clint Howard	The Corbomite Maneuver		Past Tense, Part II	
Sherman Howard		Suddenly Human	Shakaar	
Penny Johnson		Homeward	Family Business	
DeForest Kelley	regular; STII:TWoK; STIII:TSfS; STIV:TVH; STV:TFF; STVI:TUC	Encounter at Farpoint		
Kay E. Kuter		The Nth Degree	The Storyteller	
Iva Lane	ST:TMP	11001001		
James Lashly		Brothers	The Passenger; Move Along Home	
Mark Lenard	Balance of Terror; Journey to Babel; ST:TMP; STIII:TSfS; STIV:TVH; STVI:TUC	Sarek; Unification, Part I		
Judy Levitt	STIV:TVH	*Star Trek: Generations*		
Richard Lineback		Symbiosis	Dax	
Jordan Lund		Redemption, Part II	The Storyteller	
Scott MacDonald		Face Of The Enemy	Captive Pursuit; Hippocratic Oath	Caretaker
Jeff McCarthy		The Hunted		Caretaker
Robert Duncan McNeill		The First Duty		regular Jan. 95-??
Dennis Madalone		Heart of Glory; Identity Crisis	Crossover; Visionary	
Barbara March		Redemption, Part I & II	Past Prologue	
Brian Markinson		Homeward		Cathexis
Colm Meaney		regular 87-Dec. 92	regular Jan. 93-??	
Dick Miller		The Big Goodbye	Past Tense, Part I	
Katherine Moffat		The Game	Necessary Evil	
Diana Muldaur	Return to Tomorrow; Is There in Truth No Beauty?	regular 88-89		
George Murdock	STV:TFF	The Best of Both Worlds, Part I & II		
Julia Nickson		The Arsenal of Freedom	Paradise	

Table B.1 Crossover Actors *(continued)*

Actor/Actress	Original Star Trek	The Next Generation	Deep Space Nine	Voyager
Leonard Nimoy	regular 66-69; ST:TMP; STII:TWoK; STIII:TSfS; STIV:TVH; STV:TFF; STVI:TUC	Unification, Part I & II		
Natalija Nogulich		Chain of Command, Part I; Descent	The Maquis, Part II	
Tricia O'Neil		Yesterday's *Enterprise*; Suspicions	Defiant	
Robert O'Reilly		Manhunt; Reunion; Redemption, Part I & II; Rightful Heir	The House of Quark	
Alan Oppenheimer		Rightful Heir	The Jem'Hadar	
Michael Pataki	The Trouble with Tribbles	Too Short a Season		
Vidal Peterson		Unification, Part II	Cardassians	
Ethan Phillips		Ménage à Troi		regular Jan. 95-??
Richard Poe		Journey's End; Preemptive Strike	Playing God; The Maquis, Part I; Tribunal	Caretaker
Steve Rankin		The Enemy	Emissary; Invasive Procedures	
Duncan Regehr		Sub Rosa	Shakaar	
Ray Reinhardt		Conspiracy		Ex Post Facto
Daniel Riordan		Coming of Age	Progress	
Marco Rodriguez		The Arsenal of Freedom	The Wounded	
Joseph Ruskin	The Gamesters of Triskelion		The House of Quark; Improbable Cause	
Tim Russ		Starship Mine; *Star Trek: Generations*	Invasive Procedures; Through the Looking Glass	regular Jan. 95-??
William Schallert	The Trouble with Tribbles		Sanctuary	
John Schuck	STIV:TVH; STVI:TUC		The Maquis, Part II	
Judson Scott	STII:TWoK	Symbiosis		
David Selburg		The Big Goodbye; Frame of Mind		Caretaker

Table B.1 Crossover Actors *(continued)*

Actor/Actress	Original Star Trek	The Next Generation	Deep Space Nine	Voyager
Carolyn Seymour		Contagion; First Contact; Face of the Enemy		Cathexis
Jack Shearer			The Forsaken; Visionary	Non Sequitur
Armin Shimerman		The Last Outpost; Peak Performance	regular Jan. 93-??	Caretaker
James Sloyan		The Defector; Firstborn	The Alternate	Jetrel
Michael Snyder	STIV:TVH	The Perfect Mate; Rascals		
Patrick Stewart		regular 87-94	Emissary	
Brian Thompson		A Matter of Honor	Rules of Aquisition	
Susanna Thompson		The Next Phase; Frame of Mind	Rejoined	
Noley Thornton		Imaginary Friend	Shadowplay	
Malachi Throne	The Cage; The Menagerie	Unification, Part I & II		
Tony Todd		Sins of the Father; Redemption, Part I & II	The Visitor	
Scott Trost		Unnatural Selection; Schisms	A Man Alone	
Peter Vogt		Tin Man	A Man Alone	
Gwynyth Walsh		Redemption, Part I & II	Past Prologue	
Lou Wagner		Chain of Command, Part I	The Nagus	
Erick Weiss		Conundrum; Realm of Fear	Paradise	
Edward Wiley		The Mind's Eye	Profit and Loss	
Rudolph Willrich		Ménage à Troi	Paradise Lost	
Paul Winfield	STII:TWoK	Darmok		

Key to Abbreviations:

ST:TMP	*Star Trek: The Motion Picture*
STII:TWoK	*Star Trek II: The Wrath of Khan*
STIII:TSfS	*Star Trek III: The Search for Spock*
STIV:TVH	*Star Trek IV: The Voyage Home*
STV:TFF	*Star Trek V: The Final Frontier*
STVI:TUC	*Star Trek VI: The Undiscovered Country*

Multiple-Actor Characters

Characters played by more than one actor/actress:

CHARACTER	ACTOR/ACTRESS	EPISODE
Alexander	Jon Steuer	"Reunion"
	James Sloyan	"Firstborn"
	Brian Bonsall	all the rest
Guinan	Isis Jones	"Rascals"
	Whoopi Goldberg	all the rest
Jean-Luc Picard	David Tristan Birkin	"Rascals"
	Marcus Nash	"Tapestry"
	Patrick Stewart	all the rest
Ro Laren	Megan Parlen	"Rascals"
	Michelle Forbes	all the rest
Sarek	Jonathan Simpson	Star Trek V: The Final Frontier
	Mark Lenard	all the rest
Spock, Age 9	Carl Steven	
Age 13	Vadia Potenza	
Age 17	Stephen Manley	
Age 25	Joe W. Davis	Star Trek III: The Search for Spock
	Leonard Nimoy	all the rest
Toral	J.D. Cullum	"Redemption," Part I and II
	Rick Pasqualone	"The Sword of Kahless"

Notable Guest Stars

Mick Fleetwood: drummer for Fleetwood Mac; played Antidean dignitary, an alien with a fish head and webbed fingers.

Mae Jemison: former space-shuttle astronaut, first African-American woman in space, Trek fan; played transporter operator.

Bebe Neuwirth: actress best known as Lilith on *Cheers,* Star Trek fan; played alien nurse.

Michelle Phillips: singer formerly with The Mamas and the Papas, actor on *Knots Landing,* not an avid fan of the series; played Jean-Luc Picard's long-lost first love.

Joe Piscopo: *Saturday Night Live* alumnus, actor; played a comic from the past who taught Data how to tell a joke.

Ben Vereen: actor, Star Trek fanatic; played Geordi LaForge's father.

Ray Walston: TV veteran whose work ranges from the 1960s *My Favorite Martian* to the 1990s *Picket Fences;* played Picard's Starfleet Academy mentor, Boothby.

Paul Winfield: actor; played human captain in *Star Trek II: The Wrath of Khan,* and alien Capt. Dathon on the *Tamarian.*

James Worthy: L.A. Laker forward ranked third overall in steals, fourth in field goals, fifth in points, eighth in assists, lifelong Trek fan; played Klingon, Koral.

Bibliography

"The All-Time Best TV," *TV Guide,* June 19, 1993.

Asbury Park Press, October 8, 1991.

Associated Press, April 29, 1994.

Associated Press, July 22, 1994.

Associated Press, July 25, 1994.

"Authorized Biographer Says He Shows Roddenberry: Warts and All," *Charlotte Observer,* June 11, 1994.

"Beam Up to a Better Future: Politicians Could Learn Much by Using Gene Roddenberry's Vision as Their Goal," *Charlotte Observer,* February 20, 1995.

"Beam Up the Emmys," *TV Guide,* June 16–23, 1990.

"The Best and Worst," *TV Guide,* July 7–13, 1990.

"The Best and Worst," *TV Guide,* July 6–12, 1991.

"The Best and Worst," *TV Guide,* July 20–26, 1992.

"The Best and Worst," *TV Guide,* May 29, 1993.

"The Best and Worst," *TV Guide,* June 11, 1994.

The BIX (Byte Information Exchange) Computer Network

"Boldly Going Where No Show Has Gone Before," *USA Today,* July 1991.

"Boldly Not Going," *Broadcasting,* July 22, 1991.

"To Boldly Go with an Imaginative TV Finale, Star Trek Zooms Off to a New Enterprise—The Movies," *Charlotte Observer,* May 24, 1994.

"A Bronx Cheer, Please, for the Worst Star Trek TV Episodes," *Charlotte Observer,* November 25, 1995.

"Cheers to Patrick Stewart," *TV Guide,* March 3–9, 1990.

"Composer Dennis McCarthy Sets the Mood on Next Gen, DS9," *Charlotte Observer,* September 18, 1993.

Convention Transcripts, various

"Crash Course Launches Writer/Producer into Next Generation," *New York Times Syndicate,* January 29, 1994.

"Deforest Bones Kelley, the Real McCoy, Discusses His Ongoing Treks," *Charlotte Observer,* August 12, 1995.

"Directing Films Fulfills 30-Year Dream for Nimoy," *Dallas Morning News,* December 8, 1987.

"Dispute Over New Series Grounds Old Money Star Trek on WBTV," *Charlotte Observer,* January 8, 1987.

"Enterprise Crew Returns to Save Earth," *Charlotte Observer,* July 10, 1986.

"Enterprise Launched 20 Years Ago This Month: Star Trek—Its Optimism Gave Young Viewers Hope," *Los Angeles Daily News,* September 17, 1986.

"Enterprising Ideas Make Star Trek more than a Phenomenon," *Los Angeles Daily News,* January 4, 1989.

"Enterprising! Undiscovered Country Goes Where No Star Trek Movies Have Gone Before," *Charlotte Observer,* December 6, 1991.

Entertainment Weekly, May 6, 1994.

"Ethics are Alien to Galaxy's Greed-Meisters," *Knight-Ridder Newspapers,* July 2, 1995.

"Exit the Enterprise," *TV Guide,* May 14, 1994.

"On 15th Anniversary, Director Recalls Making First Trek Film," *Charlotte Observer.*

"Final Frontier Box-Office Flop Won't End Star Trek Movies," *Knight-Ridder Newspapers,* October 19, 1990.

"4 in First Trek Crew Win Royalty Settlement," *Los Angeles Times,* September 15, 1995.

"4th Film May Be Best of Star Treks," *Video Review Magazine,* December 18, 1987.

"Full Throttle at 63, William "Captain Kirk" Shatner Has All Systems Engaged," *Charlotte Observer,* April 16, 1994.

"Gene Roddenberry, Creator of Star Trek Series Dies," *Los Angeles Daily News,* October 25, 1991.

"Good Science Fiction Walks Tightrope, Says Trek Creator," *Associated Press,* October 14, 1987.

"Heavenly Help Pulls Yeoman Whitney from Addictions," *Charlotte Observer,* May 7, 1994.

"He's Not Spock, but Nimoy Relishes the Role," *Charlotte Observer,* November 9, 1986.

"His Mission: Seek Out New Fans," *Charlotte Observer,* November 15, 1986.

"Hour Drama Boldly Going to First Run," *Broadcasting,* February 17, 1992.

"Insider Cheers N' Jeers," *TV Guide,* July 13–29, 1991.

"Insider Cheers N' Jeers," *TV Guide,* September 7–13, 1991.

The Internet Movie Database

"Is Paramount Making Money on TNG & DS9?" *Broadcasting Magazine.*

"It's Kirk vs. Picard in Trek Set Showdown," *Charlotte Observer,* June 22, 1994.

"Kirk Beamed into Mythology?" *Associated Press,* June 15, 1989.

"Leonard Nimoy Looks Back," *Charlotte Observer,* October 10, 1995.

"Logically, Mark Sarek Lenard Remains Part of Trek Universe," *Charlotte Observer,* February 11, 1995.

Los Angeles Daily News, October 25, 1991.

"Majel Nurse Chapel Barrett Hasn't Had Time to Mourn Roddenberry," *Charlotte Observer,* August 7, 1993.

"Many of Trek Series Most Memorable Moments Never Air," *Charlotte Observer,* January 20, 1996.

"McDowell Says It's Good to Be the Bad Guy (Sorry, Capt. Kirk)," *Charlotte Observer,* December 3, 1994.

"Monday Guidelines," *TV Guide,* September 22–28, 1990.

"Movie Music Must Work on Many Levels, Says Trek Composer 1987, *Washington Post,* March 25, 1987.

"Mrs. Roddenberry Speaks Her Mind," *TV Guide,* May 14, 1994.

"My Appointment with the Enterprise: An Appreciation," *TV Guide,* May 14, 1994.

"New Star Trek Series Keeps Old Spirit Alive," *Los Angeles Daily News,* July 19, 1987.

New York Times Syndicate, January 29, 1994.

"Next Generation Cast Shares Final Thoughts at Taping of Finale," *Charlotte Observer,* May 14, 1994.

"Next Generation Photographer Relies on His Sense of Integrity," *New York Times,* October 29, 1994.

"Nichols Says Kiss-and-Tell Autobiography more than a Trek Book," *New York Times,* October, 22, 1994.

"Nimoy Finds Joy after Time of Loss," *New York Times,* December 8, 1988.

"Nimoy Spock-less in Lecture to Star Trek Fans at UNCC," *Charlotte Observer,* November 12, 1986.

"Previews: The Next Generation Finale," *TV Guide,* May 14, 1994.

"Robin Curtis, Who Played Saavik, Finally Returns—As a Romulan," *Charlotte Observer,* October 9, 1993.

"Roddenberry Leaves a Legacy of Hope and Love," *Charlotte Observer,* October 26, 1991.

"Sci-Fi Rides High," *TV Guide,* November 4–10, 1989.

"Shatner Direct Trek V?" *Los Angeles Times,* December 18, 1986.

"6 Star Trek's Later, Kelley 1991 Still the Real McCoy," *Charlotte Observer,* December 6, 1991.

"Star Spotlight on Trek V Spock," *Los Angeles Times,* September 18, 1988.

"Star Trek Beams Back as New Series: 1986 for TV," *Associated Press,* October 11, 1986.

"Star Trek Boldly Goes to 100th Episode," *Boston Globe,* June 22, 1991.

"Star Trek Boldly Going, 25 Years Later," *Associated Press,* September 8, 1991.

"Star Trek: The Casino," *Comicsworld,* (Issue 5) May 1996.

"Star Trek Creator Took Posthumous Space Trip," *Associated Press,* April 29, 1994.

"Star Trek V Goes West for Modern Shoot-Out," *Knight-Ridder Newspapers,* November 11, 1988.

"Star Trek IV 1986," *Charlotte Observer,* November 28.

"Star Trek IV 1986 on Mission to Save Earth," *Knight-Ridder Newspapers,* July 15, 1986.

"Star Trek VI Script Continues Voyage with New," *Los Angeles Times,* June 27, 1990.

"Star Trek: The Graphics Generation," *Publish,* April, 1991.

"'Star Trek' Only a Show? Is This Guy Serious?: Rick Berman was Hand-Picked by Gene Roddenberry to Take Over the Star Trek Empire. Now, As He Guides Another Starship into Theatres, Berman Provides a Reality Check on that Ever-Expanding Universe," *Los Angeles Times,* November 13, 1994.

"Star Trek: TNG 1987 a Worthy Enterprise," *Charlotte Observer,* October 3, 1987.

"Star Trek Role Still Holds Magic for Veteran Actor Deforest Kelley," *Dallas Morning News,* December 2, 1986.

"Star Trek Rumors Fly," *TV Guide,* October 2, 1993.

"'Star Trek' Tops 'Wheel'," *Broadcasting,* December 2, 1991.

"Stephen Decker Has Some Regrets About the First Star Trek Movie," *Charlotte Observer,* January 13, 1996.

"This Week on TV," *TV Guide,* July 13–19, 1991.

"The Torch Has Passed Off-Camera, Too," *Time* (Domestic),Volume 144, No. 22, November 28, 1994.

"Trekkies Beam as Scotty 1990 Sends 'Em Back," *Charlotte Observer,* August 19, 1990.

"Trekkies or Trekkers, They Cover the Globe," *Los Angeles Daily News,* September 17, 1986.

"Trekking Onward," *Time* (Domestic), Volume 144, No. 22, November 28, 1994.

"Trekking to the Top," *L.A. Times Magazine,* May 5, 1991.

"Trek Star Memories," *TV Guide,* May 14, 1994.

"TV Guide Presents 40 Years of the Best," *TV Guide,* June 19, 1993.

"Video, the Final Frontier: How Star Trek Films Rate," *Seattle Post-Intelligencer,* November 28, 1994.

"Vulcan Emotional About Becoming Spock on the Map," *Chicago Tribune,* September 23, 1990.

"The Vulcan Lives on in His Psyche, Says Leonard Nimoy," *Charlotte Observer,* October, 10, 1995.

"We May Have the Trimbles to Thank for Trek's Longevity," *Charlotte Observer,* April, 16, 1994.

"Who Knows How Long the Star Trek Mystique May Live and Prosper?" *The Hartford Courant,* December 3, 1991.

"Why Do Trekkers Go So Boldly? It's Love," *Charlotte Observer,* December 17, 1994.

Index